D1601183

Practical Guide to Using Video in the Behavioral Sciences

Practical Guide to Using Video in the Behavioral Sciences

PETER W. DOWRICK

University of Alaska, Anchorage

and Associates

A WILEY-INTERSCIENCE PUBLICATION
JOHN WILEY & SONS, INC.
New York • Chichester • Brisbane • Toronto • Singapore

Library of Congress Cataloging-in-Publication Data

Dowrick, Peter W.
  Practical guide to using video in the behavioral sciences / Peter W. Dowrick.
    p. cm.
  "A Wiley-Interscience publication."
  Includes bibliographical references (p.) and indexes.
  ISBN 0-471-63613-4
  1. Video tapes in psychology. 2. Psychology, Applied. I. Title.
BF637.A84D68 1991
150′.28—dc20   90-19418

  Printed in the United States of America

91 92 10 9 8 7 6 5 4 3 2 1

To:
*Students at UAA who
participated (1981 through 1990) in a variety of video projects,
contributing their enthusiasm, energy, and insight.*

Contributors

ROBERTA L. BABBITT, PH.D., Kennedy Institute for Handicapped Children, Johns Hopkins School of Medicine, Baltimore, Maryland

SIMON J. BIGGS, PH.D., Central Council for Education and Training in Social Work, London, England

ROBERT J. CAVALIER, PH.D., Center for Design of Educational Computing, Carnegie-Mellon University, Pittsburgh, Pennsylvania

PAUL EKMAN, PH.D., Human Interaction Laboratory, University of California, San Francisco, California

HEINER ELLGRING, PH.D., Institute for Psychology, Free University of Berlin, Berlin, Germany

IAN M. FRANKS, PH.D., Department of Physical Education, University of British Columbia, Vancouver, B.C., Canada

ALAN FRIDLUND, PH.D., Department of Psychology, University of California, Santa Barbara, California

FRANK P. GONZALES, PH.D., 97th General Hospital, U.S. Army, Frankfurt, Germany

DARBY JESDALE, M.S., Department of Psychology, University of Alaska, Anchorage, Alaska

HENYA KAGAN, PH.D., Counseling Education, University of Houston, Clear Lake City, Houston, Texas

NORMAN I. KAGAN, PH.D., Department of Educational Psychology, University of Houston, University Park, Houston, Texas

THOMAS J. KEHLE, PH.D., Department of Educational Psychology, University of Connecticut, Storrs, Connecticut

PATRICIA J. KRANTZ, PH.D., Princeton Childhood Development Center, Princeton, New Jersey

GREGORY S. MACDUFF, M.A., Princeton Childhood Development Center, Princeton, New Jersey

LAWRENCE J. MAILE, M.S., Department of Psychology, University of Wyoming, Laramie, Wyoming

DAVID MATSUMOTO, PH.D., Department of Psychology, San Francisco State University, San Francisco, California

LYNN E. MCCLANNAHAN, PH.D., Princeton Childhood Development Center, Princeton, New Jersey

STAN L. O'DELL, PH.D., Department of Psychology, University of Mississippi, University, Mississippi

JOHN M. PARRISH, PH.D., Children's Hospital of Philadelphia, University of Pennsylvania School of Medicine, Philadelphia, Pennsylvania

OLLE WADSTROM, OLL, Ostergot Landsting, Linkoping, Sweden

Preface

In 1986, Simon Biggs and I began some dialogue about following up on a book we had previously edited. After correspondence across the Atlantic and discussions with others, most notably Herb Reich of John Wiley & Sons in New York, the plan for this book emerged. Whereas it revises and expands on some parts of the earlier work, it is something of a companion volume, not a second edition. The purpose was to produce a professional text that is practical without being a cookbook and authoritative without being stodgy. It is also intended to be reasonably comprehensive; however, I confess my limitations and biases in this respect. Although I have tried to sample from many areas, I am a psychologist with a bent toward training and therapeutic issues, and the selected examples, even the conceptual summaries, are bound to reflect this background.

The organization of the book is possibly unique and, I hope, a worthwhile experiment. I have written Part I as a "book within a book," to set out the major uses of video in the behavioral sciences as they seem evident to me. Part II consists of invited contributions that are intended to illustrate applications in each of the purposes identified in Part I, nearly matching on a chapter-by-chapter basis. Thus, Chapter 1 (in Part I) on equipment is matched by the first chapter (Chapter 9) in Part II, which describes applications in interactive video, an area of advancing technology; Chapter 2 examines video for assessment and documentation; its companion chapter (Chapter 10) in Part II describes the analysis of facial expression and emotion; and so on. All chapters in Part II are contributed by scientists and practitioners who are experts in their fields. (At the beginning of Part II, the relationships between chapters and their special contributions are set out in a table.) A frequent disadvantage of edited books is the unevenness of style and the gaps or overlaps in content; I hope that this concern will become a nonissue by the arrangement of companion chapters, at the same time preserving the advantage of diversity and range of expertise that cannot be encompassed by a single author.

The task of being comprehensive is somewhat formidable. I examined some 6,000 references as a significant sample of those available, in addition to much personal networking, and took the precaution of making one 15-month computer search (among others) of every item containing any words beginning with *video*. This search on the PsychInfo database turned up nearly 3,000 articles and dissertations, which I classified into different uses. Even so, I can see now where the book could have been organized differently. For example, *documenting* is sufficiently important in its own right and differs enough from *analyzing* with videotapes so that it really

ix

deserves a separate chapter, even though the amount written about the principles and effects of video documenting in the behavioral sciences is relatively limited. Chapter 5, on the use of video *vignettes,* could also benefit from a split into two chapters, separating research from therapeutic and educational issues. In addition, there are some areas of video application in which I see a significant potential, unfortunately not supported by a quantum mass in the available reports. In particular, I was most disappointed not to find more evidence of use for video at the community level. In 1983, Leonard Henny described fascinating video applications in the Netherlands and Austria that were pivotal in grass-roots community and political change. I had hoped to add new information from this area, but resort to referring interested readers to the original, which remains (to my knowledge) the definitive chapter in the area.

Many people contributed to the production of this book—not the least, the 18 authors of Part II and their supporters. For my own part, I acknowledge a particular debt to the students who have worked with me on video projects since I came to the University of Alaska 10 years ago. Our graduate students choose their own research topics, and I am very flattered that no less than nine of them have finished a thesis in self-modeling or a related area in that time span and others are underway. The work of these and other students is described, sometimes featured, within this book. They have assisted me in workshops (especially Shirley Perry), challenged and aided my conceptualizations, even helped me to write some of the book, for which I specially thank Darby Jesdale. I also thank those who helped in putting the book together, including Debra Lachinski (for her dedicated help with the references), Tedi Schilling (for her persistent pursuit of reprints and the interlibrary loan), and many others.

PETER W. DOWRICK, PH.D.

Anchorage, Alaska
February 1991

Contents

INTRODUCTION

The Use of Video for Behavior Description and Intervention

HEINER ELLGRING

Video provides fascinating perspectives for the behavioral sciences within research and application. The more video becomes accessible, the more one is puzzled, however, by a considerable gap that exists between the available technical potential and the reserved application of video in the behavioral field. Despite a first or even a second trial, very often video recordings are made and then put aside without any further application. This book aims to bridge this gap. Moreover, it guides the various professions interested in human behavior to make use of the video "tool" in a creative way to accomplish a variety of tasks in behavioral assessment, documentation, changing cognitions and emotions, and enhancing behavior.

Part I of this book outlines the basis for video application, including the technical equipment as well as the goals to be pursued, the psychological theories, and the procedures and techniques derived from these theories. Part II deals with various applications in behavioral analysis, instruction and teaching, and therapeutic interventions.

Behavioral sciences need more instruments for analyzing and documenting behavior as well as methods for inducing change in the individual. There are three levels on which human behavior and experience may be approached: (a) the subjective level, where cognitions and emotions are accessible via verbal reports; (b) the physiological/biochemical level, where the biological reactions are taken as signs or indicators for psychological processes; and (c) the behavioral level, where actions of the individual are the relevant clues. It is obvious that the behavioral level deserves as much attention as the others. Given the current state of the art, this approach can be best achieved by observation with the help of video. One of the fascinating aspects of this tool, however, is its potential for inducing change—a primary focus of this book.

TECHNICAL EQUIPMENT

Chapter 1 on equipment fundamentals is a must for those who are beginning to work with video in the behavioral field. There are specific requirements for a scientific use

1

of video that differ considerably from many of the fancy functions that consumer or even semiprofessional equipment provides. Reviewing this chapter will help to avoid the frustration that otherwise causes many video users to give up after a few trials.

GATHERING INFORMATION

For many video users, Chapter 2 on documenting and analyzing should also be read before starting a video enterprise. It is not the recording but the video software handling that makes video useful. Some well-known videotape graveyards result from attitudes reflecting the stage in our cultural development of hunters and gatherers. But since it is so easy to collect the prey, too little effort is generally put into cultivating the goods. As becomes quite obvious with video, the problem today is not collecting information but rather selecting and filtering it. The basic principles of these processes are dealt with in this chapter.

THEORY AND GOALS

Although an accepted, comprehensive theory for the psychological effects mediated by video is still lacking—an advantageous state for continuous development at this point—the concepts advanced in this book are of considerable appeal and fascination in their applied perspective. This holds especially true for the concept of feedforward and self-modeling as opposed to feedback and self-confrontation (Chapters 6 and 7).

The two main processes whereby influence on the individual is mediated by video are learning from the observations of others (Chapters 3 through 5) and self-information and personal change (Chapters 6 through 8). Both domains integrate psychological theory and practical goals achieved by using video. Within these domains, self-modeling and the theory of feedforward processes appears, in my opinion, to be the most fascinating and future-directed perspective for the creative use of video in therapy and training.

APPLICATIONS

Part II on selected applications covers a variety of topics, clearly showing that video has become an indispensable tool in the behavioral sciences.

The analysis of nonverbal behavior, especially facial expression (Chapter 10), would be impossible without the technical help of video. Providing information and instruction on an interactive basis has become feasible by video disc (Chapter 9); in medical settings, patients can be prepared better for painful, embarrassing medical procedures; they can be taught to comply with new measures and can be trained in social skills with the assistance of video (Chapter 11).

For those who want to produce videotapes for instruction or training, suggestions for the development of modeling films (Chapter 12) and trigger tapes (Chapter 13) will be especially useful. Both chapters give instructions for video dramaturgy, which must take into account not only the intricacies of the medium but also the psychological aspects of actor/model effects on a receiver, concepts of social interaction and communication, and so on.

Specific techniques are presented and evaluated that directly aim at changing cognitions, emotions, and behavior; these are interpersonal process recall (Chapter 14), video review for athletic skills (Chapter 15), self-modeling in childhood problems (Chapter 16), and developmental disabilities (Chapter 17). Here, one can keep in mind that further critical evaluations of the effects of video are still needed, particularly studies on the mechanisms that are essential for change.

After Milton Berger's (1978) *Videotape Techniques in Psychiatric Training and Treatment,* Peter Dowrick and Simon Biggs edited a comprehensive overview on research and applications in their 1983 book *Using Video: Psychological and Social Applications.* The technology has developed considerably since then, making most of the technical devices more available. (Video was quite expensive for clinical use at that time.) Fortunately, the psychological concepts have grown, too, as becomes apparent throughout this book. The emergence of practical procedures and the advice for applications and their integration into a framework of psychological theory are essential, given the current state of the art. Thus, the potential use of video in analyzing behavior and in training and therapy can be made fully available.

PART I

The Applicability of Video

CHAPTER 1

Equipment Fundamentals

OVERVIEW

Selecting equipment based on one's requirements, not on "state of the art" temptations, is advocated. This chapter offers some suggestions about what to look for in a video system, information about basic technology, and operating hints. Some specific recommendations are made regarding the configurations of a beginning system and for one level of extension (for better editing). More generic recommendations about how to make choices and what capabilities to seek are presented for enhanced systems, including a modest studio, field recording, and production and editing techniques (e.g., considerations of one-way screens, ambient sound, fades and wipes). Issues of standardization, format wars, and quality are discussed.

Simple explanations of common technology, such as helical scanning and indexing, are given in the context of the rapid developments of the last 20 years— primarily Beta, VHS, 8mm, and their hi-band extensions. The current capabilities of camcorders, consumer VCRs, and videodisc players are summarized, with brief reference to differences among international systems.

The last section of Chapter 1 covers guidelines for operating video equipment: dealing with cooperation or confidence problems behind and in front of the camera, basic production (recording) techniques, simple editing methods, and trouble-shooting irksome problems that do not need a technician but are not apparent in the manual. Some suggestions are offered for preserving and cataloging these precious video documents.

P.W.D.

The most frequently challenging undertaking for anyone who considers using video is the specter of selecting, operating, and otherwise tangling with the equipment. However, social scientists and human service practitioners with little technical expertise need not be daunted. A relatively simple set of guidelines can help identify basic systems to meet most needs. This chapter addresses the selection and operation of video equipment and the basics of using and protecting videotapes. Knowledge of fundamentals simplifies the ongoing task of keeping up with the latest twists and wrinkles of available technology and predicting its future trends.

SELECTION

The objective of identifying a video system for professional use is not to find the ultimate best in current technology, but rather to find a very good system that does everything that is necessary. To seek perfection is a trap, because there is always a more clever piece of engineering in prototype, previewed in the trade magazines. The task is to decide what capabilities are desired and what equipment will meet those needs. Frequently, last year's model—not next year's—will do what is wanted, will have proven reliability, and will probably have a discounted price.

The first step, therefore, is to build a careful plan of one's requirements, with thorough attention to immediate objectives and an eye to the future. This plan cannot be built in a vacuum. A technical expert who understands the priorities of the clinician/researcher and has knowledge of the available equipment options, can facilitate planning. An interchange of ideas is usually necessary to design a workable, economic arrangement.

Minimal System

Many applications described in this book can be implemented with a minimal system—see Figure 1.1. A basic system includes:

- A color video monitor, 12 in. to 23 in. ($500)
- A camcorder with replay capability, **zoom lens,** batteries, AC converter, and headset ($1,500)
- A video cassette recorder ($900)
- Videotapes (20 at $5 each = $100)
- Cables ($50)

(Prices throughout this chapter are estimates for middle-range, top brand products available in U.S. stores in 1990). This system can be used for some data gathering for research and personal analysis, especially for short, preplanned sequences such as opening lines at a mock job interview or gymnastics on the high bar. It will also be suitable for gathering footage in preparation for documenting, teaching, training, or therapy. These recordings will need at least minimal editing, which is why the video cassette recorder **(VCR)** is included. (Terms in **bold** are listed in the Glossary.)

A television set is recommended only when it is a monitor. The term **monitor** indicates that it will accept a *video* signal (through sockets usually designated "video in" and "audio in"), rather than, or as well as, a *broadcast* signal (through the antenna). A connection can usually be made from a video player to any TV set through an **RF converter** and **VHF** connectors, but it provides an inferior picture quality and is not as flexible as a monitor in an expanding system. A 12-inch screen is adequate for small groups, say four people. Larger groups will appreciate a larger

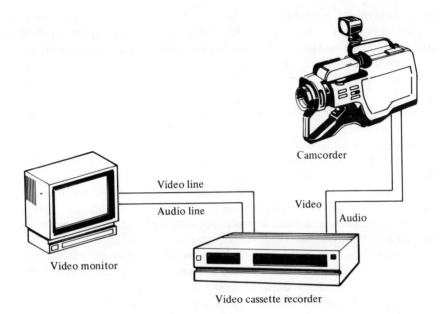

Figure 1.1. Configuration of a "minimal basic system."

screen, although the picture quality is often compromised. (The larger the picture, the larger the flaws.) More detail on technology is given in a later section on Standardization and Quality. Readers who wish to become their own technical experts may examine reference books according to their needs, whether they be for a practical introduction (e.g., Gaskill & Englander, 1985; Lewis, 1987), maintenance and simple repair (e.g., Thomas, 1989), more technical recording information (e.g., Robinson, 1981; Utz, 1982), or an overview of interactive video (e.g., Miller, 1987). Magazines available in bookstores such as *Videomaker, Video Review,* and *CD-ROM Review* and, perhaps, membership in a specialty association such as the Society for Applied Learning Technology are also recommended.

The replay capability of a **camcorder** (camera and recorder in one unit), allows the instrument to double as a player. It is important, therefore, to select a model that has convenient *scan, review,* and **pause** controls. Better quality, generally speaking, may be obtained with a camera and separate recorder; however, I recommend the camcorder for a beginning system because this unit is readily available and quality is improving rapidly. Because of stability problems, it is a mistake to be seduced by cuteness and buy a very small camcorder; one that sits on the shoulder and can be held comfortably with both hands is better. The camcorder should have video and audio line outlets that can be connected to the VCR for rough editing or to the monitor. (Usually, there is an RF connector for the latter purpose.) Power zoom and autofocus, both with manual override, are standard features on many units. Other special features are unnecessary, unless the unit will be used in one of the more demanding systems described later in this chapter. Decisions concerning tape **format** (Beta, VHS, 8mm, etc.) should be based on compatibility and quality considerations (see "Standardization and Quality").

A *video cassette recorder* (VCR) has crude editing capabilities as well as some convenience and versatility for playing tapes. One common error is to expect that tapes can be recorded without needing at least minimal editing. (See *Point, Shoot, and Cut* for editing operation with a minimal system.) And there is obvious wisdom in copying a tape for general use, while keeping the original in a safe place. Another common mistake is to buy the cheapest VCR available. Whereas a carefully selected middle-range unit will probably have the quality and features needed, a low-end unit almost certainly will not. A minimum standard is three video heads; **flying erase heads** are essential for smooth transitions. Buy the unit with the best picture quality (i.e., maximum lines of horizontal resolution) affordable. At the top end, the VCR becomes an *editing recorder* (with indexing, frame advance, etc.).

Any name-brand *videotapes* made by reputable electronics or camera companies that are designed for the camcorder in use are suitable. Differences between grades of tape (e.g., high-grade vs. standard) are negligible for most purposes, although price differences can be quite substantial. *Cables* (i.e., patch cords) other than those supplied with the equipment may be necessary. It is useful to have ready replacements for those cables that break just before a crucial performance and to have cords with alternative plug fittings—for there are myriads in the video industry.

Much can be done with a basic system, which costs about $3000. More can be spent on this system just to increase its quality and versatility; indeed, it may be money wisely spent if future expansions are envisioned. Larger or better definition screens or different projection systems can be bought for thousands of dollars. But these can be added to the system later (the smaller monitor will still have its uses); they are unlikely to be necessary for an initial setup. However, with camcorders the return is most often reflected in the price. Spending up to 100% more should buy better quality and more features (the first ED-Beta camcorder marketed in the United States for $7,000). The most valuable additional features are **flying erase heads** (for high-quality transitions), *manual* **iris** (for backlit subjects), and *high-speed shutter* (for high-quality slow motion).

Extended Basic System

There are numerous ways to improve the quality of minimal operations and the system's ease of use. One possibility is to add the following items (see Figure 1.2):

- tripod ($100)
- microphone ($100)
- editing recorder ($1,500)
- editing controller ($500)
- copying recorder ($400)

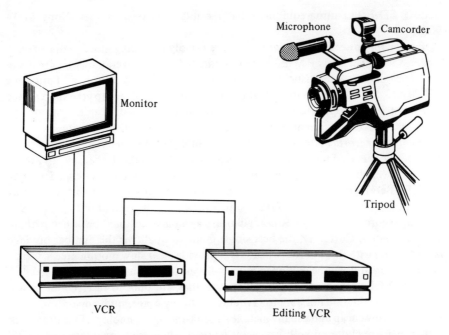

Figure 1.2. Configuration of an "extended basic system." If an editing controller is available, a setup similar to that shown in Figure 2.1 (without the computer and data entry) can be used.

In any static setting, a *tripod* is better than a shoulder. Stability, smooth swivel action ("fluid head"), easy height adjustment, and, for some, portability are important features. Almost certainly, the camcorder will have a built-in *microphone* (mic), but no matter how high the quality is, the microphone will be most sensitive to noises originating close to the camera (e.g., mutters and snuffles of the camera operator) and from the camera itself (especially the zoom motor). The best effects are usually obtained either with a directional microphone mounted on a stand or with a boom closer to the subjects or by using small clip-on wireless microphones. The choices are too complex to describe concisely here, so reliable advice should be sought in consideration of position and movement of the subjects, the microphone range, matching impedances, and interference from fluorescent lights and local radio transmissions.

The inclusion of an *editing recorder* considerably enhances the capacity of a minimal system. At this stage, it is wise to invest in a unit that might become part of a full editing system. At the same time, the recorder should be able to make copies or do simple editing as needed. I have used a Sony HF1000 (Super Beta) because it has flying erase heads, frame-by-frame advance (using a jog-shuttle or remote), simple titling, some other features useful to our activities, and plays all earlier formats of Beta. We have recently added a Sony Hi-8mm EVS-900, which is even better. Recommended VCR editing units in other formats include Sony 8mm EV-S800, Panasonic VHS AG1950, and JVC S-VHS HR-S8000U. For a slightly bigger budget, ED-Beta editing equipment has recently been released (e.g., Sony EDV-9000).

Reasonably priced *editing controllers* are rapidly becoming more available (e.g., Azden VPC-10 or Sony RM-E300, both under $500). However, they vary greatly in their capabilities. A sophisticated system can be added for a price (e.g., Panasonic WJ-MX12, $3,000 or Videonics ProEd, $5,000). It is a good idea to get expert advice and insist on the opportunity to try out or observe a system operating on the prospective tasks. See remarks on editing toward the end of this chapter.

A *copying recorder* is a useful addition because (1) any edited tape should always be kept aside in a safe place while copies are used for teaching, therapy, and other tasks and (2) the editing system should be of a superior quality (e.g., Hi-8mm, S-VHS, Beta) compared to the format most commonly available on replay equipment. (This is currently VHS—which should be the format of the copier). A copying recorder, or any VCR in regular use as a player, should be of better-than-average quality. Currently, the best single guide to quality is the number of *video heads;* VCRs with three or more **heads** will provide clear slow motion, freeze frame, and scanning and will be equipped with other useful sophistications.

These VCRs are "home" systems; that is, they are built to receive and record broadcast TV; they are not built for a multiuser, heavy usage, studio operation. They are remarkably cheap and usually include state-of-the-art technology. One drawback is that they are cluttered with irrelevant features, such as channel selection, MTS decoders, programming controls and the flashing "12:00" that is usually impossible to turn off. The equipment should be protected from overuse, or plans should be made for early replacement (a wise strategy given the rate of advancing technology).

Laboratory System

Expansion beyond a basic system depends on the user's main purpose. Following are some guidelines to help determine what is needed.

Some uses of video can be best achieved in circumstances in which the user has considerable control over the environment—dramatizations or analysis of fine motor behavior, for example. At other times, a contrived environment may provide a workable compromise with reality, while predesigned equipment settings are imperative (e.g., split-screen imaging). In both these circumstances a video laboratory or studio is called for.

Setting

It is assumed that the home of this system will be a stable environment, dedicated to its purpose. The design of the setting will vary greatly, depending on the objectives, and the following elements should be taken into consideration:

- *Room dimensions:* Height affects reflected light, acoustics, suspended equipment; floor space affects camera angles.

- *Coverings:* These affect light and sound as well as movement of subjects and picture background.

- *Location:* The most troublesome sound tracks usually come from extraneous noises, often unnoticed at the time of recording. (Soundproofing is very expensive; radio interference can usually be masked with technical help.)

- *Fixtures:* Drapes, mounted lights, and mounted cameras may need remote or individual operation.

- *Entry points:* Windows create lighting problems and distractions; doors should be designed to allow timely entry and exit and to prevent untimely events.

- *One-way screens:* Sound and light transmission problems are quite complex.

In the observation room, a single layer of plate glass will block whispers but not normal conversation; a one-way screen will act as a mirror only if the light is much brighter on one side than on the other. A room beyond a one-way screen should be as acoustically soft as possible (using carpet, vinyl-padded counters, etc.) and all sources of light must be controlled. The room should also have a bright overhead light to be used when not recording, shielded 15-watt lamps for note taking and unobserved movements, a sound system with a speaker for general monitoring, and phone jacks for recording. There should be an exit that does not lead directly into the studio, equipped with a warning light or other system to prevent untimely interruption.

Such a room is the ideal location for a video control center, to monitor, switch, and mix cameras during recording. It is also ideal for in vivo observations, especially when these are used to guide the laboratory activity (e.g., instruct trainees and terminate trials). In either case, an appropriate two-way sound system may be designed. Such a room is not suitable for group observations. For master clinician demonstrations and the like, it is preferable to take a closed-circuit TV to another room where observers can make comments, cough, and shuffle normally.

Equipment

In modest applications, the extended minimal system just described may be sufficient. The camcorder can be operated through the one-way screen, but this poses problems for picture angle, quality, and sound. Sound can be improved if the camera low light rating is 10 lux or less, and if an external microphone is wired through the wall. The best picture is achieved when the camera is mounted on a tripod and operated inside the studio. (Some camcorders, once set up, can be crudely operated by remote control.) A more ambitious enterprise will benefit from an arrangement designed with individualized technical assistance. Following are the *functional* amenities for which equipment advice should be sought:

- *Multiple angles.* Two or more cameras (not camcorders) can be mounted on tripods or wall brackets (industrial quality should be considered).

- *Camera movement.* A dolly (tripod on wheels) provides a common means of smooth movement during recording.

- *Shutter controls.* Some camcorders now feature high-speed shutters (1/500–1/1,000 second speeds are most useful) that allow unblurred slow motion playback; also available are timers for delayed action or interval recording.

- *No-light recording.* Some cameras boast a minimum illumination of 1 lux (for candlelight dinners, I presume), and infrared cameras, often used in sleep research, are available.

- *Picture mixing.* Two camera sources can readily be combined in one recording, often using an *insert* (e.g., a close-up of an individual in the corner of a picture showing the whole group) or a **split screen** (e.g., a person in profile is seen simultaneously from the front).

- *Digital coding.* Some recorders now translate video signals into digital code that makes it possible to store pictures and manipulate them for high-quality special effects—in particular, still frame, slow motion, reverse action, and picture in picture.

- *Indexing.* A variety of systems are available to access preidentified recorded sequences and to store simple information with them (e.g., time codes).

- *Computer analysis.* Sophisticated data analysis from videotapes (Krauss, Morrel-Samuels, & Hochberg, 1988; and Chapter 2) is greatly enhanced by computer interface, which can also considerably augment special effects and indexing functions.

A well-equipped studio or laboratory has far-reaching implications for what can be achieved by a behavioral scientist using video. The previous list is intended to indicate the opportunities that are most accessible. Unfortunately, as sophistication increases, so does cost—somewhat exponentially. The cost of equipping a studio may range anywhere from $10,000 to $1 million. Once established, the costs of running the facility should include the wages of some expert personnel, since the more capable industrial equipment is not very user friendly.

Field Recording

Pedestrian behavior at intersections cannot be brought into the laboratory, nor can soccer at the Olympics. And if you bring an abusive (or loving) couple into a special setting, it will be extremely difficult to get them to act naturally. These are examples of situations in which the camera must go to the people—because, for whatever reason, the activity and its context are more readily accessible in another environment. The basic and extended minimal systems are better suited to the field than to the laboratory. Following are some special considerations in field recording.

- *Portability.* Weatherproof, high-impact plastic carrying cases are available, but I prefer a shabby suitcase that does not look worth stealing, and a trundler of the type used by airline travelers. Some equipment is designed for use in adverse weather, such as Sony's 8mm Sportcam. Note that many recorders have humidity and temperature sensors and will not operate under potentially damaging conditions.

- *Batteries.* Always carry a spare, fully charged battery and a charger/AC converter with extra-long leads.

- *Recording and monitoring.* Different microphones suit different purposes; these include uni-, bi-, and omnidirectional, windproofed, or cordless. Cheap headphones for personal stereos are perfect for monitoring sound. Most portable recording systems have an electronic viewfinder for built-in replay.

- *Special fixtures.* Some recording tasks require on-site fixtures, and these will benefit from ingenuity and imagination. A good example is a system for filming from inside a moving vehicle through a fixed point of the front windscreen (see Casswell, 1983).

- *Portable replay.* A portable recorder can often be played through a TV set via an RF converter for occasional replay in a home or school setting—but beware the variety of possible connectors. Self-contained player-monitor systems are available in different degrees of portability and screen size from $500 up; player-only units (VCPs) are generally available only at the bottom end of the market. (Avoid relying on someone else's VCR—half the time it will play the wrong format or the wrong speed.)

Editing and Production

Editing potentially serves different purposes, and a system that is ideal for one purpose may not be so convenient for another. Most video tasks aspired to by behavioral scientists and practitioners can be accomplished with an extended minimal system comprising high-quality equipment. Often a form of crude editing is required. That is, sequences of recordings from one or more tapes are collected onto another tape—to provide temporary documentation for a conference presentation, perhaps, or assessment sequences for random order judging. This task can be achieved easily with a basic system, even when the sequences are quite short and transitions need to be relatively glitch free, as, for example, constructing a self-model tape. (See Chapters 7 and 16.)

If video documentation is destined for repetitive use or an audience concerned with technical quality, *fine* editing is necessary (e.g., procedure descriptions for dissemination and outcome illustrations for funding support). The advent of flying erase heads that allow smooth transitions between sequences and the easy addition of simple titles and audio dubbing have made it possible to create fine-looking products with simple VCR-(or camcorder-)-to-VCR editing. For more sophisticated effects or large volumes of editing and reediting, a system with an editing *controller* and special effects components is warranted. With unlimited resources, unlimited creativity is possible. Following are some worthy items to consider in editing and production:

- *Transition continuity.* Most VCR equipment that is designed for use with a controller will provide a 5-second preroll that brings the tapes up to speed before copying, so that the "joins" are technically perfect.

- *Inserts.* Editing into the *middle* of a sequence, so that a clean transition is made at both ends of the inserted material, is nearly impossible without a full editing system.

- *Programming.* A moderately advanced system will allow a series of editing decisions to be memorized and the planned sequences displayed on the monitor and selectively modified before being executed.

- *Titles.* Recorders or editors that have built-in title generators are very useful for keeping track of sequences as they are recorded (e.g., labeling each segment in a single tape used to collect 5-minute samples of eating behavior every Monday lunchtime for 2 months) or for an occasional documentary (e.g., a class presentation), but they are cumbersome to use. For title variety and frequent use, an accessory title generator can be added for about $200.

- *Dubbing.* Sound (one or two tracks) or picture can usually be dubbed (merged with other recorded material) quite readily without additional equipment.

- *Wipes and fades.* Soft transitions (melting a picture into white or into another picture) are technically complex; they are achieved with camera controls at the time of filming, with special effects accessories, or some editing controllers.

- *Split screens and picture-in-picture.* These effects are readily achieved with suitable mixing equipment at the time of recording. The advent of *digital* recorders has made the mixing of recorded sources quite possible in a moderately endowed system.

- *Borders.* Some manipulation of the picture itself is now possible; the simplest manipulation is a colored border of any width that can be achieved with a superimposer.

- *Picture enhancement.* Modest quality adjustments such as image sharpening and visual noise reduction can be made, sometimes as a feature of the editing recorder itself. *Digital zoom* enables a piece of the picture to be enlarged to screen size (with associated loss of detail).

The amenities just listed are made easier with either a sophisticated controller or a simple one to which selected special effects components can be added. If the system is to be used frequently, or if the range of effects is at all extensive, it is better to identify a comprehensive special effects controller at the outset. Some processors developed for the high end of the home video market are remarkably sophisticated for their price (e.g., Sansui VX-99, $600; Showtime AV Processor, $2,700).

Standardization Wars and Quality Considerations

Wherever there is technology, behavioral and social scientists are there to try it. Use, therefore, has been proportional to availability. In the mid-1960s, advances in technology made video available to many institutions where it became popular for teaching, large research projects, and hospital-based clinical services. The breakthrough was the development of the **U-matic** system, which used 3/4-in. tape in a self-loading cassette and mass production that greatly reduced costs. This format became the quality standard in the behavioral sciences for about 20 years. (Larger formats are used in broadcasting and commercial studios.) Many institutions still maintain their U-matic recording and editing facilities because, until 1987, none of the smaller formats could match the quality.

However, there have always been several different systems of video recording competing for the consumer's attention, and the incompatibility situation has never been worse. Currently, there are three major small-format systems available. Within these three, there are substantial variations; most of these variations are incompatible with each other. In addition, there are three major (and other minor) television **display** systems worldwide—so that, for example, a VHS tape recording produced in the United States is unplayable on a regular VHS recorder produced in Britain, and a tape recorded in Britain cannot normally be played in France.

The price and convenience of the small formats have made them tremendously sought after. Intense consumer interest (over 40% of homes in the United States now have a VCR; one family in ten owns a camcorder) has fueled the competition, resulting at last in the availability of better-than-broadcast quality. For anyone who wants to rent video movies, the choice of VHS is clear. However, VHS dominance of this market is due to marketing wizardry and some luck on the part of the VHS interests (primarily JVC). Choosing equipment for live recording and editing purposes is much more complex. To make purchasing decisions and to be an informed user, it is worth examining the elementary technology (Medoff & Tanquary, 1986; Speed, 1988).

The possibility of small (and therefore portable) formats, even 1-inch tape, came with the development of the **helical scan.** Simply put, helical scan is the ability to record information diagonally on magnetic tape. The moving video image, as in the cinema, is made up of a series of still pictures flashed on the screen for a fraction of a second. Each still (frame) comprises over 500 lines; each line is composed of tiny dots; each dot is coded for its intensity in one of the primary colors. One way to keep frame-by-frame information together on a narrow tape economically and coherently is to lay it out diagonally. The problem of how to record and read back diagonal coding on a moving tape was solved by pushing the tape against a drum, in which the read-record heads are spinning (in a helix) at a slight angle to the direction of the tape. The heads are exposed to the tape through a slot in the side of the drum that takes the head diagonally from near the bottom to the top edge of the tape. One or two simple sound tracks can be coded along the tape, using stationary read-record heads as in a conventional audio tape recorder. The video recording system is ingenious, yet complex enough that the conditions of equipment uncertainty and quality variations that have plagued the field for many years should surprise no one.

The first system to put half-inch tape in a self-loading cassette was invented by Sony, but it was set aside because both the encoding and tape handling were thought to be too cumbersome. Ironically, this system was later adopted and developed by

JVC, who called it Video Home System—VHS. In the meantime, Sony developed a technically simpler half-inch system, called Beta, with quality that was surprisingly close to U-matic. VHS arrived on the market with cassettes slightly bigger than Beta, partly because the coding system uses more space and partly to gain an edge in the length of available recording time. It is rumored that VHS's domination of the market stems from the fact that it was the first home system programmable for 2 hours of recording—the usual slot for broadcast movies and some major sports events. It is likely that JVC's willingness to franchise VHS to many manufacturers, thus increasing its availability, was an even more important factor. Beta continued to provide superior recording and editing quality, but battles for off-the-air recording convenience led to a distressing number of variations within the major formats.

Sony then focused on the development of 8mm video, using superior electronics to retain picture quality with considerable reduction in tape (and therefore recorder) size. These electronics and other advancements have recently been incorporated into Super VHS and Extended Definition Beta—to retain tape size with greatly enhanced picture quality. Following are the current formats of consumer equipment in descending order of quality to be expected, with additional relevant information. (Consideration of professional equipment may be referred to the media specialists.)

Extended Definition (ED) Beta

The first review of a production model VCR (Sony EDV-9000) using sophisticated laboratory testing equipment (Feldman, 1988) indicated 500 lines of horizontal resolution, beyond anything else currently available in half-inch formats—indeed, far beyond the industry standard for U.S. broadcast television (330 lines). *Horizontal resolution* is the technical attribute that contributes most to picture quality. Other technical attributes (color, contours, steadiness, and sound) are also top of the line, although more marginally so. The ED quality requires the use of ED tape with a more expensive metal coating. This machine will record ED at two speeds (Beta II and III); it also records Beta IS (Super Beta) on regular tapes. It will play back any other Beta recording. It has useful editing features: a **jog/shuttle** wheel that provides frame-by-frame movement control, a memory in which to store the location of sequences for semiautomatic editing, and digital control of still frames and flash motion.

An ED-Beta camcorder (Sony EDC55) capable of producing live recordings of the quality just described is available. It carries state-of-the-art features for a top model: flying erase heads, high-speed shutter, continuous white balance, automatic iris with manual override, and a 10:1 manual and motor zoom. This model has more appeal to the "prosumer," as it requires more light than most camcorders, manual focus, and a strong arm. (The camcorder weighs 15 lb.) The term *prosumer* has recently been coined to refer to the market between professionals and average consumers.

There are two things to watch out for in camcorder evaluation: (1) resolution of the camera section is quite independent of (and usually much higher than) resolution in the recorder, which is the section that matters, and (2) many camcorders back up as much as 2 seconds at the end of a recording sequence to provide glitch-free continuation, touted as an advantage. However, for data sampling or unrehearsed documentation, it can be quite an inconvenience.

Super Video Home System (S-VHS)

The JVC VCR HR-S10000U, described in a test report by Feldman (1989), is about the same price as Sony's ED-Beta VCR but it is more expensive than more modest S-VHS decks. (It was first released at $3,500.) It has a horizontal resolution of barely 400 lines, but the quality of its other technical features if reportedly comparable to the ED-Beta VCR. The editing and special effects are quite sophisticated: not only is there essential frame-by-frame control in review mode, but the VCR is capable of editing extremely short sequences and multiple sequences may be programmed with preroll. As with ED-Beta, S-VHS recording requires special tapes. Most units will record regular VHS on regular tapes and will play back any tape recorded on an earlier VHS system.

The Olympus VX-S405 camcorder delivers a "mere" 350 lines of horizontal resolution (other S-VHS camcorders rate up to or slightly over 400) but it includes some special digital effects that might be useful for ambitious documentary or stop action enterprises. It has the important state-of-the-art camcorder features listed earlier and it claims a low-light capability of 1 lux.

Hi Band-8mm Format

Hi-8 is on a par with S-VHS for picture quality and has the advantages of the smallest format tape size and top-of-the line audio. I use a Sony CCD-V99 (bought for under $2,000), which has 400 lines horizontal resolution, an 8:1 zoom ratio, high shutter speeds, automatic and manual iris, and continuous white balance. Titles can be recorded and superimposed, even scrolled, over other materials. The disadvantage of its miniaturization (it weighs 3.5 pounds with battery) is its instability and controls that are difficult to use when the camera is operating. The Canon A1 has a completely different grip, like a still photography camera, which may be an advantage. (It also has a 10:1 zoom.) There is likely to be a marketing push in Hi-8 camcorders for the "prosumer" (e.g., the Sony CCD-V5000; Beckner, 1990). Although this market is designed around the amateur videophile, it could encompass the nonmedia professional (e.g., behavioral scientist) who needs video as a part-time tool.

Optical Disc Format

Although it is not economically feasible for most readers to create original videos on optical discs, some may be able to use commercially produced laser videodiscs in their applications. (See Chapter 9). Manufactured on the same principles as audio compact discs (CDs), videodiscs deliver a very high-quality picture (over 400 lines) and superb audio reproduction. Several excellent laser players are now on the market.

The Pioneer Laser Vision Player, Model CLD-1080, is remarkably priced at $600, delivers highest image quality, and can play discs with either analog or digital sound tracks. Toward the other end of the price spectrum ($2,000) is Pioneer's CLD-92 LaserVision Player, which incorporates the features just cited and others, including a time-base corrector and a digital memory that allows such extras as still picture with sound, strobe motion with sound, totally noise-free scan, and special effects on CLV discs. In 1989, the first prototype of a recordable videodisc was demonstrated at a trade show for future consumer products.

Limited interactive video capability can be programmed onto a videodisc, requiring no further equipment. But full use of the medium requires a computer. The term hypermedia is often used to refer to a configuration including a Macintosh run with Hypercard software, although Amiga and some IBM-type systems are also popular. For technical and production information, see Optical Recording Project/3M (1981) and Miller (1987); for comment on interactive video in schools, see Seal-Warner (1988).

Super Beta

This system is clearly superior to the ones described below; it is even more clearly surpassed by those just listed. The Sony HF1000 has editing features similar to those of the more advanced systems, but picture quality at 270 lines is not comparable to the newer formats that use metal evaporated tape. It now has the advantage of being "previously best" in convenience and reliability, and has a remarkably good price. The top-of-the-line camcorder, Sony BMC-1000, lacks some features important to home users—in camera replay, low-light sensitivity, auto focus—that may or may not also be important to users of this book. If more convenience features are necessary, the BMC-660K offers nearly as good quality.

Beta, VHS, and 8mm

The best of these are comparable in quality, and choices can be determined primarily on the convenience of features offered by individual models. In Beta, look for the versatility to replay (if not record) at different speeds; in VHS, HQ circuitry is a must. The appeal of 8mm is its size; therefore it is important to double-check for a full range of the features required. In all recorders, flying erase heads and digital circuitry have great advantages, and some types of indexing may be helpful. Camcorders in these formats can have all the features just listed as state of the art, except that (only) 6:1 zoom is common in 8mm.

VHS-Compact

VHS-C (also S-VHS-C) was JVC's camcorder counter to the size challenge introduced by 8mm. The VHS-C uses a smaller cassette with a much shorter playing time; it can be played in a full-size machine, usually with an adapter. These camcorders may be of modest quality and may lack features available on other models.

International Incompatability

As previously indicated, compatibility problems are even worse internationally. The picture (screen) format is determined by broadcasting conventions. These arose in different parts of the world at times when compatibility was not nearly as important as quality. There are three major conventions, and a few minor variations, in use worldwide. The United States reaped a disadvantage when it became the first country to broadcast television; the **NTSC** (National Television Standards Committee) standard of 550 lines to the screen seemed plenty at the time. The British followed a few years later, adopting **PAL** (Phase Alternation Line) with 625 lines and an improved (but not quite compatible) color system. The French and the Russians later adopted **SECAM** (Sequential Couleur à Mémoire) with an even more stable color system. For years, there has been talk about adopting a high-density television **(HDTV)** picture convention (over 1,000 lines) for worldwide use. In the meantime, programs beamed by satellite are translated at receiving stations and rebroadcast in the local standard, and some studios offer services to translate recorded materials. Larger institutions in many parts of the world (though fewer in the U.S.) often have access to U-matic or VHS machines that can switch among NTSC, PAL, and SECAM. Reasonably priced players and recorders have recently become available that are capable of switching between international formats. For example, Instant Replay 620 IT3 is a 3-1/2-kilogram VHS player-only (priced about $700) that plays NTSC, PAL, and SECAM on almost any TV set. The World Traveler will play or record almost any national system in VHS most places worldwide (under $2,000).

OPERATION

Each piece of equipment has its own principles of operation. The best way to learn about the equipment is from someone who already knows how to use it, and by referring to the user manuals. In this section there is short discussion of issues not described in user manuals—namely, psychological barriers, tips about recording and editing, and troubleshooting.

Equipment Phobias

In universities and other large institutions it is often tempting to say, "Let's get someone from media services to do the filming." This solution is not always best—it depends on the purpose of the intended product. If the objective is to document relatively predictable behavior, such as a 30-minute meal session with a selective food refuser, then a visit to the studio or the use of a technician is wise. For more complex activities, it is necessary to develop a relationship with the technical personnel, to educate them about the needs of the specialty. For example, body language that is obvious to a psychologist may be overlooked by a media specialist—as easily as a white balance indicator may be overlooked by a clinician.

For some activities, it it relatively easy to train students or interns to become fluent with equipment and to capitalize on their ready appreciation of the variables that are of value to the purpose of the project. This is clearly true in self-modeling, for example, where cases are highly individualized and the technical quality is of minor importance. For behavioral scientists or clinicians who are not working in large institutions, employing media services may not be an option. Overall, some autonomy in the use of video equipment is desirable and there is little need to be daunted by the undertaking.

It is surprisingly common to find professionals whose attitude toward operating electronic equipment is tantamount to phobic. That is, they discount the possibility of acquiring the necessary skills, and their avoidance ensures it. Prevention of the avoidance response is required, but expected performances must be graduated. Unlike some phobias for which fear of harm or the anxiety itself is the issue, here there is a fear of not knowing what to do, making possibly irrevocable errors (erasing a tape) and looking foolish. It is worthwhile to ensure much successful practice in the basics, as early as possible. Hopefully, as home videos become more widely used by family members, these "phobias" will become less common.

A less negotiable crisis is to encounter subjects who are phobic or excessively inhibited at the prospect of being filmed. However, this situation is surprisingly less common than one might expect. When I first started working with physically handicapped children over 10 years ago, I was very cautious about the prospect of their not wanting to participate or see themselves on video. However, they were generally exuberant. Even greatly overweight (Prader-Willi syndrome) adolescent boys quite pestered me to see their videos. Teenagers in delinquency programs have typically preened themselves and participated in group processes more fully in the presence of a camera. I have encountered only three exceptions: one was a 10-year-old boy with severe acquired cerebral palsy, who had been knocked down by a truck several years earlier; the others were both teenage girls with histories of abuse.

A major strategy to help overcome these fears (successfully used with the 10-year-old boy) is to give the subject experience as an operator in the medium. This tactic presumably gives the individual a greater sense of control, especially if he or she can film the would-be photographers and see them on the monitor first. Also, by making the filming a nonissue, desensitization is allowed to occur, most readily when other members of a group are participating freely. If a subject reluctantly agrees to participate, skillful use of the camera can make the picture more flattering.

Point, Shoot, and Cut

The most common technical faults in recording (which are not avoided simply by following the user manual) are a wavering picture, unsatisfactory focus, uneven lighting, jerking transitions, and poor sound.

Picture Stability

Some people are naturally good at holding a camera still on their shoulder, some can achieve stability with practice, and others should always use a tripod. The steps are obvious: (a) hold the camera with both hands, with one elbow pressed against the torso; (b) move very slowly and only if necessary—preferably stop recording, move, then restart; and (c) breathe evenly with the diaphragm.

Focus

Most automatic systems bounce an infrared beam at the middle of the picture. These systems will, therefore, be inaccurate if the center of the picture is black (absorbs infrared) or "hollow" (a more distant object is focused on), or if something like an elbow projects between camera and subject. A manual focus can be adjusted with the zoom on "telescope" (maximum close-up) for the greatest detail; it need not be readjusted when the zoom angle is varied as desired.

Back Lighting

Video cameras adjust to the total amount of light in the picture, so that a bright background (e.g., a window) renders a person in the foreground much too dark. One solution is to dim the light source. It is better to have a slightly grainy picture than not to be able to see the main subject. Better cameras have a **manual iris** that allows the user to determine the overall exposure, or a backlight switch. If possible, film with the major source of light behind the camera.

Camera Transitions

Beginning users turn the camera as they would turn their heads, which produces confusion in a video picture, particularly when the movement is not drawn by peripheral vision. Suppose an exchange between two people is being recorded and the one on the left is framed, head and shoulders in the picture. The best solution is to open the angle to include both people, holding the top left corner of the picture steady (it takes some practice to do it smoothly), then shrink the picture down to frame the other person, keeping the top right corner steady.

Sound

If a monitor is connected to the camera, it can be turned off during recording, otherwise it causes audio feedback (and the picture distracts subjects). As mentioned earlier, built-in microphones pick up noises closest to the camera disproportionately louder than other sounds, and plug-in microphones are susceptible to interference or may lose the connection and not work at all. Expert advice is often necessary when sound quality is important. An essential practice is always to monitor the sound with headphones.

More sophisticated filming techniques are described in Chapter 12; sample script extracts are included in Chapters 2 and 3.

A recording worth keeping is a recording that has been edited. Some brochures boast "in-camera editing," with which it is possible by careful planning to record one scene at a time, check its accuracy, rerecord if necessary or add another scene, and thus assemble a complete recording. In most professional settings, it is much easier to record scenes as they become available and then assemble them on an editing recorder. (The reference to "cut" in the section heading above is facetious; unlike cine film, video recordings are not edited with a scalpel, but electronically—by rerecording onto another videotape.)

The use of a full editing system (two editing recorders, two monitors, and a controller) requires some training and cannot be described here. But most readers will have use of a player (or camcorder), one monitor, and, at best, one editing recorder—the minimum system for crude editing. For those who simply want to tidy up some reasonable footage, the following information will help.

Minimal Editing and Copying

Connect the equipment (as shown in Figure 1.2) so that video and audio signals go out of one recorder (call this the *player*) into another (call this the *editor*) that is connected to the monitor. If one recorder makes better picture "joins" between stopping and starting the record function, use it for the editor; otherwise, the better quality machine should be used for the player. Put a new tape in the editor and wind it on 30 seconds. Play the tape to be edited in the player (it will show on the monitor with the other machine switched on but not playing), and review it once or as often as necessary. Use a cue sheet to note exactly the counter numbers and descriptions of parts to be deleted. (See Figure 1.3.) Rewind it to a few seconds before the beginning of usable footage. Set the editor to record-pause, start the player, and release pause on the editor exactly at the beginning of the usable sequence. Hit pause again for footage to be deleted, releasing it the instant that another usable sequence begins. If a sequence beginning or end is misjudged, both tapes can be rewound to a suitable restarting point, although the transition may not be as clean. A simple copy may be made with these connections, and it does not matter if the formats are mixed (e.g., 8mm to VHS).

Titles

Titles, planned and prepared ahead of editing, may be added during the editing and copying procedure. Some recorders have built-in or auxiliary titlers. These enable titles to be stored in numbered memories and called up at any time for recording directly onto blank tape or they can be superimposed while copying. Alternatively, simple titles may be made by printing them on letter size (approximately A4) paper and recording them with a camera. Superior results are obtained using a laser printer, colored paper, and the reverse color feature, if the camera has one.

Troubleshooting

Following are some common problems that often are not mentioned in user manuals, along with their possible solutions. It usually pays to double-check cables, plugs, power supply, and switch settings first. (Adapted from Dowrick, 1986, pp. 191–192.)

Problems During Recording with Camera or Camcorder. (If recording with VCR, tape-to-tape or off-air, check monitor settings, VCR settings—especially "input" and "VTR/TV"—and cables with the user manual.)

No Picture

- Check the lens cap, camera cable, and camera/VTR switch.
- Check the power supply of the recorder (and camera if separate).
- Check the brightness control on viewer/monitor.
- Try again; check that the recording signal inside viewfinder is on.

Sequence	Start #	Pre-event Cues	Behavior for FF or PSR	End-Event Cues	End #	Comments

Figure 1.3. Editing cue sheet.

Faint Picture

- Check the iris controls.
- Check the aperture speed settings.
- Check for insufficient light on the subject.
- Check the brightness controls on the viewer monitor.

Unstable Picture

- Camera may be switched to "VTR."
- Record heads may need cleaning.
- High-speed aperture may be on.
- A tearing-like distortion may be resolved by a **tracking** adjustment, or it may be the result of a weak signal.

No Sound

- A loose microphone cable will cut off the automatic without engaging the remote microphone.
- If a remote microphone is being used, it may require a fresh battery.

Poor Sound

- Wind or camera noises may be picked up by microphone.
- The microphone may be too far away.
- The monitor sound may be on.
- Cables or connections may be faulty.
- There may be mismatched impedance between the microphone and the recorder.
- Radio waves or fluorescent lighting transmissions may be picked up by unshielded microphone cables.

Recorder Switches Itself Off

- Batteries may need recharging.
- The end of the tape may have been reached.

Record Function Does Not Operate

- End of tape.
- Record protection on the cassette may be operating.

Problems on First-Time Replay. Play a previously recorded tape on the VCR (or the new tape on another VCR) to determine whether the fault is in the tape (see above) or the machine (see below).

Problems on Replay of Tape Previously Problem-Free. First play another tape on the VCR to determine whether damage (heat, humidity, magnetism, liquids, stretching or scratching from a faulty player) has occurred to the tape since the last use.

No Picture

- Check the input selection on the monitor.
- Check the VTR/TV settings on the monitor.
- Check the channel selection if using an RF conversion.
- Check the starting point of the recorded material.
- Check the brightness control on the monitor.

Poor Picture

- Check the brightness control.
- Check whether the skew or tracking needs adjustment (probable if the recording was made on another machine).
- Check whether the replay heads need cleaning.

Poor Color

- Check the hue and contrast controls.
- Color "temperatures" may have been on the wrong setting during recording.

No Sound

- Check the channel 1/2/mix settings.

Poor Sound

- The monitor may be malfunctioning.

Replay Function Does Not Operate

- The end of tape may have been reached.

For more serious problems, useful information can be found in books such as McComb (1988) or service manuals, usually available from manufacturers at a moderate cost.

COPYING AND STORAGE

Occasional copying may be done as previously described. Large quantities of copying are best done at a media center, where banks of machines are used simultaneously. Such facilities often have film trains (to copy 8mm and 16mm **cine film** onto video) and color correctors or other image adjusting equipment. If it is anticipated that many copies will be made, the original can be kept and used *only* for copying. If a copy is to be given to someone to make further copies, it may be desirable to "copy up" into a superior format, so that the copies suffer minimal loss of signal.

Protection

Magnetic tapes are susceptible to deterioration from regular use, age, humidity, and other magnetic fields (such as the area near the back of the refrigerator and walk-through metal detector units at airports). They are not affected by X-rays, but X-ray machines generate magnetic fields when switched on or off. (Note that increases in both terrorism and agricultural bug control have led to the formality of x-raying most checked baggage, especially on international flights.) If a tape is physically damaged (or spliced), the rough surfaces will damage the VCR read heads. Thus, a damaged tape containing valuable recorded material should be copied once onto a new tape and not used again.

By contrast, videodiscs, manufactured using the same principles as audio compact discs, are almost indestructible. They should not, however, be hit with hammers or drilled with dental equipment.

Cataloging

A large library of tapes deserves a sophisticated system for storage and retrieval (see Betts, 1983). Collections of 500 or fewer tapes may be conveniently stored in drawers or on shelves and ordered by date within topic area. Given the loss in quality from copying in most formats used today, the logical planning and documentation of content is most important. Common sense guides the following:

- Squeezing unrelated material onto underused tapes is a false economy.

- Use short tapes (1 or 2 hours), recorded at the fastest available speed, unless archiving long events (e.g., talks) that need to be accessed only occasionally.

- Systematically label both the cassette *and* its jacket, since these often become separated.

- Include on the basic label an explanatory title, date(s) of recording, originator, and further information about contents as necessary (e.g., types of subjects, procedures, or activities).

- Position the spine labels like those on books (across or down, not up); labels may be attached to cassettes to be read conveniently as loaded into the VCR.

- Attach additional labels to indicate explicit content. (Problems can arise because machines have different counter systems and some use frame numbering or minutes:seconds that operate only on the recorded portion of the tape.)

CONCLUSION

New technology has been described as often as possible throughout this chapter. What is now "high tech" will increasingly become accessible to more users; for example, color correctors, animators, and mixing from multiple sources. The dedicated amateur will be able to do anything only the big film studios could do in the past. International differences may become either more important as the world shrinks or less important with the increased availability of switchable machines. Once the market is saturated, multinational industries will compromise and accept limited standards of compatibility in recording formats because, as with computer operating systems, too many consumers will have something they do not want to change. HDTV may come simply to produce international standards, or to create a market to match the advanced recording systems. Interactive video is ready for a boom cycle, with computer and laser technology dragging it along.

CHAPTER 2

Analyzing and Documenting

OVERVIEW

Capturing and analyzing visual images of the behavior of humans and other species are the most prolific uses of video in the behavioral sciences. This topic and the video documentation of research, training, and clinical procedures are the subject matter of Chapter 2. In video analysis, applications are divided into five broad areas: motor activity, nonverbal expression and communication, social interaction, medical diagnosis, and surveillance. Examples of applications are briefly described in different areas, including sports, facial expression in brain-damaged patients, family interactions, and video X-rays. Common methodology and equipment consider- ations are described for the systematic measurement and subsequent analysis of videotapes generated in these types of studies. An overview of essential measurement issues is offered: dimensions and types of measurement, macro and micro analysis, observer issues, and computer interface to facilitate indexing and coding. Surveillance (e.g., sleep, driving research) is described as distinct from the structured observations of the research previously cited.

Much less behavioral science literature exists on documenting with video. Principles on quality, content, format, length, bias, and tone are offered. To assist practical implementation, two examples and some recommendations are presented. The first concerns an economical system of documenting children's progress during hospitalized treatment developed for Johns Hopkins Medical Institutes. The second is a public relations video for a supported work program in an Anchorage agency for people with developmental disabilities; it includes a storyboard-style script synopsis. The chapter ends with a short list of recommendations for using video to enhance talks and conference presentations.

P.W.D.

Perhaps the greatest use of audiovisual recording in the behavioral sciences is that of data collection and analysis. This use of video includes documentation of research activities or clinical and educational procedures. In both cases, video is used to capture and describe behavioral events, but the treatment and purposes are different. (More recently, videotapes have been used as stimuli to produce reactions for further data collection—see Chapter 5.)

ANALYZING

Any type of recording, even a pencil-scored checklist, serves the purpose of preserving certain elements of an event, so that the event can be analyzed later—with the concomitant advantages of obtaining multiple opinions, scrambling the order of events, and so on. All recordings necessarily preserve the events in selective ways, and interpretation during the recording process is difficult to avoid. Video recordings are not helpful when a simpler system will suffice (e.g., Garb, 1984), but they do offer supreme advantages when maximum information and minimum bias are desired.

Types of Application

The opportunities for electronically aided visual analysis seem limitless. However, only a half-dozen major areas of application have substantially drawn the attention of the video camera. These are primarily areas of study in which *direct* observation has become a highly developed art and video recording has been brought in to supplement (or even surpass) it.

The first area of consequence is the analysis of motor activities (see Chapter 15). The use of high-speed cine film has been a key in the development of movement analysis, especially for the complex and precise activities of dance and athletics. Until recently, the celluloid medium was unrivaled for its clarity and its ability to photograph large numbers of frames each second. The advent of low-cost video cameras with high-speed shutters is quickly making this newer medium the one of choice. (Specific applications illustrating this and other areas of video analysis are described in subsequent sections.) Increasingly, comparative psychologists use video to study animal behavior such as courtship and aggression of the Chinese praying mantis (Liske & Davis, 1987); three-dimensional movement patterns of water fleas (Young & Getty, 1987) and rats (Kernan, Mullenix, & Hopper, 1987); and paw preferences in squirrels (Costello & Fragaszy, 1988).

The second area of major importance is the analysis of nonverbal communication and the expression of emotion (see Chapter 10). Attempts to verify the exact patterns of muscle movements and their consistency across individuals—in the facial expression of disgust, for instance—would be extremely protracted, to say the least, without the availability of video analysis.

A third area in which video analysis has been used successfully is the study of social interaction (Summerfield, 1983; Ginsburg, 1979). Again the medium excels by capturing events of some complexity. Unlike the above situations in which slowing down the action is a key to the analysis, here the key is the opportunity for repeated reviewing to establish the elements of salience that would otherwise be unpredictable.

Recently, video has been incorporated into medical diagnosis, the fourth area of consequence. For example, it is now possible to make a "video X-ray" of the esophagus during swallowing by an infant with feeding problems, or to record a patient's face and simultaneous EEG readings for concurrent display on the same videotape. Although reports on its development thus far are limited, the technology is so different that it warrants some description.

Quite a different application is surveillance; that is, a camera is used to cover an area, usually for extended periods of time (sometimes intermittently) to record whatever takes place. (See Casswell, 1983.) Video in this manner (the fifth area of application) is useful for research in such diverse areas as pedestrian behavior at intersections and the tossings and turnings of individuals suffering from insomnia. Diverse applications are also gathered within the burgeoning fields of visual sociology and visual anthropology (e.g., monograph series in Henny, 1987, etc.).

Systematic Evaluation

A systematic analysis of human behavior is warranted when enough is known about an issue so that a clearly defined hypothesis can be formed. Studies of a more exploratory nature are suited to a *surveillance* evaluation.

The first step is to determine exactly what to evaluate. Decisions must be driven by state-of-the-art knowledge in the field of study, not on what fits the capacity of available video recording technology. Video can greatly enhance good research, but it cannot compensate for inadequately chosen experimental variables. For example, the study of hyperactivity in the classroom has drawn attention to numerous observable behaviors that define the disorder. Several systems have been developed for "measuring" hyperactivity, some of which have been widely adopted (e.g., O'Leary, Romanczyk, Kass, Dietz & Santogrossi, 1979). If video analyis is to be undertaken, it will be necessary to deal with the problem of the hyperactive child's high mobility, the added distraction caused by the presence of the camera, and so on, without compromise to the measures themselves. The following examples illustrate choices of evaluation *targets*.

Examples of Movement Analysis

An Oxford University psychologist studied the great British sport of cricket (McLeod, 1987). Using high-speed film, he analyzed the reaction time and the accuracy of bat-swing adjustment to an awkwardly bouncing ball. The target for analysis was the time elapsed between the bounce of the ball and the first indication of change in position (or interrupted smooth movement) of the bat. Time elapsed was easily measured by counting the number of frames in the interval. It is interesting to note that the reaction time of professional cricket players was around one fifth of a second—fast, but no faster than some novices. This finding, therefore, implies that the experts' superiority probably lies in the movement of the bat following the reaction, therefore implying a new target for analysis.

A different kind of sport analysis is illustrated by Ripoll (1988). He used a video-oculographic technique to track gaze direction during volleyball problem situations, comparing coaches and players of national ranking. Movements associated with degrees of pain have been carefully analyzed using video, leading to an "audiovisual taxonomy" (Follick, Ahern, & Aberger, 1985) in which patients are videotaped engaging in a series of specific everyday activities (sitting, removing shoes, etc.) and exercises (toe touching, sit-ups, etc.). Tapes are scored on a seven-item pain behavior protocol: guarded movement, bracing, position shifts, partial movement, grimacing, limitation statements, and nonverbal sounds. Another type of movement analysis using video is applied to ergonomics—for example, Melin (1987) described the use of VIRA (video registration and analysis), a Swedish video-computer technique, to study neck disorders in the telephone industry.

Example of Facial Expression Analysis

Facial expression of emotion is complex and fascinating—particularly when considered in the context of brain function. Bucco-facial apraxia is a condition in which the components (verbal comprehension and motor control) appear to be present, but the ability to make facial movements upon verbal instruction is absent. Borod, Lorch, Koff, and Nicholas (1987) studied patients with left-brain damage and this type of apraxia; right-brain damaged patients and intact adults served as controls. The video was set up to record the whole face, to preserve evidence of any facial responses to instruction, and six movements were targeted. Three movements involved the upper face (one eye closed, raised eyebrows, and lowered eyebrows) and three involved the lower face (protruding tongue, corners of mouth raised, and puckered lips). Instructions to perform these movements were given neutrally (e.g., "lower your eyebrows") and with what the authors referred to as an emotional component ("lower your eyebrows like a frown").

The videotaped responses were rated on their accuracy (location, shape, and direction of movement) and their quality (very clumsy, slightly clumsy, and smooth). These relatively simple methods of rating allowed a high level of agreement between two independent judges (84–100%). They also presented some clear-cut findings (most notably that left-brain damaged patients were more significantly impaired than the others in accuracy and quality, but these two aspects of facial expression were poorly correlated). This experiment is a good example of how a data gathering system that could conceivably be used in vivo can be made highly dependable and fuss free by the use of video. Studies with similar methodology continue to be used with implications for diverse populations such as autistic children (Mirenda, Donnellan, & Yoder, 1983) and the elderly (Malatesta, Izard, Culver, & Nicolich, 1987).

Example of Family Interaction Analysis

Research by the Marriage and Family Studies Group at Catholic University of America in Washington, DC, has used videotape to examine patterns of communication during attempted conflict resolution by couples and families. According to co-directors Notarius and Pellegrini, they "take a microanalytic view of the family that can't be tracked well with the naked eye, and couldn't be reported on accurately by family members" (DeAngelis, 1988, p. 12). Thus, for the type of analysis they seek, video is essential—but not without cost; they report that each hour of interview time requires 26 hours of analysis. Their research is attempting to contrast three different types of family: those in which a parent has a chronic medical illness (viz, diabetes), those in which a parent has a chronic psychiatric disorder (e.g., bipolar disorder), and those in which neither parent has suffered severe mental or physical illness.

Different sources of information have led the researchers to specific hypotheses about expression of thoughts and feelings under different circumstances of interaction. In the analyses, couples were videotaped (through a one-way screen) while attempting to solve a problem of some importance to the family. The whole family was also videotaped under similar circumstances. The videos were transcribed and elements of interaction were then categorized into 34 classifications. A computer analysis has been planned to try to find patterns. For example, is a depressed-sounding comment treated with concern, is it ignored, or is it positively or negatively challenged?

Example of Medical Diagnosis

It is possible to take "video X-rays" of patients, allowing internal reflexes to be examined for diagnostic clarification. For example, a video X-ray may be used if an infant cannot take food orally or does so with extreme difficulty (Logemann, 1986). An investigation of this kind is described by Griggs, Jones, and Lee (1989) for 10 patients, mostly children with severe disabilities including spasticity and mental retardation. The technique is similar to the regular barium-meal X-ray, except that movement is anticipated (chewing and attempted swallowing). The image is displayed on closed-circuit television and recorded on videotape. The results assist in providing "practical advice to parents and carers on how to ensure that feeding (is) efficient, safe and nutritious" (p. 303; also see Jones, 1989).

Setting Up the Target Events

Systematic evaluation depends as much on careful planning of how to draw out the phenomena to be observed and recorded as it does on a predetermination of what to look for. With the cricketers previously mentioned, the balls were thrown by a machine so the speed of approach could be exactly controlled. The balls were made to bounce off a matting, in which hard pieces were concealed to make the bounce unpredictable to the batsman. In Borod's analysis of apraxia, she elicited facial expressions using carefully standardized instructions. The different types of instructions were presented in a specific order (neutral to standard to emotional), which had both advantages and disadvantages.

For the communication analysis by Notarius and Pellegrini, families participate in about 2 hours of preparation before videotaping. An interview, questionnaires, and audiotape recordings are used to identify specific areas of conflict. The tapes are further used to help select a key issue of particular emotional value. In family studies, the validity of naturalistic behavior is approached in different ways. For example, Worden, Kee, and Ingle (1987) told parents, "Please read this alphabet book to your child as you would at home"; Hoffman (1987), also studying parent-child interactions in literacy development, took his video recording equipment into the homes of six selected families. With the medical X-ray, the conditions are straightforward because the reflex in question does not depend on subtleties of the stimuli or underlying conditions. If this were not true, it would be necessary to provide various types of food and perhaps control the level of hunger.

Equipment Considerations

Different equipment is required in each of the examples just cited. The sport study needed a high-speed shutter for a frame-by-frame analysis. Such detail is sometimes required in facial expression analysis too, but Borod and colleagues were concerned with a more global rating, so no special equipment was necessary. In the family communication research, it was necessary for video to be recorded through a one-way screen, so a camera receptive to low light and microphones wired or broadcast through the walls were used. For the medical study, specialized equipment developed and used solely for such purposes was necessary.

The four main areas of research just illustrated do not always demand the four types of equipment exemplified. For example, some sport analysis will do quite well without a high-speed camera, and not all social interaction demands a hidden camera. However, diverse applications are likely to require diverse equipment configurations. A creative approach to the study of Braille reading was reported by Millar (1988). She videotaped from behind a transparent surface encoded with Braille of different textures and accuracy. Another specialized arrangement involves the recording of video plus simultaneously received digital information (Barnes, Haith, & Roberts, 1988) or video output from a computer with simultaneous audio (e.g., student commentary; Krajcik, Simmons, & Lunetta, 1988). These systems greatly alter the usefulness and complexity of the analyses of the recordings.

SUBSEQUENT ANALYSIS

It is after the video data collection is made that the most (or the most tedious) work remains. Whatever is recorded can be analyzed along different dimensions, in different ways, and at different levels of detail. It is usually humans (computer assistance is considered in the next section) who do the analysis; their precision and the value of the data they produce deserve careful consideration.

Events and Context

Dimensions of Measurement

Some basic guidelines are given here. (A thorough discussion deserves a chapter of its own; e.g., see Hersen & Bellack, 1981.) *Frequency* is the most common measurement. Often it is simple (how many times did the ball hit the bat?), but it loses its advantage when other dimensions of the phenomenon are important. This problem is illustrated by the famous reply to the question, "How often have you two argued since I saw you last week?"—"Once: we started the minute we left and we haven't stopped since." Here we have frequency confounded by duration. In a video analysis of arguing, it is more convenient to count the frequency of "you" statements or interruptions—fairly discrete events. If *duration* is important (e.g., the length of silences), the events can be measured in their entirety, or sampled at set intervals if they are frequent enough. The latter method can lead to a "proportion of total time" measure, often used when low incidence events are not important; that is, samples are categorized (maybe simply, as in "tantrum" vs. "not tantrum") at predetermined intervals, and the incidence of each category is measured as a percentage of the total sample. Finally, *magnitude* may be important. In some aspects of human performance, it may be the major dimension—the force of a strike, the length of a stride. In other events, such as social behavior, magnitude may be difficult to measure, and therefore is avoided (wisely or otherwise). For example, in a study of noncompliance (Dowrick, 1978b) I observed a dramatic change that went unmeasured because we were counting the frequency of the response "no" to reasonable requests without taking into account the volume, indeed the ferocity, with which it was said. With this 3-year-old boy, as was easy to see in retrospect, it was his manner, not the content of what he said, that set him at such loggerheads with the world.

Types of Measurement

Frequencies are determined simply by tallying the presence (vs. absence) of an event at the moment of sampling: did the eyelid close at the moment of kissing—yes or no? A duration is simply the elapsed time from onset to offset. Magnitude is much more difficult to measure. Physical magnitudes, such as galvanic skin response or decibels, can be precise and unambiguous. But often in the behavioral sciences, a subjective magnitude is more meaningful (or more available). The most common method is to assign a value on a discrete scale ("on a five-point scale, rate the intensity of disgust") or a continuous scale ("mark the line in proportion to your judgment between the anchor points of total failure and complete satisfaction"). Such scales, as can be inferred from the last example, may be used not only to measure magnitude of discrete events, but also to make global judgments about larger, more complex situations.

Global judgments often enhance the validity (e.g., may help to underscore the clinical significance) of measurements when used in conjunction with more detailed or microanalytic judgments. Video recordings are very useful in this process, because tapes can be stopped during the review to give time for multiple judgments, or the event can be reviewed many times. For example, in a personal safety training program (Dowrick, McManus, Germaine, & Flarity-White, 1985), we videotaped standardized role play situations in which we wanted to know whether clients had put themselves at risk or not. Each event was scored first on the basis of discrete elements: eye contact, body movement, language content (did the client say "no"?), and so on. Then the judges made an overall rating for the client in the event: safe or not safe.

Macro and Micro Analysis

The personal safety evaluation example illustrates, in simple fashion, both micro and macro analysis. It is often valuable to do both. Micro analysis in the extreme can be very detailed. For example, a *Psychology Today* article (Douglis, 1987) claims that William Condon spent "several years analyzing 4.5 sec film snippet of a family dinner." Condon's painstaking work has been instrumental in identifying rhythms and synchronies in human communication patterns, in which elements are measured in hundredths of a second. Such detailed analysis is worthy—but worth the effort only if a specific, testable hypothesis is being pursued.

Reliability and Validity

Video recordings are fundamentally helpful in checking the reliability and validity of observations (e.g., Ross & Leichner, 1988; Runco & Schreibman, 1988). The ability to obtain independent judgments is obvious; the more judges used, the stronger the case that can be made for interjudge reliability. Test-retest reliability measurement becomes quite easy with video; it is simply not possible with live observation. Sometimes video recordings indicate that another data collection system is inaccurate. For example, Collett (1987) compared video recordings of people watching television at home with self-recorded viewing diaries. He found serious discrepancies—during "viewing," people watched the screen only 65% of the time.

Not all aspects of validity can be facilitated using video, but some checks on social validity are accessible. Video is frequently used to sample expert opinion to validate either the judgments of other (less expert) observers or the appropriateness of what is being taught or studied. For example, in the personal safety training, we sampled expert opinion from those who personally knew the clients on their safe or unsafe behavior; Frisch and Froberg (1987) identified women students rated by peers as "most effective in handling criticism" and then had them validate the coping skills of others in terms of whether they were effective, appropriate, or likeable.

Training Observers

Inextricably tied to reliability (and to less extent, validity) is the training of those who do the measures. Here is a typical scenario for training observers to use an established protocol. Sufficient taped examples are identified from pilot studies (any source not in the data pool) for training purposes. The investigator (observer-trainer) goes over one or more examples with the protocol to demonstrate for, say, two observers. Observers may then want to practice on these examples and then perhaps three more (in the same room, but unable to see each other's scoring). Reliability is calculated using the number of identical ratings as a percentage of the total number of ratings made, followed by a discussion between the two observers about how they made their decisions and clarifications by the trainer. This process is repeated until it proves possible for the observers to rate a predetermined number of events, independently and without discussion, at an acceptable level of reliability (e.g., at least 90%). Training observers to criterion in such a manner helps to avoid loss of consistency in the early stages of observation or an overall unacceptable reliability level.

COMPUTER INTERFACE

The term *computer analysis* is sometimes misleadingly used in this context; unfortunately, computers do not analyze video recordings—people do. Essentially, the computer interface allows much sophisticated control of video recorder operation and enables data to be stored and accessed in synchrony with video images. With advances in video and computer technologies, more of these functions are gradually becoming available on the VCR. The computer interface with videodisc is the heart of interactive video (see Chapter 9). Computer accessing of recordings can also be used for other purposes. Krauss, Morrel-Samuels, and Hochberg (1988) described a versatile system that first allows an observer to indicate, by adding codes onto videotape, the beginning and end of any number of event categories and then processes the durations and sequences of events on a computer. This book provides an overview of the analysis of video recordings; computer-video interface requires expert technical support.

Indexing

Computer control of video materials depends primarily on all points of a tape being "addressable." Ability to locate recorded data unambiguously is usually achieved by marking a point of origin near the beginning of the tape, and using an eight-digit code to mark the distance from the origin in terms of hours, minutes, seconds, and frames. Note that this or any other addressing system depends on conventions of how to "mark" the tape; problems will obviously arise when there is discontinuity of recorded material.

All tapes are implicitly addressed by setting the origin at the beginning of the recorded material (or other identifiable place, using the reset function), and by using the VCR to measure elapsed time. Results are imprecise, but can be helpful when the tapes must be used on different equipment systems. Explicit addresses can be recorded on the second audio track or the unused lines of the video signal. (See Chapter 1 for descriptions of tape encoding.)

Data Coding

Further data can be stored on tape in association with each frame. For example, Clarke and Ellgring (1983) gave a detailed description of their longitudinal studies, in which speech, gaze, gesture, facial expression, and verbal content information was coded onto video recordings of depressed clients in structured interviews. These data must be generated by skilled observers, just as with any other observations, except that the precise timing of each event is coded onto the tape via keystrokes on a computer that has been programmed for the specific task. The advantage is that data analysis (also by computer) can show the exact patterns of timing as these different events (looking away, talking, etc.) overlap with one another. Identified patterns of observable behavior are then correlated with other known conditions, such as mood ratings or medications. The computer also can be used to search the tapes and display particular combinations of events that may be of interest. Or the computer can assist in editing sequences of specified characteristics.

Hardware and Software

As indicated in Figure 2.1, different levels of sophistication for tape searching and event notation are available with or without a computer. A common laboratory setup includes a controller hooked up to two VCRs for editing purposes, and to a computer for additional control and data input and on-line analysis.

No system can get by without high-quality video recorders, capable of frame-exact access, digital coding, and high-speed search. Built-in VCR indexing may be

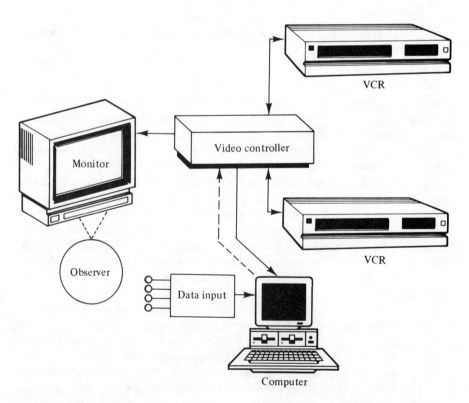

Figure 2.1 Tape searching and notation are possible with and without accessories (adapted from Clarke & Ellgring, 1983, p. 54).

useful, but it is usually redundant with computer control. An editing controller's main purpose is to simplify the operation of multiple VCRs to search and display (or record) tape sequences. As controllers become better and cheaper, they are likely to include more computerlike features, such as greater memory and programming capabilities. Microcomputers have opened up extraordinary possibilities in the video field. Some computers have built-in VCR and videodisc connections, or interface modules are available options. Software for readers of this book will most often need to be custom written. (Krauss et al. at Columbia University, who were mentioned previously, offer their software gratis.)

SURVEILLANCE

Video can play a role in the exploratory phases of research by gathering information from which to generate hypotheses, as opposed to testing them. Three features of video technology make it useful for this purpose:

- Repeated viewing and review of detail through slow motion, freeze frames, and so on.
- Video recording from a viewpoint that is awkward for live observers to obtain.
- Time sampling.

A simple example illustrates the use of the first feature. I was once consulted by a sport psychologist whose client had developed training injuries. "Wes" was a middle-distance runner of international caliber who had had a minor right foot operation from which he had completely recovered. During his attempts to build long, slow distance for stamina, he developed left side pain. Neither he nor his coach could find a cause or a solution. After watching and videotaping his running from a variety of angles, initially there appeared to be no explanation. It was only after repeated viewing that an asymmetry in his running suddenly became evident—once observed it looked so obvious that it was a wonder that it had not been noticed weeks before. Presumably the repetitive viewing of an identical stimulus (as opposed to multiple observations of similar behavior) creates habituation to distractions in the picture, and enables a piece of the pattern to be recognized that would otherwise be unnoticeable.

The fields of visual anthropology (e.g., Heider's studies in Indonesia, see Ekman & Heider, 1989) and visual sociology use video in surveillance mode as a primary means of data gathering. For example, Schaefer (1975) used video to study social transactions connected with the use of marijuana in Jamaica. For some anthropologists, the video recording *is* the analysis; as such, this approach provides the perfect example of video as the only means of observation. Schaefer also reports an early example of video surveillance of family interactions. In this case, the objective was to study transactions in the cramped environments of small dwellings. As others have found, the families soon became habituated to the presence of cameras, and their behavior became natural in a way not possible with observers present.

Other examples of video data gathering in natural situations include studies of infants (see Resch, 1981), their mothers (Harmon, Glicken, & Gaensbau, 1982), interactions between both (Kuczynski, Kochanska, Radke-Yarrow, & Girnius-Brown, 1987), and full families in verbal conflict (Vuchinich, 1984). An interesting study is reported by Holmes, McKeever, and Russman (1983), whose video recordings of profoundly mentally retarded individuals with abnormal EEGs enabled them to make discriminations of true epileptic seizures (vis-à-vis behavior) that were not possible from previous observation.

Sometimes a camera can be positioned where a person would not want to be. For example, Casswell (1983) did a series of studies with drivers under the influence of marijuana. Subjects drove on an abandoned grand prix racetrack in a car equipped with a specially mounted video camera. The recordings from the stable "automobile viewpoint" combined with landmarks painted on the track enabled precise analysis of driving behavior. Although another person traveled in the vehicle as a safety precaution, it was prudent that the passenger did not have to think about data collection.

Time sampling is another example of the camera gathering a type of information that is very difficult for a person to obtain; it is worth singling out for special mention. More and more camcorders designed for the home market are equipped with time-lapse and interval-recording features. The use of video surveillance in sleep laboratories illustrates this approach. Infrared light and modified video circuitry allow recordings to be made in the dark. Crowell and Anders (1985) reported the use of a time lapse video sonogram for a 10-year-old girl with severe sleep disturbances. From the recordings it was determined that the girl suffered from a rare disorder called hypogenic paroxysmal dystonia. Because the syndrome is unusual and similar to epileptic seizures, Crowell and Anders established the importance of this method of diagnosis because therapies for these disorders are not interchangeable.

DOCUMENTING

Video can be useful for a variety of documentary purposes. A myriad of events deserve to be recorded: a facility's activities, notable interventions, "normal" behavior, problem behavior, and progress over time. Video has certain advantages over other media. If a picture is worth a thousand words, then a moving picture is surely worth a million. But there are disadvantages, too. Who wants a million words if they are repetitious, predictable, and out of sequence? Planning a video document requires attention not just to the content, but to the audience. There also are a myriad of uses a recording may be put to: consumer information, staff orientation or training, funding applications, and public dissemination.

PRINCIPLES

Some readers will have access to media production staff. Others may have aspirations for themselves or someone on their staff to take basic training in video production (see Huwiler, 1983). For simple documenting (e.g., a physical therapist demonstrating an exercise for a patient's foot), only basic video operating skills are necessary. A more challenging documentary (e.g., a presentation to a funding agency) requires sophisticated media skills as well as the scientist's or practitioner's detailed knowledge of the content. These different areas of expertise are most likely to come from different people, so much dialogue is necessary. A media-oriented person may be overly concerned about polish and technical quality, but will nevertheless have indispensable advice about the structure of the final product. The content-oriented person may rightly insist on some real examples, but may have no appreciation of how quickly a "talking head" becomes boring.

Overall, video documentation is best when it is brief. It benefits from "real" examples, even if these are of technically poor quality; however, the total package needs to convey a sense of professional competence. Following are some basic guiding principles that are illustrated in sample applications at the end of the chapter.

Quality

A net effect of high quality is essential, because it will be seen as reflecting the professionalism of the documented enterprise. However, glitz is no substitute for content. Amateur or noisy footage can be included if it makes a powerful point and comes wrapped in a technically superior package. In the extreme, a technically poor video will be appreciated if it is part of a presentation delivered by an organized, articulate speaker who is careful to explain why the quality of video is worth tolerating. (However, to distribute the tapes without a speaker is inadvisable.) The impression of quality can often be enhanced in simple ways, such as by adding professional-looking titles, balancing sound levels and correcting color, or by introducing a fade or dissolve between scenes of awkward transition.

Content

The strength of video lies in its ability to bring to an audience images that are otherwise unavailable. Its weakness is that it proceeds at its own pace and cannot be referred to without an interpreting device (cf., a brochure or a manual). Content and structure can be designed to maximize the strengths and minimize the weaknesses.

Format

Structure will depend on the extent to which the video is to be supplemented by other media. If videos are used as part of a spoken presentation, supplemented by charts, pamphlets, and/or handbooks, then the recordings may be simple disjointed examples. If the video is a documentary to be broadcast on television or disseminated through the mail, it will need to follow the self-contained structure of any presentation: an introduction, a statement of purpose, a major point, illustrative examples, and a conclusion (with a mailing address for further information).

Length

It is better to underestimate the attention span and overestimate the quick-wittedness of the audience rather than the other way around. Illustrations that are interspersed with explanations (recorded or otherwise) are quite long at 2 minutes unless they have a story line of their own; 30 seconds is often sufficient. The maximum tolerance for a complete documentary shown to politicians or business people is 10 to 15 minutes; half an hour may be tolerated by students who view a description of a program or facility (especially if the alternative is a lecture). An hour-long video needs a storyline or ebb and flow of tension crafted by a scriptwriter who understands entertainment. An overall impression of pace is helped by sharp transitions between scenes, with contrasting sound and camera angles, and titles displayed just long enough to be read comfortably.

Bias

Cameras may never lie, but the people who use them always do—in the sense that every recording, even before it is edited, is an interpretation. There is no such thing as an "unbiased" documentary. Ethically and professionally, there are two important considerations. First, any bias in the product should honestly and deliberately, if not consciously, reflect the philosophy and considered opinions of the authors. Bias should not occur through carelessness or chance. Second, selective perceptions should be as forthright and transparent as possible; if the worst case in a hundred is chosen, it cannot be passed off as representative or random.

Tone

Tolerance for the manner or tone of the document is in the eye (or ear) of the beholder. Exaggerated exuberance will be understood, even expected, in a fundraising pitch to potential sponsors in the business community. But a low-key, understated approach will be appreciated by students or colleagues. A flippant, explanatory, read-my-cathode-ray-tube style might be fun for children, but will prove irritating or patronizing to adults. Thus tone, and the other qualities just listed, cannot easily be changed in a video product and should be considered in terms of a specific audience during the planning stages.

Filming

It is a common misperception that quantities of previously collected footage can be turned into a documentary. A small amount of fortuitously collected video recording can sometimes be used as the centerpiece, or judicious extracts of previous material can be included in a documentary. But by and large, filming is to be planned. An outline can be broken down into segments, each piece to be filmed separately following a specific script or storyboard. In addition to general technical considerations of filming (see Chapter 1), planning will take into consideration the intended audience.

Editing and Copying

For videotapes designed to persuade or inform, editing is essential. General principles of editing described in Chapter 1 apply to documentaries, with the considerations about quality just noted. The edited master will wisely *never* be taken out of the studio, but kept and copied as necessary for distribution. Thus, the original recording will need to be of sufficient picture quality for two generations of copying.

Cost

If a commercial production company is contracted to make a no-frills documentary, a final bill of about $1,000 per minute of finished recording is typical. In view of the overhead for professionally equipped studios, these costs are inevitable. However, I have long held that commercially produced videos in the behavioral sciences have traditionally been much too expensive because of emphasis on the wrong type of quality—gloss rather than educational power. Now that commercial quality equipment has entered the home video market and adequately trained personnel are more numerous (from university-based broadcast journalism programs, for example), costs may at least halve in the near future. If commercial distributors would print videodiscs instead of tapes, and if educational institutions had disc players for them, widely usable products (e.g., Bandura's "Who Did What to Whom?"; see Chapter 3) would be available for the price of a book.

EXAMPLES OF VIDEO DOCUMENTATION

Three types of examples are described. The first one concerns a procedure to document client progress, while building necessary public relations information for referring agencies. The second example describes a video produced for an agency that wanted to promote awareness of its community work programs for people with severe disabilities. Finally, a brief set of guidelines is offered for video used in support of talks and conference presentations.

Client Progress in a Children's Hospital

While on sabbatical leave at Johns Hopkins Medical Institutes in Baltimore, I was asked by one of the units to develop routines to support their record keeping and produce videos that would help convey to others, especially units within the hospital, exactly what treatment results they were capable of. As Kendall and Hollon (1983) have suggested, samples of therapy can be used to create archives and to maintain and improve quality. Following are the guidelines produced for the psychology department of the Kennedy Institute for Handicapped Children, to meet the objectives of simplicity, brevity, and systematic data collection.

Video samples are taken at the beginning, middle, and end of treatment. The initial screening has established a limited number (usually three) of standardized conditions for systematic observation. For example, a 9-year-old boy, "Raymond," had been admitted for extremely overactive and aggressive behavior problems. His conditions of observation included being in a room alone, being with one adult who would ask him to comply with reasonable requests (e.g., "come here," "turn on the light"), and being in a room with several adults who would ask him not to do things that were objectionable or destructive (e.g., spitting, knocking over a chair).

First a title is recorded onto the tape that includes the name or code name, date, and phase of treatment, followed by an observation condition title (e.g., "Alone condition"). (A camcorder with a built-in titler is ideal for this purpose.) Each condition is videotaped for 60 seconds as follows.

After a short setting-in period, the camera is started unannounced and stopped after 60 seconds. The therapist in charge is asked, "Was that behavior reasonably representative of (Raymond) just now?" If the therapist answers no, the tape is rewound 60 seconds and after a short interval the process is repeated.

Thus about 10 minutes of tape, without editing, summarizes the entire treatment progress. Clearly, the simplicity of the procedure has some trade-off with accuracy, given the sampling method and error potential in the therapist's judgment. However, simplicity and brevity are vital to the survival and usefulness of videotape archiving. Many agencies have hours of treatment videotapes sitting on the shelves collecting dust and magnetic disturbances—precisely because there are hours of them. Other practicalities to be dealt with include adequate light and sound when recording through a one-way screen, reduction of extraneous noise, and the possibility of the camera's presence bringing out atypical behavior.

Public Relations Video for a Supported Work Program

The following is a description of a video (Dowrick, Orth, & Ward, 1988) produced for Alaska Specialized Employment Training Services (ASETS) in Anchorage. The purpose of the video was to provide an up-to-date overview of the realities of employing people with disabilities—ASETS provides state-of-the-art training and supervision—for prospective new employers. The video was also intended as a showpiece for legislators and others who might influence funding. Therefore, it was short, to the point, and relatively upbeat. In 12 minutes and approximately 50 scenes (10–25 seconds each), the following were illustrated: employment supported by a job coach, the enclave, and the mobile crew. Careful consideration was given to creating a balance between employer testimonies, narration, and on-the-job vignettes, while illustrating as much diversity as possible using simple, economical recording techniques.

The narrator, Michael Hood, was a professional actor, and the testimonies were elicited by asking questions that, with a little coaching, would produce an answer that sounded like a spontaneous remark. A sample question was "What is it that you like most about the ASETS employees?" The employer was prompted to wait two beats, then begin, "What I like most about the. . . ." Visual footage was of three types: titles without sound, workplace vignettes without sound, and talking head testimonies (live sound on track 1). After editing, the narration was dubbed directly onto track 2 over the titles and vignettes. Following are some elements of the script, similar to a storyboard (see Chapter 12), except that synopses are used instead of drawings for the "picture."

Picture		Sound
Title:	*ASETS' Supported Employment Program*	*(none)*
Teasers:	Female employer talking head testimony	"They are really great, . . . in the 4 years I have been employing handicappers, I have not yet been stood up . . ."
	Male employer testimony	"The thing I like most about ASETS workers is they're dependable; they're very consistent . . ."
	Female employer . . .	. . .
Overview, employment scenes 10-second shots, e.g., kitchen, making tacos, mopping and vacuuming		*(Voice-over)*: "These are very good evaluations for any employees but the unique thing about these employees is that they all experience disabilities. . . ."
Title:	*Supported Employment Options*	*(Narrator's overview)*
|=| *Supported Job*		
|=| *Enclave* or		
|=| *Mobile Crew*		
Title:	*Supported Job*	
Supported job vignettes: For example, sorting and stacking coat hangers for a drycleaner		*(Voice-over)*: ". . . The job coach will help do the job while the employee is in training, so there is no loss of productivity—ASETS guarantees . . ."
Talking head: employers		"The ASETS employee starts as soon as . . ." "The other employees enjoy working with . . ."
Vignette: kitchen employee		*(Voice-over)*: "These are jobs in which you might have a very high turnover . . ."

Picture	Sound
Title: *Enclave*	
Enclave vignettes: e.g., supermarket shelving hospital cleaning, kitchen washing	"This is a crew of four to eight employees with a supervisor . . . who trains and remains with . . . ." (Some testimony is also used as voice-over, followed by the narrator)
Title: *Mobile Crew*	
Mobile crew vignettes: e.g., packing and window cleaners	(*Narrator's voice-over*)
Talking head testimony	(*Live, same person as in teasers*)
More vignettes	(*Narrator*)
Title: *Misconceptions Dispelled* (A series of captions shows six contradictions to common myths)	*Narrated comment:* For example, "Workers' compensation rates will not rise if you hire a worker with disabilities. . . . A recent study shows that less sick leave . . ."
Titles (*series*): *Additional Benefits* Exs: Tax breaks and community recognition	(*Summarizing comments*)
More vignettes of employees: e.g., animal care, then back to the first kitchen	(*Continues*)
Title: Phone number for ASETS.	"If you think you would like . . ."
Credits: [Script, recording, editing . . . thanks to employees]	
Prototype Production by the Image Center Inc. for ASETS	

The entire production, using modest technology and donated time, was contracted for a mere $1,000—about one tenth the realistic price from a for-profit company.

Video-Enhanced Talks and Conference Presentations

The use of video to accompany a primary oral presentation is taught to scientists about as well as preparing a lecture is taught to university professors.

Philosophy

Plan the structure of a video-illustrated talk as carefully as any other presentation; use video to take over some of the presentation, but only when it is clearly better than a speaker. Challenge every piece of video with the question: Why am I using video instead of verbal description, overhead projection, or some other medium?

Recommendations

- Edit a tape specifically for the purpose.
- Use very short pieces; if multiple facets are called for (e.g., a client's mood, reaction time, or self-disclosure), put clips of 30 seconds or less in sequence.
- Intersperse with simple titles or leave brief gaps for an announcement.
- Plan the video to pace itself, to avoid stopping or fast forward search, etc.; rehearse for timing.
- Erase sound from the relevant sequences if there is a need to talk over the tape.
- Adjust sound levels during editing.
- Do not use talking heads (a live one is always better).
- Present recordings only with a stable picture and sharp detail (the larger the screen, the worse the detail).
- Edit or copy onto the most common video format available.
- Determine beforehand the screen size and how far people may be from it.
- Make contingency plans in case the equipment fails.
- Go to the presentation room half an hour early to try out the equipment (especially "tracking") and position all tapes at about 10 seconds before the starting point.

In a 15-minute "procedure"-oriented talk, half of it could be video *if* the procedure is illustrated in comprehensive detail, but less than 5 minutes video should be presented if using multiple-sample extracts. Before-and-after scenes help the appreciation of any procedure, and these may be shown before and after the intervention, or both placed before it. In a 15-minute "data"-oriented talk, a maximum of 4 minutes on video is ample. The extracts may include interventions or pre- and postsamples—probably more of the latter.

CHAPTER 3

Instructing and Informing

OVERVIEW

Videotapes can be informative whether they are designed specifically for that purpose or for some other use, such as modeling or confrontation. In this chapter, an effort is made to highlight the didactic function of educational recordings, although evaluative research is historically sparse. Some evident benefits of video as an instructional medium include its moving visual image (that can be readily reproduced) and its potential ability to gain attention, to be interactively controlled, and to create a personal involvement. Specific considerations to maximize these attributes are noted.

Most of Chapter 3 is devoted to the description of promising applications under six major headings. The first is classroom education—*for school-age children (e.g., interactive video in mathematics), in university settings (e.g., illustrations of attribution theory), and for on-the-job training, including broadcast teleconferencing. The second area is* treatment preparation, *which includes the use of video to preview an upcoming therapeutic procedure (cross-referenced with Chapter 11). A related area is* health education, *for which video is often used in alcohol and other drug-related issues; also related but distinct is* safety education. *A significant use of video is made in* child care education, *but this topic is discussed more in Chapter 4 because of the modeling element. A modest amount of use, but considerable promise (especially for interactive video), exists for* special populations. *The chapter ends with script extracts from a video for people anticipating day surgery, "through the eyes of a patient."*

P.W.D.

There are thousands of instructional films and videos. This chapter provides an overview of informational video—the availability, use, and development of recordings, and a brief mention of live videoconferencing. Video in this context is intended to educate about "facts" (e.g., the history of social work), or to influence attitudes (e.g., is nuclear war a Good Thing?). Sometimes instructional video is intended to promote skill development, such as in long division or in living with autistic children. Effective skill-promoting films or video programs often include all three elements. For instance, a personal safety film for children might include facts about inappropriate touching, attitudes about individual rights, and skill information concerning what to say and to whom to say it. Educational films that emphasize skill acquisition through demonstration or modeling are discussed in Chapter 4.

THE VIDEO MEDIUM

Marshall McLuhan's proclamation that "the medium is the message," which was widely discussed in the 1960s, may now be largely forgotten, although the effect of television on society is irrevocable. Indeed, some individuals claim that the medium is irrelevant, at least to the effects of deliberate instruction. In a review of comparison studies, Clark (1983) concluded "the best current evidence is that media are mere vehicles that deliver instruction but do not influence . . . any more than the truck that delivers groceries causes change in our nutrition" (p. 445). Only the content, he notes, can influence learning, although choice of a medium may influence the cost or extent of distribution.

Systematic evaluation of didactic film or video material is undertaken almost as infrequently as it is for textbooks, presumably for the same reasons. These products are expected to be of commercial quality, and are therefore expensive to produce and driven by marketing forces. Recordings proliferate because publishing companies promote them, and because instructors and students say they like them. Occasionally, sales and the frequency of use will be influenced by empirical measures of knowledge gains, attitude change, and skill acquisition.

Some studies have been published in which authors have concluded that video was no better than or even inferior to some other mode of instruction. For example, Houts, Whelan, and Peterson (1987) evaluated different modes of full spectrum home training for primary enuresis (bed-wetting). Families were randomly assigned to either live-mode or film-mode treatments that were equivalent in information content and length of presentation (1 hr). The results clearly indicated a superiority for the live delivery. In a rare comparison of video and print applied to consumer opinions in home economics (Eubanks, 1988), minor differences between the formats were reported. There are other studies; for example, Peterson's study (1986) on the use of video instruction in elementary school mathematics indicated the ability of the medium to hold its own and to offer special advantages in some circumstances.

However, these specific examples are valuable because they explore the parameters of individual applications. Whatever the attempts at comparative evaluations have shown, there remain good reasons to consider the use of information-oriented, video-based instruction. For example:

- *Attention.* The attention-gaining power of a video program is widely evident, particularly in contrast to audiotape or print media. Part of the reason is the ability of video to produce a close approximation to human presence, one of the most compelling stimuli, even in today's crowded world. A recorded video has other potential for drawing attention, such as the use of special effects or dramatic pacing, especially in the hands of a talented moviemaker.

- *Cost.* The video medium does not have exclusive rights to any of the properties just mentioned, so choice may depend on effect relative to cost. A room full of people can be paced through the same video material together, sometimes an advantage over print. Video may be broadcast to different sites or screened multiple times, with advantages over live presentation. However, the initial production costs of quality recordings are usually very high, and with current technology revisions can be almost as expensive as starting from scratch.

- *Interactive potential.* The computer-based video, especially videodisc, is a burgeoning field of instruction. It combines the advantages of traditional film with the random access capability of books and some features of personalized instruction. Because of its cost and complexity, the combination of accessibility and quality will continue to be a challenge. In Chapter 9, Robert Cavalier describes in detail some examples of this fascinating new technology.

- *Visual and moving.* Video has an underdeveloped potential as an instructional medium for people who are deaf or who have other reasons to benefit from moving, visual images more than spoken or written language. In these circumstances, a true advantage of the medium may emerge.

- *Personal.* All forms of media allow the audience members the opportunity to project themselves into situations that are being described. Books on pedestrian safety printed so that children can write in their names and those of their loved ones have been shown to double the comprehension and engagement with the materials. Moving, visual recordings have a different potential. Although there is stiff competition from well-chosen words and printed photographs or slides, a movie is frequently superior in its ability to transport an observer into the depths of the ocean, the height of a family argument, or the sex life of the flea (see documentary about Oxford Scientific Films, Gerber, 1989).

If none of these reasons prevails, the use of a didactic video recording or the contemplation of making one could be called into question. However, anything that is effective can be dangerous. For example, Shipley, Butt, and Horwitz (1979) reported a study in which patients were shown an explicit videotape of an invasive medical procedure (endoscopy). Results indicated both positive and negative effects on anxiety for different patients that were relative to their independently measured coping styles. When I was first asked to produce a video for prospective outpatients (described at the end of this chapter) I sat through 6 hours of on-location tapes primarily depicting explicit hand surgeries. These videos were much more graphic than any other medium would have been and, frankly, gave me a far greater sense of being there than I wanted to have.

In summary, the effect of the video will be a sum of the *use of the medium* and the *value of the information it carries.* In deciding whether to use (purchase or create) an instructional video the following should be considered:

- Are attitudes and facts, rather than skill acquisition, the primary targets of the instruction (or is this a component of it)?
- Will the video create a sense of personal presence comparable to a live presentation without the boredom of too much "talking head"?
- Is good use made of dramatic pacing and audiovisual effect (e.g., short scenes and a variety of camera angles without a loss of continuity, a mixture of close-up and wide angles, and artistic appeal of picture composition, color, and sound)?
- What will it cost, compared with other viable options?
- How many times will it be used, relative to its costs?
- Is the subject matter such that the fixed pacing and length (for noninteractive video) will not be a disadvantage?
- Will there be an opportunity to broadcast to multiple sites?
- Will the subject matter be long-lived (requiring infrequent revision)?
- If the video is interactive, will access to work stations allow other learning objectives to be met?
- If the video is interactive, does the programming allow sufficient individualization, and how will response to student choices compare with access to a teacher or a book?
- Do the spatial presentations and the portrayal of actions convey information superior to or strongly reinforcing of words?
- Can the video be used with deaf, learning disabled, or other populations that may have a special response to the medium?
- To what extent are the personal situations depicted so that the intended audience will identify with them?
- Is there substantial reference to activities that are difficult to bring to the classroom (e.g., rare behavioral disorders, highly personal events, or foreign cultures)?
- Can the video effectively stand alone, with minimal added staff time?
- Or does it dovetail efficiently with other instructional resources for an effective package?

In the remainder of this chapter, selected applications are described. These descriptions should provide an overview of current trends and typical findings of evaluation studies. They are divided into six groups, which seem to characterize the field:

1. Traditional classroom education.
2. Patient education, especially preparation for treatment.
3. Health behavior, including drug problems.
4. Safety education.
5. Child care.
6. Programs for the deaf and other special populations.

Readers interested in producing long-life, multiple-use videotapes may note that although Chapter 12 is intended primarily as a companion to Chapter 4 (modeling films), much of Stan O'Dell's excellent procedural description is of value for the making of all types of instructional videos. Specialty books on video production will also be useful (e.g., Hirschman & Procter, 1985; Lewis, 1987; and Speed, 1988).

APPLICATIONS

The greatest imaginable variety of videotapes and films have been created for use in the classroom—from kindergarten through university, and specialty and on-the-job training.

School-age Instruction

Some studies have examined developmental considerations in the methodology of instructional television. For example, Calvert and Gersh (1987) measured how well children in kindergarten and 5th grade (c. 11 years old) tracked TV stories under different conditions. They found that sound effects, but not visual inserts, increased selective attention and inferential recognition, particularly for the younger children.

A number of applications from 1st grade (Peterson, 1987) and upward have targeted mathematics. Interactive video has an obvious potential for this task. For example, Kelly (1987) describes a system for teaching fractions to struggling high-school students; Henderson, Landesman, and Kachuck (1985) developed a system for fractions, prime numbers, and factors. The positive results of Sherwood, Kinzer, Bransford, and Franks (1987) using simple video technology to teach science concepts to junior high-school students led them to suggest interactive video in this context also. As the field of interactive video grows (Pioneer Communications announced agreements in 1990 to produce 400 new educational videodisc titles, more than doubling its catalog), studies are increasingly reported that examine specific features of design strategy. These are often well-suited for that purpose, but they cover such diverse instructional objectives (e.g., economics for high-school students, Dalton & Hannafin, 1987; installing computer boards by university students, Ho, Savenye, & Haas, 1986) that generalizations are difficult.

Interactive video is constantly drawn closer to programmed instruction with computer graphics, so the future may best be predicted by a knowledge of both fields. For example, the computer program *Operation Frog* generates color-coded displays of internal organs and body systems, providing students with a graphic but bloodless alternative to dissection. The instructional approach to this program is very similar to those for training behavioral and social scientists described in Chapter 9.

University Settings

Innumerable video productions are aimed at this market, and some of the variations are intriguing. In a Canadian survey of methods used in teaching introductory psychology, Ross, Anderson, and Gaulton (1987) concluded that video presentations had varying success, not an unexpected result given the variability in the materials and how they are used. It is rare that objective evaluations are performed and published on didactic videotapes. One good example is provided by St. Lawrence (1986), who reviewed *Sample Diagnostic Interviews* by John M. Neale. This set of three 1-hour tapes presents acted interviews to illustrate six major diagnostic categories including schizophrenia, bipolar disorder, and attention deficit with hyperactivity. In addition to her positive subjective appraisal of the tapes, St. Lawrence evaluated examination responses and reported a significant benefit to those parts of the curriculum supplemented by the videotapes.

Videotapes produced by major distributors are usually expensive. The set just described lists at $375 (but is free when bundled with a text adoption), or about $2 per minute. Commercially developed tapes frequently cost five times that much. These costs traditionally reflect very high overheads in movie production. Prices may fall dramatically in the next few years for three reasons. First, new equipment is available that produces commercial quality images at a fraction of previous costs. Second, more publishers and other producers are entering the market; and third, educators and students are beginning to value "content" over "gloss," which shifts some of the labor costs to less expensive professionals. At least one distributor now lists in its catalog recent feature movies with authenticity and relevance for the behavioral sciences. (*Mississippi Burning, Ordinary People,* and *Rain Man* are examples.) A consortium of more than 50 university media libraries in the United States has been formed to produce a catalog listing thousands of educational videos, audiotapes, and films (Bowker, 1986) available at minimal borrowing costs; another group (Berger, 1989) publishes an annotated list of free audio and video materials.

One example of the trend toward content rather than gloss is present in the description by White and Lilly (1989) of a video for a social psychology classroom. The video was produced in Ball State University's television studio. White and Lilly designed examples of interpersonal behavior and associated questions that lead students to analyze information through the framework of Kelley's (1973) attributional theory. One example of a pattern of behavior shows dance partners who do or do not get their feet stepped on and by whom. The authors claim that the video enables students to understand Kelley's model and apply it to situations in their own lives. The reasons White and Lilly chose their subject matter may be of general value to anyone considering this type of production: The theory is highly complex, students consistently have trouble with it, and it lends itself to systematic visual representation.

Another strategy was suggested by Berrenberg and Weaver (1989) at the University of Colorado at Denver, who brought the potentially dry topic of scientific method to life for introductory psychology students with visual presentations of actual research. Because they also noted that commercially available films and videos present landmark studies rather than those representative of mainstream research activity, they made videotapes of research by their own colleagues. They produced three 45-minute videos for the cost of blank tapes and their own efforts. The first tape introduces science concepts and presents six diverse topics, from circadian rhythms of fish to job performance, in which faculty explain development of testable hypotheses in their work. The second tape defines and illustrates four different research strategies; it extends the topics already introduced and refers to ethics. On the third tape, faculty describe their procedures for data analysis and interpretation, and one project is followed into its preparation for publication.

Advanced Training

Videotape production for advanced and continuing education is another big industry. Such films are apparently most often designed for, and presumably best confined to, providing overviews of issues, problems, and techniques. They lead to understanding and motivation to learn more, rather than changing immediate work performance. A number of specialty production houses exist with an enormous variety of tapes, usually a half hour to 1 hour long, costing $100 to $500 each, on topics from feminist therapy to the treatment of autism. Most tapes can be rented and some companies allow "rent to copy."

It is increasingly common for institutions (e.g., Carrier Foundation) to videotape a series of invited lectures and to make inexpensive copies available. Some speakers like to receive a copy for themselves, which is a very reasonable "honorarium."

Perhaps the largest part of the advanced training video market has been aimed at the medical professions. The American Psychiatric Association, under the leadership of Milton Berger, has progressively developed its video sessions to a very high profile. The informational video and the conference venue seem to be a good fit. In practitioner-oriented conferences and other specialty training settings, the major potential value of informational video may be in illustrating actual clients and practitioner interactions (e.g., vignettes of physician-patient visits, Buschbaum, 1986; teachers of children with disabilities, Stone, Wolraich, & Hillerband, 1988). Such videos may be expected to reduce practitioner anxiety related to job-role changes and to assist curriculum decisions by educators.

An interesting variation (also for training in a medical setting) in which behavioral science trainees record their own videotapes was described by Lewis, Stokes, Fischetti, and Rutledge (1988). One way they use video is to tape exit interviews with patients. They ask a number of selected questions such as, "What were your reactions to our involving your son in your treatment? Would you recommend that approach? How could we obtain cooperation?" They presumably gather more information this way than by using written questionnaires. They review these tapes, sometimes in edited form, with residents who have worked with the client and also with others in training.

On-the-Job Training

Closely related to advanced training video programs are those designed for employed personnel. In-service training has many virtues, and there are claims that, in British industries at least (Downs, 1985), there is a trend away from traditional training settings toward learning at the workplace through computer and video systems. Behavioral scientists have two stakes in this claim: implications for training within the profession and contributions to the development of training systems for other professions.

However, the type of training in these situations usually emphasizes skill acquisition, which is not well served by informational types of instruction. Successful on-site training that includes instructional video is most often part of a package. This point is well illustrated in Latham's (1987) review of interviewee training. Reported training methods include an important place for video, shared with other modes and media, and subdivided among many contributions within which informational video is most modest. Even using an interactive videodisc system (for training leadership in junior army officers), Schroeder, Dyer, Czerny, Youngling, and Gillott (1986) concluded the video should be combined with, not to replace, existing methods of training. Most video-based training packages (e.g., Burch, Reiss, & Bailey, 1987) emphasize modeling and other strategies.

Perhaps the most promising approach to on-the-job training using video is not to record it, but to broadcast it, in *teleconferencing* (or videoconferencing) where the audience has an opportunity to participate. Business television, the most popular type of videoconferencing, enables companies to deliver messages to thousands of employees simultaneously; this is particularly valuable for high-tech business. Employee viewers can watch demonstrations, listen to experts, and usually ask questions. (Business TV networks allow call-ins from viewers.) Business TV is popular primarily because of its cost-effectiveness. For example, the J. C. Penney Company uses videoconferencing to display clothing to its 50 or more regional buyers at viewing sites across the country, which costs much less than the $5 million the company used to spend annually to send out clothing samples (Zygmont, 1988).

Advanced systems allowing two-way communication (dubbed "interactive" telecommunications, unfortunately likely to be confused with videodisc terminology) have also been developed for education. These systems use fiber optics and microwave broadcast technologies (Mid-Minnesota Telecommunications Consortium, Hannu, 1990; Utah State University Developmental Center, Stowitscheck, Mangus, & Rule, 1986). The Utah project (Pitcher, Rule, Cocklin, Stowitscheck, & Swezey, 1987) has provided training to teachers of handicapped children in rural preschools close to state television relay stations. The system allows trainee teachers to be observed on the job, to attempt activities, to seek advice, to receive immediate feedback, and so on.

Treatment Preparation

Videotapes are frequently used to assist medical patients and others to become better prepared for treatment. Such preparation is expected to reduce anxiety or to improve a variety of other responses before, during, or after intervention. In Chapter 11, John Parrish and Roberta Babbitt provide an excellent review of studies that measure the effects of video on preparing patients and their families for surgery and other procedures. At the end of this chapter is a description of a videotape for patients anticipating outpatient surgery at a specific facility. This section, therefore, will be brief.

Video has become established as reasonably effective in patient education. In a review of studies in this area from 1975 through 1985, Nielsen and Sheppard (1988) concluded that video was as effective as any other presentation method and more effective than the print medium. They recommend that uses of video be built into an education package to reinforce the videotaped information.

Most treatment preparation videotapes are for children and parents anticipating surgery, or for dental patients; most of these are modeling, not informational tapes (e.g., Greenbaum & Melamed, 1988; Robertson, 1988). Clearly not all videos are created equal, nor should we expect a videotape to be as effective as a teacher with opportunities for live interaction (Twardosz, Weddle, Borden, & Stevens, 1986). Plavin (1988) found that mothers benefitted from his informational videotape, but their children (4 to 14 years old) did not; Rasnake (1987) has begun to examine developmental considerations for children's preparation media. Some researchers have found important response differences on the basis of personality. For example, Shipley, Butt, and Horwitz (1979) and others have found that "sensitizers" (those whose vigilance increases when under threat) benefit from informational videos of impending surgery, whereas "repressors" do not—they may even recover more slowly from surgery.

For informational video to be effective in medical settings, Parrish and Babbitt (see Chapter 11) suggest not only incorporating modeling but providing supervised practice for the skill elements. Barbara Melamed (1989), a leader in this field for over 15 years, has recommended interactive video in preparing patients for surgery, especially children ("kids like it, because they play video games"). One of the virtues of interactive video is that the user can skip over unwanted material; those who wish to can seek out explicit details, while others can choose to avoid them.

Two other applications in the preparation of treatment have interesting possibilities. One is to assist consumers to make an informed choice about potential providers. For example, Manthei (1983) suggested a system of video vignettes that would enable clients to choose between available therapeutic approaches and individual therapists. In a similar vein, the University Affiliated Program in Eugene, Oregon, has been developing a set of short video recordings of local pediatricians for parents whose children have been identified as having a developmental disability.

Another type of application with interesting potential was illustrated by Corder, Whiteside, Koehne, and Hortman (1981). They prepared videotapes (and other materials) that described a psychotherapy group for adolescents to help newcomers to the group settle in more quickly. This approach could be particularly useful for group training or therapy in which the individuals enter or depart at different times. Both these types of applications are promising as low-cost, user-developed video education programming with benefits to service providers and referral agencies.

Health Education

A number of moderately encouraging video-based educational programs have been reported in other health-related areas. Again, the programs consist of a mixture of modeled health behavior and information. Most of the studies concern alcohol treatment, smoking, or other addictions.

A good example was provided by Stalonas, Keane, and Foy (1979), who compared live, videotaped, and printed presentations of equivalent didactic material for inpatient alcoholics. The information highlighted the concepts and data related to the active elements of the treatment, of which there were five major components. They found, using multiple-choice tests, that the videotape (simply a recording of the live lecture presentation) was the most effective medium. Their explanation for this surprising result is that video was not used in any other part of their intensive program, whereas personal verbal explanations were frequent. Although probably not as effective in situations where video is less of a novelty, the recorded lecture may be worthwhile as an inexpensive alternative. Another description of video education in alcohol abuse is reported by Efron and Veenendaal (1987) for emotionally disturbed, 7- to 14-year-old children of alcoholics. They used preprepared videos to present facts, and also had the children develop and present their own video vignettes about their family dynamics. (For further remarks on video production as a component of therapy, see Chapter 8.)

At the University of London (Denmark Hill), Stephen Sutton and his colleagues have been conducting programmatic research on cigarette use. Their review of six early studies on the use of informational videotapes found this use of video ineffective as worksite interventions for smoking (Hallett & Sutton, 1988). However, a subsequent study (Sutton & Hallett, 1988) indicates that an informational videotape can contribute to motivational factors for quitting. They used a 25-minute video called "Dying for a Fag?" that featured a middle-aged, former heavy smoker dying of lung cancer and a physician describing the hazards of smoking. The effects of this video and an accompanying booklet were contrasted with a control condition (video plus pamphlet on the use of seatbelts). They found that the video produced stronger intentions and more attempts to quit in those smokers who were already sensitive to the dangers of serious illness. Given that the video they used, although an "impressive film," was produced in 1975 for broadcast television, there is cause for optimism that a video deliberately constructed with current knowledge could be designed for specific motivational effects.

The studies cited are representative of the probable effects of informational/motivational videos in a variety of health and safety concerns receiving major public attention (e.g., drugs and seatbelts). Scare tactics always suffer the liability of indicating why not to do something without proper instruction on how to avoid it. Such campaigns can contribute negatively to the problem when survivors are used as witnesses to the effects. ("If he can fry his brains with LSD and cocaine and then become a counselor and upright citizen, I can try it, too.") Thus, it is a relief to see more public interest television spots that choose to illustrate tragic consequences, rather than glamour or happy endings.

Overall, video can be an effective medium for conveying useful health information. Children can learn more about the dangers of illicit drugs (Eiser & Eiser, 1987) or the causes of toothache and the contagion of colds (Siegal, 1988); the elderly can learn more about the potential roles of mental health professionals (Woodruff, 1988). Occasionally an informational video will directly affect the viewers' behavior (e.g., medication compliance by patients with sexually transmitted disease, Solomon, DeJong, & Jodrie, 1988). Most often these videos influence attitudes only and as such need to be part of a package when health behavior is important. There are probably several reasons that Jane Fonda's exercise tapes are more popular than any tapes on the physiology of metabolism. One reason is the emphasis on direct instruction and modeling of relevant behavior—but this approach, too, is only a piece of the puzzle. (See Chapter 4; Saylor, 1988.)

Safety Education

There is often an overlap between safety and health, and many of the principles are the same. One area of application already mentioned is traffic safety, especially the use of seatbelts and infant car seats. Studies of video-based education so far are not encouraging (e.g., Tietge, Bender, & Scutchfield, 1987). Again it can be expected that informational videos will contribute to intellectual understanding and attitude change, and that behavior change will respond better to modeling, practice, and other forms of instruction.

The most reports of applications recently have been in the areas of child safety and sexual victimization. A newspaper article (Meyer, 1988) summarized seven commercially available videotapes, priced from $15 to $40. About half of the content of these tapes is devoted to avoiding or responding to hazards at home (or getting home) for children who are unsupervised by adults (e.g., *Home Safe Home,* LCA/New World). The other half concerns sexual harrassment by strangers or acquaintances (e.g., *Strong Kids, Safe Kids,* Paramount). The tapes focus appropriately on providing information such as who to call if the gas is leaking and children's rights. Most of the information is action-oriented, demonstrated by child actors or cartoons. Some tapes are supplemented by workbooks, and all are intended for parents who want to discuss the issues with their children.

As pointed out by Kolko (1988) in his review of educational programs to prevent children's sexual victimization, there is a proliferation of videotape material, largely unevaluated. He finds moderate encouragement in the results of classroom-based applications. When videotapes present information, they tend to produce increases in knowledge and some changes of attitude, as does any video-based classroom teaching. Sigurdson, Strang, and Doig (1987) provide an example that typifies the field. They evaluated a program of four videotapes (one for instructors and parents and three for children) and other materials entitled *Feeling Yes, Feeling No,* available from the Canadian National Film Board. The program, which is used with children in grades 4 to 6 (ages 9–13 years), took 4 weeks (a minimum of 9 hours) and included extensive discussions, problem solving, and different kinds of instruction. The objectives contained in three 15-minute videotapes are listed under three headings: (1) enable the children to identify and communicate their feelings, (2) recognize and assess situations of sexual risk, and (3) develop skills for seeking help. The results of the program indicated a big shift in attitudes and knowledge for girls (but not for boys) in about one quarter of the areas tested—mostly on issues of boundaries and children's rights. In their findings, typical of the area, the authors concluded that the children enjoyed the program, were engaged by the videos, and were expected to be somewhat less at risk than before. (The program also provides a half-hour film and 3-hour workshop for parents and professionals.)

This and other studies make it clear that there are significant challenges in making the information and the instructional strategies developmentally appropriate and individual enough to benefit the majority of children. This challenge is unlikely to be met by a single-shot 30-minute video, no matter how clever it is. See the last section of Chapter 7 for the description of a program that has a minimal emphasis on the education of facts and attitudes, and centers around video feedforward for personal safety training.

A characteristic of safety issues is the necessity to teach about events we hope will never occur. The decision to educate is usually based on a trade-off between the probability of an event occurring and the importance of its effects if it does occur. At one extreme is nuclear war (Borgenicht, 1985; Campanelli, 1988). Educational videos may be well suited to issues that are so difficult to access. Popular attitudes are important in determining whom to vote for, how people with visible, public responsibility will act, and in some of the small ways that people can contribute to global events (e.g., protecting the ozone layer).

Child Care

A large number of videotapes have been produced about child care. (See Chapter 4 for descriptions in the context of modeling.) Perhaps the most important information component in child care concerns developmental issues. For parents, teachers, physicians, and daycare workers alike, social and physical development norms on which to base expectations and personal interactions are not always obvious. Some training programs for family physicians (e.g., see Fischler, 1983) include videotapes that are more than just refreshers on child and family development. The tapes or other parts of the training can include information on diagnosis, consultation, and referral. A self-instructional training program for daycare providers described by Aguirre and Marshall (1988), incorporating written and videotaped material, targets information on child development, nutrition, health and safety, and business management.

Special Populations

A little attention has been given to the possibility that video as an educational medium may have special advantages in some learning situations, especially with deaf and hearing-impaired students (Dillingham, Roe, & Roe, 1982). An interactive computer-video system is described by Stapleton (1985) for the development of language and technical skills. The author describes the particular advantage for deaf students in providing visual examples of vocabulary and concepts not readily understood from the written word.

Visually impaired students can be helped with computer-generated large print (Meryer, Correa, & Sowell, 1985), and with higher definition video screens these students may have new advantages. Interactive computer-video systems also have special application to students with learning disabilities and other handicaps. One well-evaluated program for teaching daily living skills to young adults called *Project LIVE* (Learning through Interactive Video Education) has been developed at the University of Oregon at Eugene (Browning, Nave, White, & Barkin, 1985).

Video can also bring otherwise inaccessible information from or to remote sites, although this information could arguably be conveyed in another form. One example is the bringing of international examples to the classroom for problem-solving in human rights (cf., Wessitsh, 1988). Another example is provided by McConkey and Templer (1987), who took a video-based program developed in Ireland and refilmed and redeveloped it in Zimbabwe. Their *More Than Care* package has six video programs (a total of 2 hours) and a handbook with information and activities related to the videos. Its purpose is to train care providers to teach self-care and communication skills to children and young adults with developmental disabilities. It is packaged completely so that tutors need little or no experience in the specific subject matter. The course has been nationally adopted for all nurses specializing in mental health and mental retardation, with prospects for special education teachers and parent groups.

EXAMPLE APPLICATION

In 1987 I was asked by Joe Chandler, anesthetist of the Alaska Surgery Center, to develop a video to assist prospective outpatients. Development of the video is described here not as a model in the exemplary sense, but simply to provide some practical detail in the hope it may be useful to those readers who are contemplating making their own educational videos. After visits and consultations at the surgery, the following objectives were agreed to:

- Include advice and instructions given to all patients before and after surgery.
- Show the patient the most likely experiences he or she will encounter.
- Maximize the patient's understanding and appreciation of the planned procedures in about 20 minutes of video.

- Provide reasonable reassurance of the event, while properly informing the patient of the risks.

- Make one video to serve all adults (including foot and hand surgery).

The suggestion of showing actual surgery on video was rejected for reasons of potential sensitization described earlier. Instead, the surgical procedure is portrayed as a brief blackout, based on the reality of what the patient would experience. Another point of departure from the usual style of making patient-education films was to shoot entirely from the patient's perspective. The video shows the day's activities as the patient would see them: viewers never see the patient, only what she sees while the camera moves as her eyes would. The point of this strategy (cf., self-modeling, Chapter 7) is to maximize identification with the patient in the video, without respect to color, sex, age. . . . Following are extracts from the script, which was developed with the assistance of Connie Orth, who filmed and edited the final product (Dowrick, Orth, & Chandler, 1988).

1a.	Title: *A Visit to Alaska Surgery Center Through the Eyes of a Patient*
1b.	Head and shoulders of narrator: "Hello, I'm Dr. Peter Dowrick. I helped plan and prepare this video. The Alaska Surgery Center wants to make outpatient surgery as comfortable and stressfree as possible. . . ." (*Explanations and instructions not to eat, and so on.*)
2.	Fade up from black as alarm clock rings; hand reaches in front of camera to turn off alarm; sounds of groans and sheets; view of feet sliding into slippers.
3.	Medium shot of refrigerator, moving in at walking pace; hand moves in to start to open refrigerator door.
4.	Cut to close-up of sign on door (*IMPORTANT:* Connie—*NO FOOD OR DRINKS* 12 hours before surgery!); voice off (*note: patient's voice is always off camera*) reads sign and says "Well, I guess that limits my breakfast menu, huh!" (*sigh*).
5.	From moving car, through windscreen, 100 feet of road, turn with car toward "Alaska Surgery Center" sign. (*Note: ambient noises here and throughout.*)
6.	Through windscreen, trees, etc., as car is parked.
7.	Middle-distance shot of Surgery Center front door, close-in with walking movement, hand reaches to open door.
8.	Receptionist says, "Hello, are you checking in for surgery today?"; she checks appointment book; she asks about food and drink; and asks who will take her (the patient) home today.
9.	Close-up of forms to be filled in, receptionist's voice off, fitting of a wristband.
10.	View of magazines being rearranged on reception table. Track up to lab technician saying, "Connie? Would you like to come with me?"
11.	Camera continues to follow the action from the patient's eye view for the blood tests (blood sampling is shown) and urine tests (sampling is not shown) into the locker and dressing room (blue gown); waits with instructions from the nurse, consent form, questions about allergies, and so on . . . lots of detail; "IV" is explained followed by cut to IV mock-up ("That wasn't too bad at all").
12–34.	There is more waiting indicated by a cut to another room and entry by the

anesthetist, with more questions and explanations; led by another nurse into the operating room, as the camera follows the IV bottle.

35. Cut to nurse wearing sterilizing mask, from view of operating table, camera looking up. Anesthetist's voice off, "You're going to start going to sleep now, we'll take good care of you . . . ."

36. Quick fade to black and silence.

37. Slow fade up, voice off (*also fades up*) "Connie . . . are you awake? . . . this is the recovery room."

38. Wobbly view of ceiling, curtains, etc.

39–55. Views of people and room tilt for a while. Video proceeds through recovery with occasional views of clocks, a fade during a nap, return to waiting room, arrival of Connie's husband, all the closing ceremonies, and instructions on how to care for herself.

56. Head and shoulders of narrator: "Well, it looks like our patient is on her way home and doing just fine. Now, remember what you have just seen on this video is a very general picture of what will happen at the Alaska Surgery Center. Everybody's experience is different." (*Repeat of three key points made at the beginning.*) "Now if you have any other questions about your surgery or the video, don't hesitate to ask your doctor or the nurse."

CHAPTER 4

Modeling

CO-AUTHORED BY DARBY C. JESDALE

OVERVIEW

The principles of modeling most consequential to using video are summarized at the beginning of this chapter: similar models, coping models, and many of them. These and other virtues in a video help to focus attention on the important elements of modeled behavior and to ensure that these elements are relevant and within the capacity of the trainee (observer). Some suggestions are made for creating modeling tapes for a limited number of clients, making use of readily occurring events: how to structure the content, priorities of content over form, and so on. (To create modeling tapes that deserve a wider distribution, see Chapter 12.)

Most of this chapter describes selected applications to illustrate a range of typical issues and the methodologies used in developing and using the tapes. Among applications for professional training, *divorce mediation and training for teaching assistants are included; in* social skills and daily living, *children are mostly featured, but not exclusively. Another productive area is* parent training, *related to which child self-management also appears promising.* Motor performance *(e.g., sport) training is also an extensive area of application. Some reference is made to the potential of appropriately designed modeling videos for* special populations, *such as people with mental retardation. The conclusion focuses on the excellent empirical evidence for the value of video modeling as an intervention in its own right. Packaging it with other training elements, especially an opportunity to practice, is even better.*

P.W.D.

A considerable amount of human learning takes place vicariously; that is, we learn a lot simply by watching others. Observation provides information about what we potentially could learn; when it occurs under the right circumstances, the observation results in immediate personal change. Excellent reviews of the theories, range of application, and efficacy of modeling are in print elsewhere (e.g., Bandura, 1977, 1986; Masters, Burish, Hollon, & Rimm, 1987; Thelen, Fry, Fehrenbach, &

Frautschi, 1979). Following a brief summary of the major features of consequence to this book, this chapter illustrates some of the methods and applications selected from the hundreds of videotape modeling reports available.

Two terms consistently applied in this field are *observational learning* and *modeling*. Observational learning is undeniably one of the most important influences on personality development. Whether used therapeutically for training, or occurring spontaneously, this process refers to cognitive and behavioral change that results from the observation of others engaged in similar actions (Bandura, 1986). Modeling is the process by which an individual (the model) serves to illustrate behavior that can be imitated or adapted in the thoughts, attitudes, or overt behaviors of another individual (the observer). The model may be live, filmed, described in any other medium—or even imagined.

We are exposed to hundreds of potential modeling influences every day and respond to only some of them. For a videotaped model to be effective, careful structuring of the content, the conditions of exposure, and a consideration of the observer are crucial. A modeling procedure focuses on the skill to be learned, its context, and its consequences. Albert Bandura (1969, 1977), the foremost proponent of modeling strategies, identifies four components that mediate observational learning: attention to modeled events, retention of what is observed, ability to replicate modeled behaviors, and motivation to reproduce those behaviors. The characteristics of the model contribute to the effectiveness of the procedure. The use of similar models, multiple models, and coping (as opposed to mastery) performances have all been shown to potentiate effectiveness, and they provide straightforward principles to apply in the development or selection of modeling videotapes. The ability of the viewer "to identify" somehow with the model is frequently cited as a pivotal factor, and the principles mentioned all presumably contribute to identification.

Some observational learning studies (e.g., Kazdin, 1974b) indicate that behavior change is enhanced by model similarity. Observers will pay closer attention and will have a greater ability to replicate behavior of a person similar to themselves. A model who is distinctive by being unusual (e.g., a clown) may capture audience attention but detract from the potential relevance of the action. Whereas similarity of appearance and personal background make a modest contribution, the main effect is from behavioral similarity (Masters et al., 1987). The use of multiple models has been shown to promote both the effectiveness and the generalization of modeled actions. For example, Charlop and Milstein (1989) devised a filmed modeling training program to teach autistic children conversational speech. They concluded that the considerable generalization achieved by their program may have been partly attributable to the use of multiple models in the videotapes.

Coping models (those who initially demonstrate flawed performance that gradually improves to criterion) tend to produce more desired change among viewers than mastery models (whose performances are "perfect" from the beginning). For example, Meichenbaum (1971) reported an influential study that indicated a coping model (on film) was more effective than a mastery model in the reduction of anxiety. However, a number of studies (e.g., Ginther & Roberts, 1982; Zachary,

Friedlander, Huang, Silverstein, & Leggott, 1985) have failed to produce specific support for coping models, and raised questions about the distinction. Coping models are behaviorally more similar to people who may learn from them. They tend to demonstrate behaviors more easily replicated, or a series of skills in attainable steps rather than a distant target performance.

The characteristics of the observer and the setting also mediate the receptivity to modeled events. Observation requires capable and alert faculties, and the development of abilities to learn from modeling opportunities. Sometimes, observational learning must be first taught as a skill in itself (e.g., with autistic children, Carr, 1985). An optimal level of arousal, as in most learning settings, is to be stimulated moderately above rest, with minimal distractions and supportive company. Individuals who have been cued in advance to heed specific modeled sequences will be more likely to focus appropriately.

Two other factors are often mentioned in the observational learning literature. One is the status of the model (McCullagh, 1986). The evidence for greater efficacy from models of higher status may seem to run counter to the findings of similarity and coping just described. The paradox may be reconciled by considering that a model's higher status is useful when it contributes to some mediating factors (e.g., attention, retention), provided that it does not detract unduly from other factors (especially the replicability of demonstrated performance). Some teaching films, for example, *Three Approaches to Psychotherapy* with Rogers, Perls, and Ellis each working with "Gloria," (the client) serve less for modeling and more as informational films, because the discrepancy between the trainee counselor and the therapist on film is too great (discussion by Weinrach, 1986). However, there is as yet no empirical effort to test these suggestions. The other factor of interest is that seeing examples of target behavior being rewarded lends potency to the modeling effect (e.g., Stokes & Kennedy, 1980). The enhancement of modeling by the inclusion of vicarious reinforcements on videotape is unsurprising. What may not be so obvious is that the data are equivocal on the effects of negative modeling examples when undesirable consequences are depicted. Whereas it might seem likely that demonstration of a negative outcome would act as a deterrent, the reverse is frequently the case, sometimes with tragic results: for example, televised dramatizations of teenage suicide were followed by an increase in actual suicides among young people in the greater New York area in 1984 and 1985 (Gould & Shaffer, 1986).

METHODS

There are two major strategies in the making of modeling videotapes. One has the objective of a widely distributable product and usually requires a major enterprise of planning, scripting, actors, technicians, and other professional support. The task of making a full-scale video product is described by Stan O'Dell in Chapter 12.

The second type of project has the objective of serving just one client or a limited number of students or clients and is necessarily a low-tech affair, capitalizing as much as possible on naturally occurring events. To engage in the development and application of a modeling "home video" requires the right circumstances. Some production elements are suggested based on principles described at the beginning of the chapter. A review of selected applications for their methodology will also help to illustrate some of these elements in action.

Circumstances

The first prerequisite is, of course, that the intended modeling is the intervention of choice for the case in point. Since there is good evidence for the efficacy of modeling in issues as disparate as snake phobias, family communication skills, and athletics, it is probably true that modeling is an underused treatment modality. Another prerequisite is that the person in charge of the program has the skills and resources (or is prepared to acquire them) for a video-based approach. A camcorder and basic editing system (see Chapter 1) and some talent (preferably in-house, but can be hired) for the medium are required.

A less obvious circumstance, I suggest, is that the training issue should be a recurring one in the setting (unless available personnel are already highly experienced in the use of video). For example, if parent training is called for, it may be best to borrow or rent commercially available tapes (see O'Dell et al., 1982; Webster-Stratton, 1989), unless parent training is frequently taught. A related consideration is whether suitable videotapes already exist. (Many tapes of parent skills do.) Thus, a clinic specializing in assisting parents of adolescents at risk for suicide, or rural Yupik families whose children have become influenced by middle-class America, might benefit most from developing their own modeling tapes. Personnel in such a clinic might begin with *self-modeling* (see Chapter 7) and use these tapes for peer modeling when similar cases arise, or they might estimate a range of family circumstances likely to be encountered and produce modeling tapes with the strategies noted in the next section.

The circumstances of viewing the tapes may also be considered. Does the program have its own facility where students or clients routinely and conveniently watch videotapes? When clients take videos home to watch on their own equipment, do they need a system for prompting and checking?

Characteristics

Following are some specific strategies summarizing methods that can be used in creating modeling tapes for in-house use and the characteristics to be looked for in selecting tapes from other sources:

- Identify a small set of specific skills to be demonstrated.

- For each skill, identify (and portray) a challenging context as well as the appropriate behavior.

- Use someone who has recently acquired the skills to act as the model in naturally occurring or easily prompted circumstances. (Avoid using a primary model who is younger than the anticipated clientele.)

- For each skill, plan the event to begin with a little stumbling, followed by self-correction and a strong finish; rehearse if necessary.

- Clearly show or imply a positive outcome for each skill demonstrated.

- Add one to three further models to vary the task, the solution, and model characteristics; consider skill level, age, gender, and ethnic and social background, depending on the purpose of the tape.

- Include one "high-status" model if possible.

- Limit the length of the tape (or any segment to be used in a single phase of intervention) to 5 to 20 minutes. (Modeling tapes can be even shorter than informational films, see Chapter 3.)

- Limit the number of concepts to about four, depending on complexity and audience.

- Consider content above form.

- Look for theatrical impact (not to be confused with gloss).

- If the recording will be longer than 10 minutes, plan some ebb and flow of tension (dramatic pacing).

- Use special effects of camera and editing (close-ups, slow motion, etc.) only to add or focus information.

- Plan (and check up on) viewing conditions and a timetable.

- Bundle the modeling with a comprehensive intervention—allowing for practice, discussion, systems change, or other elements as appropriate.

It is not uncommon in modeling tapes to show a negative model (ineffective response) first, although there is no evidence to support such a practice. One possible virtue may lie in its engagement value; seeing someone make a common error and generally mess up may be disarming enough to improve the receptivity of the audience. Some humor may be well worth including. John Cleese (of Monty Python fame) has marketed a series on management that is extremely popular (and very expensive)—but, alas, empirical studies on the resultant behavior change have yet to be done.

APPLICATIONS

A sample of applications follow. They have been selected to illustrate a range of different issues that are typical of the field; they are described to illustrate some of the methodology in the development of modeling videotapes. Six broad categories are used as headings: professional training, social skills, children and parents, preparation for treatment, motor performance, and special populations. Although videotape modeling is well established in all these areas, these categories, even broadly interpreted, do not represent the limits of the field.

Professional Training

Video modeling is frequently used in the training of professional skills such as teaching and human services (e.g., Clark, 1988). An informative example is provided by Schoonover, Bassuk, Smith, and Gaskill (1983) in their videotape series for training health care personnel to handle psychiatric emergencies. They illustrate the value of theatrically compelling story lines, action sequences, and characters for viewers of widely diverse learning styles. They found that dramatic videos were even more effective in influencing skill acquisition than live role plays. First they defined clear instructional goals. In an attempt to portray each scene as realistically as possible, they attended to the authenticity of detail in the selection of equipment, style of dress, use of colloquialisms, cultural and professional values, and symbols. Deviations from orthodox medical protocol (e.g., incorrect use of medical equipment) seriously interfered with learning by distracting attention and decreasing identification with the model.

Schoonover et al. (1983) used multiple models with full character development. They composed short descriptions of each person and his or her social context before writing any dialogue. Each character was given a unique verbal and behavioral style, in an attempt to avoid two-dimensional, unrealistic personalities. The script illustrated coping rather than mastery in a suspenseful story line with specific instructional sequences, leading to the solution or containment of problems. The authors suggest maintaining a moderate level of uncertainty with dramatic pacing: "It must be fast enough to maintain interest but slow enough to allow the student to consider new ways of behaving" (p. 808). Following an anxiety-provoking scene, a low-key interlude lets the viewer reflect on her or his own feelings and mentally rehearse the modeled activity.

Another valuable example is provided by Sharp (1981) who successfully designed and evaluated a modeling videotape to train graduate teaching assistants. Factors examined in the study included viewers' interest in, and the relevance of, the subject matter presented in the video. Surprisingly, he found the interest and relevance of the topic made no significant contribution to skill acquisition. In fact, it was suggested that modeling videotapes purposely designed to maintain high viewer interest may cause so much attention to be focused on the issue presented that the modeled behaviors themselves may be overlooked. This conclusion, in context with Schoonover's viewpoint, implies an important, subtle difference between interest maintained by the *behavior* (e.g., what can be done with this man threatening to kill himself) versus interest piqued by arbitrary *subject matter* (e.g., how the dinosaurs became extinct).

Video modeling is frequently used in various types of counselor training (e.g., Hargie, 1988). In a well-designed investigation of the relative effects of role playing, videotape feedback, and modeling, Bailey, Deardorff, and Nay (1977) found modeling to be consistently associated with the largest behavioral gains in specific counseling skills. Although there are always problems in "equating" different interventions for comparison of effectiveness, modeling may frequently be the treatment of choice when time is limited and the learning objectives can be explicitly identified.

In 1985, Taylor reviewed different uses of video in the training of mediators. She presented a set of criteria that provides a useful example of training content for a specific type of counseling. Following is an abbreviated list of content items that might appear in a modeling tape (Taylor, 1985, pp. 122–123):

- Introductions, comfort established.
- Preliminary statement, qualifications, confidentiality, time frame.
- Legal process.
- Mediation rules and ethics; roles and commitments.
- Equal verbal and nonverbal expression by both participants.
- Expectations, best and worst, open and underlying.
- Background case data, precipitating events, other parties.
- Agreement to proceed: costs, duration, process.
- Fact finding: note-taking, control of interview.
- Reflecting, clarifying, summarizing.
- Acknowledging conflicts, reframing.
- Areas of agreement, acknowledgement of hard work.
- Creating options, use of direct communication.
- Brainstorming without judgment: ideas, and outcomes (list).
- Presenting mediator suggestions without pressure.
- Identifying sources for additional data.
- Assuring standards and fairness.

A different use of video modeling with considerable potential is to record in a clinic, a specific treatment that is to be applied by others in a home setting. During my 1-year visit to Johns Hopkins Medical Institutes, we used this approach a number of times with parents of children with severe eating disorders of different kinds. The content illustrated various ways of helping the child at mealtime or between meals. Some videotapes showed the therapist, and others were filmed while the parent was given suitable off-camera support, with some editing later. In a similar spirit, Michael (1984) described the use of videotaped physical therapy demonstrations for use by parents and teachers at home or school. She suggested that, from time to time, the in-progress tape of the parent working with the child be sent to the therapist for follow-up purposes. If large-scale changes are required, the therapist may make another video. Clearly this approach need not be limited to services for children, but could conveniently be used with accident victims, stroke patients, and others.

Social Skills and Daily Living

Video is widely used in a variety of ways for social skills training with children (see Dowrick, 1986) and adults (Hosford & Mills, 1983). Video modeling is the staple of many packaged programs (e.g., Hazel, Schumaker, Sherman, & Sheldon-Wildgen, 1983; Liberman, 1987; Walker et al., 1983) and is probably underused in other settings. Often part of packaged training, it has been the primary component for situations as diverse as teaching young, isolated children to overcome their shyness (O'Connor, 1969) to teaching gay men to be socially assertive in the face of ridicule (Duehn & Mayadas, 1976).

Sometimes modeling is used to teach specific skills to people who may already have good general social abilities. For example, Sims and Manz (1980) conducted a series of studies on the verbal behavior of "leaders." Through one-way glass, tapes were created by recording subjects who role played in a room simulating the leader's office. Two subjects sat at a table so that the leader's face was fully visible to the camera and the subordinate was seen in profile. A protected recording area was used so that a trained camera operator could be directed by the experimenters when to shoot close-ups and so on, to maximize the emphasis needed to meet instructional goals.

Video modeling is often used to train people in general social competence—even when natural peer models exist in the environment. Presumably, the tendency for some children to remain shy at school, for example, surrounded by socially adept peers reflects an inadequacy in the observational learning situation that can be remedied by systematic control in symbolic modeling. To this end Schneider, Raycraft, Poirier, and Oliver (1986) designed an instructional program in four phases: a videotaped modeling sequence, a leader-facilitated discussion of the modeling video, another display of the tape, and role playing by the participants. The children were then taught to imitate, using video feedback and instruction. They were videotaped role playing in pairs. After they viewed their tapes, feedback was elicited from: the main actor, the supporting actor, and an observer (in that order). The process of videotaping and discussion was repeated until each child performed one role play to predetermined criteria. Schneider et al. (1986) emphasized the importance of each modeling sequence displaying the behaviors to be imitated with clarity and detail, avoiding as much irrelevant matter as possible. They recommend the use of different modeling sequences with repeated displays to the point of overlearning. They recommend against the use of negative examples (to avoid the imitation of nonadaptive behavior) although they suggest "the negative example may be *occasionally* helpful if the discriminating features of the modeled skill are not clear to the children" (p. 11).

Social skills training, with a modeling component, is also frequently used to provide alternatives to undesirable behavior, such as drug abuse, aggression, and other illicit or unhealthy activity. For example, Evans et al. (1981) reported an antismoking program for junior high-school students. Evaluation of this program over a 3-year period indicated the efficacy of multiple intervention components. A significant piece of the intervention was the use of films of age-appropriate student models coping with the social pressure to smoke cigarettes. A number of video packages are now available for teenagers emphasizing the resisting of social pressure to take drugs, while minimizing the chance of losing friendships. Fortunately, public service spots on television now seldom show a reformed junkie testifying about the evils of life past—actually serving as a model of how to do drugs and get away cleanly and honorably. Most often they dramatize negative consequences—taking drugs as a high dive into an empty pool, a parent by a gravesite—which is at least a small step forward. Better still is the occasional use of a celebrity who has not used drugs, testifying to why he never has, never will.

In 1985, the Institute for Mental Health Initiatives (IMHI) investigated anger on prime-time television and recommended ways to incorporate more constructive modeling into the plethora of incensed TV personnae. In two studies, they demonstrated to the television industry that anger can be resolved without compromising good drama. In fact, successful conflict resolution was shown to increase overall dramatic effect. Subsequently, as part of a media campaign called "Channeling Children's Anger," IMHI collaborated with an advertising agency to produce TV spots and a music video showing models variously expressing anger and turning it into a source of creative energy. Integrated with this effort were anger management workshops held in local communities.

Parent Training and Child Self-Management

Another area in which video modeling has received much attention is parent training. An early leader in the field was Stan O'Dell (see Chapter 12). One of his studies (O'Dell et al., 1982) compared live modeling plus rehearsal with prepared media materials: a written training manual, an audiotape, and videotaped modeling. He and his colleagues replicated two previous findings. First, all training methods were comparably successful. Second, video training demonstrated a superior ability to train parents possessing a wide range of individual characteristics, presumably because of the video's use of multiple models and its capacity to focus attention on specific behaviors.

Carolyn Webster-Stratton has also developed and evaluated parent training videotapes. In a study with parents of conduct-disordered children published in 1988, Webster-Stratton, Kolpacoff and Hollinsworth compared three interventions with a waiting list control group; self-administered videotape modeling; group discussion; and video modeling with group discussion. All treatment groups produced significant effects relative to the control condition, with few differences relative to each other. Although the combined treatment showed an overall edge, the investigators point to the cost-effectiveness of the videotape-only intervention.

Most parent training is precipitated by conduct problems of children. One approach is to address the child's impulsiveness directly by teaching self-management. For example, Manning (1988) used adult modeling plus videotaped peer modeling for successful self-instructional cognitive training with children. Adults first demonstrated the self-instruction, then students watched modeling videos of age mates using specific strategies related to the classroom setting. These strategies included *problem definition* (what is it I have to do?), *focusing attention* (now look at this), *self-guiding* (carefully cut along the line), *self-reinforcement* (good, I'm doing fine), and *self-coping* (even if I can't finish, I can try). These conditions were contrasted with a control procedure that was entirely similar except that the self-instruction components were replaced by classroom compliance instructions. That is, the children in the control group saw the same peer modeling tape dubbed with different commentary. The effects of the two interventions were significantly different. The students with the self-instruction training component showed substantial gains in on-task classroom behavior. It may be noted that symbolic modeling (or any other intervention) without some attention to parent training or other aspects of the social environment is unlikely to be effective in the overall treatment of attention deficit disorder with hyperactivity or more severe conduct problems (cf., Henry, 1987).

Preparation for Treatment

Few areas of application have seen greater use of videotape modeling than in preparing people (especially children) for different kinds of treatment, from group psychotherapy to endoscopy. Much of this effort has combined modeling with informational film material in medical settings, and is discussed in this context in Chapter 11—also see Chapter 3. Information (e.g., how long an operation may take and how it affects the physiology) is important to emotional responses and long-term attitudes, but modeling is more essential to immediate behavioral change (cf., Klingman, Melamed, Cuthbert, & Hermecz, 1984). Modeling is effective and economical in preparing children for dental procedures. A child model on video is as effective as say, puppets in vivo (Peterson, Schultheis, Ridley-Johnson, Miller & Tracy, 1984). Filmed demonstrations by personnel of dental procedures are significantly less effective in the absence of a child model as a patient (Melamed, Yurcheson, Fleece, Hutcherson, & Hawes, 1978). This is presumably because given a model children learn how they can respond to minimize the unpleasantness of the procedure. (Those who observe modeling videos are rated higher on cooperation and lower on disruptivenes.) The effectiveness is not on the basis of general coping ("here's how to be tough") but on the specificity of the situation, and symbolic modeling can be facilitated by participation and other environmental support. In a brief review of pretreatment modeling specifically for children's dental anxiety, Greenbaum and Melamed (1988) cite approximately 40 studies reporting successful procedures; they also note with some curiosity a survey indicating only 17% of pediatric dentists (in Minnesota; Glasrud, 1984) have ever used a preparatory film. They advocate the availability of standardized videos that are suitable for routine use in the waiting room.

Motor Performance

The principles that apply to teaching motor skills through modeling are similar to those already described in this chapter. The use of multiple models is not as common, nor is it as important except where performance anxiety is an issue. Higher status models may be of particular value where competitiveness is important (McCullagh, 1986). Coping models are specially emphasized, perhaps because behavioral similarity and the exact relevance of the demonstrated skill are of greatest salience to motor performance. Sport and other movement applications are the most likely situations in which special technical effects will be useful (e.g., slow motion, still frames).

An ingenious study by Carroll and Bandura (1982) illustrates the value of modeling early in the skill acquisition process. They examined the learning of a novel action pattern (moving a lightweight paddle through nine separate maneuvers) under conditions of modeling, practice, and visual feedback. The results indicated that the opportunity to monitor these action patterns in real time on a television screen assisted learning *only* after the skill had been adequately conceptualized through modeling.

Other studies have confirmed the value of modeling in the beginning stages of skill acquisition (e.g., Ross, Bird, Doody, & Zoeller, 1985). Modeling has demonstrated value for advanced skills also. For example, Hall and Errfmeyer (1983) adapted video modeling to improve the free-throw accuracy of highly skilled women college basketball players. The model tape showed a female basketball player executing 10 consecutive foul shots with perfect form. She was filmed from behind and the observing players were encouraged to imagine themselves to be taking the shots; they viewed the tape for 2 minutes, then closed their eyes to imagine themselves making a perfect shot, repeatedly over a 20-minute period. The tape included sounds of the bouncing ball and swish of the net to enhance realism and was shown in a dimly lit room. Over a relatively short period of time, with some repeated applications of the video modeling, these players increased their foul shooting percentages from 72% to 82%, while other players using imagery only over the same period remained at exactly the same level of performance. (Other applications of video modeling to sport skills are described in Chapter 15.)

Special Populations

Appropriately designed video modeling would seem to have obvious application to "special" populations who by definition may lack the opportunity to observe naturally occurring models or have different learning needs. In their review of social skills training for people with mental retardation, Davies and Rogers (1985) concluded that "active rehearsal in combination with other instructional methods, *particularly visual modes of instruction* and practice have been demonstrated most effective" (p. 194, emphasis added).

Multiple models and situations, relatively easily captured on video, may be especially valuable to some populations. For example, Haring, Kennedy, Adams, and Pitts-Conway (1987) used video effectively to promote generalization of shopping skills for young adults with autism. Whereas training (in vivo) in one setting (a cafeteria) failed to produce generalization to three probe settings, the use of videotapes showing models buying items in these settings did result in generalization to three different neighborhood shops. Although the models were nonhandicapped (but the same chronological age as students, 20 years) they demonstrated the same sequences as the shopping training: entering a store, selecting items for purchase, walking to the checkout, placing items on the counter, greeting the cashier, paying cash, receiving change, thanking the cashier, and leaving the store. The videotapes were 1 1/2 to 3 minutes long (one complete purchase) and varied in the content of the social responses ("Hi," "How are you?," etc.). Students watched four episodes at each session, and were asked such questions as "What store is this?", "What is he doing?", and "What will she say next?".

An interesting program was developed and evaluated by Durham et al. (1981) first to teach adolescents with handicaps, using video modeling, to be trainers, and then to have the adolescents, using video modeling and peer tutoring strategies, teach recreational skills to younger children with handicaps. Disabilities included mental retardation, physical handicaps, and learning, emotional, and behavioral disorders. In creating the modeling videos, an "advisory content committee" selected the activities as appropriate for physical impairment, limited to a single concept, and able to be portrayed visually. The activities were differentiated by ability level, task-analyzed into discrete elements, and there was an equal mix of gross and fine motor skills (swings and basketball vs. painting and cooking, etc.). A series of 12 videos was used to train the trainers; trainers were quizzed on each tape before viewing the next. Each of the younger trainees was shown selected videotapes (from a pool of 29), three times each, in small groups conducted 4 days each week by the trainers. (Trainees were also given cross-age peer tutoring by the trainers, who were given feedback and instruction from supervisors of the recreation facility.) As judged by observers, trainees achieved approximately 80% of criterion on their recreational skills, while trainers demonstrated significant increases in job skills and knowledge (compared with a control group).

CONCLUSION

An impressive range of modeling videotapes are available from commercial distributors and individual producers. Many more can be made for new and sometimes individualized purposes. The characteristics to seek in selecting or creating such videos are documented at the beginning of this chapter, and illustrated throughout. (See also Chapters 11, 12 [especially], and 15.)

Video modeling is well documented in the research literature as a powerful intervention in its own right. Nonetheless, it is generally used in conjunction with other procedures. The most powerful modeling-based treatments emanating from Stanford (the "home" of observational learning) in the treatment of snake phobias are packaged as participant modeling (e.g., Bandura, Blanchard, & Ritter, 1969).

Video modeling can very naturally include nonbehavioral information. It has an advantage over live modeling in some cases by incorporating multiple models and focusing selective attention by use of the camera and other technical advantages. It will normally take its place early in the learning sequence, following instruction but before practice, feedback, and feedforward. But it can also be modified in its application to play a part in sophisticated and advanced development of personal change.

CHAPTER 5

Scene Setting

OVERVIEW

The use of video vignettes to promote discussions, memories, emotions, or judgments is a common but little studied practice. This chapter surveys these practices and attempts to provide a taxonomy of use in therapy, training, and different kinds of research. First, principles (e.g., conciseness and provocation) are identified, including some from the art of advertising. Vignettes in training are described for interviewing, counseling, and training observers. (Chapter 13 covers professional training.) Vignettes have been used surprisingly little in therapy, but promising examples exist in social skills training, exposure therapy, and sex therapy. (A related use of budding importance but not discussed in this chapter is to evoke responses for assessment purposes; e.g., Flarity-White, 1988.)

A vast number of research studies mention the use of video vignettes within the methodology. In this chapter, the different roles of the vignette are classified and examples are given to assist the practical application of video, and perhaps to set the stage for establishing some methodological principles. Examples are presented in which video content is the independent variable *(depressed affect in one vignette but not in another); or video is contrasted with another medium (closed circuit video of oneself vs. a mirror). Video can even be a* dependent variable, *as when subjects adjust a distorted image to meet some criterion by instruction. It is common to use a* single vignette *but to create different conditions by labeling (e.g., "this boy is disabled" vs. "this boy has been in trouble") or to use subjects who belong to different categories of interest (e.g, coaches vs. players). Quite often these strategies are combined, sometimes to examine an interaction effect that is essential to the research question being asked.*

P. W. D.

Of all the uses of video identified in this book, scene setting is second only to video analysis as the most commonly identified practice in the literature. Or at least that appears to be the case on the basis of computer searches done on the *PsychInfo* database. This fact is surprising, given that there is virtually no literature on the methodology and principles, unlike the accepted classifications of modeling, instructional films, and self-confrontation. Scene setting has established a place of growing importance to the behavioral sciences.

In the present context, scene setting refers to the use of video vignettes to elicit a variety of responses for training, therapy and research purposes. These responses include:

- discussions
- memories
- emotions
- judgments

Sometimes the anticipated responses of interest are very short, such as a statement of preference for one character or another in the vignette, or relatively brief and finite, as in a viewer's description of how he or she would proceed on the basis of the portrayed scene. Or the responses may "trigger" a chain of events that then comes under the control of some other training or evaluation paradigm—this strategy is detailed by Simon Biggs in Chapter 13.

The characteristics of scene setting sometimes overlap with methods discussed in other chapters. For example, any form of self-review (Chapters 6 and 7) leads to emotions and judgments. An interesting example of overlap with modeling (Chapter 4) is provided by Webster-Stratton's (1984) program for families of conduct-disordered children. She used 2-minute videotaped vignettes of parent-child interactions. The program included 180 scenes of everyday situations—at the supper table, in the living room or bathroom, during phone calls, and the like. Although the scenes primarily illustrated effective parents, they were not used to prompt modeled rehearsals, but group discussions led by a therapist. Videos and films discussed as "instructional" in Chapter 3 can also be used to promote these kinds of responses.

Therefore, this chapter focuses on examples of using video vignettes that do not meet the purposes described in other chapters. The purposes of these videos fall into three broad categories:

Training and therapy vignettes: provide economic presentation of situations for observer reaction that are structured for the viewer's developmental level or point of progress.

Research of differing stimulus conditions: presents situations in which elements on video are systematically varied for comparative evaluation.

Research with differing observer conditions: presents videos in which the conditions of viewing (or the viewer) are systematically varied.

Because this type of classification has not been examined before, this chapter describes examples in each category. Chapter 13 provides some detail for production of video vignettes in the first (largely underdeveloped) category. Before presenting sample applications, a few general principles are summarized.

PRINCIPLES

Scene-setting vignettes are, by definition, part of a larger program. Video qualities of special relevance may (or may not, depending on the purpose of the program) include the following:

- conciseness
- controversy
- provocation
- predicament
- sentiment
- fantasy
- realism

The best source of information about methods to obtain these qualities is found in the literature on television advertising. The short duration of commercial presentations (usually 30 seconds or less) does not allow the development of an intellectual argument, but calls for a message at the emotional level. There may be room for a brief storyline (a crowd of children stand in front of vending machines for Soda A and Soda B—which one will they choose?) or a few succinct facts, but most of the impact comes from aesthetic factors: screen space, motion, framing, editing, lighting, color, and sound (Zettl, 1987).

Using a large number of shots creates a high-density display to be perceived rather than critically examined. Close-ups carry maximum energy and suit the small screen. A series of close-ups can lead inductively to a composite picture, even when an overview is not presented. This technique and others that require the viewer to provide closure (but make it easy to do so) draw an investment from the viewer in the scenario presented. Colors have the ability to arouse emotions. Although the strength of the effects are often overstated, the potential should not be overlooked. Some attempts to drive consumer interest through use of color may seem corny (e.g., "before" in monochrome, "after" in bright color), but they do serve as reminders of simple nonverbal ways to demark event categories, time transitions, and so on.

Sound can also be important in setting the mood, focusing attention, or holding multiple visual images together. When Zettl (1987, p. 107) likened a video sound track to a rubber band that "holds the various pieces together and makes them into a manageable perceptual package," he was referring to narration or music that provides continuity and context. Music, human voices, or other sounds, especially at the beginning of the sound track, may easily set a tone of high drama, frivolity, sentiment, or whatever, chosen for the piece or in contrast with the picture to create irony. Selective use of sound against a silent background can be used to draw attention to highly specific elements of the vignette.

Aesthetic presentation can reawaken interest in everyday objects and situations.

Lighting from an unusual angle or to create patterns of light and dark contrast may be useful. Motion is usually most exciting when it is created by the subject, not by the movement of the camera (the camera or the picture moves with the subject), but it is occasionally dramatic when the rule is consciously broken. As with still photos, distance shots benefit from something in the foreground—usually to one side or overarching the distant subject. But unlike still photos, aesthetic factors can be added temporally in video, as with a man facing the camera from a middle distance and an adversary stepping past the camera into one side of the picture to face him. All these effects of distance and close-up, light and dark, complementary or clashing colors, and quiet and discord can be dramatically contrasted by editing. Or editing can be deliberately unobtrusive to ensure minimal distraction from the message. A useful summary of aesthetics in instructional media is provided by Martin (1986).

In the following pages, sample applications are presented in the use of vignettes for training, therapy, and different kinds of research.

VIGNETTES IN TRAINING

Some vignettes, as distinct from video methodologies described in other chapters of this book, are used for skills such as parenting (example described earlier), interviewing, or making systematic observations required of research assistants.

Interviewing and Counseling

An example of a simple but effective methodology in the training of interviewing was provided by Robinson, Kurpius, and Froehle (1979). Prepracticum graduate counseling students responded to a videotaped client and then evaluated their own responses on the basis of a specified performance standard. Videotapes used in the program were developed from a pool of written statements role played by two men and two women. Each video ran 45 seconds: 15 seconds of scripted role play followed by 30 seconds in which the actor-client appeared to be listening to the response. The 30 seconds allowed the interviewer trainee to respond. An example of a client statement is, "I'm really afraid to be by myself. My imagination is going wild. I keep thinking of all these terrible things that could happen to me" (p. 95).

The program was evaluated with some minor variations designed to reduce supervision time. For example, criterion performance standards were displayed on the screen and spoken (voice-over) by the actor-client. During the silence that followed, the trainee evaluated the woman's response by comparison with the standards. These self-evaluations were audiotaped for later supervision. In this way, trainees were able to practice their interviewing skills on their own. The performance standards provided a framework in which viewers were able to shape their own counseling behavior with minimal supervision.

A different example was described by Rodolfa (1987). He described a program to train faculty and staff in a type of crisis intervention that has been used at Humboldt State University in Arcata, California, for a number of years. The video vignette's contribution to the training program is in the accurate identification of emotionally troubled students and as a springboard for workshop discussions and problem solving. There are seven vignettes, 2 to 5 minutes long, illustrating depression, dependency, intrusiveness, aggression, orientation to reality, hostility, and acting out. The tapes were developed in a collaboration between the theatre and counseling services departments.

In a 2-hour workshop, three or four vignettes are selected on the basis of issues raised by participants. After a vignette is shown, a series of questions is asked:

1. How are you feeling while watching the vignette?
2. How would you feel if you were in the situation?
3. How do you think the student feels?
4. If you were the faculty or staff member dealing with the student, what would your goal be?
5. What are the possible actions that you can take? (p. 183)

A semistructured discussion follows, lasting up to half an hour. Participants are encouraged to draw on their own experiences and ideas, while group leaders provide additional information and lead toward the identification of effective action.

Observer Training

In settings where video recordings are routinely made for observation and evaluation purposes, the use of vignettes for observer training is obvious. Observers are often trained using tapes from previous studies or pilot sessions. However, this approach provides no guarantee that a full range of observation circumstances will be met in the training. To meet this concern, Naumann (1987) developed observer training tapes to illustrate the full range of preschool children's free-play activity under examination in her study. Partly because of the age of the children and the complexity of behavior, she captured and edited actual interactions, in preference to simulations or role plays.

The technology may be taken a step further by using interactive video, as illustrated by Bass (1987). He trained college students in a 10-second partial interval system for the observation of videotapes. Video training was preceded by using a computer program to ensure the ability to identify written descriptions of target events correctly (teacher and student behaviors in a special education industrial arts class). Students viewed videotapes and responded on a computer keyboard that provided immediate feedback on errors. Observation intervals with errors were corrected, and the tape was rewound and reviewed before continuing to the next interval. This training proceeded through three levels of complexity based on the number of target behaviors and individuals observed. An interactive training program of this nature requires equipment that includes an interface that can encode and read frame numbers on the VCR under the control of the computer. Such control interfaces are available as options on most major computers and from specialty hardware suppliers. Most better quality VCRs now have frame-indexing circuitry that will assist this interface.

Other Examples

Further examples of vignettes in training described in the recent literature include: other mental health training (Alger, 1984); medical training in the recognition of cultural issues (Mao, Bullock, Harway, & Khalsa, 1988) and interactions with elderly patients (Robbins, Fink, Kosecoff, Vivell, & Beck, 1982); burn unit staff for improved liaison; military personnel for perceptual-motor skills (Jones, 1981); sign language for special education teachers and deaf students (Newell, Sims, & Myers, 1983); and interviewing skills for rehabilitation clients (Anholt, 1987). Some vignettes developed in assessment and research strategies may be applicable to training, for example in police situations (Rand, 1987). A system of training police cadets who "interact" with life-size video projections is described by Doyle (1981). The vignettes are filmed from the (police) participant perspective, rather than from an onlooker's point of view, with careful attention to appropriate silent intervals during which the trainee makes a response.

VIGNETTES IN THERAPY

Surprisingly little has been written about vignettes used for therapeutic purposes, although descriptions appeared in print some time ago (e.g., Mayadas & Duehn, 1981). To the extent that skills training is often a significant part of therapy (e.g., social skills, coping skills, and problem solving) and the way in which video recordings of one's own behavior are often replayed vignette-style (see Chapters 13 and 14), the potential application is clear. In this section, one application of social skills training helps to illustrate the connection between the two areas. Reports on vignettes in flooding (exposure treatment) and sex therapy are also described.

Social Skills

Training programs for social skills frequently use video vignettes (e.g., Cooper, Biggs, & Bender, 1983). Most of the commercially available programs that include videotapes in their packaging (e.g., ACCEPTS by Walker et al., 1983; ASSET by Hazel et al., 1983; and *Alcohol Trigger Films* by the American Automobile Association) are deliberately constructed, or end up being used, according to the vignette principles described in this chapter.

A program that features these strategies for soon-to-be-released inmates of two prisons in Great Britain is described by McGuire and Priestley (1983). One segment of the "release courses" involved critical incident analysis. Small groups of prisoners made 2- or 3-minute videotapes depicting single, problematic social encounters as experienced by group members, with negative resolutions. Each recording was then replayed so that participants could stop the tape at crucial points of the exchange to discuss more effective alternatives. A natural extension could be to have the inmates then make a video recording of an enactment to each original situation, with positive resolutions. However, the authors produced effective results with the program as described.

Flooding: Exposure Therapy

Therapies for a wide range of anxiety disorders (flooding and response prevention, participant modeling, systematic desensitization, implosion) require exposure to stimuli that provoke the anxieties. The exposure is usually very systematically organized, often in a hierarchy, and may be described, actual, or in some form of media such as photographic slides. Perhaps video has been used infrequently because of the expense (trouble) in using the medium and the general advantage of individualization. In settings where treatment issues are repeatedly encountered with exposure themes in common, such as fear of flying or height phobias, the development of video vignettes that could be selectively used with different individuals would now seem both feasible and advantageous.

An example of this approach was described by Beidel, Turner, and Allgood-Hill (1989) in the treatment of an obsessive-compulsive woman. The client's primary concern involved contamination of her kitchen by food particles. The therapists considered imaginal flooding to be the treatment of choice. However, the woman reported she was unable to sustain the images for the necessary duration. To address this difficulty, a number of videotapes were made showing her family in their kitchen preparing various foods. Videos were 8 to 10 minutes, viewed by the client during daily flooding sessions. The combined procedures, including in vivo, were reasonably effective in about 6 weeks of treatment. Similar principles were used under the somewhat different circumstances of a 5-year-old girl who had phobic reactions to thunderstorms. In the exposure component of treatment, Matthey (1988) included a videotape of a weather report and audiotape recordings of storms. Audio recordings of combat sounds have been used in the assessment of post-traumatic stress disorders in Vietnam veterans (Blanchard, Kolb, Taylor, & Wittrock, 1989) and would seem to have potential use in the flooding treatments often recommended with those clients.

Sex Therapy

The use of "blue movies" has brought some inevitable notoriety to clinical psychologists who treat sexual dysfunction. But there are several ways that video recordings can be used in this context, beyond simple arousal. Tapes used by sex therapists typically have informational and modeling value; arousal stimuli are used in the treatment of impotence, for redevelopment of sexual preferences, and as part of assessment systems. Vignettes can be used to provoke discussions, in problem solving, or in the treatment of sexual anxiety (Annon & Robinson, 1981; Dauw, 1988).

VIGNETTES IN RESEARCH

Dozens of reports appear every year in which video vignettes make a significant contribution to the experimental design in the reported studies. A selection of studies is described below to illustrate different strategies. Sometimes different vignettes are presented to groups of subjects so that the videos differ from each other in ways that address a research question, or a video presentation may be contrasted with a nonvideo condition, such as a group discussion or lecture. Sometimes the same vignette may be presented to different individuals or groups, so that the subjects are classified differently or they observe under systematically varied viewing conditions. The video may even contribute to the dependent variable measures or other interesting innovations.

Video Content as Independent Variable

A clear example of this strategy was provided by Gurtman (1987) in a study of depressive affect and disclosure as factors in interpersonal rejection. In three different videotaped segments, an actress was shown from the waist up, sitting in front of a neutral background and apparently conversing with an off-camera interviewer positioned in front of her. The actress, a college student who had been given extensive coaching, portrayed three different affective responses—happy, sad, and flat—in segments 1 1/2 minutes long. Each video was accompanied by one of two audiotapes (or none as a control condition) commenting on recent negative events concerning dating and studies. The response varied, to illustrate either a depressive or a nondepressive condition; for example: "It's obvious now that I'm a failure; there's no point in disputing it. I've got another exam coming up soon, but what's the use? Why even bother trying to get into grad school? The only good grades I've ever gotten were pure luck. After getting the exam back, I stayed in my seat until everyone left . . ." (p. 91). The commentaries were kept as similar as possible in length and content. With this economical design, producing nine different but systematically related conditions, Gurtman was able to demonstrate that depressive disclosure was most strongly influential in producing a negative impression in viewers, while sad or flat affect was a secondary influence.

Instead of varying single elements only, the vignettes may vary in their entirety. One type of example is provided by my own research with colleagues in Alaska (Raymond, Dowrick, & Kleinke, 1990). The purpose of this study was to examine reactions to seeing oneself on video for the first time. Video recordings were made of all subjects in a short (3-minute), structured interview situation. A third of the subjects saw tapes of themselves; another third saw tapes of a different person in the same situation; and the others viewed a control tape of the same length showing outdoor scenes with no people. During and after viewing, physiological and self-report affective measures and behavioral observations (also using video) were made of all subjects. (Results indicated that for this group of college women aged 18 to 45 years, seeing themselves on video for the first time was a mildly anxiety-provoking, perhaps embarrassing experience, but the effects were moderate and mostly transitory.)

Video has been used quite often to study various aspects of attitudes toward counselors. A review by Manthei (1983) described studies in which experimental subjects observed videotaped interviews of clients by different therapists. One study, combining several approaches by Littrell, Caffrey, and Hopper (1987), investigated the effects of student opinions on preferences among counselors. Seven experimental conditions were created with professionally prepared videotapes. Rather than use scripts, students' spontaneous comments were edited to provide a representative sample. In addition to the reputational comments (positive, negative, or neutral), footage of a counselor in an 8-minute interview was included in some of the experimental conditions—a female counselor with a female client, or a male counselor with a male client. In a review of studies involving the manipulation of expectancies about counseling and psychotherapy, Tinsley, Bowman, and Ray (1988) concluded that audiotape and video interventions are most often effective.

An interesting variation is to present two (or more) video stimuli simultaneously. An intriguing illustration is provided by Golinkoff, Hirsh-Pasek, Cauley, and Gordon (1987) in their development of an assessment methodology for infant language. In their system, two 17-inch video monitors are separated by a 12-inch speaker that plays a message to match only one of the screens. Infants sit 2 feet away while their direction of gaze is recorded. For example, the voice through the speaker might say "Where's the boat? Find the boat," while the display on one monitor shows a boat and the other one shows a stack of blocks. Clearly the video medium with a moving picture has special advantages in the discrimination of verbs (e.g., push the ball vs. bounce the ball). The sound track was recorded on one of the videotapes and equipment (a Sony VP-5000 tape deck) was used that could ensure the synchronicity of the two tapes; several pairs of stimuli were presented in succession spaced with black rest periods. During the rest periods, a light came on above the speaker to attract the infants' attention back to the center.

Other recent studies using video to provide the independent variable include one by Howe (1987) that concerned attributes of cause in marital conflict observed from different perspectives. Three 3-minute videotapes were made of wife-and-husband arguments (acted) from the perspective of the husband, the wife, and a counselor. The influences of excuses on attitudes toward rapists has been studied by Kleinke, Wallis, and Stadler (1990) by varying the amount of remorse expressed in videotapes by a role-played offender. A study by Keane, Nelson, and Herbert (1987) examined mothers' reactions to video displays of compliant versus noncompliant child behavior. The authors also studied contextual variables by adding different descriptions of the child's circumstances and by considering the adult's mood. These other sources of independent variations are part of another strategy described later in this chapter.

Video in Contrast with Another Medium

In one of its mainstream purposes (e.g., assessment, instruction) video may simply be contrasted with some other procedure (e.g., live observation or written manual). Examples of such studies are cited in pertinent chapters throughout this book. One study (Grabe & Tabor, 1981) contrasted small-group learning experiences provided to students of developmental psychology. Half the subjects participated in a traditional discussion of children's behavior related to the topic of the week; the other half viewed carefully structured videotapes of children engaged in such behavior. Grabe and Tabor measured not only academic outcome (video group students performed better on examinations) but also related processes: Students who saw the videos rated the course as more interesting and they attended the small-group sessions more regularly.

An application of greater pertinence to this chapter was reported by Bigelow (1981) in the measurement of young children's self-recognition. She contrasted three recorded video conditions (self, another child, and parent—each 3 minutes), closed-circuit TV, and mirror images. (She also made video recordings of children's reactions for later analysis, and repeated the experience monthly for 8 months.) The results indicated that these infants recognized their parents' images before their own, and recognized themselves in a mirror more readily than on a screen. A number of interesting studies have been done on self-recognition using other strategies, to be discussed later in this chapter.

Video as Dependent Variable

An interesting variation that has received limited development is to examine the subject's manipulation of the video screen or other equipment as a measurable outcome. The one area of major use has been in the measurement of *body image*. The usual setup, which has met with modest success, is to project a still photograph onto a screen by means of a camera with an adjustable distorting lens. The system can expand or shrink the width, sometimes ranging as much as double to half the width, but cannot differentially alter, say, the torso or hips. Technology has recently become available through inexpensive special-effects generators to "digitize" any picture for manipulation by computer software (see Dispezio, 1990), which will make this measurement strategy more diverse and effective.

The video distortion technique currently in use has been described by Cash and Brown (1987) in their review of body image in anorexic and bulimic individuals. Typical of this procedure, the subjects are asked to reset their on-screen picture after it has been arbitrarily distorted. The technique is often used for estimates of ideal (personal or social) body image (Lindholm & Wilson, 1988; Taylor & Cooper, 1988). Because distortion may favor overestimation, screen size may affect judgments, and because of other technical problems, careful use of control groups and cautious comparison between studies are necessary. But used with care, valuable results can be obtained (e.g., Gardner & Moncrieff, 1988).

It will be interesting to see if other strategies emerge in using subjects' interactions with video to create dependent-variable measures. In a sense, perceptual interactions such as direction of gaze fit this category. And the number of times subjects play a tape or where they choose to stop it, to avoid or to indulge the content, are other possibilities. More creative opportunities may rapidly emerge with advances in image-manipulation technology.

Contrasting Conditions Created by Labels

A popular methodology in some areas of research is to use a single vignette and to create varying conditions by describing aspects of the video differently for different viewers. This strategy was incorporated into the study, previously described, by Keane et al. (1987). They gave the mothers who watched a boy on videotape one of nine descriptions of chronic disabling conditions and/or recent events affecting the child to see if these descriptions altered how the women would react to the boy's behavior.

A prototype for this research strategy is provided by Woolfolk, Woolfolk, and Wilson (1977), who showed a film of a teacher using contingency management in the classroom. For one group of university undergraduates, the tape was described as being illustrative of behavior modification. For another group of students, it was described as an example of humanistic education. Results indicated that both the teacher and the teaching method were rated more favorably when the method was described as humanistic.

Other recent research using the methodology of vignettes with labels has addressed attitudes toward rape victims (Tetreault & Barnett, 1987), political candidates (Sigal, Hsu, Foodim, & Betman, 1988), and children with mental retardation (Van Bourgondien, 1987). Topics of studies that address the effect of labels on perception and judgment include: prematurity and gender of babies (Stern & Karraker, 1988), mental illness diagnosis (Czajka & DeNisi, 1988; Herbert Nelson, & Herbert, 1988; O'Connor & Smith, 1987), and leadership and management (Foti & Lord, 1987). A number of studies have examined factors concerning eyewitness testimony and jury decisions; for example see Smith and Ellsworth (1987) and Tanford and Cox (1987).

Categories of Subject (Viewer) as the Major Variable

Another popular and straightforward strategy, the last to be identified in this chapter, is to measure reactions to video vignettes in subjects differentiated by naturally occurring or induced distinctions. A computer search revealed about 40 studies emphasizing this strategy, published in journals in approximately 1 year (late 1987 to late 1988). These can be classified into seven subcategories (see Table 5.1). These classifications are somewhat arbitrary and are not presumed to be definitive or intended to limit the approach. These classifications plus sample studies from the computer search are listed in the table to assist readers who are looking for examples that may parallel their own interests.

A common approach is to contrast subjects of different *levels of training* in a video review task expected to reflect that training. For example, undergraduate psychology students and experienced clinicians may be asked to rate certain dimensions of an interview. Quite often the research design is given a little more complexity by adding variations (e.g., clients of different diagnoses) to the vignettes. Situations in which the variations to both the categories of viewer and the contents of vignette are central to the research, are discussed in the next section of this chapter. A

TABLE 5.1. Video Vignettes in Research: Sample Studies in Which the Subject Conditions Create the Independent Variable

Author	Topic	Comparison Variable
1. Level of Training		
Borgeaud & Abernathy (1987)	Skill specific memory	Volleyball players *vs.* nonplayers
Jackson (1988)	Confidence levels	Laypersons *vs.* professionals
Peterson & Comeaux (1987)	Classroom instruction	Novice *vs.* experienced teachers
Sipps, Sugden, & Faiver (1988)	Counseling self-efficacy	Graduate training *vs.* counselor training
Wilkinson (1988)	Psychiatric decision making	Trainee general practitioners *vs.* trainee psychiatrists
2. Other Related Experiences		
Adamson, Bakeman, Smith, & Walters (1987)	Interpretation of infants' acts	Mothers *vs.* fathers *vs.* other men *vs.* other women
Childress, McLellan, Ehrman, & O'Brien (1988)	Responsivity	Methadone outpatients *vs.* detoxifying methadone inpatients *vs.* abstinent opioid users *vs.* abstinent cocaine users
Dodge & Coie (1987)	Attributional biases & aggression in children	Reactive aggression *vs.* proactive aggression *vs.* nonaggression
Dodge & Somberg (1987)	Hostile attributional biases	Aggressive boys *vs.* nonaggressive boys
Dozier (1988)	Interpersonal information processing	Socially rejected 5th-graders *vs.* average 5th-graders
3. Relationship to Subject Matter		
Barnett, Tetreault, & Masbad (1987)	Empathy	Raped undergraduate women *vs.* nonraped undergraduate women
Noller & Callan (1988)	Rating interactions	Mother *vs.* father *vs.* adolescent
4. Clinical Diagnosis		
Hobson (1987)	Recognition	Autistic children *vs.* retarded children *vs.* normal controls
Van der Meere & Sergeant (1988)	Sustained attention deficit	Hyperactive *vs.* control children

5. *Age or Gender*

Walk & Samuel (1988)	Interpretation of nonverbal behavior	Females vs. males

6. *Conditions Immediately Before or During Review*

McCann & Sheehan (1987)	Recall pseudomemory	Video vs. hypnotic suggestion
Morokoff, Baum, McKinnon, & Gilliland (1987)	Chronic stress levels	Unemployed men vs. employed men
Murphy & Constans (1987)	Bias in rating	Reading scales before vs. after viewing videotape
Quackenbush (1987)	Social perception	Male undergraduates vs. female undergraduates
Salvemini (1988)	Rating accuracy	Rater rewards vs. prior ratee performance

7. *Conditions of Review*

Balamore (1987)	Moral decision making	Audiotaped dilemmas vs. videotaped dilemmas
Fortenberry, Kaplan, & Hill (1988)	Adolescent health care	Structured interview vs. questionnaire vs. videotape
Gibling & Davies (1988)	Recall	Correct vs. misleading information
Siegal, Waters, & Dinwiddy (1988)	Conservation	Two-question vs. one-question procedure
Srinivas & Motowidlo (1987)	Rater stress	Stressful vs. unstressful video performance

related approach is to contrast the reactions of viewers who are differentiated on the basis of other kinds of *relevant experiences,* also related to the video content. For example, soccer coaches from different countries may be asked to respond to scenes of controversial game movements. A slightly different approach is to contrast subjects on the basis of their *relationship* or extent of identification with the individuals portrayed on the video (e.g., family vs. nonfamily).

The fourth approach identified here is one in which subjects differ on the basis of some *clinical or social grouping*—for example, hyperactivity or androgyny. Or subjects may differ *developmentally* or by *gender.* A different type of approach is to *create differences* immediately before or during the viewing (e.g., introducing different levels of short-term stress). The seventh strategy includes studies in which the *conditions of review* are systematically varied—for example, different rating instruments are used. Clearly these categories are not mutually exclusive. Studies listed in Table 5.1 are selected because they emphasize one of the identified approaches in their design; in a number of instances, they arguably fit other categories or combine approaches.

Two-Way Designs: Video Variables and Subject Variables

Many studies combine the strategies just listed in significant ways. For example, in a developmental study of *self-recognition,* Hill and Tomlin (1981) examined reactions to different forms of image for children with different disabilities. In a minimum of four sessions of 10 minutes each, preverbal children watched video images of themselves, either prerecorded or in real time, with faces either unmarked or marked with finger paint. Data collection included mark-directed responses and video viewing time. Down syndrome children indicated self-recognition more readily than age-matched multihandicapped children. In a review of the literature on self-recognition, Anderson (1984) has pointed to the advantages of video in developmental and comparative studies.

Particular value emerges from two-way designs when there is some kind of interaction. Such was the case in some research of mine with colleagues at Smith College, Massachusetts (Frost, Benton, & Dowrick, in press). Our first interest was to see whether or not people would rate themselves differently on the basis of memory versus video replay of an event that occurred a week previously. We also divided the subjects by affective state (dysphoric vs. nondysphoric). There was an interesting interaction effect in which dysphoria combined with the video replay condition to produce the most critical self-appraisals. The event in which self-appraisal was called for was a structured format, mock job interview similar to that used in the Raymond et al. (1990) study described earlier in this chapter.

Another example of a study in which this type of interaction is of central importance is described by Weaver, Masland, Kharazmi, and Zillman (1985). They examined the effect of alcoholic intoxication on the appreciation of different types of humor. After drinking specified amounts of ethanol, subjects saw 2-1/2-minute videos containing examples of both "blunt" and "subtle" humor. The blunt material was taken from a "Carol Burnett Show" featuring Tim Conway and Harvey

Korman. Conway played an old and feeble pediatrician, examining an adult, Korman, who was dressed in pajamas. Conway treated him like a small child; he wore a monkey mask and shook a rattle. The so-called subtle material was taken from a televised comedy routine by George Carlin, playing a newscaster. His announcements included "Twenty-one killed in 21-gun salute" and "Boomerangs are coming back." As indicated by an analysis of facial movements recorded by a hidden camera, appreciation of blunt humor was greater with a higher consumption of alcohol; subtle humor produced more smiles with less alcohol consumption.

From these and other examples, it can be seen that having two sets of variables—one in the vignettes to be presented and one in the subjects who do the viewing—is sometimes essential to address the research question. Sometimes another factor (gender, age, mood, or years of service) is included as a secondary interest, occasionally from thoroughness or as a kind of insurance in case the main effect is not significant. Of the many studies recently published that incorporate this combined strategy of research design using video, most fall into three broad areas:

1. *Communications* (e.g., laryngectomy speech ratings, Watson & Williams, 1987) and *social/personality* (e.g., perceptions of sexually interested behavior, Shotland & Craig, 1988; effects of shyness, Asendorpf, 1987).
2. *Developmental* (e.g., childhood attitudes toward Down syndrome, Graffi & Minnes, 1988), *clinical* (e.g., sex therapy, Strassberg, Kelly, Carroll, & Kircher, 1987), and *clinical training* (e.g., teacher perceptions of problems, Safran & Safran, 1987).
3. *Human performance in work* (e.g., job applicant evaluation, Gordon, Rozelle, & Baxter, 1988) and *sport* (e.g., eye movements in baseball, Shank & Haywood, 1987).

CONCLUDING REMARKS

The use of video vignettes as reported in the behavioral science literature has been simmering for long enough; it now looks to have boiled over. In this chapter I have attempted to characterize some major trends. Now it seems the uses of vignettes are diverse enough and the reports so numerous that further conceptualization and review are in order. Many interesting practices were not even commented on in this chapter (e.g., research without independent variables, as in correlations between counselor characteristics and reactions to client vignettes, Wachowiak & Diaz, 1987). The conceptualizations put forth in this chapter are merely a beginning taxonomy of a developing field. Some comments on possible future trends are made in Chapter 8.

CHAPTER 6

Feedback and Self-Confrontation

OVERVIEW

Descriptive and evaluative reports on video "feedback" have dwindled in the last 10 years, even though its practice is more firmly in evidence than ever, and despite the lack of an accepted theoretical basis for its use. This chapter presents a reexamination of the potential purposes of "unstructured" video self-review and sets out some principles of application. I argue that what is generally called video feedback can be effective as self-assessment *or as* motivation. *(Observational learning from oneself is described in Chapter 7.) Feedback is defined and its usefulness in assessment to promote self-correction is described. Confrontation as motivation is also examined, including the circumstances contributing to deleterious effects. A theory is presented for a* video review effect, *in which the emotional response is predicted on the basis of the reaction to the (recorded) event as if it were in the present, complicated by the event actually being past. Methods are then described to maximize self-assessment: identifying self-correction information (especially simple errors of commission and readily attainable errors of omission); enhancing exposure to key information (e.g., client or trainee receptivity); and monitoring the effects. Video recording techniques related to these methods are described. Strategies to maximize motivation, as different from those identified for self-assessment, are noted. The chapter ends with a selective review of some promising applications and their effects as relevant to the conceptualizations presented here (e.g., self-monitoring, refocusing of efforts, and recognizing progress).*

P.W.D.

People are profoundly affected by seeing images of themselves. When video became reasonably accessible for use by behavioral scientists and clinicians in the late 1960s, it was a natural, perhaps glib, assumption that this profundity was good. Video replay (VR) became widely used in educational and therapeutic settings. (Numerous and diverse examples are published in collected works: Berger, 1970; Geerstma, 1969.) But as more and more reports were published, successive reviews voiced enough reservations that a tug of war developed: Is VR *beneficial* or *damaging?* Most reviewers reached the conclusion that it could be either, neither, or both (Danet, 1968; Bailey & Sowder, 1970; Fuller & Manning, 1973; Griffiths, 1974; Hung & Rosenthal, 1978). This chapter presents a reexamination of purposes that might be served by showing people themselves on video and a description of what is known about the circumstances that most facilitates these purposes.

It is worth making a distinction between *structured* and *unstructured* video replay. The use of unstructured VR, in which subjects see themselves as "realistically" as possible in footage replayed without adulteration or emphasis, raises such questions as "what kinds of psychological processes does video replay help?", "who will benefit?", and "how will these benefits accrue?". Structured VR refers to the result of any method that selectively emphasizes the perceived content of tapes during replay. Structuring can be initiated during recording, while rerecording, or while presenting the VR. The most common methods, illustrated later in this chapter and in Chapters 7 and 14 through 17 include scripting, specialized camera work (e.g., angles, close-ups), editing, split-screen (multiple-image) replay, and supervisor- or therapist-led discussions during replay. Structured VR poses the additional question "What kinds of recorded episodes will help a person change?"—broadening the enquiry to include not only the subject but also the use of and interaction with the technology.

It can be seen that "unstructured VR" is somewhat hypothetical. Contrary to popular adage, the camera always lies; some selective emphasis is inevitable, although it may not be deliberate or planful. Thus, the distinction is not categorical, but one of degree. I believe the failure to note the amount (and type) of structuring in various VR applications has led to the confusion in findings.

Some previous reviewers have concluded that when VR is relatively unstructured (or used without regard to its structure), and is effective, then the effectiveness derives from the process of *observational learning from oneself* (Dowrick, 1977; Hung & Rosenthal, 1978). To the extent that this may be true, it is worth pursuing VR to maximize this instructional approach—fully described as "self-modeling" in Chapter 7. I will argue, however, that VR has at least two other potential effects that assist personal change. These may be loosely referred to as assessment and motivation and are the major topics of this chapter.

FEEDBACK AS ASSESSMENT

When video replay is relatively unadulterated, it can be a rich source of information about current performance capability. It can also provide examples of detail from recent activity. On the global level, the video provides a source of objectivity, an opportunity to observe without participation, and a view from a different perspective. (Robert Burns' "O wad some Power the giftie gie us/To see oursels as ithers see us," was for some years the most consistently cited quotation in the VR literature.) On the micro level, there is the opportunity to be reminded of, and perhaps to reexperience, past events and to observe more closely (enhanced by slow motion, repetition, the chance to stop and discuss, etc.). It is a mistake, especially in therapy, to assume that this information is necessarily desirable as presented and received.

The term "feedback" is freely used by psychologists. Various types of feedback have been examined and reviewed, in some cases extensively, in other contexts (e.g., Balzer, Doherty, & O'Connor, 1989). In the physical sciences and biology, the term is used in a wisely narrow sense to refer to the connecting of output to input of a system such that there is potential for immediate change in the system's ongoing activity (as in the furnace controlled by a thermostat, or the blink reflex that moistens a dry eyeball). Visual feedback that influences behavior might then be restricted to mirrors and closed-circuit television. The event that in general parlance is called *video feedback* is most often considerably delayed (as is true of other "feedback" in clinical or educational settings.) Worse, the term carries with it the automatic premise that it is part of a self-correcting system. Whereas in other sciences, output information that is fed into a system is not called feedback *unless* it allows self-correction to take place, behavioral scientists (at least those concerned with training, education, and therapy) seem to assume that if they call information "feedback," self-correction shall take place. Given the widespread use of the term, it seems that "feedback" will continue to be used to refer to any information provided to a system about its functioning, no matter what the interval of delay. But we should at least avoid the error of assuming that such information automatically leads to self-correction.

Thus, the question becomes "how does information (improved self-assessment) promote self-correction?". In biological and physical systems, self-correction usually takes place when feedback indicates to the system that it is somehow off-target. This feedback is commonly interpreted as "error-information" (although error is an odd connotation for natural loss of heat from a room or the drying of an eyeball). So when a therapist offers you "feedback" on the way you interact with your spouse, you can expect to hear about some of your errors of miscommunication, and this information may serve as "true" feedback (i.e. with potential for self-correction). But potentially you will receive two other kinds of information. One, which she will call "positive feedback," will concern the things you did well and should continue to do, maybe do more often (see Chapter 7). The other will be errors you are unable to self-correct, but may provide a springboard for further intervention (see the next section). If the therapist is skillful, she will provide a judicious mix of the three types of information, depending on the setting and her appraisal of your strengths and her resources. At the other (damaging) extreme, the error information will be impossible to self-correct and will produce strong negative, unsupported emotions; the on-target information will be fatuously redundant or negatively presented.

The major conclusion to be drawn at this time is that feedback is not necessarily therapeutic or educational in and of itself. It is often mislabeled to encompass any kind of information about process or outcome, but even when the feedback is true to the narrow sense of the word, the individual must have the ability to self-correct. It seems that the early enthusiasm for the use of video was related to its obviously vast capacity to convey information, and the assumption that more was better—despite early warnings to the contrary. Over 20 years ago, Reivich and Geertsma concluded that "video-tape self-viewing *per se* is not likely to effect an optimal therapeutic response and that clinicians . . . should be prepared to take an active role . . ." (1968, p. 41). In passing it may be noted that information obtained and processed as described in this section is sometimes quite correctly called "insight." Whatever terminology is preferred it remains important to remember that feedback/self-assessment/insight is not a technique of change in itself—but it may provide the conditions for change. Sometimes self-correction is neither possible nor intended, but the information and, more particularly, the emotional impact may be a catalyst for other changes as described next.

CONFRONTATION AS MOTIVATION

When video replay information does not lead to self-correction, to be a useful change agent it needs to fit into a support package. It may also be possible to use the emotional loading beneficially. If not, the self-image video confrontation carries considerable risks.

Damage sometimes occurs, apparently as a result of information that cannot be acted upon and the associated negative emotional reactions, without the support that could possibly turn these events to an advantage. It can be expected that if the video confrontation is stressful, people will turn to their most usual coping strategies—for people in therapy, their ineffective coping mechanisms may be the main reason for their seeking help. For example, Schaefer, Sobell, and Mills (1971) found that alcoholics were greatly moved by seeing their own drunken behavior on videotape. Most of the subjects were appalled and expressed great "motivation" to change, but subsequently drank even more alcohol—presumably as their most practiced way of coping with upset emotions.

An even more dramatic outcome was reported by Alkire and Brunse (1974) who described marital separation and even suicide among couples provided with unsupported VR. Their study, published as a cautionary notice, in retrospect reads like a recipe for disaster. As experienced family and group therapists, they set out to measure the effects of different therapy components, including VR, in a relatively systematic manner. Their subjects, who had all been in group therapy for some time, were divided into three groups of three couples each. (Singles groups were also used as controls.) The procedure incorporating video began with group members identifying other individuals' most representative problems. Derived scenes were then role played by these individuals and their partners for the camera. During replay to the group, no comments or interruptions were allowed; it was followed by 5 minutes of discussion by *other* group members only. Immediate and long-term results made it clear that virtually none of these clients benefitted from this confrontation, and for some the effects were tragic. Table 6.1 sets out the seven procedural faults that now seem evident with the advantage of hindsight. Consistent with the point intended in this section, effective alternative procedures are set out in juxtaposition.

Following is an overview of three major strategies of effective confrontation.

Sometimes information from VR can alter the therapeutic relationship. Some users have described VR as breaking down the resistance of clients who have denied the existence of a problem or their responsibility in it, as seen by others. Variations of

TABLE 6.1. The Do's and Don'ts of Unstructured Video Replay*

Don't	Do
1. Behavior to be reviewed chosen by other people (clients).	1. Involve the client/trainee in the selection of issues, under the guidance of a therapist/trainer.
2. Issue selected on the basis of worst, noncoping behavior.	2. Select *either* an ineffective but redeemable behavior *or* an effective but low frequencey one.
3. The target problem had a history of unsuccessful treatment.	3. Show only errors of which the subject is unaware (or incompletely aware).
4. Tape reviewed without any control by subject.	4. Maximize subject control of replay.
5. Reviewed in the presence of others (clients).	5. Reduce the public exposure, relative to the sensitivity of the material.
6. Discussed only by other clients, experienced in confrontational therapy.	6. Train discussants to make constructive comments and brainstorm with primary client/trainee.
7. No therapist intervention during or after video.	7. Monitor and structure all VR events and build in other treatment components (package) as necessary.

*The *Don't* column is derived from Alkire & Brunse, 1974; the *Do* column is consistent with the point that effective feedback indicates a solution, not just a problem.

this approach have been pursued in eating disorders seen as body image problems (e.g., McRea, 1983; Probst, Vandereycken, & Van Coppenolle, 1988). In family systems and other settings where communication is important and difficult to monitor as a participant, VR can be used to provide another perspective (Whitaker, 1978). It is dangerous, however, to use VR just to make a point without a therapeutic plan. As the resident video person in various settings, all too often I have had to turn down or modify requests to provide a videotape for a colleague who says, "I just want to show the kid how awful he is. . . ." VR that is effectively designed to change an attitude toward therapy or a training program will provide carefully selected information, minimizing the emotional loading.

Another major strategy is to use VR to reprocess recent events. In Chapter 14, the details of procedures for "interpersonal process recall" are presented, as developed and widely used by Norman Kagan and his associates over the last 2 decades or more (Kagan, 1978; Kagan, Krathwohl, & Miller, 1963). In this approach the replay, which is frequently stopped and discussed, is used to elicit memories of thoughts and feelings associated with the recorded events. Opportunity to reexamine past events in this way promotes both self-analysis and motivation. A related approach is to apply consequences during the replay. (See Chapter 17 for examples with autistic children.)

A third strategy is to turn the potential for emotional reactions to VR from a liability into an asset. Because many therapists expect to elicit emotions as part of the therapeutic process, it is surprising that this strategy is not used (or reported to be used) more often. Clearly there are risks in drawing out emotions such as anxiety, anger, and depression. Although these feelings may in turn produce changes in verbal expression (e.g., self-disclosure) and emotional display (e.g., crying) often considered therapeutic, they may alternatively increase alienation, leading to further defensiveness or quitting therapy altogether. There is much speculation but limited evidence for negative emotional reactions under certain viewing circumstances. For example, Trower and Kiely (1983) point to the important possibility that depressed people will become more depressed on seeing themselves on video, at least in conditions where they are likely to select negative information about themselves. There is also limited evidence that VR is anxiety-producing for most people when they are unused to it (Raymond, Dowrick, & Kleinke, 1990, described in Chapter 5). It is possible that other viewing circumstances may lead to positive emotional reactions with concomitant changes in the therapeutic or educational process: for example, euphoria and surprise that produce energy and work. Data and concepts are sorely needed to provide some predictability for emotional reactions that can be supported in a structured way when they occur.

A THEORY OF VIDEO REPLAY

The experience of video replay is somehow different from simply reactivating a memory. The question is, "What is the nature of that difference, and what evidence is there?" As memories fade, they acquire a "positive glow" (Markus & Wurf, 1987). That is, people selectively forget elements of the past that damage their reputations. With even quite recent events, individuals tend to explain their own roles more generously than others do (Alloy & Abramson, 1979; Snyder, 1985). If not, the effect is called clinical depression. The flip side of this aspect of human nature is that people are selectively more vigilant, even self-critical, during ongoing activities. For example, self-awareness increased when performance deteriorates (Pyszczynski & Greenberg, 1985). These attributions and selective attentions make sense in evolutionary terms. There is survival value in being vigilant about the current circumstances because of the opportunity to influence events. Since the past cannot be changed, there is further survival value in a selectively positive memory.

Video recording is one of many technical aberrations that disturb evolution. VR has the peculiarity of capturing a past event (which cannot be changed) that is experienced in the present. The level of vigilance and self-evaluation appropriate to the original event will occur reflexively. It would seem, then, that a testable theoretical basis for understanding the effects of video replay would be to expect that the emotional reaction to seeing oneself on video will be variable, but may be predictable based on the reaction to the event as if it were in the present, constrained or complicated by the event actually being past (cf., Dowrick, 1986, p. 201).

We have made a small beginning to collecting data on this hypothesis (Frost, Benton, & Dowrick, in press). We videotaped 46 Smith College students in mock job interviews. A few days later they evaluated themselves, based on *either* their memory of the interview *or* a review of the videotape. Mood measures were taken using the Beck Depression Inventory. The results indicated limited evidence for a *video review effect* in which people evaluated themselves more critically from videotapes than from memory, exacerbated by negative mood at the time of appraisal. That is, people feeling dysphoric (not really depressed, but not quite happy either) are overly self-critical when faced with videotapes (where nothing can be done to adjust the observed situation), but not when recollecting memories, which have already been filtered to enhance a "positive glow."

METHODS

For the two general purposes of video self-review—self-assessment and motivation—as identified in this chapter, some basic strategies are now described. Where possible, procedural details of specific techniques are listed.

Self-Assessment

When video replay is used to provide feedback with potential for self-correction, the following three strategies are helpful. First, it is necessary *to identify* what information can be acted upon. For example, facial expressions are easier to control in a stressful situation than quickness of thought. Therefore, feedback on what a person looks like during an angry confrontation may be more useful than recordings of what he or she says in the heat of the moment. Second, useful information selected for self-correction can be presented in ways that *maximize* its exposure and receptivity. Sequences can be preselected; slow motion, still framing, and supervisor commentary are common tactics. Third, it is valuable to ensure that self-correction can and does take place through some form of *monitoring*. Sometimes it is not possible to predict self-correction with real certainty, and a risk may be worth taking for the opportunity of greater gains—if a safety net is provided. Elaborations of these methodological strategies are described next.

Identifying Self-correction Information

The strategy of showing people their errors (in the belief that it allows for self-correction) is the most obvious and the most abused. As previously stated, reviewing undesirable performances on video can have damaging effects. Following are some categories of information about less-than-ideal performances that promote self-correction. (See Figure 6.1.)

Some *errors of commission* can be eliminated relatively easily when one becomes aware of them: for example, fidgeting during an interview. If a counselor trainee has found it difficult to recognize exactly what she does that is distracting or annoying to clients when she is talking to them, seeing herself on video may provide exactly the information she needs. However, if all she needs is to be told, "you play with your hair a lot," the video is superfluous. It is not always easy to stop a behavior that one is

A. **Identifying self-correction information**
   1. Errors that can be eliminated (e.g., fidgets of a courtroom lawyer).
   2. Errors in which correction is self-evident and possible (e.g., racquet angle for an intermediate tennis player).
   3. Omissions for which correction is self-evident and possible (e.g., "I" statements of a spouse who has had some communication training).
   4. Behavior needing practice, but potentially useful/adaptive.
   5. Emphasis on relevant elements in the general context.

   Technical considerations: zoom lens, camera angles, high-speed shutter, second camera, wireless microphones.

B. **Enhancing exposure of key information**
   1. Cognitive understanding established prior to feedback.
   2. First viewing by self or coach (etc.) only, perhaps record/analyze behavior.
   3. If review with others (e.g., group), structure their support.
   4. Examples selected to minimize emotional reactivity (events and appearances).
   5. Explanation of associated events (memories of thoughts, feelings).
   6. Errors/omissions, for which self-correction not evident, tied to explanations or other training/therapy.

   Technical considerations: repetitions, still framing, slow motion, reverse play, split screen.

C. **Monitoring the effects**
   1. Prediction that self-correction is probable, progress monitored.
   2. Support by other training/therapy.

Figure 6.1. Video replay for self-assessment that promotes personal change.

aware of and wants to eliminate. Sometimes a person is helped by a recording that really highlights how often he says "um" while speaking. Then again, this habit may be only slightly reduced, but not eliminated, by "conscious effort." Under these circumstances it is better to train a replacement behavior by some other method, perhaps feedforward rather than feedback (see Chapter 7).

Other kinds of error may be easily corrected. These include *errors in which the correction is both self-evident and within the repertoire* of the reviewer. Suppose someone is a tennis player of intermediate ability who has a problem of hitting the ball too often into the net instead of over it. By examining video replay, he may solve the problem by identifying a rectifiable cause: his grip on the racquet may be skewed anticlockwise, the timing of connection with the ball may be late when attempting to apply topspin, and so forth. If the video shows only the *product* of the error (the ball hitting the net), he is no better off than he was on the court. For the video to be effective it must show the process of the action. Furthermore, the player needs enough knowledge of tennis-ball physics to infer what he must do differently and he needs the skill to do it. Or he needs a supportive coach to provide the information and assist the skill development. This use of video replay is very common in sports (e.g., McCallum, 1987; Rothstein, 1981).

Sometimes errors of *omission* also have remedies that are self-evident and achievable. It is risky to show distressed couples VR early in therapy, or at any time without the right planning and support. (Besides the disastrous study described earlier of Alkire & Brunse, 1974, proponents of VR in family therapy such as Berger, 1978, and Whitaker, 1978, temper their enthusiasm with caution and describe extensively supportive frameworks for their clients in the therapeutic process.) However, after a spouse has become sufficiently educated in some manner of interaction, such as "I" statements, and is actively seeking to increase her use of them, she may well benefit from the opportunity provided by VR to identify occasions when she did not use an "I" statement and could have. In emotionally laden circumstances such as these, a clinical judgment is necessary to determine if the viewer has the skill to do whatever the omission points to, and if she will feel safe enough to be self-critical. In less emotional circumstances, such as reviewing a chess game, these precautions may not be necessary.

Not all errors that provide useful feedback fit into the above categories. There are also those less than satisfactory actions that nonetheless are along the right lines. Most skills at some time in their development simply need practice. There may be some advantage in the self-assessment of partially eliminated fidgets, improved footwork at the baseline, or a well-placed if slightly stumbling "I" statement. There is no advantage in further analysis, however, if the skill is underpracticed. Video review may serve as useful self-assessment if it provides a relatively value-free picture of the current status, allowing the observer to judge where to focus continued practice and what associated goals to set. Videos that show current status in the context of overall progress can contribute to motivation, described later.

There are two major aspects in the construction of video information. One is the context of information elements; the other is the element itself. For example, foot positioning is crucial to many sports. But illustration of feet positions *per se* is relatively useless in the absence of information about others players, ball movement, distance from the net, and so on. Similarly, voice volume, language content, and facial expression are important in themselves, but are also highly dependent on who is being spoken to and what else is being communicated. Thus, some care can be taken to present specific elements identified as being of value to self-assessment, in the relevant context.

Although this idea may sound obvious in theory, it is frequently overlooked or inadequately executed in practice. Most coaches, therapists, and teachers will (hopefully) be accomplished at providing both context and detail in their verbal communications with trainees, clients, and students. Translation into the video medium simply requires a little planning and conscious effort. (Farmer, 1987, has written about the need for "visual literacy" in supervisors.) Indeed, when some detail of action is captured for VR, the context may be provided verbally by an alert supervisor. But it is better to provide it on video. Typically, the recording will alternate between context and detail, using wide angle and zoom, different camera angles, and fast and slow motion, or context and detail can be shown simultaneously using a split screen. Trainers can plan this aspect of VR from a self-analysis of how they provide verbal feedback in the absence of video. If necessary, trainers can do this analysis via video recordings of themselves giving verbal feedback to their trainees. An example is provided by Fosnot, Forman, Edwards, and Goldhaber (1988) who examined different uses of VR in teaching 4- to 8-year-olds to balance blocks. They found an interaction between developmental age and the effectiveness of video replay drawing attention to action versus placement of the blocks.

The other major aspect of constructing the video concerns emphasis of the informational elements. Often this emphasis is left until the video is being reviewed. But there are several technical advantages to planning the emphases at the outset. Close-up detail and elimination of distractions are most easily and efficiently taken care of during recording. It is technically possible to enlarge a piece of the screen image or to superimpose a mask on one part of the screen, but only with expensive equipment and some awkwardness at the time of review. It is technically impractical to offer another perspective (camera angle) to a picture unless it has been recorded as such. Slow motion deteriorates during replay unless the original action was recorded with sufficient light and a higher shutter speed. It is impossible in common usage to enhance one person's voice if it is recorded onto the same audio track as other voices or background noise.

Following are some common *technical considerations* for recording video information that will be used for self-assessment and self-correction. More information on equipment is given in Chapter 1.

- A zoom lens provides detail, focuses attention, and can eliminate some distractions to the context, but it may distort the apparent depth of field.

- The camera position can offer different angles on the same subject to add both redundancy and new information.

- A variable-speed shutter can improve the quality of slow motion replay (the higher the speed, the smoother the motion).

- Multiple views (split screen or otherwise) of one event require multiple cameras.

- Multiple microphones (the wireless type are usually the most convenient) can focus the sound sources in different parts of the field; if different recording tracks are used, the relative emphasis can be modified at replay.

Enhancing Exposure of Key Information

There are several ways in which the information just described can be made more salient to the viewer (see Figure 6.1.) First, feedback of self-corrective information is relatively useless if the student or trainee has an incomplete appreciation of the ideal or target performance. Carroll and Bandura (1982) provided definitive research evidence on this issue, at least for the acquisition of a motor skill. In their study, they carefully separated the effects of modeling and video monitoring at different stages in the learning process. They found that visual feedback during ongoing performance was effective, but *only* after adequate conception of the modeled performance had been established. In studies of different training tasks and where video feedback has been delayed, others have also found that VR was inferior to modeling in early phases of acquisition (e.g., Bailey, Deardorff, & Nay, 1977; Erbaugh, 1985; Ross, Bird, Doody, & Zoeller, 1985). Thus, modeling or some other method of establishing a clear comprehension of the task is advantageous prior to feedback, and it may be advisable to measure the level of understanding rather than taking it for granted.

Another means of maximizing receptivity to feedback is to avoid an audience during replay. Many training and therapeutic programs using VR successfully report allowing the trainee or client to view the tape alone first (e.g., Bailey & Scott, 1982) or with only a supervisor present (e.g., Kagan, 1978; this book, Chapter 14). A helpful variation is to have viewers record or analyze their own behavior in some structured way (see Booth & Fairbank, 1983).

The value (and economy) of video review in a group setting should not be ruled out. The power of group participation (sometimes dangerous, as noted earlier) may be used to positive advantage. To do so requires planning and structure. For example, Kivlighan, Corazzini, and McGovern (1985) reviewed a trend in group therapy for clients to be pretrained in expression of feelings and receiving feedback, whether or not VR is used. Also in group therapy, Skafte (1987) made reference to a less specific procedure of distancing the group from its video image, encouraging the perception of the video recording as an "objectself" (cf. Kohut, 1978; Mead, 1934).

Both of these strategies help to safeguard against unwanted emotional reactivity during VR. A further safeguard is to be selective about events that are shown or emphasized, either by pre-editing or by manipulating the tape during replay. For instance, Mastria, Mastria, and Harkins (1979) described the selection of a balance between positive and negative examples in child-management training for abusive parents. In sport, Rothstein (1981) provided a careful analysis of VR as effective feedback, including a distinction between the training of "closed skills" where the environment is stationary (e.g., gymnastics) and "open skills" where the environment is moving (e.g., football).

In some cases, control of the replay is given to the subject. The supervisor may use these opportunities to explore the observer's associations recaptured by the video. Memories of perceptions, thoughts, and feelings will be heightened by the VR. The most extensively developed and described use of this approach, interpersonal process recall (IPR), is articulated in detail in Chapter 14. Rehabilitation following traumatic brain injury is a new area where IPR may have a valuable future, given the particular challenge to the memory processes (see Begali, 1988).

The sixth consideration is to deal with errors or omissions, apparent on video, for which self-correction is not so apparent. The majority may be edited out, skipped through using "fast forward," or otherwise ignored. But some errors may be selected, by the nature of the obstacles they present, for special treatment. These examples can be tied into other specific strategies of training or therapy. Most of the procedures described by authors cited in the previous paragraphs include elements of this strategy. It is widely used in sports (see Rothstein, 1981, and Chapter 15). Berger

(1978) and Whitaker (1978) used many elements of video replay including errors as springboards for family and individual therapeutic processes, which they tightly control. This approach is in stark contrast to using video to emphasize shortcomings that are then left as loose ends, with more potential for damage than good.

Following are some *technical methods* commonly used to enhance exposure of selected video information (to assist self-assessment and self-correction):

- *Still frames* draw attention to specific events, allow absorption of multiple aspects by the viewer, and allow time for discussion. Sometimes there are advantages to one but not all of these virtues. Alger (1978) has documented "freeze frames" as a major vehicle for an approach to psychotherapy. (Still frames will be intelligible only when the player has at least three video heads or, better still, digital capability; for further equipment details see Chapter 1.)

- *Slow motion* also focuses attention and provides more detail.

- Similar effects can be achieved by *scene repetition* as an alternative or enhancement to still frames/slow motion.

- *Reverse motion,* partly through its novelty, can assist in the perception of information that is otherwise overlooked. It can also show "new" information, such as a reaction away instead of toward, or a movement upward that was performed down, providing feedforward rather than feedback (see Chapter 7).

- Split screens are invaluable for comparing two movements (across time, different parts of the body, or different individuals), or for juxtaposing a close-up onto a wider setting. The technology for split screens is rapidly becoming more accessible, but their use always requires detailed planning (Rynearson, 1982).

Monitoring the Effects of Video Replay

Using video as real feedback always involves an element of guesswork. Sometimes the most obvious "feedback" fails or backfires; sometimes it is a clinical judgment to guess which video elements might support effective self-correction. Thus, it is both advantageous and responsible to monitor the impact of video review. It may simply require alert observation of immediate reactions, setting up a tracking system for use by the client or someone in the environment, and emergency telephone support, if a strong emotional reaction is conceivable. Presumably such standard procedures will avert the most dire results, since reports of severe deleterious consequences have dwindled and disappeared during the 25 years following Alkire and Brunse's (1974) tragic study.

Most often video replay is bundled into a larger training or therapeutic program. In a review of clinical studies, Hung and Rosenthal (1978) concluded that there was no clear empirical support for VR used independently; the identified therapeutic benefits derived from VR packaged with other treatment elements. They noted that about one-third of the studies in their review included a VR-only condition. But not one of the 20 training and treatment programs in Berger's (1978) book entitled *Videotape Techniques in Psychiatric Training and Treatment* nor the dozens of practical applications described in more recent collections and book length reviews (e.g., Dowrick & Biggs, 1983; Dowrick, 1986; Heilveil, 1983) actually recommends the use of unedited video replay as a stand-alone intervention.

A good example is provided by Asendorpf (1987) who described the use of VR for the reconstruction of emotions and thoughts during reactions of shyness. Subjects were met by Asendorpf and a confederate in a structured social situation that was videotaped through a one-way mirror. Immediately afterwards in a 30-minute interview, the subjects were shown themselves on video. The tape was stopped at planned moments of potential anxiety (e.g., request for personal evaluation) and the subject was asked "to remember his or her thoughts and feelings at that particular event as accurately as possible and to verbalize them" (p. 545). (In several ways, this approach is similar to that of Norman Kagan's interpersonal process recall, see Chapter 14.) The Asendorpf study illustrates a simple point. If the primary value of the video replay is for self-assessment, why not set about it systematically for that purpose?

Motivation

When video replay does not provide feedback in the strict sense of the word, it may, if suitably managed, assist motivation. For our purposes, motivation includes the recognition of goals in the therapeutic or training interests of the individual, and the energy and tenacity with which the person applies himself or herself to those goals.

VR can motivate individuals in productive engagement primarily by refocusing their attention and by optimizing their arousal levels. (See Figure 6.2.) It is common practice during different kinds of skill training (e.g., sport and social skills) to offer generally encouraging remarks during video replay. Such remarks (mentioned by Davies & Rogers, 1985; Marzillier & Winter, 1978) tend to increase arousal and, by their timing, may direct attention to productive issues. The explicit purpose described by McCrea and Summerfield (1988) in using video replay with people who were extremely overweight was to help their clients develop realistic, nonnegative evaluations. Similar reasoning was given by Probst et al. (1988) in their use of VR for people with anorexia nervosa.

Some of the strategies and technical considerations identified in Table 6.1 and Figure 6.1 are applicable. They may be used to support the following purposes:

1. Increase arousal of individuals who express no interest in change.
2. Direct attention to productive issues.
3. Decrease arousal of individuals whose anxiety interferes with the task.
4. Direct attention away from counterproductive issues.

Figure 6.2. Video replay for motivation.

Occasionally, video is used to promote motivation, or at least therapeutic compliance, when major issues are somehow denied by the client. For example, Metzner (1978) advocated VR as an adjunct to narcotic-induced abreactions that are not otherwise remembered; Caul (1984) used it in similar spirit with multiple personality disorders. Such uses of video to cross barriers of state-dependent learning carry with them well-documented dangers—for example, see studies with alcoholics by Schaefer, Sobell, and Mills (1971)—and strongly demand to be tied into supplementary training or therapeutic support. Sometimes video is selectively used to maximize arousal and nothing else. For example, McCallum (1987) described hockey players who, just before going into a new game, watched themselves coming off worst from body checks. In this case, the value of arousal depends on the immediate opportunity to expend it.

Examples of video replay to decrease arousal or to direct attention away from counterproductive issues are hard to find, although such uses would seem logical. Booth and Fairbank (1983) described using video in the behavior management of a 9-year-old emotionally disturbed boy, in which part of the strategy was for the teacher, also watching the video, to prompt alternatives to observed misbehavior. An interesting twist was provided by Badura and Steinmeyer (1984) in what they dubbed "hetero-confrontation." In the treatment of patients with anorexia, rather than using self-confrontation, they presented a video of a carefully selected, similar patient to avoid overarousal but also to direct attention to self-relevant issues.

APPLICATIONS AND EFFECTS

Following is a selective review to illustrate some applications and effects that have shown particular promise (although many others exist). It is hoped that this sample will assist in the appreciation of the diversity of methods of video replay that can serve as effective feedback or confrontation. These brief descriptions are arranged not by broad topic or population to be served, but by the effect of the video replay in bringing about change in the viewer. There are at least four areas where video replay is extensively used; descriptions written by developers and reviewers exist in most of these areas. VR is currently most widely used in:

1. Social skills and other personal communications (Trower, Bryant, & Argyle, 1978).
2. Professional communication skills (e.g., teacher and counselor training: Ivey & Authier, 1978; Kagan, Chapter 14).
3. Sport, where it is called "feedback" (Franks & Maile, Chapter 15).
4. Group or individual therapy—where it is called "confrontation"—for emotional disorders (Berger, 1978; Heilveil, 1983).

The following discussion identifies some of the personal change effects readily promoted by self-assessment and motivation, in the hope they may be used more predictably and productively and in further areas of application. For each of the effects listed, one application is briefly described as an illustration.

Self-Recognition

Ever since the classic report by Cornelison and Arsenian (1960) that described the therapeutic use of Polaroid photographs for hospital patients with schizophrenia, there has been a fascination for studying the effects of mediated self-images. With nonhuman primates (Gallup, 1987) and in some extremes of human developmental delay (e.g., autism, see Chapter 17), video is occasionally used in an attempt to teach self-recognition in the most encompassing sense of the word.

Video is more frequently used to assist learning about a part of oneself, expressively (as in personality disorders) or physically (as in weight disorders). For example, Probst et al. (1988) described "body-oriented therapy" for anorexia using video and mirrors at the University Psychiatric Center in Kortenberg, Belgium. On admission, each client is videotaped in a bathing suit in a standardized procedure of movements, camera angles, and close-ups. These tapes are shown and discussed in group sessions. The treatment includes further videotaping and self-observation in mirrors during weight gain, with the objective of learning to like their new body images 10 kilograms heavier. The authors indicate positive effects on both physical and mental health with this therapy, but caution that the video confrontation should be carried out only in the context of further therapeutic support.

Self-Monitoring and Self-Evaluation

Self-observation almost inevitably produces self-evaluation. When intended, as in interpersonal process recall, it can provide the major basis for discussion and problem-solving-oriented teaching or therapy. A report by Booth and Fairbank (1983) illustrates a case in which treatment effects are most clearly attributable to self-monitoring and evaluation during VR. A 9-year-old boy with emotional disturbances, including hyperactivity and aggression, was videotaped in mathematics class. During immediate replay (10 minutes), the boy recorded the frequency of his on-task, talking, out-of-seat, and noncompliant behavior. Effective and alternative behavior was briefly discussed with the supervising teacher. Independent ratings of on-task activity rapidly changed in the desirable direction, and the child evidenced "willingness to accept responsibility" and improved "perception of self-control" (p. 58). The impact of this strategy is presumably dependent on the trainee or client's inability to self-evaluate by simpler means (cf., Palmer, Henry, & Rohe, 1985, who found physical therapy students able to evaluate themselves equally well with or without VR).

Refocusing Effort

Recognizing discrepancies between where a person has been expending effort and where the effort might be better spent is often the thrust of social skills training programs (Rubin & Locascio, 1985) or sport (Chapter 15). In a related application, Jackson and Beers (1988) used repeated VR in parent training (see Dowrick, 1986, for a discussion of parenting as a social skill). As part of their 16-week program for parents of oppositional children, weekly video samples (three, 7-minute interactions) were recorded of parent-child dyads and triads. In sessions up to 60 minutes in duration, these tapes were immediately reviewed, at first without comment, then gradually with increasing levels of parent- and therapist-initiated interruptions, to assist parents "in developing, for themselves, ways of improving their interactions with their child and with each other" (p. 17).

Recognizing Consequences

A closely related positive effect of VR can be to enable the recognition of the outcome of one's action—at least, when those consequences might otherwise be incompletely or inaccurately understood. Recognition of consequences probably played a role in the interventions just described and with other applications involving hyperactive children (Boggs, 1989; Spiegel, 1977; note these and other studies—see Chapter 16—clearly indicate the superiority of reviewing positive over negative outcomes). In a different type of setting, Cooper, Biggs, and Bender (1983) used video as a component in social skills training of adults with severe mental illness. They describe one man's efforts to practice dating conversation. On VR, the group discussed his overzealous talk, nervous mannerisms, and "the effect the behaviour had on female members of the group" (p. 91). Observation of these effects led to the man asking questions, paying attention, and subsequently observing the effects of those behaviors.

Recognizing Progress

When progress is made over an extended period, it may not be appreciated, especially if it has been gradual and hard-earned. Probst et al. (1988) make an "admission tape" of anorexics and an "exit tape," typically 4 months later. These two tapes are reviewed together, not only to confirm the effects of treatment, but for additional therapeutic impact. This strategy can revitalize engagement for clients or trainees who have become jaded, or it can be used to support maintenance of effects (see Chapters 7 and 8).

Response Elimination

To use video simply to point out errors in the expectation that the undesired responses will simply go away by being identified is based on a most dangerous misconception—this point cannot be overemphasized. There have been dramatic casualties, in circumstances that seemed logical at the time, such as the attempt by Schaefer et al. (1971) to show alcoholics their drunken behavior. Response elimination can occur using VR only when the response is easily eliminated and does not require a substitute, complex behavior yet to be mastered. The strategy is suitable for skill refinement by people who are reasonably accomplished and confident in the skill area, such as experienced athletes, but unfortunately, clear descriptions in the literature are scarce. (They are absent in video research that I have been able to find, but supported by implication in self-monitoring and self-regulation research, reviewed by Kirschenbaum, 1984.)

Emotional Reactions

As discussed earlier, emotional reactions to seeing oneself on video are unpredictable; therefore, deliberate attempts to provoke such reactions remain risky. Despite the risks, this strategy remains popular in group therapy; a positive example was described by Corder, Whiteside, McNeill, Brown, and Corder (1981). They selected and structured the videotape replay so that 2-minute sequences of tape were reviewed specifically to identify examples of behavior related to group goals. (When examples of rule violations were noted, the therapist moderated and emphasized positive modeling.) Among the major effects of this strategy were greater group engagement (discussion) and expression of feelings in contrast to a control condition of unstructured VR. These effects encouragingly illustrate a procedure that is safe and effective.

CHAPTER 7

Feedforward and Self-Modeling

OVERVIEW

Video replay can be deliberately structured through planning and editing in various ways. This chapter describes the application of self-modeling, in which recordings show only adaptive behavior. The term feedforward *is coined to refer to video images of target skills not yet achieved, created by editing together component behaviors that are manageable for the trainee or client. Principles are presented for creating video feedforward and* positive self-review, *which refers to selectively compiling the best recorded examples of target skills already manageable but infrequently achieved. Applications of self-modeling are reviewed and issues raised about mechanisms, limitations, and strengths are discussed. These issues include subject participation and awareness, efficacy compared with other interventions (including peer modeling and unedited replay), and when and when not to use different forms of self-modeling. The methodology is summarized based on successful applications in different areas: disruptive behavior, selective mutism, depression, anxiety, sports, social skills, physical disabilities, and provider training. The chapter ends with a step-by-step description of developing and implementing a self-modeling-based package for the training of social safety skills in young adults with developmental disabilities: assessment, task analysis, video capture, editing, viewing the tapes, and evaluation.*

P. W. D.

As indicated in Chapter 6, to be most productive, video replay is structured in different ways for deliberate effect. The most distinctive use for predictable behavior change purposes is undoubtedly *self-modeling*. This use is conceptually, as well as procedurally, distinctive. Self-modeling is operationally defined as "a procedure in which people see themselves on videotapes showing only adaptive behavior" (cf., Dowrick, 1983, p. 105; 1986, p. 201). Logically, the concept is not confined to videotape, but may refer to any system in which people can observe themselves as models for future action. For example, audiotapes, still photographs, and print have been used. (In the imaginal medium, self-modeling becomes indistinguishable from mental rehearsal.)

The term *self-modeling* was first coined by Creer and Miklich (1970) in a brief description of an intervention for a boy, "Chuck," with severe social deficits. After several other interventions had failed, these psychologists hit upon the idea of making a videotape in which the boy would be his own model. Chuck rehearsed several adaptive coping scenes and then played them for the camera until a satisfactory scene was captured. A multiple-baseline evaluation showed that Chuck made remarkable gains from repetitively viewing his 5-minute tape and his progress did not appear to derive from the rehearsal or other miscellaneous aspects of the procedure.

A similar procedure dubbed "self-as-a-model" was developed independently around the same time by Ray Hosford. (See Hosford, Moss, & Morrell, 1976; Hosford, 1980.) Hosford's first application was with an adult who stuttered; an audiotape was made under conditions to minimize stuttering and then edited to remove dysfluencies. Again, repeated review of this adaptive recording produced positive results where other interventions had failed. Both these examples illustrate the use of supportive conditions to maximize a one-time performance by the subject. Hosford enhanced these effects by editing to remove errors and distractions. Both examples illustrate forms of maximized "positive self-review" (the best of possible current performance) discussed in detail later in this chapter.

In 1975 I began a series of studies to investigate different ways to produce self-modeling tapes (see Dowrick, 1976; 1983; 1986). In the first of these studies (Dowrick & Raeburn, 1977) a 4-year-old boy, "Paul," was taught to be less "hyperactive." Observations had indicated that Paul's hyperactivity could be reinterpreted as an inability to play by himself, so specific skills were targeted for acquisition. A video was constructed to illustrate these targets: solo play (family members were actually in support but out of the picture during recording) and extended time on task (e.g., sequences with Play-Doh® that lasted 10 seconds were repeated twice for an apparent 30 seconds on task). Systematic self-review of these tapes, as with other reported self-modeling studies, showed clinically significant gains where other interventions had not. With hindsight, this procedure can be seen as conceptually distinct from the earlier approaches, although it comes under the general definition of "showing only adaptive behavior." In this case, the construction of the videotapes went beyond maximizing the best current performance. Potential future behavior was identified and deliberately constructed on videotape from components of the existing repertoire—a strategy for which the term *feedforward* is coined.

FEEDFORWARD

Feedforward is a term invented deliberately to contrast with *feedback*. Whereas feedback denotes information about current or recent performance, feedforward depicts the future. Most usefully, it refers to future adaptive behavior not previously evident. In general, it may refer to any kind of instruction, including peer modeling or self-modeling. It seems most admirably suited to the audiovisual medium, partly because the medium provides such a complete description of the "instruction"—if a picture is worth a thousand words, how many for a moving picture with a sound track?

The procedure of video feedforward has related inherent advantages. The methodology builds a picture of future behavior based on existing skills. The process of using the subjects themselves determines that. For example, a 14-year-old gymnast can do a perfect takeoff, one-and-a-half flips in the air, and a perfect landing—but never in a single sequence. Perfect landings are achieved only after a single flip; one-and-a-half flips are accessible only on the trampoline, not from the boards. Filming the components from separate angles and editing together the sequence provides the perfect set of instructions for this gymnast because the presentation is visually complete and entirely in the subject's own terms.

Another inherent advantage is that procedural expediency usually ensures that instructional elements are of the optimal scope. To explain by way of analogy: If I give directions for someone to get to the airport, I am careful to do so in the "largest" terms useful to that person. If the person knows the major roads and intersections, I refer to those; if the person does not, I might begin with "go out the parking lot and turn right" and use such ploys as "ask the toll attendant for further directions." In all instances, I try to use elements already in the repertoire: If the person cannot tell left from right I help him or her call a cab. Nor do I say "stand up, put your left foot in front of your right . . ." because although those skills are in the repertoire, it would be tedious and inefficient to break down the instructions to that level. In video self-modeling, capturing the "largest elements" occurs naturally because anything else would create more work. Thus, in a sense, the optimal task analysis is automatically (or at least, readily) achieved.

Principles for Use with Video

A detailed example that incorporates feedforward is described at the end of this chapter, and a laundry list of principles is given in Figure 7.1. In general, video feedforward has been used when more typical approaches have failed, if dramatic changes are pressingly required, or if a "self-image" issue seems to be standing in the way of progress. First, perhaps even more than with other interventions, a clear analysis of *what* change should take place is necessary. The creation of a video image of the desired adaptive functioning is then achieved by a combination of strategies including maximizing the environment, providing support that is off-camera or can be edited out later, planning separate pieces that can be put into a different context by editing, and taking advantage of technology such as mirrors, voice-over, and slow motion.

Self-modeling, particularly its feedforward element, has obvious implications related to self-efficacy. Bandura (1986, p. 403) described self-modeling as providing both skills information and the basis for strengthened self-belief, the essential elements of self-efficacy. According to Bandura, self-efficacy is a major mediating influence in support of generalization and the maintenance of behavior change, particularly in the face of adversity. Whereas the data are not yet all in, the early signs are that an unexpectedly high level of generalization and maintenance results from some self-modeling interventions. For example, mentally retarded young adults have been trained with self-modeling to make safe decisions in interactions with strangers. Even though their training involved only six viewings of a 2-minute tape,

A. VIDEO FEEDFORWARD

Advocated in one or more of these circumstances:

Individualization of intervention is called for.

Rapid or extensive personal change is necessary.

A major factor is seen as a "self-image" problem.

Other approaches ("treatments of choice") have failed.

Task analysis:

Analyze in visual terms the precise outcome behavior desired.

Use video recording to establish the current capability (approximation to the goal).

Begin to consider how the components of missing capability can be achieved on videotape.

Establish an individualized list of the task's components with trainee/client participation.

Achieving the "future" image, potential strategies:

Maximized conditions for best performance (primarily environmental, but may include "psyching up," even psychotropic medications).

Support (physical or social) off-camera.

Checklist and/or storyboard-style planning for required elements.

Off-camera coach and camera operator collaboration to achieve these elements.

Components captured in alternative (but not clearly visible) settings.

Slow motion and/or still-frame emphasis.

Mirrors to transfer right-side capability to left side, and vice versa.

Editing to resequence events, and so on, for planned complex behavior image.

Voice-over dubbing to point out crucial and positive attributes.

B. POSITIVE SELF-REVIEW

Advocated in one or more of these circumstances:

Trainee's/client's skills are at a very low level.

Skills/confidence/motivation have fallen off previous level.

Video recording and review routines are already in place.

Trainees/clients are able to edit their own tapes.

Goal specification:

Identify currently desirable skills occurring at low frequency.

Rank order the importance or benefit of the goals.

Maximizing the video image, potential strategies:

Maximize conditions for best performance.

Moderate amount of practice by trainee/client before recording.

Record from the subject's viewpoint and selected other viewpoints.

Avoid recording unwanted material.

Edit to select and repeat adaptive sequences.

Dub self-instructions and affirmations.

Figure 7.1. Guidelines in the development of self-modeling applications.

and there were no opportunities to practice, adaptive use of the training was reported months or even years later in circumstances tangentially related to the original training scenarios (see Dowrick, 1986, pp. 116–121). For a more detailed discussion of generalization possibilities, see Chapter 17.

POSITIVE SELF-REVIEW

Procedurally simpler than feedforward is what may be termed *positive self-review* (or PSR; cf., "positive self-monitoring," a term used in sports psychology, Kirschenbaum, 1984). PSR refers to the selective review of superior performances drawn from the current repertoire. Conceptually, the difference between PSR and feedforward lies in the definition of the behavior that is targeted for change. For example, if the gym instructor has determined that a takeoff jump needs to be perfected, he or she may follow the trainee with a camera all day to capture a few exemplary jumps. Repetitive review of these exemplars will in all likelihood increase the frequency and consistency of their occurrence (and subsequently increase the opportunity for the gymnast to concentrate on the rest of the floor exercise). The use of PSR is increasingly but anecdotally reported in gymnastics and other sports such as tennis and skiing (see Chapter 15 for more formal studies). By contrast, feedforward as just described targets behaviors that have *not* occurred before. (Sometimes it is the *combination* of components that is important and therefore the identified target of change.)

Principles for Development and Use

Figure 7.1 contains a list of considerations, and procedural details of applications are described at the end of this chapter and in Chapters 15 and 16. PSR is useful for beginning skill acquisition or when there has been a drop-off in performance. It might also be cost-beneficial in settings where video recordings are routinely made for other purposes (e.g., counselor training) or where trainees are taught to edit their own tapes. Unlike feedforward, the identified targets for performance enhancement do not require component analysis. The effort in producing PSR tapes will be reduced primarily by optimizing the conditions of performance. (The presence of a camera is itself often a major contributor.)

As previously stated, PSR should be applied to adaptive but infrequently occurring behavior. Of course, if a target were not infrequent, why would we want to increase it? We might, however, inadvertently expose behavior that already occurs frequently to repetitive self-review—and herein lies a trap. Paying additional attention to a well-established skill is most likely to lead to its deterioration (Johnston-O'Connor & Kirschenbaum, 1986). In general, this effect may be seen either as an interruption by conscious attention to automated activity (the racing driver thinking about timing the clutch with the stick shift), or it may be carelessness induced by inattention to areas of vulnerability (the tennis player standing flatfooted, overconfident of a strong forehand).

This difference has led to a distinction in treatment between "beginners" and "experts" that may be oversimplified. With beginners, almost any skill is likely to be low in naturally occurring frequency, so there are good prospects for simply recording much footage and editing out the errors. This is exactly what we found in a study of pool players (Gonzales & Dowrick, 1982). In our study, the better players tended to get worse rather than better, and with hindsight it is easy to see why: By selecting *all* successes, most would have typified "easy" shots—that is, the shots that were frequently successful. It would be a mistake to suppose that PSR does not work with experts; however, it is more difficult to apply. Although it has not been put to an empirical test, the implication is that we need to identify the more difficult shots for the better pool player and edit together those shots only. The more skillful a person is, the more his or her training must be individualized.

Positive self-review does not appear to have the same potential for generalization as feedforward, but it does have implications for maintenance. The possible impact on learning and memory of repetitively seeing oneself being successful in difficult circumstances is tantalizing but unexplored. The potential for maintaining skills that are infrequently used (or have deteriorated for other reasons) is more transparent and is supported by at least some evidence. In personal safety training for people with disabilities, early findings showed quite unanticipated effects over time (see Dowrick, 1986, pp. 116–121). It turned out, fortuitously, that trainees from the program had kept their self-modeling tapes and would watch them every couple of months, "to remind themselves how to talk to strangers," as it were. The fact that these tapes were originally of a feedforward nature is probably irrelevant. After the feedforward training, the skills were acquired, so the subsequent use of the tapes was more like positive self-review. Reacting to strangers who tried to pick them up at bus stops and so on occurred with fortunate irregularity, so later reviewing of the tapes possibly acted as booster training to a skill that otherwise could be expected to fade with disuse.

This possibility was put to practical advantage in a military hospital setting by one of my students. This student supervised technicians who repaired medical equipment, sometimes under urgent conditions in the middle of the night. She observed inevitable delays while technicians familiarized themselves with procedures related to equipment they had been trained to repair some time previously but which infrequently broke down. Therefore, she made videotapes at the peak of training. When technicians were called at 2:00 A.M. for emergency repairs, they took a few minutes to review the tape and went straight to work. (The military personnel were apparently grateful enough for this procedure that they calculated the cost savings and paid her 10% as a bonus.) Other procedures in the literature, using video PSR to support maintenance of learning, are described in Chapter 8.

APPLICATIONS

Self-modeling has demonstrated behavior change with a variety of populations and applications. In a previous review (Dowrick, 1983) and more recently, self-modeling treatments have been documented for *personal and social adjustment* in the following areas: depression, eating disorders, hyperactivity, tantrums, cross-gender behavior, sexual dysfunction, dressing, eating, bed making, class disruption, anxiety, phobias, and aggression. They also have been documented in *communication:* public speaking, stuttering, selective mutism, sign language, assertiveness, social skills, interviewing, and job seeking. Self-modeling has also been used to teach physical and vocational skills such as walking, swimming, basketball, billiards, running, gymnastics, figure skating, kayaking, weight lifting, juggling, walking with prosthetic devices, physical therapy, reading, writing, arithmetic, and increased job productivity.

These applications have been systematically evaluated with populations that included professional and amateur athletes (Maile, 1985; also Chapter 15), depressed adults (Dowrick & Jesdale, 1990), offenders and ex-offenders (Hosford, Moss, & Morrell, 1976; Batts, 1978), counselors and teachers (Hosford & Johnson, 1983; Hosford & Polly, 1976), college students (Germaine, 1983; Holman, 1990), abusive parents (Barmann, 1982), adults with developmental disabilities (Dowrick & Hood, 1981; also Chapter 17), children with disabilities (Dowrick & Dove, 1980; Pigott & Gonzales, 1987; Scraba, 1989), gifted children (Greelis & Kazaoka, 1979), disturbed children (Dowrick, 1978; Gonzales, 1988; also Chapter 16), depressed children (Kahn, Kehle, Jenson, & Clark, 1990), school children with conduct disorders (Kehle, Clark, Jenson, & Wampold, 1986; Murray, 1982), and children struggling with fractions (Schunk, 1987). No specific population seems to be unable to profit from self-modeling, although certain populations may experience higher gains.

Neither does the scope of application seem limited by age. Published studies report the use of self-modeling from preschool to adulthood; I have used it clinically with children under 3 years old (eating disorders) and with a great-grandmother in her 70s (child management training). Nor does cognitive functioning seem any more important here than in other forms of modeling or instruction. In Chapter 17, work is described with severely impaired individuals, and, with colleagues at Johns Hopkins, I have used self-modeling with a highly gifted child with social deficits.

The published studies just listed, among others, are empirical demonstrations. That is, some are descriptions of case studies where other approaches had failed, and some are reports using individual and multiple-subject designs. A few are group or individual designs in which self-modeling is shown to be superior to other interventions or placebos. It is instructive to consider some of these studies and related findings that raise issues about the mechanisms, limitations, and possible strengths of the procedure.

Awareness

At conferences and other settings where self-modeling was discussed during its early days, there was much curiosity about the subjects' awareness of the methodology and how that might affect their performance. Were they being tricked into thinking something that was not true? Did they simply need an external perspective on what it was they were supposed to be doing? My own early work was almost exclusively with young children experiencing disabilities that limited debriefings and discussions about the procedure, so I was pleased to discover Ray Hosford's successes with adults who were sophisticated enough to understand exactly what was going on.

One consideration has been that self-modeling taught discrimination of "appropriate" behavior and provided additional opportunities for reinforcement. For example, in a procedure they referred to as "self-modeling" (although it differs from other definitions), Olson and Rardin (1977) showed slides to hyperactive children of themselves on-task or off-task (out-of-seat, etc.) to teach discrimination. In conceptually related procedures with videotapes, Schwarz and Hawkins (1970) replayed recordings from the classroom to apply consequences (praise, rebukes) to a child watching himself on tape (they referred to "delayed reinforcement"—see also a similar study with adolescents by Mayhew & Anderson, 1980). The discrimination notion has much in common with the current concept of self-modeling as an instructional procedure. The possibility that contingent consequences might be necessary in self-modeling has been contradicted by many studies (e.g., Dowrick, 1978b; Dowrick & Raeburn, 1977; Dowrick & Dove, 1980) in which any commentary while watching the tapes was deliberately avoided. Providing consequences in the context of a recorded event (Van Houten & Rolider, 1988) may be a helpful procedure in its own right, and it may be usefully incorporated into situations in which an individual needs to be taught how to model from oneself (see examples in Chapter 17), but it is not a *necessary* component of self-modeling.

Another aspect of awareness was investigated by Miklich, Chida, and Danker-Brown (1977). They applied self-modeling to institutional compliance with bed making in an asthma hospital, such that the children thought the videotaping was to help a university student with a media project. That is, Miklich and colleagues showed that self-modeling did more than just focus attention on the target of treatment as in a placebo effect by demonstrating the procedure to be effective without subject awareness.

At the other end of the scale, self-modeling has been confused with "false feedback"—that is, are we tricking people into thinking they did better than they really did? This apprehension is the result of thinking that all video replay is somehow "feedback." There is no doubt that the procedure can sometimes result in deception, but ethics aside, the scientific question is whether the deception is a necessary contribution to the efficacy. The answer is definitely no; indeed, it seems certain that false feedback is an inferior technique. A student of mine did a thesis study in which pool players saw themselves on videotapes that showed successful outcome shots only (Gonzales, 1982). One group saw exclusively their own successful shots, as performed (PSR); another group saw bad shots that were faked to appear successful. Both groups did equally well. Subjects in the second group were under the impression they were reviewing real performances—one person, following what seemed to be an obvious fake, actually remarked "Yeah, I remember that one." But the gains were modest, and only the beginners (in both groups) did significantly better than a no-treatment control group. (See earlier remarks on the dangers of PSR with well-established skills.)

By contrast, deliberate involvement of the trainee in creating the "future image" has proved considerably advantageous. Ray Hosford once told me how one of his cases of assertiveness-anger management training was at an impasse until he involved his client in selecting some of the crucial sequences to be edited. The possibility that trainee participation may enhance the procedure's effectiveness has impressive implications both procedurally and theoretically. Another student's thesis study concerned the use of self-modeling to train national-class power lifters (Maile, 1985). Using a multiple baseline across lifts, the gains were so great during self-modeling that no gains were registered for weeks afterwards, even though other training continued. Of most interest was that the trainees helped to select the weights that they would appear to be lifting—just as they participated in other aspects of planning their training schedules and goals.

In clinical applications (e.g., rehabilitation) and with students in video training courses, I consistently stress the value, *not* the disadvantage, of client participation. The procedure is best presented as a straightforward depiction of potential future behavior, not a bogus past. If the emphasis is on positive self-review, then the message is, "Here are good examples of what you should do more often." If using feedforward, the message is, "Here is your goal; this is what you will look like when you've mastered this difficult situation."

Relative Efficacy

A few studies have compared self-modeling with other interventions. In many of the reported case studies, self-modeling was found to be successful after other approaches had failed. It is difficult to *equate* interventions for direct, fair comparison, but some have tried.

An obvious target for comparison is peer modeling. The circumstances of an early study with selectively mute children (Dowrick & Hood, 1978) were fortuitous in this respect. For two children who would not speak at school but would speak in their homes, a self-modeling program was designed after an unsuccessful attempt to set up contingency management interventions. Both children had constant exposure to classmates who spoke freely but did not serve as effective models. After self-model tapes for each child had been constructed, both children watched one tape only, a number of times. The other child's self-model tape was then used, and the procedure was repeated for two more phases. At each session, one child saw a self-model while the other observed a peer model. The overall effects, compared with other attempts at intervention, were rapid and educationally significant. Systematic observations revealed that changes accrued during self-modeling only. The procedures to create the self-modeling tapes, recently replicated by Kehle, Owen, and Cressy (1990), are summarized in the "Methodology" section of this chapter.

Other studies have found self-modeling at least as effective (teacher training, Hosford & Polly, 1976; attention-deficit disorders, Murray, 1982), or somewhat more effective, in comparison with peer modeling (disruptive classroom behavior, McCurdy & Shapiro, 1988). Thus, in some circumstances, peer modeling may be as effective and more economical (cf., Petroski, Craighead, & Horan, 1983); but when individualization is necessary, self-modeling may be more accessible (Creer & Miklich, 1970), or the self-element may have special significance (as in selective mutism), making self-modeling the intervention of choice.

Another target for comparison is contingency management because of its established efficacy in skill training. The only reported study that directly addresses this issue concerned productivity in a sheltered workshop (Dowrick & Hood, 1981). Fifteen subjects were randomly assigned (within their level of disability) to one of three groups: self-modeling, cash incentives, and attention control. We attempted to make intervention time equal across the groups. In the case of cash incentives, a daily points system with weekly backup was provided at a level of elaborateness that required the same supervisory staff effort as the self-modeling. Improvements in productivity following brief intervention showed the active treatments to be statistically superior ($p < .05$), the self-modeling group producing the greatest changes. These were maintained at a 4-month follow-up.

Another obvious comparison is with unedited video replay. An early study with a child diagnosed as "hyperactive" (Dowrick & Raeburn, 1977) produced results similar to those reported for the selectively mute children: positive gains during self-modeling and no progress with unedited videotapes. In another intervention with attention-deficit children (Kehle, Clark, Jenson, & Wampold, 1986), the unedited replay condition led to an increase in disruptiveness. These and similar findings from other studies in which these comparisons can be made (e.g., Boggs, 1989; Dowrick & Dove, 1980; Johnson, in press) are most readily explained by the self-modeling paradigm: Video is a medium for instructional potential such that whatever is shown increases the probability of that behavior occurring in the future. These probabilities can be outweighted by other influences such as self-correction or support, described in Chapter 6; otherwise, there is every reason to believe that the positive and negative influences of video self-review will be directly proportional to the adaptive and counteradaptive behavior evident in the recording.

The question, "Is self-modeling better than intervention X?" is too broad to be useful. We need to ask, "*When* is self-modeling likely to be more effective, more cost-beneficial, or easier to implement?"

Limits

Much can be learned about the mechanisms and characteristics of a procedure by scrutinizing its limitations, most of which are not in the published literature. As just noted, when self-modeling is limited to positive self-review, the procedure is effective only when the videotaped exemplars occur infrequently in the current repertoire. When the approach has been simply to edit out all the mistakes without reference to the individual's ability, only "beginners" are likely to benefit. Thus, an individualized approach to PSR and feedforward is often warranted.

Because of the individualization, self-modeling as a group treatment has not been attempted. Application to a genuinely collaborative process (e.g., problem solving, team sports) seems logical. But to apply the procedure to a setting of several relatively independent individuals (e.g., a classroom) simply for economy's sake, the prospect is a little daunting—like trying to get a family photograph in which not one person is scratching or looking the wrong way. There are other ways to make the procedure more economical. Since effective tapes are usually only 2 or 3 minutes long, the time spent on the "active ingredient" (subject watching video) is incredibly brief. Making the tapes longer does not usually make them more effective, so setting up can take more time than viewing. One approach has been to show several tapes at one sitting, as was done with a number of co-workers from the same workshop (Dowrick & Hood, 1981). Presumably watching their workmates' tapes did not do any harm. If watching someone else's tape might do some good, there is the powerful possibility of combining self- and peer modeling by carefully choosing one member of a setting with whom to make the video recordings. Another approach is to arrange for trainees to watch their tapes at home, an increasingly available option, provided it is monitored and prompted.

As with any technique, there will be those individuals for whom it is developmentally inappropriate. For people with mental retardation, self-modeling has enjoyed considerable success—perhaps because it is visual rather than language-based, because the "self" element makes it engaging, or because of the inherent individualization. But the question has frequently been asked, "What are the lower limits of cognitive functioning for which self-modeling is effective?" Such a question cannot be answered in terms of a developmental age or an IQ score. It is better to ask, "*How* can we teach individuals to learn from observing themselves if they are not already able to do so?"

The following case illustrates one approach. At the Johns Hopkins Medical Institutes I endeavored to help teach a boy of 30 months (developmentally much younger) to feed himself using self-modeling. He had just learned, after intensive therapy, to take food orally, having since birth depended on a tube inserted directly into his stomach for all his nutritional requirements. He expressed obvious delight at seeing a videotape (for feedforward, fittingly enough) that showed him feeding himself with a spoon, constructed from components of the task, some in slow motion. However, he made no attempts whatsoever to use a spoon except to wave it in the air and wait to be fed. I then made more recordings with his therapist and re-edited the tape to break the action into segments. Between each segment, the therapist commented on what had just happened and prompted what was about to happen; for example, "Good, good holding the spoon; now put the spoon in the food." This tape proved a clinical success. Apparently, in this boy's case, his attention needed to be drawn to specific activity on the recording. In Chapter 17, Pat Krantz and colleagues describe other approaches to extending the usefulness of video applications to clientele experiencing severe disabilities.

SUMMARY OF METHODOLOGY

Few attempts have been made to standardize the methodology of self-modeling. Until recently, much work has been exploratory with inventive methods to create videotapes to meet the self-model definition. In his dissertation research, Gonzales

(1988) used a uniform approach, applied to the same four behaviors (bed making, eating, saying "thank you," and peer interactions), with four different children in an inpatient treatment unit for emotional disturbances. The interventions were applied to each child in a different order and carefully monitored; the results showed clear evidence of efficacy. Whereas the main purpose of the study was to add to the empirical foundation of self-modeling, it also served to clarify the methodology by setting out parameters and procedural steps in making the tapes for each behavior. Tapes were a predetermined length, reviewed at specified intervals. The content was produced by supporting the natural occurrence of desired behavior, followed by editing and repeating target sequences, for enhanced positive self-review effect.

In my own dissertation research (Dowrick, 1976), self-modeling was used with 18 children who had physical disabilities and was applied to different behaviors according to clinical priorities. The study sought to explore different methodologies within the parameters that the tapes would be 2 minutes long and would illustrate only those behaviors that the collaborating physical and occupational therapists indicated were developmentally appropriate for acquisition. Thus, tapes were created by editing together preplanned components, primarily for a feedforward effect.

There have been many other explorations of methods to create the effect of future images and variations in the conditions of review. Some elements of a consensus have emerged:

- Careful preplanning of tape content.
- Subject participation whenever possible.
- "Capture" recordings using one or more of the strategies discussed next.
- An edited 2- to 5-minute tape.
- Self-review about six times spaced over 2 weeks.
- Repeated process for further improvement.
- Review after 3 months or as necessary for maintenance.

Procedural Strategies

Following are synopses of applications for which methodological strategies are evident. These strategies are tentative, emerging as they do from a limited number of studies in each case. Meanwhile, the list serves to document a variety of successful approaches. More detailed methodology in a specific application is described at the end of this chapter; others are in Chapters 15 through 17.

Disruptive Behavior

More studies have been reported in self-modeling interventions with hyperactivity, attention deficits, and so on than in any other area (review by Woltersdorf, 1989; other examples cited in this chapter and described in Chapter 16). The main approach has been to "catch 'em being good" in the classroom and edit for positive self-review. Some labor can be saved by providing incentives during filming. (In a suitable context, the presence of the camera can be an asset.) Quickly stopping the recording of unsuitable material helps to extinguish acting out and also reduces the amount of editing required.

Selective Mutism

Sometimes a child who speaks freely at home will not talk at school (the mutism is setting-specific). A self-model film can be made by recording the child in the home but with school display boards in the background and an interviewer out of sight. Using a transcript of this recording, and with the child dressed in the same clothes as on the film, an attempt is made to recreate the recording in the classroom with the teacher as interviewer in sight. (It is expected that the child will remain mute during the second recording.) These two tapes are then edited together; collated, as it were—readily done if two video players can be fed into one editing recorder.

In other cases, a child may be disinhibited to talk when a significant person, usually a parent, is present (the mutism is person-, not setting-, specific). Here the recording can be done in the school setting, and it may be enough that the parent is simply present but out of view of the camera. In this case, the only editing necessary will be to maximize (e.g., by variety of demands or responses) the selection of sequences to produce a 3-minute tape. If the child will talk only to the parent, another recording with the teacher, using the "collator" editing strategy, will be necessary.

Depression

Most depressed people can be helped to identify a situation pleasant or exciting enough that, during its recounting, they become more animated than usual. Video recordings can then be edited for self-modeling using criteria to maximize the display of nondepressed behavior. Clients can help to identify how they would like to see themselves, including dress and deportment (see Chapter 16 for more details). Social deficits can also contribute to depression, in which a different approach is used—see "*Social Skills Training*" in this chapter.

Anxiety Disorders

A person can be seen, on video, to cope with a normally threatening situation by using the *hidden support* technique—that is, physical or emotional support is planned so that it is not evident in the recording or can be easily edited out afterwards. (Psychotropic medication has been used on rare occasions; Dowrick, 1979.) The only phobias reported to be treated by self-modeling have been those of medical or dental treatments. In such cases, a brief hierarchy (up to five items) has been useful. Subject participation may again have particular value, because anxiety and coping reactions are so individual.

Sport

Good results for some sports and other physical activities have been obtained using the *displaced-outcome* strategy. That is, an outcome or other difficult component is recorded from a relatively easy situation (e.g., below-maximum-weight squat, without showing actual weights; flip and twist from a trampoline, without showing the trampoline). The action from a situation slightly beyond current capacity that leads up to the desired outcome is also recorded (e.g., loading weights and getting into position; floor exercises run-up). These components are then edited together in the correct order. A reminder of the value of selecting and planning the exact target behaviors is provided by Scraba (1989) in her study of self-modeling to teach swimming to physically handicapped children. Her outcome measures included stroke quality and speed, the first of which improved greatly. It is clear from an examination of her procedures that the self-modeling tapes carefully illustrated the desired elements of quality, but showed nothing to reflect elapsed time. Presumably speed, in this case, will be affected in the long term as a product of practice with improved strokes.

Positive self-review (as previously described for "disruptive behavior") can also be used for beginners, or for advanced players and athletes if edited to included only infrequent successes that occur during competition. Note that positive effects can often be enhanced technologically—for example, by using slow motion, close-ups, certain camera angles, or the distance distortion of a zoom lens.

Social Skills Training

Self-modeling tapes frequently have been created using the strategies of "hidden support" for anxiety-related performance deficits, or "displaced outcome" for anger management. When the key *situations* that need social resolution have been identified, the choice or combination of strategies usually follows. For example, a teenager has a reflexive outburst when criticized, no matter how warranted or gentle the criticism. But if someone else gets angry, he or she can at least be coached to say quite reasonably, "Let's cool it—I'd like to talk about this later," and calmly leave the situation. This reaction (by the teenager's choice) is recorded and then edited in place of his or her uncontrolled anger in response to criticism. Feedforward effects can often be created in this way when social competence is greatly dependent on the person to be interacted with (e.g., an older sister vs. a friend). When prompted role play of components of effective social interaction is possible, edited video may take the place of the behavioral rehearsal and practice across different situations normally expected. Further details about the application to personal safety as a social skill are described in the "Methodology by Example" section of this chapter.

Physical Handicaps

Again, self-modeling tapes may be created with a combination of the hidden support and displaced-outcome techniques (see demonstrations on film, Dowrick, 1978a). Determining the key *components* of the skill to be acquired is usually the prerequisite task. For someone learning to walk with prosthetic devices or to button clothes despite cerebral palsy, a feedforward picture of the complete action may be put together from several isolated components. Physical support is commonly used (e.g., electrical stimulation from an unseen source) and optical tricks are useful—for example, filming the mirror image of the left foot movement to show what the right foot should look like or copying a recording played in reverse to show an upward movement when only a downward movement can be executed. Again it should be stressed that superior results are achieved when clients are aware that these are *targets* of therapy—future images not representative of current performance—and are aware of how these images are achieved. A 30-year-old woman, with whom I used a mirror image (she had a lifelong spinal injury affecting torsiflexion at one ankle), then started using a mirror at home at her own initiative for other asymmetrical difficulties.

Direct Service Providers

Training for teachers and counselors using self-modeling has mostly relied on PSR tapes edited from supervision videotapes. This approach is most useful with beginning trainees, although it is time-consuming to search through tape recordings that are generated in this way. These edited tapes might then be effective for peer-modeling and thus pay a return for the effort.

An alternative suited to advanced trainees, is self-directed PSR. This strategy would be applied to generally accomplished providers learning new skills, for example, a classroom teacher learning incidental teaching for a setting with autistic children. The teacher would video record himself (or herself) attempting the new task, edit (simply copy) together the best examples from a task analysis checklist, and review the edited tape every day for a week. Suppose there are 20 items on the checklist, and the first week the teacher demonstrates 8 items effectively. This process continues until it appears that the teacher has demonstrated mastery, at which point the tape is checked by a supervisor. This approach has a number of potential advantages; the most obvious is to minimize supervision time.

METHODOLOGY BY EXAMPLE

Some methodology will be described in detail through a specific application. Further details of the procedural review and model program development in self-modeling can be found in the thesis completed by Perry (1989). The work is part of a long-term project for training the social safety skills of young adults with developmental disabilities. Contributions have been made from a number of student assistants and providers at service agencies (Hope Cottages and Association for Retarded Citizens of Anchorage; Dowrick, 1986; Dowrick, McManus, Germaine, & Flarity-White, 1985; Perry, Dennis, Bolivar, & Dowrick, 1988).

Programs designed for people with developmental disabilities need to be flexible in order to address distinctive behaviors and unique environmental problems in the integration of the individual into the community. One of the primary limitations for such integration is a lack of social safety skills (Stuart & Stuart, 1981). This population is especially vulnerable to exploitation because it lacks basic safety knowledge, judgment, and skills that provide protection. In a review of programs to teach social skills to developmentally disabled adults, Davies and Rogers (1985) showed the importance of visual instruction, repeated practice, individual situations, and social reinforcement—elements readily provided by self-modeling.

There are six major steps in the general self-modeling process: assessment, task analysis, video capture, editing, viewing the tapes, and evaluation. From a review of the self-modeling literature, discussions with other practitioners, and our own experience, we developed an initial methodology for our program, which we called the "best guess" framework. We then applied our best guess with intensive evaluation at each step, refined it, reapplied it, and so on, until our evaluations confirmed that no further refinements were necessary—that the program was the "best possible" under the system we had.

Assessment

The program's efficacy rests on effective assessment. Assessment includes operational definitions, a behavioral task analysis of the components of the desired behavior, observations of the behavior in question, and an individual assessment of skills to determine the selection of target behaviors.

The task at hand was limited to training the clientele to stay safe with strangers in a public place. The use of operational definitions served to clarify function and outcome. Safe behavior was defined as avoiding inappropriate overtures (e.g., request for a phone number, offer of a ride) while maintaining sociability in normal conversation. Role play baselines to elicit behaviors that could be evaluated for vulnerabilities were videotaped. Responses to six types of situations—charm, trick, harassment, verbal threat, physical force, and small talk (nonthreat)—served as a baseline for comparison with post-training role plays, at the same time providing information about specific skill deficits. Following is the script for a trick situation.

S: Hi! My name is _____. I'm a friend of your mom's (or other person)
C: (Response)
S: She sent me here to pick you up. My car is right over there. (Gesture)
C: (Response; if negative, continue)
S: Oh, it'll be okay. I'm an old friend of the family. You can trust me.
C: (Response; if negative, continue)
S: Are you sure you don't want a ride home?
C: (Response)

Task Analysis

A behavior analysis approach to the assessment of skill deficits and target behaviors was selected. A generic analysis of safety skills was combined with an individual assessment. Verbal and nonverbal behaviors from social skills inventories (Dowrick, 1986) were used to compile a checklist of elements contributing to the individual's safety. For each person we developed a semistandard questionnaire incorporating the checklists, which included the client's existing skills and provided information about his or her functioning in the environment, idiosyncratic vulnerabilities, and high-risk situations. Specific target behaviors and circumstances for training were chosen on the basis of preassessment role plays to address individual skill deficits during the video capture session. For example, one client who had been through another personal safety program would call the police whenever an unknown man spoke to her ("Hi, my name's Mike"); another would accept rides from anyone when she was walking home, loaded down with shopping bags ("My name's Robert—you don't know me, but I'm a friend of your mother's . . ."). In each case there were different components of effective social responding (engaging in small talk without giving away a home address; turning away without smiling, after saying "no thank you") that the women could or could not do under different circumstances.

Video Capture

Based on individual skill deficits, the video capture session was preplanned to elicit examples of specific behaviors and sequences of action. (Preplanning the video capture session clarifies content, ensures that necessary components are present, and reduces the amount of video capture needed.) Individually tailored role plays with a male "stranger" (usually a service provider known to the client) were used to address these deficits and unique scenarios. Capture footage was limited by selective taping of complete acceptable sequences, insertion of desired components (e.g., gaze, body posture) at desired times, and nonverbal cuing (directions and gestures off-camera) if the client was unable to produce the desired component behaviors. Video capture includes all skills and components identified in the analysis, as well as the role play situation pertinent to the individual. Recording only the behaviors identified in preplanning in the approximate sequence desired reduces the amount of tape to be reviewed during editing.

Editing

In the video editing process, we selected and arranged the component behaviors to present complete sequences that showed the individual responding in a safe manner. The task was to construct in a predetermined manner selected elements from the video capture to produce a 3-minute self-modeling tape with specified content and format. Each tape began with an introduction by the client herself ("Hello, my name is Robyn, and this is my safety tape") and ended with a still frame of the client's smiling face in close-up. The content of the tape included two situations of major importance in which the client conducted herself gracefully and effectively stayed safe in her own terms. Key elements, especially those of difficulty, were emphasized with slow motion, still framing, or by abrupt elimination of sound if the nonverbal aspect was important. Each little scene included an escalation of effort by the "stranger" to put the client at risk.

Viewing Schedule

Optimal viewing was three times per week (one viewing each time) for 2 weeks, a total viewing time of about 20 minutes. Written schedules included planned dates and viewing times, dates and times actually viewed, and the initials of the client and the person responsible for the tape. Thus we could monitor compliance with the schedule and restrict access to the tape, while this part of the program was delegated to the client or other individuals. Written instructions for viewing conditions were necessary to ensure standardization in this case.

Evaluation

Post-evaluation role plays conducted after the 2 weeks of intervention provided evidence of behavior change. Questionnaires and interviews with house parents and co-workers provided us with validation of safer behavior in the community and enabled us to evaluate the overall integrity and viability of the program, as well as the effectiveness of the self-modeling procedure. Exit interviews were used for debriefing and to obtain information about the clients' perceptions and reactions to the self-modeling process.

CHAPTER 8

Expanding Horizons and Professional Issues

OVERVIEW

The purpose of this chapter is to look at future directions for the field based on the strengths that have emerged and some recent, novel applications. Technological advances are noted, particularly as auxilliary to medical assessment and in interactive video applications. There is an increasing (and productive) trend toward packaging—that is, including video, in one or more of the forms identified in earlier chapters, with other procedures. Increased attention to the interface of packaged investigation and intervention will be a useful trend for the future. There also may be more and better use of video in the courtroom, with people who have special needs (e.g., the deaf), in animal studies, in underexplored areas of assessment, and for dissemination in professional development. Major challenges that can be served by video are those related to maintenance and generalization of training and therapeutic gains (some examples are noted); video-based distance education is also up-and-coming. Video, despite the "cold" image of technology, has the potential to increase personal participation. The last part of the chapter covers professional issues (agreement, consent, and doing no harm) and includes a brief conclusion.

P.W.D.

Years ago I was taken with a comment made by Ivan Illich, author of *Deschooling Society, Medical Nemesis,* and other provocative works. He playfully referred to public suggestions about him as a prophet and said, "A prophet is someone who can predict the future by seeing the present very clearly." I do not see the present as clearly as I would like, but in this chapter I will attempt to summarize recent activities and developments in video so that some future directions may be inferred. In general, video (like other technologies) has not been sweepingly unique in its contribution to behavioral science, nonetheless, it offers a sometimes powerful new dimension to existing strategies of influence and measurement. Thus, video bundled into a *larger package* is a development that is increasingly researched and reported. The avenues of application have been uneven, so there are many opportunities to extend the range into new areas. Teaching and remedial endeavors, community-based treatment, generalization, maintenance, and other issues *beyond the clinic* are

127

becoming increasingly recognized for their importance; video has the potential to play a significant role in these developments. One dimension brought by video, especially given the recent advances in consumer technology, is the enhanced potential for *personal participation.* These "horizons" are each discussed briefly in this chapter. *Professional issues,* such as those concerning the distribution and use of video recordings, will also invite increasing attention.

TECHNOLOGICAL DEVELOPMENTS

Innovations and changing costs in the technology help to determine what is possible and what is popular. The general trend is toward smaller components and better quality at a lower cost. Such a trend encourages more widespread use of the technology in research, training, and therapy—but without necessarily justifying the increase in use. In recent years, still photography equipment has become better, cheaper, and friendlier, but very little change in its use has occurred (notwithstanding flourishing pockets of activity such as "phototherapy"; Weiser, 1990). To capitalize on the hardware, software—the procedures, the systems, and effective theories that readily allow replication and adaptation to a useful range of circumstances—must be available. I have some cautious optimism for the eventual systematizing of knowledge surrounding how and when to use video, but developments over the last 2 or 3 decades have been slow and their acceptance even slower. Growth is also reliant on personnel, so that the spread and development of use will be as dependent on system's articulation and training as it is on technology.

Some remarkable technology has been invented. Video X-rays are now in relatively common use to assess the swallowing capabilities of infants unable to eat, for example. Other medical-analysis equipment compatible with standard video includes a videometry processor by Glonner that records electroencephalograph readings, capable of displaying the brainwaves with or without a simultaneous picture of the patient on a split screen. Some research now makes use of touch-sensitive screens (Bailey, Deni, & Finn-O'Connor, 1988) or monitors that are capable of altering size or even visual angle of stimuli (usually words; Jordan & Martin, 1987). Many of the advances come from computer developments such as the capacity to convert pictures into line drawings that can then be displayed tachistoscopically (Fraser, Lishman, & Parker, 1987). Analytics, Inc., has developed a system for tracking eye movements with an infrared beam as a person watches a screen (*Effortless Computing,* 1986). Eye movements and voice can then be used to control equipment and tracking devices.

It is the combination of advances in magnetic and optical recording and in computer technology that is bringing interactive video into its own (see Chapter 9 for details; further examples are in Chapter 3). As indicated by the content of DeBloois's (1988) status report, the SALT (Society for Applied Learning Technology) conferences, the NTIS (National Technical Information Service), and other sources, medical and military training have been at the forefront in this medium. The worldwide reductions in developmental defense spending may curtail the military-sponsored applications, but growth in medicine will continue, while business and education will rapidly attempt to catch up. Some examples of interactive video training that seem to be indicative of the future include the identification of suicide risk (Denton, 1988), client simulation (a computer application ready to be translated into video is described by Lamberg, 1987), and sign language and other education for deaf people (see Newell et al., 1983—also described in Chapter 5). It is even possible "to train" voice recognition systems and to drive interactive video choice points using keyword vocal commands instead of screen menus (Harless, 1986). The field is now ready for more research on efficacy (e.g., Petty & Rosen, 1987) and other elements such as the interactions between the student and the videodisk system (Silverstein, 1987).

However, the greatest influence in the near future will probably derive from the fact that there is at least one video format widely available and in frequent use. The impact of TV and home video is enormous, altering life styles globally. But notwithstanding its role in spreading violence (Eron, 1987), the *specific* influences of the TV medium are generally overstated. The general effects (absorption of leisure time, homogenizing society) and some unexpected effects (its contribution to the downfall of single-party governments) are far reaching. In its specific and deliberate influence, TV is good for selling soft drinks, motor vehicles, and underarm deodorants. The influence is not on total consumption, but on brand switching—even on who becomes president. TV election campaigns do not increase the voter turnout; they influence the relative results for each candidate. There is much to be learned about the effective use of the medium. Video workout tapes are bestsellers by a fluke—they happen to help people do something while watching the screen. Video gardening or golf will never compete—but they could be effectively packaged with print materials that have the advantage of random access and self-pacing. The next generation in many parts of the world will grow up with videotapes and cameras, will expect them, accept them, and think of using them more often.

PACKAGES

The vast majority of successful applications described in other chapters of this book are packages in which video plays a significant role. I expect there will be increasing attention to packaging, in which, if it is approached correctly, a major task will be to develop better understanding of the interface among components.

A few examples, described with more detail elsewhere in this book, will suffice. One is the video-based provider training for developmental disabilities in Zimbabwe (McConkey & Templer, 1987; see Chapter 3). Their approach was to take a proven package (successful in Ireland), refilm the video locally (six 20-minute programs), and ensure that the other components were culturally and educationally suitable. Other components included a handbook of learning activities structured around the videotapes, experiential goals, and local tutors. Another example of provider training (daycare) is described by Aguirre and Marshall (1988). A self-study manual was written around four content areas: child development, nutrition, health and safety, and business management; four videos (averaging 30 minutes each) were professionally prepared to illustrate the same topics. These materials, along with study questions, activities, supplementary readings, and pre-post quizzes, were made available for home use. The program was evaluated as effective, especially for participants with stronger educational and economic backgrounds, although the videotapes were rated "very useful" by less people (53%) than other components (the manual was top rated by 94%).

Modeling (on video or otherwise) can be very powerful in its own right, but there is widespread recognition that it is usually better in combination with practical experience. In their examination of video in medical settings, Parrish and Babbitt (see Chapter 11) draw firm conclusions about the limited effects of informational or modeling films as single interventions and illustrate with a description of packaged training for parents of children with disabilities.

As noted in Chapter 6, video self-confrontation is often ineffective or even damaging when used alone, but can be quite powerful when incorporated into a properly devised context of support. The widely used programs of interpersonal process recall (Chapter 14) emphasize the total package of implementation, including such features as student or client control over interruptions in replay. Packaging is taken a step further in scene setting (Chapter 5) and trigger tapes (Chapter 13). In these systems, the strategy is to use video as a stimulus or a catalyst to other elements in a training or research structure.

Self-modeling appears to be the most consistently powerful video intervention that can be used without packaging for personal change (see Chapters 7, 16, 17)—although some will challenge my bias in this appraisal. Nonetheless, its future, too, is in packaging. The farthest reaching intervention in my own experience has been the personal safety training for young adults with disabilities (described in Chapter 7). Whereas it is evident that the feedforward tapes provide the crucial element of successful training, the development and implementation of self-modeling for consistent effects depend on other elements such as assessment, task analysis, discussions, coaching, and monitoring the viewing of tapes and related social behavior. In my view, the biggest future for self-modeling will be as a planful supplement to existing training and therapeutic regimens.

Generally, the use of video as a significant supplement to established methodology has been slow to develop. One clear example was described by Abkarian, King, and Krappes (1987). They discovered that a 3-year-old boy with developmental problems who was totally resistant to evaluation procedures could be induced to participate in speech and language assessment through the television medium. At the end of a chain of graduated experiences of engagement with a TV monitor, the Peabody Picture Vocabulary Test was administered by projecting pages of the test manual from a camera in the next room. Abkarian et al. report using the procedure with other children and recommend its more widespread use and evaluation. My recommendation, more generally, is to explore other creative (and maybe simple) adaptations of established assessment, research, training, or therapy protocols, incorporating a video-based enhancement.

EXTENDING THE RANGE OF APPLICATIONS

Practitioners and researchers are steadily reporting new uses of video: different strategies, settings, subject populations, and purposes. In this section, a sample of recent innovations is presented in addition to those described in other parts of the book.

The use of video in courtroom trials is an area in which some years ago my colleagues and I expected to see growth (see Casswell, 1983), but relatively little has happened. However, one aspect has drawn increasing attention recently because of more public awareness and litigation concerning incest and child abuse. More courts are accepting videotape testimony by children as admissible (Gothard, 1987) bringing forth discussions in support of children's interests (e.g., Tedesco & Schnell, 1987; Yates, 1987). A single videotaped interview made available to all parties minimizes the distress to the child, but is open to challenges of bias. Thus, systematic and fair methods of interviewing for video must be developed and recognized; valuable recommendations have been proposed by Colby and Colby (1987).

In other parts of this book, I have drawn attention to the value of *video* for some special populations, including deaf and hearing impaired students. It seems reasonable to expect more program development in this field. Interactive video has been used as a natural extension of printed pictures to develop language and vocabulary skills, for example (Stapleton, 1985). Perhaps applications for this population will become more diverse and more popular through the adoption of methods used in other areas. Interactive video has special potential for adapting educational programs for different languages and cultures; an interesting example was reported by Sponder and Schall (1990) for Yup'ik Eskimo traditions in Western Alaska.

Video may seem an unlikely instrument for assistance with myopic patients. But Gil, Collins, and Odom (1986) reported a simple, effective training program to improve visual acuity, perceived clarity, and response confidence. They set up systematic practice with the video game *Space Invaders*® by Atari. Performance goals were set for each individual, and the task graduated in difficulty by altering the distance from the screen each time criterion was met.

Video games developed for fun and profit have been used for other purposes. A number of researchers in psychophysiology have used the video game as a laboratory stress analogue with children (Benton, Brett, & Brain, 1987; Murphy, Alpert, Willey, & Somes, 1988) and adults (e.g., Miller & Ditto, 1988; Turner, Carroll, Dean, & Harris, 1987). Videotapes also have been designed to induce stress or mood changes in clinical research (Consolvo, 1988; Croyle & Uretsky, 1987), although Rosenthal et al. (1989) report a study in which much higher levels of stress were induced by individualized fantasy.

Very little application has been made in research with animals. An exception was described by Pear and Legris (1987). They used a computer interfaced with a video system to track head movements and shape the keypecking of pigeons. They claim that a greater degree of precision, enabling improved analysis of the shaping process, is available with this methodology. A different use of video games has been with monkeys (Williams, 1987). A computer-programmed video game was developed, with joystick control, in the study of learning and short-term memory.

An application to research in phonetics reported a few years ago (Brooke & Summerfield, 1983) probably deserves more attention. A shuttered video camera was used to record English vowel and consonant enunciation for analysis. Special video and computer equipment was used to assist the analysis and to generate line-drawing simulations of articulatory movements, which were used to explore the skills of audiovisual speech perception. Given the extensive developments in video and computer technology and the increased availability of relevant software, further research with these types of methodology will become more attractive and accessible.

Quite a different approach to medical education has been developed by Fidler (1990), who is producing short films that have particular implications for the human and ethical concerns of the profession. The videotaped movies are short plays acted by and in front of physicians, medical students, and other health professionals. Discussions held immediately after the performance are edited in as epilogues to the plays, which address such themes as racial and social prejudice, dual relationships, and judgments of responsibility. The productions are part of a teaching program at the University of West Virginia, and the tapes are made available to other medical schools.

BEYOND THE CLINIC

A major challenge for social services in the 1990s will be to meet the need for more progress in issues of generalization and maintenance of the skills and adjustments made in education and rehabilitation. Another, somewhat related, challenge will be the development of services that are less dependent on large institutions located in the middle of cities. Video, in different ways, may play a significant role in these matters.

Generalization of skills learned in one setting to other environments is a theme addressed by Pat Krantz and her colleagues in Chapter 17 in their efforts to serve one of the most challenging disabilities: autism. As many readers are aware, children with autism are peculiarly unlikely to generalize what they learn. Children who have learned to make their beds and dress themselves in the group home bedroom will almost certainly have to be taught again from the beginning when they are transferred back to the family home. Krantz et al. have discovered some powerful effects using video (modifications of self-modeling supplemented with consequential training) where other strategies have failed. Self-modeling also has contributed to unexpected generalization and maintenance over time in personal safety training programs. At least part of the effect in this case has been attributed to the clients' tendency to replay the tapes from time to time (say, monthly) as if to refresh the skills depicted—a strategy that can be used planfully for other skills that are infrequently called upon, such as emergency equipment repair (see Chapter 7).

A related strategy is to prepare videotapes for patients to take with them when leaving the hospital or other institution. An application of "video to go" in the treatment of stuttering was reported by Daly (1987). The rationale for the strategy is based on the tendency of stuttering severity to be environment-specific. Daly reported that his first use occurred because one of his clients, a 13-year-old boy, expressed a wish that his father could see his in-session successes. He gave the boy a videotape, requesting that, "in addition to showing his progress to his parents, he carefully watch himself talking smoothly and effortlessly on tape for at least 5 minutes each day" and "that he focus on the positive aspects of his speech . . . behaviors that enabled him to talk fluently" (p. 104). Essentially, the approach is one of positive self-review, as it was for the children with eating disorders described earlier, with the added benefit of family members being able to see results that might alter their expectations of (and therefore their behavior toward) the client. A slightly different approach described by Denton (1988) is the use of the interactive videodisc as developed by Barbara Rosenberg at Missouri Institute of Psychiatry. This system teaches about medication and stress management by having the patient, soon to be discharged, make decisions on behalf of a fictitious but realistic person with a similar diagnosis. Videodisc was chosen to replace a labor-intensive workshop.

Another method in which video can go beyond the normal service setting, teleconferencing, is described briefly in Chapter 3. The field is well established and with a future enough beyond dispute that it helped to launch the *American Journal of Distance Education* in 1987. Much of the development so far has been in support of teacher training (e.g., Stowitscheck, Mangus, & Rule, 1986). In its most developed form so far, it enables trainers at a central facility to be in two-way audiovisual communication with trainees at their worksites—not just for conversation, but to demonstrate skills, observe activities, interact with students or clients, and so on. In recent years, presumably as part of a trend for the near future, issues beyond the immediate efficacy of training have been discussed in the literature, and other interests, such as business management, have begun to participate.

For example, Acker and Levitt (1987) examined the design of videoconference facilities. They described and evaluated the "Gazecam" technology that assists apparent eye contact between participants at different sites. (The system uses mirrors so that when one person looks at the receiving monitor, he or she appears to be looking directly into the camera.) Others have examined the economics of teleconferencing. In the state-of-the-art system in Utah for training special education teachers, Rule, DeWulf, and Stowitscheck (1988) produced some interesting figures. Even in the first year, costs are no greater for teleconferencing than they are for on-site training; the initial equipment and broadcasting expenditures are balanced against higher personnel and travel costs of on-site services. After 3 years, as the cost for one system goes down while the other goes up, the on-site training becomes three times as expensive as the videoconferencing.

PARTICIPATION

Contrary to any expectations that electronic equipment might decrease the personal element in human services, a developing strength of video is its potential to increase human participation and consumer control. This idea is not new; for example, Reese (1981) described the therapeutic process of having drug-abusing adolescents make their own video films. The current ways to involve participants with the medium have become more diverse and appear to be gaining in recognition and significance. For example, interpersonal process recall subjects control the replay and discussion points of their own tapes (Chapter 14); weight lifters collaborate in devising their feedforward tapes (Chapter 15).

There is a steady trickle of reports on video production by clients as a therapeutic strategy, mostly with teenagers. Darrow and Lynch (1983) described the use of video production projects, and still photography as an alternative, with adolescent girls. They considered the method to be beneficial in a culturally mixed, low-income group as a catalyst to problem-solving issues of aggression, body image, and racial and sexual identity. Working with a slightly younger group of very emotionally disturbed children from alcoholic families, Efron and Veenendaal (1987) describe the production of videotapes reflecting family issues and the use of vignettes derived from the children's productions. Student-produced videos have been advocated for children with disabilities (Fleig, 1983).

A different type of learning by producing was reported by Prager and Hantman (1987). They developed a system in which social work students created short documentaries on aging topics in collaboration with older volunteers. The films were produced in the context of a third-year gerontology seminar, and some production workshops and assistance were provided. At the University of Alaska in Anchorage, three successive instructors of personality theories have used the small group video production as the "term paper." Relatively simple self-instructional systems for single-camera video production have been reported (e.g., Fuller, 1982) that could assist the implementation and more widespread use of the strategies just described.

Interactive video, by definition, implies a higher level of student or client participation than is necessarily required in other formats. But because of the expense and sophistication required, consumer involvement in production is more limited. In the meantime, implications of different aspects of subject control may fruitfully be examined. For example, Powell (1988) studied student option versus program control in the corrective feedback available from an interactive video lesson in Spanish. She found that less able students chose less corrective feedback under their own control and performed better under program control. It is hoped that the future will bring more studies of the conditions under which participation by consumers will or will not bring about advantages in a variety of video training settings.

PROFESSIONAL ISSUES

Reports (fortunately infrequent) of video interventions with no beneficial effects (e.g., Brown, 1987, Cooker & Nero, 1987) or deleterious side effects (e.g., Alkire & Brunse, 1974) remind us of the importance of protecting our clients and our research subjects. Articles that question the direction our research is headed (e.g., Levy, 1987) remind us to consider carefully how we use our own and others' time. Reports that charge professional neglect for the safeguards that should normally be expected (McElroy, 1987) remind us to take nothing for granted. The use of video in the behavioral sciences has resulted in more than its share of professional issues, but the associated concerns have, if anything, diminished over the years as the effects have become more predictable and as people have become more used to the presence of recording devices. In a study we finished recently in Anchorage on the reactions of people seeing themselves on video for the first time, we were hard pressed to find sufficient subjects who qualified.

Education, human services, and research are issues that are not specific to video but are relevant to the general concerns of the profession. There are established, codified ethical principles in psychology (American Psychological Association, 1981; "Ethics Committee," 1990), social work (National Association of Social Workers, 1980), nursing (American Nurses Association, 1976), medicine (American Medical Association, 1980), and other professions. Books have been written (e.g., Cohen, 1980; Hannah, Christian, & Clark, 1981) and U.S. federal regulations have been established governing human rights in research (e.g., "National Commission," 1978). There also are issues that are specific to video because it involves recording or broadcasting, because the participants are highly identifiable, and because a probable purpose (or byproduct) of the video is for people to view it. Although there are national and professional differences in ethical issues, the major principles often are similar.

Agreement

Before formal consent is sought (if it is necessary), less formal agreement is obtained. Public behavior is generally accepted as offering an implicit agreement to being observed and recorded, so social and anthropological studies and some documentaries are often made without formalities—although decency suggests discretion in the recording and release of such videotapes. (Television programs based on live recordings of police activities, for example, make use of a technology for blurring faces while keeping the rest of the scene in focus.) When video is used for purely educational purposes, such as a student production to illustrate an understanding of the bystander effect, only informal agreements are expected. Under these circumstances, the institution's rules, explicit or otherwise, should prevent any exploitation of the participants. An individual or group project will be protected in the same way regardless of the medium it is in; if a professor wants to keep a copy of a student's term paper or video, naturally he or she will ask for permission. Eventually, using video in the classroom will be no more special than books and pencils. A little extra sensitivity is advisable in the meantime, while the protocols become established.

Another consideration when making videos is people's reactivity to being recorded. Human beings under some circumstances are like the subatomic particles of quantum physics; that is, their behavior under observation is altered by being observed. Therefore, professional consideration is given to the nature and effects of this reactivity and how it may be minimized. Sometimes, the reactivity is desirable. It is often found in the production of self-modeling tapes that the presence of the camera is singularly useful in maximizing the client's performance capabilities. If minimal reactivity is desired, a one-way mirror may be used or the subject may be habituated to the camera by prolonged exposure. Some very nervous or curious subjects become more settled following an opportunity to operate the camera.

Consent

Formal consent in writing is necessary for all clinical and research subjects. Participants must be informed of exactly what will be required of them, how the tapes will subsequently be used, and how their participation is voluntary. A sample consent form, worded for people of low cognitive functioning, is shown in Figure 8.1. The major elements of consent forms include:

- Communication of the general purpose of the project.
- Statement of specific purpose concerning the participant.
- Clear indication if the purpose is research.
- Statement of the steps that will be taken to protect confidentiality.
- Rights of the subject to withdraw at any time, for any reason, and without jeopardy.
- Description of how and when the tapes will be disposed of after they have served the stated purpose.

Although some tapes from the project may be useful for teaching, dissemination, or other purposes at a later date, it is nonetheless common to use wording to indicate that tapes will be routinely erased or turned over to the participant. A revised form of release can be obtained later when it is established that further use of a recording is desirable. This release is generally explicit about the *type* of exposure anticipated (e.g., to future trainees at such-and-such institution, classroom teaching, professional conferences, public meetings, or broadcast).

Research is different from evaluation. Often a requirement of therapy or education is that it be evaluated. The important distinction for the participant is not whether something is being measured, but whether the first priority of the measurement is in his or her interests or of something more abstract. In pure research, the video activity is not expected to be of benefit to the subject; in applied research, the activity is often expected to be of individual benefit, but some potential benefits may be withheld or delayed. In evaluation of training or therapy, benefits

---

Social Skills Training Program Consent Form

You are invited to join a social skills training program with Cynthia (Sis) Bolivar. She is working with Dr. Peter Dowrick, from the University of Alaska, Anchorage, to develop this program.

If you decide to join the program you can expect:

- To answer some questions about your daily life; one person who helps you will also answer questions about your daily life;
- To be videotaped while you practice certain kinds of social skills (social skills are ways of behaving that help us get along with others);
- To watch a videotape of yourself several times;
- To go to a social skills group once a week while your are in the program; and
- To tell us what you think of the program.

If you decide to join the group, you can quit the group at any time and no one will be angry with you. At the end of the project you can keep your videotape. The only people allowed to watch your videotape will be Sis Bolivar, Dr. Dowrick, and four of Sis's classmates in her University class. No one else will be allowed to see your videotape without your permission. Anything that we learn during the program will be kept confidential (it will be kept secret).

I understand what this paper says. I have decided to join the Social Skills Program that Sis Bolivar is developing.

_____	_____
Participant	Guardian (if applicable)
_____	_____
Date	Date

Figure 8.1. Example consent form, written in low reading level language for research participants of low cognitive functioning.

will be maximized at all times and some measure will be taken of the effects. These and all other aspects of risks and rights are explained to participants orally as well as in writing.

Safeguards and Benefits

It is incumbent upon the responsible professional to be aware, through a knowledge of the medium, of different potential effects that may put the subjects at risk or benefit them. Proper protection and support may be facilitated by two additional items on the consent form:

- Sources of referral for questions about the project or problems arising from participation.

- Later access to information derived from the project (supplied on request, invitation to presentations, etc.).

When research subjects have finished their contribution, it is normal for them to be debriefed on any matters that could not reasonably be disclosed earlier. The protection of human subjects' principles widely accepted in the United States were established by a national commission on the basis of human respect, beneficence, and justice. It is also of practical importance to maintain trust and cooperation between behavioral scientists and their consumers.

CONCLUDING REMARKS

Video has become established as an important agent for personal change (training, education, health, therapy, recreation) and research (documentation, dissemination, measurement, diagnosis, independent- and dependent-variable manipulation). In a few cases, video has emerged as an agent in its own right; more often its greatest value is adjunctive or serving to embellish established methodologies. The extent of use continues to escalate, given the camcorder, the computer chip, and laser technology. Those professionals with a responsibility to the field will feel increasing urgency to clarify the benefits, the harm, and the benign influences of video and to develop more useful conceptualizations for predicting the exact circumstances under which these effects may occur.

The various uses of video described throughout this book can be, and in most cases are, used independently of each other. Some notable examples of combined video applications are cited; the possibility of this trend to continue in the future has been remarked upon. For the video enthusiast, the following "ultimate" scenario is proposed:

- Video *surveillance* to establish the issues.
- Baseline recordings for *evaluation*.
- Developments or solutions proposed and shown on video for *community participation*.
- *Models* developed and observed.
- Beginning skills further developed using *interactive video*.
- Practice videotaped for *feedback* and personal exploration.
- The best examples kept for *positive self-review*.
- *Distance education* used to benefit an expanded community.

- Advanced skills planned and constructed for *feedforward*.
- *Vignettes* used in research (refine the tasks and teaching strategies).
- *Triggers* developed for ongoing professional development.
- More recordings for *outcome analysis*.
- Participants make their *own recordings* for personal growth.
- Videotapes of all elements compiled for *documentation* and *dissemination*.

PART II
Selected Applications

Relationship of Contributed Chapters to Part I

Each chapter in Part I corresponds to one or more chapters in Part II, to illustrate video applied in the context of the companion chapter. The authors, all recognized experts in their fields, provide procedural details drawn from their own work.

Part I	Part II
Chapter	Chapter
1. Equipment fundamentals (systems, decisions)	9. Interactive video (exploring the current limits of technology)
2. Video for analyzing and documenting	10. Facial behavior (analyzing expressions of emotion)
3. Instructing and informing (educational videos)	11. Behavioral information for medical patients and their families
4. Modeling videos	12. Video production guidelines
5. Scene setting (using video vignettes)	13. Trigger tapes (production and use)
6. Feedback and self-confrontation	14. Video replay to prompt recall of interpersonal processes
	15. Sport skills from video replay and modeling (also links Chapters 4 and 7)
7. Feedforward and self-modeling (structured and edited video)	16. Self-modeling with children (social/ emotional problems)
8. Expanding the usability of video	17. Using video with people experiencing serious disabilities

CHAPTER 9

The Multiple Dimensions of Interactive Video

ROBERT J. CAVALIER

OVERVIEW

This chapter begins with some background to the development of video in combination with computer technology, leading to the emergence of interactive videodisc systems. Three levels of interactivity, their applications, and advantages are described citing the managerial training program called Decision Point *as an example. An illustration of Level III interactive video is provided by a disc system concerning suicidal adolescents, in which the viewer is placed in the position of choosing interview questions and deciding treatment options. Dr. Cavalier then outlines the design and development of interactive video applications, including phases of development, roles of the project team, and problems such as personal politics and computer programming bugs. He discusses developing technologies and future applications. Some limitations of the older technology are overcome by new developments (e.g., optical read-only-memory on compact discs and other digital conventions have helped to reduce the incompatibility between systems). Advantages of digital technology include the simplicity of patching sound over still frames from video. An important direction for the future lies in the development of "multitasking" and other software. Interactive video will rapidly become more user friendly and accessible not only for regular consumers, such as students, but also as a tool for scientists, teachers, and therapists.*

P.W.D.

Interactive video is the result of merging video with computer technology. The origins of the former go back to the 1930s. The origins of the latter go back at least to George Babbage's analytical engine of the 1870s, although modern computing power began with the development of the transistor in the late 1930s. It was not until the 1970s, however, that the two fields joined forces.

VIDEODISCS

The first machines combined a videotape recorder with a small computer program that controlled access to various parts of the videotape. Later developments allowed the videotape to be processed on a plastic videodisc. Using a disc instead of tape allows for, among other things, a rapid and random access of material—the desideratum of any interactive application. The disc, in turn, becomes the visual database that is read by a laser beam under the control of a computer program. A video recording yields the frame numbers that are "randomly accessed" through commands embedded in the computer program. The 12-inch discs most used in interactive video can hold up to 30 minutes of motion video, 54,000 still frames, or any combination of the two (Miller, 1987).

The basic configuration of a computer-driven videodisc system consists of a videodisc player, a computer, and a monitor. Two-monitor systems have one monitor to display analog video signals while the computer monitor is used to display control functions and other user options. A single-monitor system combines these images through special circuitry and computer boards, thus allowing graphics to overlay the video signals (either in whole or in part). These graphics can be used to place menus or other information on the screen. A viewer can then use this interface to communicate with the system by devices such as a pointer or touch screen.

Early examples of interactive videodiscs included a "tour" of Aspen, Colorado, and a resuscitation program developed for the American Heart Association. Today, major applications of videodisc technology fall into three main categories: sales (point of purchase), general information access, and education (schools and training).

Applications disclose three levels of interactivity. These levels are above the "level 0" of regular, linear video presentations. At interactive video level I, the disc is accessed by frame number through a handheld keypad. Some level I discs also contain "chapter stops" and/or "picture stops" that automatically stop the play at certain sections. This format could be quite helpful in "trigger tapes" of the kind described in Chapter 13 of this book. Here a large number of 10 to 40 second segments could be rapidly accessed with search, playback, and jump forward options. One example of this level is "The First National KIDISC." The disc uses a well-designed series of chapters to take the viewer through 26 presentations. For instance, one section utilizes still frame and step frame (slow motion) techniques to teach the viewers simple elements of sign language for the deaf. This idea could be expanded upon to provide more extensive study of signing. The still and step frame functions could also be of great help in the study of human and animal behavior since the videodisc allows extremely clear step throughs on a frame-by-frame basis.

At interactive video level II, the disc contains a simple (and small—7K) computer program with menus and a few multiple-choice questions. The program is contained on the opening section of the second audio track and dumped into a special videodisc player containing a microprocessor for reading and executing the program code. The advantage here is that machine requirements can be simplified and a turnkey system (i.e., simple on/off procedures) can be made. This allows for easy use and transportability. A disc on AIDS was designed to take advantage of these features. Upon entering the program, viewers are asked some questions about their sex and sexual preferences. Depending on these answers, the program will branch to, for instance, a discussion of AIDS in relation to the heterosexual or homosexual community. One segment of the latter discussion takes place in a simulated small party scene, where a narrator talks about the facts of the disease, including safe and unsafe sexual practices. Viewers are occasionally questioned (in a yes/no, true/false, multiple-choice format) about the issues discussed.

Applications in interactive video level III involve the use of a computer program (of any size) located on a floppy or hard disk that has the same capacity as other computer programs, plus special drivers to access features peculiar to interactive video (e.g., the disc player). This is the level that requires the basic hardware configuration just described. A good example of this level is a program called *Decision Point*, produced by Digital Equipment Corporation in 1984 (J. Maher, personal communication). The designers created a living case study in which the viewer becomes a key participant in the case and its outcome. The program simulates organization dynamics through a series of randomly generated scenarios involving functional process, use of tools, personnel motivation, and management style (including hiring and firing). The storyline places the viewer in the role of a new associate vice president for sales. Using crisis management as a manifestation of the everyday business world, the program presents 10 major issues. Each issue (e.g., when to report certain financial figures) creates different decision-making opportunities. Furthermore, the information available is often presented as incomplete. The viewer has four ways to respond. He or she can accept the initial position, investigate further, make a change in the position (and company policy), or postpone the decision. The program's internal record keeping will follow the user's input and tailor responses and scenarios accordingly. For example, a tabled decision could come back suddenly—and require an immediate resolution. As with the real world, decisions actually made do not receive immediate feedback in terms of right or wrong.

Decision Point shows the power of the medium not only as an educational tool, but as a *diagnostic* facility. It can actually be used to determine a person's management skills. This is made possible by the adaptive ability of interactive video programs.

VIDEODISCS ON SUICIDAL ADOLESCENCE

This set of three level III discs, developed jointly by the National Library of Medicine and the National Institute of Mental Health, is designed for 3rd- and 4th-year medical students. Its purpose is to explore areas of identification, risk assessment, interviewing, physician attitudes, and intervention techniques as they relate to the topic of suicidal adolescents. It involves three case studies using different aspects of interactive video, and it provides access to such resources as a glossary of psychiatric terms, a bibliography, information about pharmacotherapy, and statistical trends in adolescent suicide.

The first case study is that of an 18-year-old male who is exhibiting depressive, suicidal behavior. The viewer engages in a simulated interview session with a confused and initially reluctant patient. The interview, which is limited to 15 minutes as clocked by the computer, is guided by four options: thoughts, questions, replay, and continue. The last two control the direction of the video. The first option allows the viewer to "listen in" to the therapists' thoughts, ideas, and hypotheses as the interview progresses (this is done by having the computer program alternate between two separate audio tracks).

The "questions" option allows the viewer to take charge of the interview by choosing topics from a menu and viewing them in separate but related sequences. Choices available include family relationships (father, etc.), school (performance, attendance, etc.), present illness (chief complaint, symptoms, when it started, etc.), physical complaints (sleep, appetite, drinking, drugs, etc.), friends, future plans, and other interests (activities, job, dating, etc.). A sample exchange, triggered by selecting "drugs" as the topic, goes like this:

Dr. Heines: What about drugs, John. Do you use drugs?
John (*with a look of disgust*):   What are you, a nark?
H: You got angry when I asked about drugs.
J: Yeah, so what?
H: That's a sensitive area for you, I can tell.
J: My dad thinks I use a lot of dope, too . . .

Throughout, the computer program is keeping track of the viewer's choices. This is done not only for feedback, but to insure continuity of presentation. In the exchange just illustrated, the context could lead the viewer to ask questions relating to either drugs or John's father. One would hope for a smooth transition from topic to topic. This continuity issue can be seen in the following exchanges relating to dating and drinking. If the viewer initially chose "dating," this is the exchange:

H: *Do you have a girlfriend?*
J: *I used to . . . she dumped me this summer.*

But if the topic of "drinking" came immediately before "dating," this is how the exchange would go:

H: Do you drink?
J: Some.
H: What do you drink? How much?
J: Beer, mostly. And I can really put it away—my girlfriend used to be real impressed by that.

[Viewer now chooses "dating."]

H: *You say your girlfriend was really impressed by how much you could drink? Tell me about her . . .*
J: *There's nothing to tell. She dumped me this summer.*

The italicized segments show two different shots accessed by the program according to the viewer's selections.

Another segment of the program shows the viewer how to conduct a suicide interview. The section combines didactic presentations with modeling of the techniques that are described. The therapist explains crucial aspects of a suicide interview; then the program shows how they are handled in an actual case.

The second case study is that of Shari, a 13-year-old who has just attempted to commit suicide. The patient took an overdose of medication and has been brought to a hospital emergency room. As in the previous scenario, the viewer is to conduct an interview. He or she will have 10 minutes to diagnose and treat the emergency situation. But this time the viewer can choose interview techniques as well as subject areas such as family history, presenting circumstances, and mood and thinking.

The interview techniques are empathy, support, and open-ended question. If the third technique is chosen, one segment would run as follows:

Dr. Clark: What happened tonight before you came here?
Shari (*sitting up, sobbing*): I already told the doctor about that.
C: I know how frustrating it must be to keep repeating yourself. But I'm really concerned about you and I want to make you feel better.
S: Will the seizures start again?
C: No. They're over now and you're going to be OK . . .

If the viewer chose empathy, this is how the same section would run:

C: I understand how upset you must be. Just coming to the hospital can be pretty scary.
S: Yeah, it was.
C: Shari, do you know what happened to you? (*Shari shakes her head, "No."*)
C: The pills you took caused the seizures. They're over now and you're going to be OK . . .

After the interview with the patient, the user sees the reasons for an interview with a family member and learns what kind of information is important to a physician's decision about intervention. At the end of this intervention unit, the user must decide whether to hospitalize Shari or send her home. Shari's case differs from John's in that it appears to be impulsive, rather than guided by a severe depression.

A third case is that of "Lisa," a 15-year-old whose mother takes her to a physician when she begins to lose weight and refuses to go to school. This case study gives the viewer practice in initial problem solving, since it soon becomes clear that the patient's behavior is due to depression rather than physical illness. Through an online chart and individual video interview segments with both Lisa and her mother, the viewer discovers that Lisa is from a broken middle-class home, that her mother's work and night classes have placed Lisa in the role of taking care of her younger siblings, and that, due to a recent move, she is mostly friendless. She is depressed and thinks of suicide, though her mother, in a later interview, is seen to be unaware of this. Lisa does have a boyfriend, but thinks that her mother no longer wants her to see him. During a segment in which Lisa is discussing her situation concerning her boyfriend (Jeff), the following screen comes up:

What do you want Dr. Mario [the physician] to do now?
1. Encourage Lisa to see Jeff more so she won't be so lonely.
2. Help Lisa explore her ambivalent feelings toward her mother.
3. Help Lisa "sort out" what limits her mother is trying to set for her.
4. Try to determine why Lisa's mother doesn't want her to see so much of Jeff.

If the viewer chooses option 2 as the way to proceed in the intervention, the following response occurs:

Remember, Dr. Mario is not a therapist; she just wants to initiate practical problem solving. A good starting place would be to help Lisa see if she can accommodate her mother's concerns and continue to see Jeff.

A video segment follows exemplifying the appropriate level of interview for this situation. In this segment the doctor helps Lisa to "reshape her thinking" by clarifying her mother's real concern regarding Jeff (e.g., getting too serious, interfering with Lisa's homework habits) and by eliciting from Lisa the possibility of a compromise with her mother. A final segment of this case study shows how the doctor develops a "no suicide contract" with the patient. That is, how Dr. Mario gets Lisa to write a promise to call or go to an emergency room if she wants to harm herself. The doctor has also set up an appointment for Lisa with a therapist.

   The Suicidal Adolescent shows one example of the multiple uses of interactive video, not only in the different approaches to each case study, but in the different tours that viewers experience as they make their choices. Interactive video, unlike traditional linear video, can integrate the components of a program in such a way as to yield a particularized and vivid learning experience. This ability alone argues well for its continued use and growth.

DESIGN AND DEVELOPMENT OF AN APPLICATION

How are interactive programs like *Decision Point* and *The Suicidal Adolescent* designed and developed? What resources and skills are necessary to create interactive applications?

Textbook procedures for designing and producing an interactive videodisc application (Miller, 1987) break down the development process as follows: analysis phase, design phase (including choice of authoring environment and hardware configuration), preproduction (including programming), production (video—still and/or motion), premastering and mastering (including check disc), and replication and distribution. Because of the many different kinds of tasks and skills involved in an undertaking that includes computer knowledge and video production, textbooks also speak of the project team as the human force behind the development. This team consists of a project director, a project manager, content experts, an instructional designer, computer programmers, and a video production team (the latter has its own cast of producers, directors, camera crews, etc.). While helpful in organizing one's thoughts on developing interactive videodiscs, this process will certainly wax and wane throughout each project. The only constants that remain are the premastering, mastering, and replication stages, since these are wholly dependent on a mechanical process.

Analysis and design stages for interactive video differ significantly from preparations for linear video production. In particular, the analysis phase involves considering delivery systems as well as hardware and software requirements. The design phase also involves decisions about programming techniques along with strategies unique to interactive storyboarding (e.g., separate audio tracks and computer-generated screen design). Production and postproduction also differ substantially from traditional video. Viewing edited tape will bear little resemblance to linear presentation since its segmentation is the result of the program flowchart rather than a linear script.

It is not easy for producers and editors to go straight from linear production techniques to interactive treatments. The standard use of dissolves, for example, can be disastrous if they occur at branching points in the program. How can two images overlap in transition when the viewer may be branched to one of three different scenes? Furthermore, audio tracks are frequently dual-independent. Sometimes an audio track will have no relation to the video images, for it could be used for a narrator voice during a part of the program when the video segment is hidden behind a graphics overlay. Some technical considerations that are unimportant in linear video, such as identifying field dominance, can be crucial in interactive applications. (Since a videodisc program can freeze accurately on a single frame, it is important to avoid the flicker that results with mismatched frames.)

When the postproduction process is complete, the videotape is prepared according to the specifications of the mastering facility. The tape is then sent to the company (disc mastering is too expensive an operation for in-house capabilities). A check disc is sent back and the disc (now the "visual database") is run in conjunction with the computer program. This final check determines whether the logic flow of the program dovetails with the visual and audio information on the disc. The mastering facility can now produce the master disc from which replications are made.

Real-world scenarios seldom follow a clean formula. There are always work, world politics, and personality conflicts that can emerge and heighten during the life of the project. Also, adjustments due to strategic changes and financial considerations seem endemic to the project. Long-term projects take on a life of their own, and each one poses unique problems and possibilities. Finally, the interactive nature of programming itself leads to much "diddling and fiddling," which in turn causes unanticipated changes in design and presentation. Often when one moves from an idea (expressed on a flow chart or otherwise) to an actual interactive presentation, flaws or new opportunities emerge that were not seen on the macrolevel of collegial exchange or even on the microlevel of detailed flow charts and/or pseudocode.

Thus reality casts a cautionary light on the recipe approach. This is not to say that general principles for design and development cannot be found and developed. But it is to say that these principles should be seen as flexible.

CHANGING TECHNOLOGIES AND FUTURE DIRECTIONS

The typical "interactive video" configurations found in the early 1980s utilized a proliferation of incompatible hardware and software environments. These configurations were characterized by a computer connected to an analog video monitor with RGB graphics overlay capabilities. The digital graphics were generated by a variety of graphics cards that required different hardware and software support. DEC, Sony, IBM, and EIDS have or have had products in this market. Their products were limited not only by the analog/digital dichotomy, but also by the fact that interaction had to take place in a single "window" (the whole screen). While thought better than a double-monitor configuration for most applications (except Macintosh using HyperCard), these single-screen designs prevented nondistorting interaction between viewer and material (e.g., a notebook function would cover part of the scene, a picture album could not be "left open" while the viewer moved to another part of the program, etc.).

Two movements in the late 1980s addressed these perceived limitations. On the one hand, exploitation of CD-ROM technology allowed for the implementation of a purely digital multimedia program. On the other hand, the growing presence of mega-pixel computer screens and multitasking operating systems made possible the utilization of "video windows" as part of a larger computer interface. The drive toward multimedia CD-ROM technology was seen, in one respect, as a way to overcome the cumbersome and incompatible hardware configurations of earlier level III systems (Microsoft Press, 1988). By having a purely digital format, it was unnecessary to divide and sync video signals and RGB computer graphics. The images and sound that would have existed in analog form on the video tape are now digitized—they share the same binary code as computer programs and computer graphics. Furthermore, this multimedia digital information could be built upon the standards established for common 5 1/4-inch compact audio and data discs. Thus the simplified and standardized format could also be "played" on appropriately adjusted low-end equipment such as the compact disc player and the CD-ROM disc drive.

General design considerations for multimedia CD-ROM applications remain similar to the "single screen" design of level III interactive video. However, the digital nature of the images and the audio allow for unique features. The possibility of "sound over still" is greatly simplified. First, an image (existing as a file containing, for example, 250K) is brought up and displayed on a part of the screen as a graphic image. The controlling program then calls up an audio file (consisting of, for example, 50K) and runs it. The result for the end user could be a Vermeer painting and a brief audio narrative describing some of its features. A mouse click on an icon at the bottom of the screen could call up another audio file, and a different feature of the painting could be described. Unless the computer program called up a specific command either to clear the screen or to locate another graphic image in place of the Vermeer, the user would be viewing the same image throughout both narrations.

The digital nature of images also allows the user to "zoom in" on a feature and even to cut and paste the graphics in a bit-mapped graphics program. Video shot through a fisheye lens can be laid out in such a fashion that the viewer can "pan" left/right or up/down. This latter technique was used in a program called *Palanque*. This program, produced by Bank Street College, creates a simulated tour of an ancient Mayan ruin. After a brief introduction by the program's guide, the viewer can use a toggle stick to "walk" through the ruins. An eye icon allows glances up or down, left or right. The walk is achieved through a series of still frames taken every 10 feet and the panning effects occur within a graphics window built upon wide-lens camera work. One can also call up information about various sights, and a camera icon can be used to capture still frames. Randomly accessed audio tracks containing jungle sounds complete the interactive environment.

Production of multimedia CD-ROM applications requires strategies similar to those for the design and development of interactive video (Microsoft Press, 1988). However, programming and production should take into account the unique features of CD-ROM that are made possible by its purely digital format. Furthermore, the premastering phase is no longer a matter of preparing a time-coded tape with appropriate lead-ins and lead-outs. All components must be carefully laid down on magnetic tape, and this requires more computer power as well as sophisticated software to simulate the final product.

Paralleling the development of multimedia CD-ROM applications were applications utilizing large-screen monitors. These monitors are characterized by displays of approximately one million "picture elements" (or "pixels"). A pixel is the smallest unit of on/off display on the screen. A monitor with $1,000 \times 1,000$ picture elements is thus a high resolution, mega-pixel display. Large-screen displays also allow for "separation" of activities. It is now possible to design a program with the video in one part of the screen, a notebook in another part, and a series of questions in yet a third. Thus overlay need be used only when essential to the purposes of the program (e.g., to superimpose perspective on a building) and not because one is limited by the display space (Brand, 1987).

If we add to this display an underlying operating system that is capable of "multitasking" (e.g., UNIX), then sections of the screen can become separate programs running simultaneously. Thus, for example, sophisticated 3-D graphics can be processing while the viewer continues to interact with another aspect of the lesson. A further advantage to a UNIX-like environment lies in its telecommunications and networking capabilities. UNIX evolved in the setting of university computer science departments, and a number of "tools" were developed to support communications among machines distributed across a campus and country network. One result is the hooking up of a computer to other computers and peripheral devices scattered throughout the campus. When these computers combine CD-ROM drives with "servers" containing dozens of programs and hundreds of digitized images, and when these peripheral devices are stacks of videodisc players, then it becomes possible to design a vast interactive multimedia environment of unprecedented power and potential.

One prototype of this environment was developed at MIT under the Visual Courseware Group of Project Athena. Here a number of programs were developed for the *Visual Workstation.* These programs covered areas in foreign language instruction, neuroanatomy, engineering, and architecture.

At MIT's Media Lab, an application in the social sciences uses similar computing strategies. Under the general title of *Reconfigurable Video,* one project allows viewers to analyze a couple's therapy session by viewing the session from various angles and "rewriting the script" by designing their own video of the situation. Movie stills and sequences stored on a videodisc are combined with computer-generated text to create an electronic book. Options on the opening screen consist of analysis, expert opinion, files and resources, interactive movies, slide shows, transcript, and video databases. Through the use of real-time editing facilities, it is also possible to mix expert commentary with the case study. One of the purposes of the project is to establish a model for the use of interactive video in social science research.

Indeed, pioneer work at the Media Lab anticipates the direction of many efforts at the turn of this century. These efforts will involve "the whole gamut of communications media—television, telephones, recordings, film, newspapers, magazines, books and infesting and transforming them all, computers" (Brand, 1987, p. xi). In fact, the convergence of computers and video has already revolutionized our relation to the visual, and the coming ubiquity of visual workstations will form a natural part of education and research in the social sciences.

Once video becomes yet another binary bit of information that the CPU can process, it can become fully integrated into machine-mediated research and learning. This, in turn, points the way for a kind of dynamic multimedia document processing called hypermedia. In its full blown sense, hypermedia represents the complete integration of heterogeneous applications into a single screen display. An application from a spreadsheet would maintain its life (i.e., its calculative capacity) even after being cut and pasted into a word processing program. And audio with video images could be hidden behind buttons in an interactive application that could be part of a research "paper". By the end of the century, we will come to see and use dynamic visual information in our "publishable" work in as natural a way as we now see and use visual information in our daily work routines

CHAPTER 10

Analyzing Nonverbal Behavior

DAVID MATSUMOTO
PAUL EKMAN
ALAN FRIDLUND

David Matsumoto was supported in part by a grant from the National Institute of Mental Health (MH 42749–01). Paul Ekman was supported by a Research Scientist Award from the National Institute of Mental Health (MH 06092).

OVERVIEW

This chapter offers some insight into the task of analyzing facial expressions with the degree of detail that is possible only with the assistance of video. It begins with a taxonomy of facial action—that is, the ways the face moves and the information it imparts. Facial expression configurations and dynamics are defined and described. Dr. Matsumoto and colleagues describe four primary methods of eliciting nonverbal behavior to be measured: (a) structured and unstructured interviews; (b) structured imagery, self-reference, and reminiscence tasks; (c) emotion-eliciting stimuli, for example, film clips; and (d) structured activities of emotional valence. The authors then review related video-based methods of measurement including open-ended observation and standardized facial measurement using the Facial Action Coding System (FACS). Selective measurement is discussed as an economic, standardized means of studying nonverbal expression. Selective observer judgment and three major direct-measurement approaches are described: the Maximally Descriptive Facial Movement Coding System (commonly called MAX), the System for Identifying Affect Expression by Holistic Judgment (AFFEX), and the Emotion Facial Action Coding System (EMFACS). Facial electromyography (EMG) is mentioned as an alternative or an adjunct to video analysis. The authors illustrate with examples drawn from their research indicating systematic differences in the facial expressions of people with different diagnoses of severe mental illness.

P.W.D.

This chapter presents guidelines for recording, measuring, and analyzing nonverbal behavior. We have expanded upon substantial portions of another article (Ekman &

Fridlund, 1987) to be of use to scientists whose interests lie in the assessment of nonverbal behavior, whether part of the clinical realm or not. As the bulk of our research has involved analyzing facial movements, we limit our discussion to the use of video technology in the assessment of facial behavior. The principles and guidelines that govern the assessment of other nonverbal behaviors including body movements, gaze, and speech are similar. A detailed discussion of the analysis of these behaviors can be found in Scherer and Ekman (1982).

We first discuss the different types of facial actions observed in naturally occurring interactions and the different types of information that can be gathered from the face. We then describe the two major decisions involved in examining facial behavior—namely, selecting the conditions under which to obtain samples and the methods for measuring the behavior. We then present several of our own studies that exemplify the use of video recording for the analysis of facial behavior. Throughout, we attempt to provide scientists and practitioners alike with the concepts and methods requisite for making informed decisions about measuring facial behavior.

FACIAL EXPRESSIONS

Types of Facial Actions

Several different types of information can be gathered from facial expressions, including emotions and nonemotion signals. For several reasons, we focus on techniques for measuring *emotion*. First, the techniques available for facial measurement were, for the most part, developed for studying emotion. Second, there is ample evidence that these techniques can accurately measure emotion. Third, there is increasing recognition of the importance of emotional displays in relation to internal state and in the regulation of social interaction.

Most facial actions, however, do not signal emotion. Three of these types of actions are particularly relevant to the study of nonverbal interaction:

- *Instrumental facial actions* are related to activities that help to satisfy bodily needs or manage emotion. Examples include lip wiping and wetting, lip biting, or grinding of the teeth.
- *"Emblematic" facial actions* (Ekman, 1973) are learned symbolic facial gestures whose meanings are language-like and widely shared within a culture. Examples include the wink, the facial shrug, and the tongue defiance display.
- *Conversational facial signals* (Ekman, 1979) include actions that highlight or punctuate language. These may help to illustrate one's own speech, regulate or monitor social interaction, encourage a speaker to continue, call for more information, or presage an interruption.

Types of Information That Can Be Gathered from the Face

Affective Phenomena

In unpacking visible facial behavior, we have suggested terminology for a distinction between *expression configuration,* the specific muscles used in an expression, and *expression dynamics,* the amplitude-time course of the configuration (Ekman & Fridlund, 1987). Both properties are related to emotion; expression configuration specifies the type of emotion and expression dynamics specify its strength.

There is consistent, robust evidence (see Fridlund, Ekman, & Oster, 1986) for the facial configurations that signify fear, anger, disgust, combined sadness and distress, surprise, and happiness. Evidence is weaker for distinguishing guilt or shame from sadness and distress and for measuring interest or different varieties of happiness (such as amusement, physical pleasure, and contentment). New evidence (Ekman & Friesen, 1986; Ekman & Heider, 1989) suggests a specific configuration for contempt (but also see Fridlund, in press, for an alternative, intention-movement account of facial displays).

Less is known about the dynamics of facial expression. There is evidence that intensity and duration of muscular actions vary with the strength of self-reported emotion (Ekman, Friesen, & Ancoli, 1980; Fridlund, Schwartz, & Fowler, 1984). Both configurative and dynamic features distinguish voluntarily produced facial signals of emotion from more spontaneous expressions (Ekman, Hager, & Friesen, 1981; Hager & Ekman, 1985).

Other than those facial actions currently identified as prototypic of emotion, there is no hard evidence for facial activity uniquely characteristic of moods or affective disorders. We have argued elsewhere (Ekman, 1984) that these phenomena are likely to be characterized by unique facial dynamics, but not configurations. For example, in a blue mood, one may readily feel sadness and that emotion can be called forth easily. Periods of sadness will generally be longer, more intense than usual, and more difficult to regulate. These characteristics will be even more pronounced in some clinical depressions for which the further study of facial dynamics holds promise.

Other Types of Information

Several other types of information can be gathered from facial expressions. These include personal identity, kinship, race, gender, temperament, personality, beauty and attractiveness, intelligence, and age (Ekman, 1977). Unfortunately, little empirical work has been done to study systematically the relationship between these dimensions and facial expressions, as the study of emotion has dominated research on faces.

METHODS OF ELICITING FACIAL BEHAVIOR

Several formats allow sampling of facial behavior. Each has its own advantages and disadvantages. We consider four types, all of which are commonly part of basic and applied research: (a) structured and unstructured interviews; (b) structured imagery, self-reference, and reminiscence tasks; (c) the use of emotion-eliciting stimuli; and (d) the use of structured tasks or activities. While unobtrusive measurement of facial behavior in naturally occurring settings is theoretically important, it is most often impractical. We will briefly review each of the formats for obtaining samples of facial behavior, and the advantages and disadvantages of each.

The first two methods require interaction of the subjects with an experimenter with possibilities of reactive impact. Subjects may show facial signs of evaluation apprehension (e.g., knitting of brows) or undue politeness (e.g., appeasement smiles), and depending on the person, exaggeration or minimization of distress. For these reasons, subjects' facial behaviors while interacting with experimenters cannot be assumed to reflect accurately the emotional or motivational state without unobtrusive verification in other social situations.

All formats for eliciting facial behavior require the investigator to choose between a hidden camera or a visible camera. The hidden camera allows measurement of less reactive facial behavior, but it may pose problems in obtaining informed consent. The use of a visible camera obviates difficulties in obtaining consent but may result in attenuated or distorted facial behavior (e.g., Kleck et al., 1976). Either videotape or film recording may be employed; Walbott (1982) presented the advantages and constraints of each.

Structured and Unstructured Interviews

The unstructured interview format carries the advantages of varying length, the flexibility to explore in depth specific features of the subject's presentation, and the ability to elicit affect from someone who would be unexpressive under more restrictive conditions. While the unstructured interview format often is used effectively in clinical settings, it has some severe drawbacks in that facial behavior is likely to be very sparse. Also, comparisons across individuals are nearly impossible given the uniqueness of each interview.

Structured interviews have the advantages that the interview format is relatively consistent and subjects' facial behaviors from question to question are more readily comparable. One liability of the structured interview, however, is the inflexible transition that must occur between questions. These transitions can be jarring and often inhibit expression. Like the unstructured interview, the structured interview readily yields conversational samples but still requires long recording epochs to obtain emotional facial behavior.

Imagery, Self-Reference, and Reminiscence Tasks

Laboratory experiments on induced mood often use a variety of imagery, self-reference, or reminiscence tasks. In imagery tasks, subjects may be asked to recall, then "re-experience" personally significant emotional events. Alternatively, they are asked to imagine "affective imagery" items culled from standardized descriptions of everyday emotional situations. Self-reference tasks such as Velten statements rely on suggestion to elicit emotion ("I feel blue"). Imagery and self-reference tasks typically employ items or statements with known (or predictable) emotional content. Reminiscence tasks do not involve prior procurement of an "item" or "situation" for eliciting emotion; they rely on free recall of material that may have varying, unpredictable emotional or motivational content.

Although imagery, self-reference, and reminiscence tasks seem to provide easy ways to elicit authentic emotion, closer analysis suggests caution. These tasks have in common the request by the experimenter to experience emotion. Thus, any expressions of induced emotion may reflect compliance as much as felt emotion, and inhibited or intensified facial behavior may occur. But these tasks have advantages over the structured clinical interview: Emotions are more potently elicited and their content specified more precisely.

These structured tasks are all economical. They can be used to evoke emotion quickly and in a relatively controlled fashion, despite their confounding with effects of compliance. The twin advantages of economy and standardization are important. Facial behavior can be very densely packed. Whatever task is employed, acquiring and measuring the facial behavior will take considerable time. Therefore, brief samples are desirable, and the fact that standard tasks can fit into brief epochs is highly advantageous.

A disadvantage of imagery and self-reference tasks is that they typically exclude conversation and thus preclude the facial expressions associated with speech. Reminiscence tasks include conversation but typically do not use standardized emotion elicitors. A good compromise is to use imagery that is guided by the subject from personal experience. Facial behavior can be sampled during the imagery. The subject is then asked to recount his or her experience of the imagery, and conversational signals (possibly mixed with emotional signals) can be observed.

Emotion-Eliciting Stimuli

The use of emotion-eliciting stimuli offers researchers a third tool with which to analyze facial behaviors. These types of stimuli are distinguished from the imagery tasks just described in that emotion is elicited by an external stimulus. Typical examples of these stimuli include film clips depicting images of particular emotional content and electrical shock.

There are several advantages to using these types of tasks. First, the same stimuli can be used with different individuals, providing a degree of standardization. Second, the stimuli are often perceived as more "real" to the subjects, as they are required to view films or experience sensations directly. In imagery tasks, there is always a question of whether the emotion is comparable to that elicited by physically real stimuli. Finally, external stimuli are readily usable in other studies.

The major caution in using emotion-eliciting stimuli concerns whether emotion is in fact elicited. For example, some researchers have used electrical shock to study facial reactions. It is questionable whether response to shock is an emotion and whether the facial reactions to shock are emotional expressions.

Second, when it is clear that the stimulus elicits emotion, it is important to know *which* emotion it elicits and whether it elicits multiple emotions. It would be ideal to use stimuli that arouse single emotions such as happiness, sadness, or anger unambiguously. Unfortunately, reactions are most often complex, and people may react with different emotions.

Structured Tasks and Activities

The final way to measure facial behaviors involves the use of structured tasks or activities for individuals or groups. The tasks may target the elicitation of emotion directly or indirectly, since the engagement and completion of most types of tasks are usually associated with some type of emotion, either during or after the event. The central question is, "What is the importance of emotion and emotion-related processes in the resolution of the task?" If, for example, one believes that facial displays of emotion during the task play a central role in the regulation of the activity, then it seems appropriate to use the task in studying emotion.

The major advantage to this procedure is that it allows the researcher to obtain naturally occurring records of facial behaviors in a relatively structured, constant format. Allowing the task to take its natural course to completion, then, becomes one of the most attractive features concerning the use of these activities. The danger, of course, is that the tasks may not elicit emotion or that they may elicit reactions that are ambiguous.

MEASUREMENT OF FACIAL ACTION

Facial behavior, as we have mentioned, is densely packed. The face contains nearly 80 muscles that act in rapidly changing patterns; the muscles are capable of forming tens of thousands of facial expressions. Consequently, choices about how much facial behavior to measure are crucial. Also crucial are choices about *which* facial behaviors to measure. Many systems have been developed to structure and analyze observations of facial action, most have been developed for studying emotion to the exclusion of nonemotional facial behavior. (See Ekman, 1982, for a detailed comparison of 14 major facial coding systems.)

Figure 10.1 shows the decisions facing the investigator in choosing a facial measurement system. The first choice is whether facial behavior is to be measured comprehensively or selectively. Comprehensive measurement, while costly, may be necessary depending upon the state of knowledge about facial behavior gathered to date. Furthermore, it is the only way to discover unexpected facial actions. Selective facial measurement is the method of choice whenever the behaviors to be measured can be specified in advance. The use of selective facial measurement assumes that the investigator knows which facial actions are most pertinent to study.

Comprehensive Facial Measurement

There are two major comprehensive methods of facial measurement. One uses open-ended inferences drawn by observers of facial behavior. The other measures

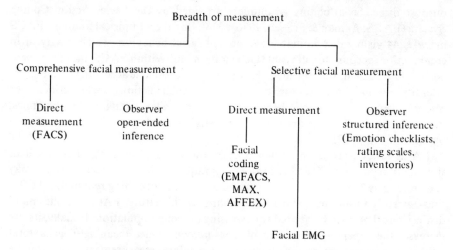

Figure 10.1. Decision tree for measuring facial behavior.

facial behavior directly. Observers may be able to infer phenomena that no direct measurement system is yet configured to detect. On the other hand, observers may miss detailed information that can be directly measured in the face.

Open-Ended Observation

Open-ended observers' reports about facial behavior are rarely employed. Yet they are among the simplest measurement methods, and they offer an unusually wide net with which to assay facial behaviors. Observers are shown videotaped facial behavior and asked to report what they see. Their responses are audiotaped and collated. The responses can be unstructured, or observers can be prompted to provide their judgments about "disorders," "moods," "traits," and "emotions." Systematically collecting observers' open-ended impressions provides valuable data on how individuals perceive subjects' affect. It allows one to incorporate into theory and research all reasonable inferences about facial behavior and affective disorders.

What kinds of observers should be used? Naive observers, trained nonexpert observers, and expert clinicians would provide different and complementary reports that could guide future hypothesis construction and testing. Should observers view videotapes that provide the full sound track? Past research has involved filtered speech or provided just the video image. However, we see no reason during initial research to forsake the ecological validity of the full audiovisual presentation. Including the sound track also simplifies separating conversational from emotional facial behaviors and the latter from referential emotion (i.e., expressions that refer to emotions felt in the past).

Comprehensive Direct Measurement of Facial Behavior

In contrast to open-ended observation in which observers supply impressions of facial behavior, here the behavior itself is measured. Comprehensive general-purpose direct facial coding is uniquely provided by the Facial Action Coding System (FACS; Ekman & Friesen, 1976, 1978). Based on empirical findings, FACS includes 44 visibly discriminable component facial behaviors which, singly or in combination, account for all visible facial movement. Within FACS, the component behaviors are called Action Units, or AUs. AUs are scoreable according to five-point intensity ratings. Because the timing of muscular actions seems critical for discriminating types of facial behavior, FACS provides coding of AU dynamics, that is, timing of AU onset, apex, and offset. High interrater reliabilities typically are obtained using FACS.

FACS takes considerable time to learn and to use, and it requires repeated, slow-motion viewing of facial actions. For example, 1 minute of facial behavior may take as long as 3 hours to code, depending on the type of coding required. FACS is thus currently unsuitable for real-time coding. By its nature, FACS includes more distinctions than may be needed for assessing any one population. Initially, its use increases the expense and tedium of measurement. Once meaningful behavioral units are derived empirically, however, elementary measurement units can be collapsed and subtle distinctions disregarded. Flexibility in retaining and discarding AUs will be critical in early research on any topic involving facial behavior, since initial hypotheses will be largely speculative.

Selective Facial Measurement

Several methods are available for measuring facial behavior selectively. Selective measures are economical and are preferred when the facial behaviors of value are known in advance. A major liability is often their inapplicability in studying particular phenomena. Their selectivity usually is based on theoretical preconceptions that may be irrelevant for the topic under study. They do not usually separate emotional from conversational facial behaviors, and some behaviors characteristic of emotion are omitted.

Selective methods of facial measurement include both observer judgments and direct measurement. Selective direct measurement can be performed using either visual coding or facial electromyography.

Selective Observer Judgment

In the judgment approach, observers are asked to rate slides, films, or, occasionally, live presentations of facial expressions. In studying the facial behaviors associated with depression, for example, videotapes of depressed patients may be shown to judges who rate each patient as having major depression with or without melancholia using a rating scale. Scales that have been used include emotion scales (e.g., Schlosberg, 1941, 1952, 1954) and discrete emotion categories (e.g., Izard, 1971, 1972, 1977; see review of scaling and categorical approaches by Ekman, Friesen, & Ellsworth, 1982). They can be used equally well in psychodiagnosis.

Unlike open-ended observation, observer-judgment methods by nature constrain observers' responses. The constraints on observer responses make judgment methods inappropriate for exploratory studies of facial behavior in affective disorders. Rather, construction of rating scales, categories, checklists, and so forth should follow pilot research using comprehensive measurement.

Selective Direct Measurement

In the selective direct measurement approach, facial behaviors are specified in advance and sampled at a predetermined level of precision. Specification of behavioral units proceeds from theory, research, or clinical inference. Selective direct measurement is performed using visible facial coding systems or by electromyography. Selective visible facial coding systems require a videotaped record of the patient's facial behavior. Electromyography does not require videotaping, but requires placement of recording electrodes to monitor the patient's physiological activity.

MAX and AFFEX. The major exemplars of selective direct measurement facial coding systems are the Maximally Descriptive Facial Movement Coding System (MAX; Izard, 1980), the System for Identifying Affect Expression by Holistic Judgment (AFFEX; Izard & Dougherty, 1980), and the Emotion Facial Action Coding System (EMFACS; Friesen & Ekman, 1983). MAX and AFFEX are based on recognition studies that established the cross-cultural association of certain facial expressions with specific emotion labels. Neither MAX nor AFFEX provides an exhaustive listing of possible facial behaviors. MAX, for example, provides only those 27 descriptors believed by Izard to be necessary to form judgments about seven "primary" emotions. No data are available to show that the excluded facial actions do not reflect emotion. Expression dynamics are disregarded; facial behavior is seen instead as "on" or "off."

EMFACS. EMFACS is a subsystem of FACS that uses standardized selective alternatives to measure broader, emotion-related facial actions. EMFACS considers only emotional expressions and, among those, only the AUs and AU combinations best supported by empirical findings or theory as emotion signals. EMFACS is a systematic derivation from FACS that permits confident statements about its omissions, indicated by numerous concurrent validation studies (Ekman, 1982).

Coding time with EMFACS is accelerated, albeit at the expense of subtler data—including those indicative of conversational signals or self-manipulations. Precise temporal dynamics of the facial actions are replaced by unitary demarcations of peak actions. To maintain an empirical approach in EMFACS or FACS scoring, facial actions are described in terms of numerical codes. Coders are requested not to interpret actions as emotion signals until they are tabulated post hoc and classified according to EMFACS criteria.

A number of predictions deriving from FACS emotion hypotheses have been supported (see review by Ekman, 1982). Studies of spontaneous emotional expression using self-report as a validity criterion support predictions about expressions that signal happiness, fear, distress, and disgust. Studies employing observers' attributions of emotion as a validity criterion support FACS predictions for these emotions as well as for surprise and anger.

Facial electromyography. Facial electromyography (EMG) is an alternative method for selective direct facial measurement. This technique most often involves the recording of tiny electrical discharges generated by contracting facial muscles through surface electrodes filled with conductive paste and attached to the skin with adhesive collars. Facial EMG techniques have been used to study affective imagery and mood states (Carney, Hong, O'Connell, & Amado, 1981; Fridlund, Schwartz, & Fowler, 1984; Schwartz, Brown, & Ahern, 1980; Teasdale & Rezin, 1978), posed expressions (Rusalova, Izard, & Simonov, 1975; Sumitsuji, Matsumoto, Tanaka, Kashiwagi, & Kaneko, 1977), and social interaction and empathy (Cacioppo & Petty, 1979; Vaughan & Lanzetta, 1980).

Facial EMG has three advantages over direct observation of the face. First, the EMG signal is instantaneously detectable and thereby lends itself to immediate recording. Second, the EMG signal offers a more finely graded measure of muscle activity than can be provided by visible facial coding systems or observer judgments. Third, EMG techniques detect muscle contractions that are too small or too fast to be observable (Ekman, 1982; Fridlund, 1988).

There are disadvantages to the EMG technique. Recording facial EMG requires an extensive electrode application procedure that limits the number of recordable sites (usually to three or four). Also, subjects usually are manifestly aware that they are participating in research concerning the face, which can result in distorted or attenuated facial behavior (Fridlund & Izard, 1983; Kleck et al., 1976). The leads, paste, and collars inhibit movement and may be torn by strong muscle actions. Attaching the recording discs can be problematic on males with heavy beards. If fine-wire recording is performed, implantation of the electrodes often produces irritation and pain.

A facial EMG signal may not be an accurate representation of ongoing dynamic muscle activity. The relationship between detected electrical output at an EMG site and the mechanical force exerted by a muscle may change over time as a function of fatigue (Mulder & Hulstijn, 1984).

Finally, conversational and emotional signals cannot be distinguished without an accompanying audio record. The typical surface electrodes show activity in areas considerably broader than the muscles directly underlying the electrode site. Thus, emotion signals may be confused with conversational signals from other muscles. Care should also be used in processing EMG signals to ensure that expression dynamics are not obscured by overaveraging of the signals (see Fridlund, 1979).

FACIAL BEHAVIORS AND AFFECTIVE DISORDERS

A variety of studies exist that exemplify the different ways of eliciting facial behavior and the different ways of measuring facial actions. Following is an example from our own research to illustrate the guidelines and issues raised to this point. This example comes from pilot studies of the facial behaviors associated with affective disorders.

The goal of this research was to examine the types of emotional expressions exhibited by clinically depressed patients. In the first study (Ekman & Friesen, 1981), structured interview settings were used to elicit expression from depressed patients at the time of intake at an inpatient psychiatric facility. FACS was used to measure the facial behaviors; this allowed for a comprehensive and direct measurement of the expressions that occurred during the interview. The DSM-II (American Psychiatric Association, 1968) diagnoses of the patients were major depressive ($N = 4$), minor depressive ($N = 3$), manic ($N = 3$); and schizophrenic ($N = 2$). Results reflect combined scores from the two interview samples.

FACS measurements identified 5,987 separate expressions. Some were composed of one muscular action; others involved co-contractions of two to five muscles. About one-third (1,770) of these expressions involved actions predicted by FACS to signal emotion. Most frequent were nonemotional facial actions such as lowering or raising the eyebrows to punctuate speech.

Patients diagnosed with major depression showed more sadness and disgust and fewer unfelt-happy expressions than minor depressives. Manics showed more felt-happy and unfelt-happy and fewer anger, disgust, or sadness expressions than either depression group (see Ekman & Friesen, 1982, for distinctions concerning felt and unfelt happiness). Schizophrenics differed from manics and depressives in showing more fear expressions and fewer of the other emotional expressions.

Patient groups also differed in their nonemotional speech-punctuating facial movements. Depressives and schizophrenics showed fewer speech-punctuating facial movements than manics. Major depressives showed much more brow lowering than brow raising in punctuating speech than the other groups, whereas manics showed the opposite pattern.

In another study (Ekman & Matsumoto, 1986), a standardized interview format again was used to elicit emotional expressions from depressed psychiatric inpatients, both at admission and at discharge. The videorecords used for this study were collected by Ekman and Friesen in 1964. EMFACS was used, allowing for a selective but direct measurement of the facial behaviors of the depressed patients. The attending physician and the ward chief agreed by the time of discharge on a DSM-II depression diagnosis for each of the 17 patients included in the study. Mean age of these patients at time of admission to the hospital was 47.5 years. Patients' hospital stays averaged 68 days.

Brief Psychiatric Rating Scale (BPRS) ratings were made independently by three clinical psychologists after viewing the first 2 minutes of the admission interview. They made a second set of BPRS ratings after viewing the first 2 minutes of the discharge film. At this time, they also rated each patient on degree of clinical improvement. A single coder measured facial behavior with EMFACS. A second reliability coder independently measured the facial behavior shown by eight of the patients in focal 1-minute interview samples. Intercoder reliability of EMFACS was 0.82.

Table 10.1 shows that more felt-happy expressions and fewer unfelt-happy expressions occurred at discharge relative to admission. The number of sad expressions tended to decrease, but the change was not significant. Patients who showed sadness expressions were rated by the clinicians as less disturbed (lower BPRS scores) both at admission and discharge (Table 10.2). At admission, patients

TABLE 10.1. Number of Patients Showing Happy Facial Expressions in Admission and Discharge Interviews.

	Admission Interview	Discharge Interview
Felt-happy expressions	3	12
Unfelt-happy expressions	14	5

$X^2 = 9.63$, $df = 1$, $p = .01$.

TABLE 10.2. BPRS Ratings of Patients Who Did or Did Not Show Any Sadness Expressions.

	BPRS Rating			
	Admission Interview		Discharge Interview	
	Mean	SD	Mean	SD
Sadness expressions	32.8	8.1	19.5	1.6
No sadness expressions	38.5	7.7	24.5	5.5
p (two-tailed)	.03		.01	

who showed sad expressions did so when describing current feelings. At discharge, patients who showed sad expressions did so when describing how they *had* felt when admitted. Sadness at admission did not predict clinical improvement by discharge.

On admission, patients who showed at least one happy expression (felt- or unfelt-happy) were rated as less disturbed (mean BPRS = 30.5) than those who did not (mean BPRS 43.2, $p < .01$). This difference was independent of whether they also showed a negative emotional expression. There was almost no overlap (1 of 17 subjects) in BPRS score distributions of those who did and did not show a happy expression.

Contempt expressions and unfelt-happy expressions at admission were independently associated with *less* clinical improvement. Each expression correlated with improvement even when variance associated with the other emotion was statistically removed (Table 10.3). Severity of disturbance on the BPRS at admission was positively correlated with subsequent clinical improvement. Table 10.4 shows that when unfelt-happy and contempt expression scores at admission were added to

TABLE 10.3. Correlations Between Facial Emotion Scores on Admission and Ratings of Subsequent Clinical Improvement.

	Rank Order Correlation	Partial Correlation
Contempt	$-.54$ $p < .05$	$-.69$ $p < .002$ (controlling for unfelt-happy)
Unfelt-happy	$-.60$ $p < .01$	$-.71$ $p < .001$ (controlling for contempt)

TABLE 10.4. Severity and Emotion Measures at Admission and Clinical Improvement

Measure at Admission	
BPRS	$r = .46,\ p = .06$
BPRS + contempt + unfelt-happy	$R = .82,\ p = .005$
Unfelt-happy + contempt	$R = .79,\ p = .001$
Unfelt-happy + contempt + BPRS	$R = .82,\ p = .001$

the BPRS scores in a multiple correlation with clinical improvement, the correlation was significant. Expression scores explained 46% of the variance. When expression scores were entered first in the multiple correlation, they correlated .79 ($p < .001$) with subsequent clinical improvement. Adding the BPRS accounted for only 4% of predicted variance.

CONCLUSION

The example just given illustrates the use of structured interviews to elicit emotional expression; in other studies we employed different techniques to sample facial behavior. For example, we used imagery and self-reference tasks, in studies of emotion and autonomic nervous system activity (cf., Ekman, Levenson, & Friesen, 1983; Fridlund et al., 1984), emotion-eliciting stimuli in our studies examining cultural similarities and differences in the expression of emotion in social situations (Ekman, 1972; Friesen, 1972), and structured tasks in a study examining emotional expressions during engagement in games posing moral conflict (Matsumoto, Haan, Yabrove, Theodorou, & Cooke-Carney, 1986).

We have emphasized the analysis of facial behaviors, but we believe that the issues outlined in this chapter are pertinent to most avenues of research examining nonverbal behaviors. As the study of nonverbal behaviors grows in popularity, we hope that the understanding of the methods employed to study them and of the issues underlying those methods grow as well.

CHAPTER 11

Video-Mediated Instruction in Medical Settings

JOHN M. PARRISH
ROBERTA L. BABBITT

OVERVIEW

This chapter provides a focused review of instructional video in medical settings, followed, as an illustration, by a usefully detailed description of one of the authors' own applications. The availability and usefulness of video is considered for a range of medical purposes, including those that inform patients about their medical conditions, prepare them for medical procedures, or teach them how to participate effectively in their own care. Uses of video are described in the preparation of patients for nonsurgical events, such as visiting the dentist or receiving injections. Different types of reaction to video, by children and adults in the processes of cooperation and recovery, are summarized. The authors then examine video in preparing patients for surgery and in patient education and skill development— teaching patients about topics such as disease, health maintenance, self-care, and drug regimens. Video is shown to be as effective as most (but not all) alternatives, if care is taken concerning the media content relative to prior hospitalizations and other characteristics of the viewers.

The authors draw conclusions about the trends in using video in medical settings and apply these conclusions in practice by describing a methodology for designing and implementing a video-mediated training curriculum. In their example, based on training parents of children with disabilities in how to interact with medical providers, they go beyond a simple instructional film to a comprehensive package incorporating modeling and criterion-based practice. Each step is illustrated: identifying skills and deficits, task analysis, composition of videotapes, scripts, behavior rehearsals, assessment simulations, skills training, maintenance, and follow-up assessments.

P.W.D.

The application of video technology to medical settings is burgeoning. Increased reliance upon such technology can be attributed to three recent trends: (a) the emergence of relatively inexpensive yet highly capable audiovisual hardware; (b) the increased emphasis upon structured, replicable approaches to patient education; and (c) the heightened concern about the extent to which quality health care can be provided in a cost-effective manner. Although initially more expensive than verbal instruction and live modeling, the development of prototype video enables the medical practitioner to extend relevant information to patients and their families in a manner that can be standardized (when applicable) across patients and is time-efficient as well as effective.

Video recordings have proven useful in both examining and influencing patient behavior (Dowrick & Biggs, 1983). For instance, databased approaches to effective patient care have advanced with the aid of video technology that permits the permanent recording of patient performance during critical medical procedures, thereby allowing medical practitioners to provide specific feedback and remedial instruction to the patient over time (Maxwell & Pringle, 1983). Educational and therapeutic applications in medical settings have included informing patients about their diagnoses (e.g., Moldofsky, Broder, Davies, & Leznoff, 1979; Minton, 1983), their indicated medical procedures and regimens (McCue, 1980; Pace et al., 1981), and their prescribed medications (e.g., Burkle & Lucarotti, 1984). In addition, video-mediated instruction, coupled with opportunities for the learner to imitate the filmed model, is being increasingly employed to promote skill acquisition among patients and medical staff charged with the responsibility of adhering to or delivering long-term regimens (Pace et al., 1981; Reith, Graham, McEwan, & Fraser, 1984).

This chapter highlights the availability and usefulness of prerecorded and customized video that informs patients about their medical conditions, prepares patients for medical procedures, and teaches them how to participate skillfully in their own care. Table 11.1 contains a brief description of selected studies regarding the use of video instruction in medical settings. We offer an example of one approach to the design and development of a training film suitable for use by health care providers and their patients. Rather than provide an exhaustive, critical analysis of previous related work, we refer interested readers to excellent reviews in the literature (Ludwick-Rosenthal & Neufield, 1988; Melamed, Robbins, & Graves, 1982; McCue, 1980; Nielsen & Sheppard, 1988; Siegel, 1986; Thelen et al., 1979). Because videos employed in medical settings often include both didactic instruction and modeling, we refer readers to Chapters 3 and 4 of this book for more comprehensive overviews of these two procedures.

USE OF VIDEO TO PREPARE PATIENTS FOR NONSURGICAL PROCEDURES

Much of the research literature on the application of video technology to the health professions has focused on preparing patients, typically children, to undergo painful or intrusive medical procedures. Video-mediated curricula typically have included modeling of targeted appropriate behaviors, as well as the provision of information. In general, the research literature supports the use of videotaped instruction and

TABLE 11.1 Descriptive Profile of Selected Studies.

Author(s)	Target Problems/ Diagnoses	Number of Subjects	Age of Subjects (years)	Training/Video Format	Skills/ Dependent Variables	Study Design	Short-term Results	Long-Term Results	Cost-Effectiveness
Vernon & Bailey (1974)	Minor elective operations and anesthesia	38	4–9	12-minute film	Global mood scale before and during anesthesia	Simple comparison (pre-post)	Decreased anxiety while waiting for anesthesia	ND	ND
Vernon (1974)	Tonsillectomies, herniorrhaphies, myringotomies, cystoscopies	30	4–9	18-minute film; model showing no pain; model exhibiting pain	Global mood scale before, during and preoperative medication injection	Factorial design	Increased anxiety among no pain movie group; pain movie more accurate, produced less anxiety	ND	ND
Machin & Johnson (1974)	Restorative dental treatment	31	3–5.5	11-minute peer model videotape	Behavioral rating scale	2-factor mixed design	No significant difference	2-3 weekly visits	ND
Melamed & Siegel (1975)	Elective surgery for hernias, tonsillectomies or urinary/genital tract difficulties	60	4–12	Peer modeling film (8mm cassette)	Self-report, behavioral and physiological measures of child's emotional state/anxiety. Parental report of postoperative behavior problems	Mixed design	Lower level of physiological arousal and postoperative behavioral problems	3-week continued reduction	ND

Study	Procedure	N	Age	Intervention	Measures	Design	Results		
Melamed, Hawes, Heiby, & Glick (1975)	Prophylaxis and dental examinations	60	5–11	12-minute peer model film	Maternal anxiety questionnaire; Palmer sweat index; behavior profile; fear surbey	Repeated measures; factorial design	Treatment group showed fewer disruptive behaviors and were less anxious		ND
Melamed, Yurcheson, Fleece, Hutcheson, & Hawes (1978)	Prophylaxis; dental examination; dental restorative treatment	80	4–11	10-minute videotape (long vs. short; model vs. demonstration)	Galvanic skin response and cardiac responses during film and treatment; questionnaires about child's behavior problems	2 x 2 factorial design	Peer model film produced less dental and general fears	ND	ND
Shipley, Butt, Horwitz, & Farbry (1978)	Upper gastrointestinal endoscopy	60	22–80	18-minute tape (1 vs. 3 viewings)	Heart rate; physician/nurse anxiety rating and self-report of anxiety	Simple comparison (pre-post)	Fear reduced as a function of number of prior viewings of preparation tape	ND	ND

Continued

TABLE 11.1 (Continued)

Author(s)	Target Problems/ Diagnoses	Number of Subjects	Age of Subjects (years)	Training/Video Format	Skills/ Dependent Variables	Study Design	Short-term Results	Long-Term Results	Cost-Effectiveness
Moldofsky, Broder, Davies, & Leznoff (1979)	Asthma	62	$M = 46$	55-minute videotape	Personality inventory; questionnaire on attitudes towards medicine and asthma; information about asthma; reports of medication use, and doctor visits; respiratory symptoms	Simple comparison (pre-post)	Increased knowledge scores	Knowledge gains were not maintained 16 months post-training	
Shipley, Butt, & Horwitz (1979)	Upper gastrointestinal endoscopy	36	22–80	18-minute tape (1 vs. 3 viewings)	Anxiety scales; frequency of gags; insertion attempts, and timing	Simple comparison (pre-post)	Multiple viewings of tape decreased anxiety in sensitizers	ND	ND
McCue (1980)	Children cancer undergoing painful medical procedures	2	2.5–4	Mixed media— play/puppet therapy, modeling, preprocedural education	Anecdotal reports of behavior	Review of literature/case studies	Reduced uncooperative and anxious behavior	ND	ND

Study	N	Age	Media	Outcome Measure	Design	Results		
Pace, et al. (1981)	68	35–59	5-minute videocassette	Adherence to protocol list and knowledge of balanced food choices (Likert-scale food habit survey)	Simple comparison	Improved dietary behavior	Not significant 2 months post-training	Yes
Padilla, et al. (1981)	50	<18	Filmstrip (information on procedure, distressful sensations, coping behaviors, or a combination)	Self-report of pain/discomfort/anxiety; willingness to repeat procedures	2 x 4 factorial design	Combination decreased anxiety	ND	2 x 4 factorial study
Melamed, Dearborn, & Hermecz (1983)	58	4–17	Slide-tape information package	Information acquisition; physiologic responsivity; self-report of medical concern; observed anxiety (rating scales and checklists)	Correlational/Factorial	Improved hospital experience and recovery; film was contraindicated for young, experienced children	ND	ND
Minton (1983)	14	16–55	11- and 17-minute videotapes vs. lecture and visual aids	Knowledge of bowel and bladder management	Simple comparison (pre-post test)	No difference between groups	ND	Yes—time

Continued

TABLE 11.1 (Continued)

Author(s)	Target Problems/ Diagnoses	Number of Subjects	Age of Subjects (years)	Training/Video Format	Skills/ Dependent Variables	Study Design	Short-term Results	Long-Term Results	Cost-Effectiveness
Pace et al. (1983)	Primary hypercholester-olemia	68	35–59	5-minute videocassette	Adherence protocol list and knowledge of balanced food choices (Likert-scale food habit survey)	Simple comparison	Improved dietary behavior	Not significant 2 months post-training	Yes
Burkle & Lucarotti (1984)	Hospital patients	ND	ND	5–10-minute videotape and file cards	Medication instruction	Descriptive	ND	ND	Yes—cost and time
Marshall, Rothen-berger, & Bunnell (1984)	Females requesting contraception	100	$M = 21.5$	Pamphlets; one-to-one dialogue; audiovisual presentation (slide/tape)	Knowledge about methods of contraception	Simple comparison (pre-post test)	Increased knowledge gain and satisfaction by audiovisual groups	ND	No—time and cost
Peterson, Schultheis, Ridley-Johnson, Miller, & Tracy (1984)	Elective oral surgery	44	2–11	Puppet model vs. local videotape vs. commer-cial film	Parental and self-report of coping; ratings of maladaptive behaviors	4 x 2 x multivariate ANOVA	All three types of modeling improved coping	ND	ND
Spindler (1984)	Total hip orthopaedic surgery	17	$M = 69$	Slide-tape presentation	Knowledge of total hip surgery	Descriptive	Increased knowledge	ND	Yes—cost, time, consistency

Study	Population	Sample	Age	Intervention	Dependent variables	Design	Results	Follow-up	Design
Reith Graham, McEwan, & Fraser (1984)	Diabetes	21/22/86	ND	Videotape demonstration vs. poster or written instruction	Urine glucose testing; attitudes toward video medium	Descriptive	85% preferred video medium; video more effective than poster or written information	ND	ND
Faust & Melamed (1984)	In-hospital pediatric surgical patients and same-day surgical patients	66	4–17	Singer Caramate II with slide carousel and audio cassette; 10-minute show (hospital related vs. unrelated)	Heart rate; Palmar sweat index; self-report of anxiety postsurgical complications	2 x 2 factorial design	Group exposed to hospital video retained more information; same-day patients reduced anxiety with distraction film	4-week maternal report of behavior	2 x 2 factorial design
Ward, Garlant, Paterson, Bone, & Hicks (1984)	Insulin dependent diabetes	36	18–69	13- & 17 1/2-minute videocassette	Knowledge about diabetes and health beliefs	Simple comparison (pre-post test)	Increased knowledge	ND	ND
Twardosz, Weddle, Borden, & Stevens (1986)	Minor elective ear, nose, or throat surgery	60	3–12	20-minute videotape of a preoperative class vs. life presentation vs. nurse's explanation	Negative vs. positive behavioral reactions to preoperative injections and trip to surgery; blood pressure, pulse, and temperature	3 x 2 factorial design	Live class was most effective in preparing children for surgery; physiological measures did not discriminate among groups	ND	ND

modeling as a successful method of preparing patients for medical as well as other procedures (see Chapters 3 and 4). Some investigators have predicted that prepackaged preparation materials will become routinely available in most medical settings (e.g., McCue, 1980; Melamed, et al., 1982; Mullen, Green, & Persinger, 1985; Williams & Kendall, 1985). Such packages have been and are likely to be increasingly employed to provide patients with relevant information about disease and stress, to desensitize patients to impending aversive medical procedures, and to guide them in the competent completion of prescribed regimens.

Because several studies have documented the overall efficacy of video-mediated instruction and modeling on behalf of patients, researchers have increasingly centered their studies on an understanding of the specific conditions under which the use of film is maximally beneficial in medical settings. For instance, Vernon (1974) examined the influence of filmed modeling on children's responses to injections. One group of hospitalized children viewed an 18-minute film depicting children receiving injections without exhibiting any emotions or pain. Another group observed a more realistic film of children responding to injections with short-lived, moderate pain and emotion (e.g., wincing and saying "ouch"). The group that viewed the latter film reported experiencing less pain, supporting the author's hypothesis that realistic modeling is more effective than noncredible modeling in reducing patient distress during moderately painful medical procedures.

Melamed, Yurcheson, Fleece, Hutcherson, and Hawes (1978) evaluated the influence of length and type of audiovisual preparation on the performance of pediatric dental patients. Results indicated that subsequent to viewing a peer modeling film, children exhibited fewer behavior problems and less fear during the dental treatment than did children who viewed a demonstration film during which the dentist reviewed the procedures without a child model. The length of the film did not appear to affect the children's behavior.

In an investigation involving adult patients, Shipley, Butt, Horwitz, and Farbry (1978) studied the effects of prior viewing (once or three times) of an 18-minute videotaped endoscopy on physiological and self-reported measures of anxiety in hospitalized adults. Results indicated that anxiety about the endoscopy was reduced as a function of the number of prior viewings of the videotape. The authors suggested that the results were consistent with an habituation hypothesis, whereby preparation that included repeated exposure to stress-relevant videotapes maximally reduced the patients' anxiety.

Padilla et al. (1981) compared the distress-reducing effects of four types of film on adult patients undergoing nasogastric intubation for gastric analysis. One film depicted the procedure only, another the procedure plus common distressful sensations (e.g., discomfort, pressure), a third the procedure plus coping skills (e.g., how to relax, increase comfort), and the last, the procedure plus coping skills specifically designed to relieve the distressful sensations. These researchers found that the last procedure was the most effective for decreasing pain and anxiety.

These studies and others of similar parametric focus obviously inform not only the scientist dedicated to the construction of theory, but also the practitioner interested in designing training films. Through scrutiny of the available research literature, the clinician can learn how best to proceed in the selection of optimal models and training stimuli. For instance, based on the aforementioned studies, preparation is likely to be facilitated by repeated exposure to a video depicting a credible model who responds to the stressful situation realistically, yet adaptively.

Other researchers have examined the comparative efficacy of video vis-à-vis attentional control conditions or alternative interventions designed to reduce patient anxiety and to promote patient cooperation during aversive medical procedures. For instance, with inner-city children undergoing prophylaxis and dental examination, Melamed, Hawes, Heiby, and Glick (1975) examined the efficacy of a brief peer-modeling film depicting a child of like racial origin coping well with the prescribed dental procedures. Children who viewed the modeling film exhibited significantly fewer disruptive and fearful behaviors during the dental examination than those assigned to an attentional control group who viewed an unrelated film.

In another study, prior to restorative surgery, Machen and Johnson (1974) exposed children of preschool ages to either a brief peer-modeling videotape showing a child behaving appropriately during dental treatment while receiving encouragement from the dentist or to desensitization therapy, where anxiety-producing stimuli were presented gradually in hierarchical order from least to most fearful until such stimuli became tolerable. Although both groups exhibited less uncooperative behavior following treatment, the video-mediated intervention was by far more cost-effective.

Researchers examining the effects of video on patient cooperation and recovery have also been concerned with the interaction of type and content of video-mediated instruction with patient characteristics. They seek a theoretical framework or patient-by-situation profile that would enable a practitioner to construct and/or select the optimal video for the specific clinical case at hand. For instance, Shipley, Butt, and Horwitz (1979) guided patients who had previously undergone an endoscopy to re-experience that procedure by viewing the same videotaped endoscopy multiple times. Patients were classified according to their coping style as either "repressing" (typically ignoring a stressor) or "sensitizing" (typically seeking information about a stressor). Viewing the videotape reduced anxiety among those classified as "sensitizers" and had either no effect or a detrimental effect on those labeled "repressors." This study not only speaks to the benefits of video, but also suggests the importance of assessing the patient's coping style when selecting the training film. Based on these studies as well as several similar ones, it appears reasonable to conclude that the use of video is frequently associated with positive differential effects. However, as will be highlighted later, refinements to previously employed methodologies are indicated in order to draw more definitive conclusions.

USE OF VIDEO TO PREPARE PATIENTS FOR SURGERY

It goes almost without saying that many, if not most, patients abhor surgery and the associated unwelcomed aspects of hospitalization. Patients hospitalized for surgery often experience a plethora of stressful and/or painful events, including physical examinations, injections, and separation from family (Traughber & Cataldo, 1983). Video has been found to be especially efficacious as a means of preparing patients to undergo painful surgical procedures and thereby to possibly facilitate recovery subsequent to surgery. For instance, an event that many patients experience just prior to surgery is anesthesia induction. Vernon and Bailey (1974) used a brief film showing children responding calmly to mock induction in order to prepare them to undergo minor elective surgery. The children who viewed the film exhibited less anxious behavior while waiting to enter the operating room than children who did not view the film.

As with aversive nonsurgical procedures, several investigators have studied the comparative efficacy of videotape in preparing patients for surgery. Melamed and her co-investigators, for example, have examined the effects of preparing children hospitalized for elective surgery through the use of audiovisual presentations and peer modeling. In one study, Melamed and Siegel (1975) compared the effects of viewing a stress-relevant peer-modeling film versus viewing a non-stress-relevant film. The dependent variables included direct observations of anxiety and behavior problems exhibited by the children, patient self-report (e.g., anxiety, fear), parental report regarding the children's anxiety, and physiological measures (e.g., heart rate, galvanic skin response). Results indicated that children who were exposed to the stress-relevant peer-modeling film exhibited significant decreases in levels of "fear arousal," both pre- and postoperatively, as compared to those children who viewed the other film. Furthermore, the parents of the children assigned to the intervention group reported significantly fewer behavior problems after discharge.

Melamed, Dearborn, and Hermecz (1983) improved on their previous study by also controlling for the children's age and previous hospital experience. Results replicated the effectiveness of using a stress-relevant audiovisual curriculum to prepare children for surgery. Their findings also indicated that the audiovisual program might be contraindicated for young children with a history of prior hospitalizations. The authors hypothesized that such children may remember the previous painful experiences and may, therefore, benefit more from viewing a distracting film.

Faust and Melamed (1984) studied the influence of previous hospitalizations or surgeries, age, and timing of preparation (e.g., the night before surgery versus immediately before surgery) on inpatient versus same-day pediatric surgical patients. Every child assigned to an experimental group viewed a 10-minute film, either stress-relevant in regard to the planned surgical intervention or stress-irrelevant with a focus on fishing. Results revealed an interaction between type of surgery and impact of the video. For instance, physiological arousal among inpatients who viewed the stress-relevant film was significantly lower than that of outpatients. Children with previous surgical experience who viewed the stress-relevant film exhibited significantly greater increases in physiological measures than those children who were naive to the impending surgical procedure, regardless of the timing of the viewing of the film.

In fairness, we should point out that not all investigators have found video to be superior to alternative interventions in every case. For instance, Twardosz, Weddle,

Borden, and Stevens (1986) compared the differential effectiveness of a 20-minute videotape of a preoperative class versus an in vivo presentation of a preoperative class or a nurse's verbal explanation for preparing children scheduled for minor ear, nose, or throat surgery. Children who attended the in vivo class displayed fewer adverse behaviors before and subsequent to surgery than those who viewed the videotape, followed by the children who received the nurse's explanation. The authors posited that the opportunity for personal interaction and active participation may have been responsible for the apparent superiority of the in vivo demonstration.

Leaving less positive results behind while returning to recent developments related to the skillful use of video, some research suggests that clinicians who wish to incorporate film into their ongoing practice may not require an extensive budget in order to do so effectively. On some occasions, the practitioner may be well advised to develop his or her own video-mediated curriculum, rather than relying on commercially available film. For example, Peterson et al. (1984) compared three different modeling programs (puppet model vs. locally made videotape vs. commercial film) in order to assess their relative efficacy in minimizing children's adverse reactions to elective oral surgery. The customized videotape was individually tailored to meet the special needs of the hospital setting in which the study was conducted. Results demonstrated that all three interventions reduced the children's distress with no significant differences noted as a function of the various modes of presentations.

This study is of interest for at least two reasons. First, it yields provisional evidence that a locally produced, relatively low-budget videotape can compensate for lack of technical sophistication as an audiovisual product by being especially synchronous with the idiosyncratic needs of a particular patient, program, or setting. Second, the findings offer some hope to practitioners who want to use video yet lack access to or money for sophisticated, state-of-the-art audiovisual equipment.

Spindler (1984) described the development of an audiovisual patient-education program to prepare orthopedic patients for total hip surgery. Patients who viewed a slide-tape presentation exhibited a high degree of knowledge about their impending surgery. Furthermore, the nursing staff, as well as the participating patients and their families, were reported to be quite satisfied with the slide-tape curriculum and preferred it over a standard verbal presentation, citing the increased consistency across slide-tape presentations, savings in staff training time, and the aesthetic appeal of a multimedia format.

Spindler's descriptive analysis is noteworthy in three respects. First, it draws attention to the potential importance of evaluating the acceptability of various video-mediated curricula, as determined by consumers. Second, it includes a detailed, replicable frame-by-frame description of the content as well as the methodology of the curriculum; such detail is rarely provided in the literature pertaining to the use of video in medical settings. Perhaps one of the reasons video is not used in medical environments as frequently as those experienced with its effectiveness might expect is that procedural detail sufficient to replicate and extend existing curricula is seldom available. Finally, Spindler (1984) precisely calculated the cost of providing her videotaped curriculum and found it to be extremely cost-efficient.

As with preparing patients for nonsurgical interventions, video is often efficacious in assisting patients to prepare for surgery. However, the conditions under which the effects of video can be optimized have not been fully explored and warrant further study.

USE OF VIDEO FOR PATIENT EDUCATION AND SKILL DEVELOPMENT

Another application of video technology has been to educate patients about their medical conditions and/or prescribed regimens. Approximately one-third of the reviewed studies fall into this category. Until recently, methods of patient education have typically included verbal instruction, in vivo demonstrations, and/or printed materials. Of late, videotaped training curricula have been used increasingly for instructional purposes. For instance, Ward, Garlant, Paterson, Bone, and Hicks (1984) were successful in using a brief video program to teach adult insulin-dependent diabetics about diabetes and health maintenance. The authors found that the primary effect of the videotapes was to stimulate group discussions.

Reith et al. (1984) compared a videotaped demonstration with an in vivo demonstration by qualified nurses with a poster presentation combined with written instruction in teaching diabetic patients to perform urine glucose tests. They reported that video instruction was as effective as a live demonstration and was more effective than the poster package. Additionally, 85% of the patients preferred the video medium. The results of this study support the position that video instruction can be as effective as live demonstration in the short term and may be more cost-effective in the long term.

Moldofsky et al. (1979) produced a 55-minute videotaped educational program that provided an overview of asthma and its treatment. This curriculum was designed to teach adults with asthma about lung function, physiological abnormalities, self-care, and drug therapy. Subjects who viewed the videotape scored significantly higher on a quiz than those assigned to the minimal treatment comparison group when assessed immediately after viewing the tape. However, knowledge gains, especially in the practical area of self-care and drug therapy, were not maintained when evaluated 16 months later. Furthermore, there was no measurable benefit in the medical status of either group. This study illustrates the importance of including an analysis of the maintenance and generalization of educative gains as a part of a comprehensive evaluation of video-mediated instruction.

Two similar investigations examined the effectiveness of a 5-minute videocassette program for increasing adherence to a prescribed diet through improving the attitudes and diet-related knowledge of men diagnosed to have primary hypercholesterolemia (Pace et al., 1981, 1983). Results of both studies indicated that although there were no significant changes in attitudes or knowledge, dietary behavior marked by adherence to a breakfast protocol did improve. However, these improvements were not evident 2 months after instruction. Videotaped instruction also has been documented as an effective medium for teaching patients about their prescribed medication regimens. For instance, Burkle and Lucarotti (1984) described a program in which hospitalized patients received closed-circuit videotape instruction and file-card summaries covering medication information (uses, precautions, administrations, and adverse effects).

These studies, among others, generally support the efficacy of video technology as a means of promoting patient education, especially if the aim is to enhance the patient's understanding of disease and prescribed treatments. However, if the goal of patient education is not only to augment knowledge and/or to adjust attitudes, but also and perhaps most importantly to facilitate skill acquisition, then the jury is still out. It is highly probable that advances in video technology will need to be combined with the methodology of competency-based instruction, including behavior rehearsals and performance-based remedial instruction, in order to accomplish skill acquisition.

LITERATURE-BASED CONCLUSIONS

The literature attests to an increasing reliance by health care professionals on video applications, be they commercially or locally produced, to prepare and inform patients regarding their medical conditions and the assessment/treatment procedures necessary to address them. Such video applications often have been shown not only to be effective, but also to be superior in many instances to alternative instructional strategies. Initial development costs notwithstanding, video-mediated curricula carry the advantages of ease of repeated implementation, consistent presentation, enhanced pedagogic impact through multimedia formats, and reduced time and effort required of costly professional trainers. Although video-based instruction will prove to be extremely efficient, at this time there exists a surprising paucity of data measuring the cost-effectiveness of this medium. Of the investigations cited here, less than 10% reported any data on the cost-effectiveness of using video, but only one study indicated negative cost-effectiveness data (Marshall, Rothenberger, & Bunnell, 1984).

FUTURE DIRECTIONS

The literature yields an extensive variety of applications of video recordings for use within hospitals and other medical settings. Many of the investigators reported above used descriptive, correlational, or quasi-experimental methods. Increased use of group comparison and/or single-subject experimental designs would greatly augment the internal and external validity of reported findings (Cook & Campbell, 1979; Kazdin, 1982).

In addition, the overwhelming majority of the cited studies relied on indirect and nonspecific measures of dubious reliability as well as validity, such as paper-and-pencil instruments and anecdotal reports. Methodological rigor could be enhanced through the addition of direct observations of targeted trainee behavior that is functionally relevant to competent performance. For example, when studying the impact of video-mediated instruction on the acquisition of self-injection skills, an evaluation of the effectiveness of the training paradigm can include direct repeated measures of trainee-administered injections with concomitant measures of trainee status (e.g., perceived self-efficacy, anxiety, locus of control) and side effects as well as main effects of the medical intervention itself. As previously mentioned, reported studies also provide insufficient procedural detail to permit systematic replication. Unfortunately, the literature appearing in journals is too inexact to be of much use to practitioners interested in capitalizing on the innovative work of others or in designing their own individually tailored curricula.

Much work is still to be done to firmly identify the conditions under which learning via video is optimal. Although several prior investigators have examined the comparative efficacy of video vis-à-vis alternative instructional methodologies, many unanswered parametric questions remain. For example, in the medical context, when is it beneficial and when is it harmful to expose a patient to the process and sequelae of an aversive medical procedure? Given the untoward and possibly lethal consequences of making an error during the course of a self-administered medical procedure, is it ever defensible to teach by negative as well as by positive video-mediated exemplars? These and other questions require programmatic investigation prior to the emergence and widespread use of video applications in medical circles. Future studies may also profitably include assessments of the long-term effects of training via video. Less than half of the reviewed studies reported follow-up data, and the majority of these collected such data only 1 month after training. Video recordings have been used to educate patients about their chronic diseases and long-term medical regimens. It would be advantageous to evaluate patients' compliance with their prescribed medical regimens over an extended interval in order to identify variables predictive of successful maintenance and outcome. These evaluations may profitably include an analysis of the extent to which competent performance generalizes to extratherapeutic settings such as homes, schools, and places of employment.

The next section discusses how to design a competency-based, video-mediated training curriculum suitable for use in medical settings. The merger of video technology with competency-based instruction derived from the science of an applied behavior analysis promises to open up a multitude of exciting and practical, not to mention effective and efficient, applications that are likely to significantly advance the quality and expediency of modern health care.

DESIGNING A COMPETENCY-BASED VIDEO-MEDIATED TRAINING CURRICULUM

One of the most ubiquitous training approaches is that of didactic instruction. Via film, the instructor often provides background information pertaining to a given disease or disability, offers a rationale for intervention, and extends general guidelines regarding what the target audience (i.e., practitioner or patient) should and should not do. Sometimes this instruction may include a brief demonstration of recommended procedures followed by commentary by previous users as well as experts. The provision of such information may effect desired attitudinal improvements in addition to expanding the viewer's knowledge base. However, skilled completion of the prescribed intervention by the viewer does not necessarily occur as a result. Indeed, there is a growing body of evidence that suggests that didactic instruction, be it film-mediated or not, often fails to produce improvement in trainee performance (e.g., Rickert et al., 1988; Ziarnik & Bernstein, 1982).

One alternative method of instruction frequently proven to be effective is that of competency-based training (O'Dell, Blackwell, Larcen, & Hogan, 1977; Parrish, Egel, & Neef, 1986). In this paradigm, the highest priority is assigned to acquisition and maintenance of skills. The defining characteristics of a competency-based curriculum, especially as they apply to video, are outlined next. Imbedded in a general case description of these characteristics is an illustration drawn from the work of Kohr, Parrish, Neef, Driessen, and Hallanan (1988). Kohr and her colleagues employed a video-mediated curriculum to train parents of handicapped children to communicate effectively with professionals, including physicians.

Specifications and Validation of Target Behaviors

During the initial phase of curriculum development, prior to the production of a training film, experts identify target skills that must be acquired by viewers in order for the latter to conduct recommended procedures proficiently. Such identification typically involves consultation with reputable health care providers and perusal of literature that describes the skillful conduct of indicated preparation, management, and/or remedial routines (Riley, Parrish, & Cataldo, 1989). Quite importantly, the curriculum designers directly observe individuals who can already demonstrate target skills and, based on their observations, develop task analyses of competent performance. Task analyses are step-by-step descriptions of exactly what the learner is to do to be in full compliance with a prescribed procedure. Each step consists of an action that is observable and measurable. Input from leading practitioners of the recommended intervention are sought throughout the development of the task analysis. Provisional analyses are typically submitted to experts with a request that they independently determine whether each identified skill is essential to the masterful performance of a recommended regimen. Revisions to the task analyses are then completed.

For example, during the process of validating a task analysis of requisite communication skills, Kohr et al. (1988) solicited input from an advisory board consisting of both professionals and parents. Each judge listened to one of two audiotapes of conferences involving a parent, a social worker, and a pediatrician. One tape presented a sample of effective parent communication skills, while the other provided a sample of ineffective communication. Tapes were assigned randomly to raters. Each judge was asked to complete a questionnaire about behaviors displayed by the parents that were or were not conducive to effective communication. The experts were also questioned whether they believed parents needed communication-skills training. Based on the raters' input, a review of literature, and direct observation of parent-professional interactions, a preliminary task analysis of skills to be trained was constructed.

The second step of the validation sequence consisted of mailing a copy of the provisional task analysis to the same judges. This time, these experts were asked to rate each item of the task analysis on a five-point Likert scale for its relative importance to effective communication, ranging from "not important" to "important." Judges were also requested to suggest additions to the provisional task analysis. The decision rule for further revision of the task analysis was (a) to exclude items receiving a mean rating below 2.5 and (b) to add any item recommended by more than one judge. Each skill in the resultant final task analysis was then defined operationally.

Such operationalization prior to filming is critical. Prior specification of the content of a training film increases the likelihood that that curriculum will be comprehensive, valid, and presented in a maximally efficient manner.

Composition of Training Videotape

Although not well researched, it appears that the juxtaposition of positive and negative examples of requisite skills facilitates learning. Within a competency-based paradigm, the training film typically demonstrates positive and negative examples of each element of each skill domain within a task analysis. For instance, in the training videotape of parent communication skills composed by Kohr et al. (1988), the order of presentation of examples was: (a) negative example of an entire skill domain, (b) positive example of the same entire skill domain, (c) a breakdown of the same negative and positive examples consisting of one negative example of each component skill followed by a positive example of the same task, and (d) a repetition of a positive example of the entire skill domain. Breaking skill demonstrations into these finite modules may not only facilitate the discrimination of appropriate from inappropriate behaviors, it may also augment the ease with which the trainer can locate demonstrations of especially difficult-to-acquire skills and expose the trainee to such demonstrations repeatedly as needed.

Scripts for Behavior Rehearsals and Assessment Simulations

In the context of competency-based training, students are given repeated opportunities to practice what they view. Practice continues until the student demonstrates mastery. The mastery criterion is usually set at 90% correct task completion, inclusive of all skills judged by the validating panel of experts to be critical to skillful performance. That is, of a 30-step task analysis, each student rehearses until he or she demonstrates mastery of 27 steps, including all critical steps.

Multiple scripts that vary in content along all significant dimensions of a situation (eliciting different skills) are typically devised. For instance, for purposes of behavior rehearsal following videotape modeling, Kohr et al. developed five scripts. Prior to each rehearsal, the parent was given a card containing information about a fictitious child. Each parent was allowed to choose among the five available scripts for each rehearsal, with the restriction that different cards were used for each practice session. In this case, companion scripts for the trainer were also employed.

Scripts for use during assessment simulations are also created. They are designed so the trainee has an opportunity to exhibit each targeted skill in the order skills are presented during the training film. During each simulation, the trainer completes an assessment instrument comprised of a procedural checklist, with space allotted for the trainer to indicate whether each skill component is demonstrated proficiently. Before training commences, the instructor gives each trainee an opportunity to demonstrate competency. Frequently termed "baseline," this assessment determines whether training is required and, if so, where the focus of training should be. Often, trainees demonstrate several skills prior to training, thereby suggesting that selected aspects of the planned curriculum can simply be reviewed or skipped, permitting the instructor more time to train where it is most warranted.

Skills Training

Subsequent to documenting each student's training needs, the instructor specifies objectives and begins to provide systematic training centered on video-mediated instruction and modeling. The trainer usually sits next to the VCR, pacing the trainee's procession through the curriculum. However, with several video-mediated curricula, training is self-administered. Usually, video instruction starts with an overview of training objectives. Target skills are then delineated one skill domain at a time. Often actors portray skills in true-to-life situations, while a narrator highlights critical skills. Sometimes, humorous vignettes are selected in order to better elicit and retain the trainee's attention, while also enhancing the entertainment value and impact of the video. A description of each skill is presented along with a rationale for the importance of that skill. Proper implementation of each skill is described. The training film typically presents examples of multiple situations that call for the practice of target skills. When negative as well as positive examples are shown, the narrator (and sometimes the on-the-scene instructor as well) discusses critical differences between effective and ineffective skills.

At the conclusion of each skill domain, important points are summarized and sometimes represented. Viewing comprehension questions are also posed from time to time. Trainees are then encouraged to ask questions and are given an opportunity to discuss how the general case skills can be applied in specific, relevant situations. Following video-centered instruction and such discussion, a written comprehension quiz is sometimes administered. If students fail to answer any quiz items correctly, remedial training ensues consisting of additional viewing, ancillary instruction, and retaking of failed items.

Next, trainer and student often role play a situation similar to an example shown in the videotape, using a script (such as the one just described) to guide the behavior rehearsal. During and subsequent to the role play, the trainer typically provides performance-based feedback to the student. When appropriate, remedial training consisting of additional video-mediated instruction and modeling, behavioral rehearsal, and feedback is extended to the trainee. Training continues until the student meets or exceeds a predetermined mastery criterion. For example, if the trainee exhibits all critical skills and 90% of the elements of the task analysis across two consecutive simulations, then the student is ready to demonstrate skills in criterion (actual) situations.

Posttraining and Follow-Up Assessment

Direct observations of trainee performance across criterion situations are taken repeatedly. If the student fails to demonstrate mastery during criterion situations, additional remedial training is provided. Training continues until the student demonstrates mastery consistently, say across at least two or three actual opportunities. Follow-up assessments and social validation of training outcomes (Kazdin, 1977; Wolf, 1978) often are completed to determine whether acquired skills are maintained over time and are applied appropriately.

Advantages of Competency-Based, Video-Mediated Training Curricula

Having described the framework for constructing competency-based curricula, it seems apropos to suggest why such curricula should be placed on film. First, because the expense of producing a film of professional quality is often quite high (typical cost estimates are $1,000 per minute of actual film), every effort is made to present curriculum content with maximum efficiency. Thus, videotaped curricula tend to be exceptionally well organized, with content presented in a logical, economical sequence. Carefully composed narration provides all critical information in a concise, readily comprehensible manner.

Second, many students benefit appreciably from exposure to a multimedia presentation. Complex information can be transmitted more clearly through a visual medium. Viewers can witness the simultaneous or near simultaneous occurrence of multiple skills in a sequence and time frame that more closely resembles actual performance. This is in contrast to an oral or written medium through which each discrete skill must be described in a laborious, sequential fashion.

Third, a videotaped curriculum can be distributed with ease, thereby promoting technology transfer and diffusion without concern about the extent to which the integrity of the curriculum is diluted as it is passed from one trainer to the next. Fourth, through some creativity and special effects, otherwise dry material can be presented in a format that captures and maintains the audience's attention and interest, thereby facilitating learning while enhancing the audience's degree of entertainment. Fifth, over the long term, the cost associated with training each student to criterion may actually fall below that incurred through other methods, because video-mediated curricula are often self-sufficient and do not require repeated labor, travel, and material costs.

At this time, we are involved in the filming of several competency-based curricula. For instance, with the help of a professional production crew, Neef, Parrish, and

Holbrook (1988) have recently produced a 50-minute, narrated, color film depicting how to provide in-home care for children with developmental disabilities and/or medical disorders. A curriculum demonstrating the competent performance of 164 child-care skills has been validated socially as well as experimentally prior to being filmed. Child and adult actors, both professional and lay, portray how to manage daily routines such as mealtime, toileting, and bedtime; medical emergencies such as seizures and choking episodes; and how to handle, position, and transfer a physically handicapped child. We are currently evaluating the efficacy of the film as a vehicle for training. In addition, we are comparing the relative efficacy of alternative methods of disseminating the film and promoting its adoption and use by training coordinators of various human service agencies. We hope to find that the training video will be sufficient, in and of itself, to promote skill acquisition. However, we may find that, given the number and complexity of skills to be acquired, viewing of the film will need to be supplemented with corresponding written handouts and repeated behavior rehearsals for skill acquisition to occur.

CHAPTER 12

Producing Video Modeling Tapes

STAN L. O'DELL

OVERVIEW

This chapter presents considerable detail in the creation of a video modeling tape. Dr. O'Dell begins with a summary of modeling principles related to the content and implementation of the video. He then provides a thorough overview of video production beginning with writing the script. The major elements of planning and visual communication are described and illustrated—storyboards, visual transitions, continuity, sequencing, and the viewer's sense of space. Elements of instructional technology are summarized: viewer characteristics, capturing interest, motivation, knowledge or skill acquisition, and retention. A detailed discussion of writing the script follows, including development and format, translating ideas into shots, and making decisions about the use of graphics, studios, and so on. The author then provides production suggestions about working with actors, locations, costs, and directing. Some detailed advice is presented for the recording process itself with respect to both picture and sound and postproduction editing.

P.W.D.

As video technology becomes cheaper and more accessible, many behavioral scientists are interested in producing tapes to train their clients or staff. Today, a nonprofessional with some training and dedication to the task can produce surprisingly good training tapes.

The purpose of this chapter is to provide information about how to produce video modeling tapes. The term *video modeling tapes* refers to a type of production in which behaviors are demonstrated in some manner to the viewer for purposes of actual behavior change, as opposed to didactic training tapes. Because of the considerable power of modeling to produce behavior change, it is in this arena that video technology has special promise. Although the chapter focuses on this type of production, many of the following principles apply to most video productions.

THEORY AND EMPIRICAL FOUNDATIONS

The success of any video modeling intervention depends on the producer's understanding of fundamental principles of learning and modeling. This knowledge includes both the theoretical foundations of the area and the empirical research on specific applications. Modeling principles are discussed elsewhere in this book (see Chapter 4); for a thorough review see Bandura (1977, 1986), Perry and Furukawa (1986), Rosenthal and Bandura (1978), and Thelen, Fry, Fehrenbach, and Frautschi (1979). The research on which these books and articles are based clearly shows that modeling and video modeling, when appropriately applied, can produce a wide range of changes in diverse populations.

DEFINING GOALS AND CONTENT

After deciding that video modeling is an appropriate approach, the first step is to define precisely the goals of the videotape. A distinction should be made between "lofty-admirable" goals and "realistic-obtainable" goals. Thirty minutes of videotape will not change a person's style of life. However, teaching three to five new discrete behaviors and when to exhibit them is probably realistic.

Usually, the goal is to teach the viewer to emit variations of a homogeneous set of behaviors in response to variations of a homogeneous set of stimulus situations. Therefore, it is most important to try to define the "universe" of both the target behaviors and the eliciting stimuli. Then, a sufficient sample from each of these two universes must be selected so that appropriate stimulus and behavior generalizations on the part of the learner will be possible. Finally, enough pairings of the stimuli and behaviors must be made for permanent learning to occur. For example, the goal may be to teach spouses to improve their communication with one another. First, each spouse must be taught to perceive and track the situations in which the new behavior would be appropriate and to demonstrate his or her own appropriate variations. Most training tapes probably fail because they do not have enough representative and varied stimulus-behavior pairings to allow for conceptual comprehension, skill acquisition, and long-term retention.

The delineation of these stimulus situations and targeted responses defines the core content of the videotape. If enough examples of the stimulus situations and range of responses are effectively presented, the production has a good chance of success whether or not it is entertaining or aesthetically pleasing. However, production-enhancement elements such as video quality, entertainment value, and motivating the learner should produce a substantial improvement. Following is a consideration of these factors.

EFFECTIVE PRODUCTION

Visual Media Literacy

It is expected that the sentences in this chapter represent units of thought, that a paragraph indentation signals some change of topic, and that the chapter has a beginning, middle, and end. These are the rules of communication via literature.

With videotape the rules change. Bits of videotape replace words and must be strung together into visual sentences and paragraphs. Videotape productions communicate effectively when the scriptwriter follows the rules of visual literacy. Since most of us grew up with television, we have some intuitive understanding of these rules. Still, the extent of our facility with them and their effective application will make a major difference in the quality of the production.

Once the exact goals and general content of the video production have been determined, they must be translated into a script. Writing scripts requires an understanding of the structure of scenes and rules for continuity across scenes. One of the best sources of information on this topic is the book *The Five C's of Cinematography* (Mascelli, 1965). It covers the critical issues of (a) camera shots—the basic unit of communication; (b) continuity—the principles that allow separate shots to "flow" together and tell a logical story across time; and (c) cutting or editing—the procedures for exactly placing the shots on the finished tape. The book also discusses (d) close-ups and (e) composition. Other useful books include those by Bensinger (1981); Gaskill and Englander (1985); Medoff and Tanquary (1986); Hirschman and Procter (1985); and Speed (1988).

The "word" of visual communication is the *shot*. It is the content of the tape from the time the camera is turned on until it is turned off. However, just as a word can tell only a part of the idea to be expressed, a shot is usually incomplete. Novices often turn the camera on and let a continuous wide-angle shot record the total action from beginning to end. However, experienced videographers know that a series of more selective shots usually can communicate the information more clearly, quickly, and with impact.

A set of such shots that expresses a complete idea or sentence is called a *scene* or *sequence*. For example, imagine that the goal of a production is to demonstrate how two spouses can communicate more effectively. First, one could establish that there is a family, living in a specific place, and that they have problems, such as the father's alcoholism. There are innumerable ways to shoot a series of shots to communicate this idea. The usual rule is that a series of shots goes from general/wide-angle (somewhat like the subject and verb) to specific/close-ups (somewhat like the adjectives and adverbs). General broad shots establish setting and character placement while more detailed shots define specific persons and actions. One could open with a shot of a house, followed by a wide-angle shot of a family in a living room, followed by a head and shoulders shot of each family member reflecting his or her current mood, and a close-up of the empty vodka bottle beside the drunken father. Shots of individuals interspersed with occasional wide shots or shots of two persons at a time might follow as the wife verbally attacks her husband and an argument unfolds. As hostilities intensify, close-ups might show the frustration on the faces of the family and the father's doubled fist as violence seems imminent. This sequence would help define the family and model its ineffective communication for purposes of later comparison. Using the same principles of visual communication, the action could jump forward to the spouses in a therapist's office. A wide shot could show all three in the office, followed by standard medium shots of the therapist modeling better communication intermixed with extreme close-up reaction shots of the spouses as they listen.

Most amateur videographers have watched enough TV and movies to have some natural sense of how to translate ideas into an acceptably clear series of shots. Much can be learned about how shots and camera angles are used to develop sequences of information by turning down the TV sound and just concentrating on how the image changes and why.

It is well worth the time to translate general visual ideas into a storyboard. A *storyboard* is a series of still pictures, usually drawn simply, that shows the basic sequence of images. The fact that the person drawing the storyboard understands it is not enough. It should be shown to others. When they can grasp the basic information only from the series of pictures, the visuals are probably communicating effectively.

In addition to making sure the separate shots contain the needed information, one must also understand the visual rules that govern their transitions. The rules are true for any two shots edited together as well as for the transitions between larger sequences. This dimension of visual communication is called *continuity;* it involves making sure the shots, when edited together, give the illusion of flowing smoothly through time and across events. When continuity rules are broken, it is usually obvious and instantly brands a production as amateurish. Unfortunately, the continuity breaks often do not show up until the editing phase.

The first rule of continuity is that the focal length of the lens (zoom) or the placement of the camera should be changed between every shot. Otherwise, with the background staying exactly the same in consecutive shots but the person having moved, the person will appear to jump across the screen (called a *jump cut*).

Another rule is not to cross the action axis. A viewer has a strong sense of spatial position as he or she watches the screen, as if the characters and scenery are on a stage with a clear sense of right and left. If a person is facing toward the left in one shot and, later, is suddenly facing toward the right, the viewer will have a sense of confusion about where the person is within the scene. Therefore, almost always, the camera shots should be made from the same side of the scene as if the camera is in the audience and cannot move into the middle or to the back of the stage. This imaginary line is called the *action axis*. There are exceptions to this rule (e.g., sometimes when cutting to a close-up), but it should be kept in mind.

Each sequence represents a certain amount of time, although the actual length of the tape sequence may be very different from the time illusion it creates. Hollywood can make a 2-second explosion last 30 seconds on the screen by showing it from different angles, focusing on details, and showing reaction shots of the actors. Viewers allow great latitude in how much time a sequence is supposed to represent and whether the action is flashing forward or backward. However, they quickly notice if the sense of time does not seem to flow logically.

Imagine that the father in the scene previously described is shown in a wide-angle shot with his left hand on the chair arm. If this shot is followed immediately by a closer shot, but his hand is now in his lap, this small change in arm placement will be noticed instantly and will appear to have magically broken the laws of time. Keeping his arm in the same place in both shots or inserting a shot not showing the father in between the two shots will be accepted by the viewer. The same principle holds for all shots that are supposed to represent the realistic passage of time. If the camera cuts from a medium shot of an actor to a closer one of the same actor, the actor had better be in exactly the same position in the close-up or it will look as if he magically moved. This problem is often simplified by making sure a shot begins and ends with some sort of action. If movement is taking place when the shot stops and the entire movement is repeated at the beginning of the next shot, matching the shots during editing is greatly simplified. Notice in commercial productions how often the actor is making some significant movement at the beginning and end of the shot. This method of maintaining continuity is called *cutting on the action*. It is one of the most difficult aspects of video production. If two or three cameras can shoot the different angles simultaneously, as in studio productions, the action and continuity will match perfectly.

Modeling tapes may also have sequences that move across time or place. If so, appropriate transitional shots will make it clear to the viewer how these have changed. For instance, if the videotape in the previous example uses a second family in the production, a shot of another house might signal the movement in time and place. Also, the action with the first family might jump forward from the family argument to the father and mother in a therapy session. Transitional shots that fade out the last shot in the living room to a black screen and fade in the first shot in the therapist's office from a black screen could represent the change in time and place. However, viewers will accept an edit that jumps time forward without such a transitional device as long as there is a clear change in time or setting in the second shot.

There are other devices that can assist in making the production a logical whole. For example, the sequences may be interspersed with an on-camera narrator or a voice-over may introduce each segment while the visual action continues. Such narration can keep the viewers straight when they otherwise might not understand the changes in visuals.

Of course, application of other principles of visual literacy will assist in successful communication. An effective script carefully applies visual literacy principles to ensure the production communicates effectively.

Instructional Technology

The fact that a video modeling production must be more than entertaining requires another type of knowledge. The field of instructional technology focuses on the principles that make any educational experience, including a media production, an effective one. Actually, the area of modeling can be conceptualized as a subset of this field. This topic also has an extensive literature (e.g., Heinich, Molenda, & Russell, 1982). While only basic ideas can be covered here, mentioning some main principles will ensure that they are dealt with in writing the script. The following issues will be briefly covered: viewer characteristics, eliciting attention, motivation, knowledge/skill acquisition, memory, and assessing outcome.

Know the intended audience. College-educated people use ideas, vocabulary, and examples that fail to produce identification and comprehension by other people.

Knowledge of and experience in communicating effectively with the types of people who will be using the videotape is invaluable. A screening of a pilot production during which persons similar to the intended audience offer reactions and show what they have learned is usually well worth the time and expense.

Capture interest quickly. In the previous example, the dramatic scene of the spouses yelling at each other could be used as an introduction, while the narrator explains that this presentation will deal with this type of communication problem. Once attention is gained, the task is to keep it. Generally, it is difficult to hold attention closely for more than about 20 minutes. Rarely should training tapes be made that last longer than 30 minutes. Many techniques can help maintain attention: frequent changes of the visual image, tight editing and rapid pacing of the material, dramatic material, narration with enthusiasm, avoiding the "talking head" where a person talks to the camera, appropriate humor, surprise elements, an unfolding "story" to build curiosity, attractive actors, simple forceful dialogue, material and/or music that elicits an emotional response, and so forth.

Consider viewers' motivations. Viewers must identify with the problems and conflicts presented in the examples and develop a sense of hope that they, too, can solve similar problems of their own. Again, showing a sample set of problems, rather than just one example, is important. Varying the types, ages, races, and so forth of actors can help. Of special impact are real pre- and postscenes that show the extent of change. Part of the production needs to focus clearly on the tangible payoffs of learning the material in the videotape.

Present for knowledge acquisition. Even with an attentive and motivated viewer, the information must be presented in a manner that will produce knowledge and skill acquisition. Usually, a conceptual overview and outline of the material is presented early in the production, possibly with explicit behavioral objectives. Text on the screen and/or graphic material may help keep the information organized and important points emphasized. If time allows, using a "slider" example in which the actor with the problem feels overwhelmed at first, has some failures, then gradually overcomes the problem may enhance viewer feelings of self-efficacy (Bandura, 1986). Testimonials or having the narrator in the tape express confidence in the viewer's ability (e.g., Mr. Rogers' "Can you say kleptomaniac? Sure you can!") may also help. As previously stated, the core teaching device should provide clear examples of the target skills and situations for use so that the viewer understands the general principles.

Repeat points for retention. Name the ideas just mentioned for getting and holding viewer attention. It is no problem to refer back and refresh the memory with a written page. However, with a videotape the viewer may have only one exposure. Therefore, devices to assist retention are especially important. The general rules to solve this problem are repeat, repeat, repeat without boring the viewer, and try not to teach too much. Material that elicits an emotional response is easier to remember than dry didactic material. Retention may also be helped by these factors: cuing important points; linking ideas to their practical consequences; multimodal presentations that combine visual, aural, and written media; mnemonic devices; numbering of main points; asking viewers to make covert or overt responses during the viewing; summaries; take-home materials; and so forth.

Assess outcome. All these ideas may assist the viewer's learning of the material. However, the best way to determine impact is to pilot test and directly assess the viewers.

Script Writing

With clear goals about content, a thorough knowledge of modeling principles, a general understanding of media literacy, familiarity with instructional technology, and a storyboard, it is time to translate these elements into a specific production script. Although many decisions will have to be made during production, it is almost impossible to have too detailed a script from which to work.

The script is primarily a highly detailed storyboard; many basic decisions about the nature of the production will have been made when the storyboard was developed. As an integral part of the development of the storyboard and script, many decisions will have to be made about the production. General decisions about production include the overall format and length. The format could range from the most basic presentation of the modeling scenes without any transitional or narrative devices (leaving these up to the therapist who will show the tape) to a fully developed dramatic presentation much like a movie or soap opera. Most productions will at least include an introduction, narration, and a summary/closing segment.

The unit of the script is the shot, or what is on a segment of tape from the time the camera is turned on and off. The final script should include everything that will be on the final videotape including the 30 seconds of blank leader at the beginning of the tape, color bars, countdown, fade-in to the title, music, narration, all production shots, transitions between segments, graphics, credits, and so forth. The script is an exact reproduction of the videotape in written form.

Usually a video script is compiled using a series of one-page forms, with one form for each shot. At the top of the form will be general information about the shot such as shot number, running length, purpose, setting, actors required, props needed, type of shot (close-up, pan, etc.), continuity issues, and room for some general notes. The lower part of the form will be divided horizontally into two columns, one labeled "video" and one labeled "audio." It is a good idea to have a blank TV-shaped screen area at the top of the video section. A simple drawing, like the corresponding picture from the storyboard, can be made in this space to remind the camera operator about the type of shot and composition. In the video section is detailed all the needed information to record the visual track; in the audio section is written the directions for the audio track, including dialogue, music, and so forth. Usually, the information in both columns runs parallel down the page in matching sequence. Special notes are made regarding exactly how the shot begins and ends. A new page is begun for each shot, including still pictures, graphics, written text, credits, and so on.

In the example being used, imagine that one of the purposes of the videotape is to model how spouses of alcoholics can communicate more effectively by using "I messages." The script for one of the modeling segments showing the mother confronting her husband by using this approach might look like the example shown in Figures 12.1 through 12.4. Notice in the figures the detail in the notes, including issues related to continuity between some of the shots.

There are many other decisions to be made as general ideas are translated into specific shots. When there is dialogue between two or more people, will both/all be shown together or each one separately as he or she speaks? The latter, or some mixture of the two, is much more difficult and expensive, but creates more of a sense of reality and intimacy. How many close-ups and reaction shots should there be? How can camera angles and composition be varied to enhance the message? When the narrator is talking while the scene is running, how can this be coordinated so that nothing too important is happening on the visual track that would detract from the message? Will special elements be used such as graphics or text-on-screen information, or camera effects such as zooms, pans, and fades? Will there be one camera or two? Should one shoot only in a studio or go on location? What actors are realistically available? Will there be music or sound effects? Shooting a first videotape following a script will teach a lot about how to write a better script next time. It is easy while working on the script to write a segment about a crying child, include dramatic fast-paced dialogue with many edits, or put three elephants in the scene. When it comes time to make the magic happen, the producer will often wish that he or she had been more conservative.

Some other dos and don'ts may help in writing the script. Because a changing image helps hold attention, having many short varied shots and short narrations is an objective. The realism of the modeling examples is very important. Vary the pace of the production by having some portions with a few long shots and then, with more action, speed up the pace with shorter shots. Finally, viewers should not be able to guess what will happen next. A predictable production is boring. Once the script is ready, there are preparations to make for the actual shooting.

Equipment

Equipment scares some people. Others love to master the buttons and dials. Fortunately, modern equipment has so many automatic features that even a novice usually can produce works of acceptable technical quality. (See Chapter 1 for basic equipment descriptions and choices.) However, before the script is written, the capabilities of the equipment to be worked with and compatibility with editing equipment must be known. To be sure of having the needed equipment, an expert can be asked to read the script to consider equipment needs.

Tips for Working with Actors

If funds for professional actors are not available, there are several other ways of obtaining "talent." Many aspiring actors will work for little or nothing on a not-for-profit endeavor for the sake of a credit. Even some professionals will donate time. Many people who were once involved in the stage or film might be talked into

SHOT #: ___83___   RUN TIME: ___5 sec___   PAGE #: ___1___

PURPOSE: ___establish setting; wife entering scene___

SETTING: ___husband's home office___

ACTORS: ___husband; wife___

PROPS: ___office materials on desk; 1/3-full bottle of vodka___

TYPE SHOT: wide

NOTES: ___

VIDEO	AUDIO
(Continuity with previous shot?)	(none, other than background sounds)
(none, fade in from black)	

(begins with husband only in scene) (wife enters scene from left, moving briskly, bottle clearly in right hand; husband looks up as she enters; she stops several feet away with firm stance, raises bottle for emphasis)

(Continuity with following shot?)

(ends with raising bottle close to face)

Figure 12.1. A sample video script with detailed notes for setting up the shot; this is shot #83.

SHOT #: _____84_____   RUN TIME: _7 sec_   PAGE #: _____1_____

PURPOSE: show wife's disappointment at finding more hidden liquor

SETTING: husband's home office

ACTORS: wife

PROPS: 1/3-full bottle of vodka

TYPE SHOT: close-up—head and shoulders

NOTES:

VIDEO	AUDIO
(Continuity with previous shot?)	(at completion of raising the bottle)
(begins with raising bottle close to face) 	Wife: "I found this... (pause) You promised!"
(Continuity with following shot?)	
N/A	

Figure 12.2. Shot #84 of the sample video script.

SHOT #:____85____   RUN TIME:__2 sec__   PAGE #:____1____

PURPOSE:__show husband's embarrassment__

SETTING:__husbands's home office__

ACTORS:__husband__

PROPS:__N/A__

TYPE SHOT:_close-up_

NOTES:____video only could be edited in during shot 86 to pro-

vide reaction shot to wife's statements as she speaks (option #2)

VIDEO	AUDIO
(Continuity with previous shot?)	Option 1: (none, other than background sounds)
N/A	
	Option 2: (voice-over of wife speaking during scene 86)
(husband drops eyes from wife to floor—embarrassed)	
(Continuity with following shot?)	
N/A	

Figure 12.3. Shot #85 of the sample video script.

SHOT #: __86__   RUN TIME: __20 sec__   PAGE #: __1__

PURPOSE: _modeling of "I-messages"_____

SETTING: _husband's office_____

ACTORS: _wife_____

PROPS: _N/A_____

TYPE SHOT: _extreme close-up_____

NOTES: _____

VIDEO:	AUDIO:
(Continuity with previous shot?) N/A 	WIFE: (with strained, frustrated, but calm voice...) "I love you. I want to help, but... (pause) I get so angry when you make promises and then break them. (sigh) I feel so helpless!"
(Continuity with following shot?)	

Figure 12.4. Shot #86 of the sample video script.

helping. Unless the competence of the actors is known, the equivalent of screen tests should be held to weed out the unacceptable actors, uncooperative children, and so forth. Many people can do a good job playing "themselves" even if they cannot take on the persona of another character. Therefore, typecasting from among friends to play roles of father, child, stressed boss, and so on may be possible. Also, when writing the script, keep the shots brief, the dialogue basic, and the direction simple; this will make acting easier.

Rehearse. Rehearse. Rehearse. This is especially true for children and for complex scenes or scenes requiring convincing emotional expression. With the right kind of training using slow shaping and rewards, children often can perform even better than adults. With children, lots of small trinkets and coins with which to reward them can keep their enthusiasm high. Determine clothing, makeup, and hairstyles ahead of time. Make rehearsal a desensitization session and include cameras, lights, and microphones.

If there is only a little money for talent, consider paying a professional narrator. If the narrator sounds like a pro, viewers will accept much more amateurism in the examples without being annoyed. Remember the extras. When appropriate, a few extras in the background can make a scene much more convincing. Usually, some of the crew can fill in here, too.

Locations

The two primary types of sites for productions are in the studio and on location. On location can mean either outside or inside. Each of these settings can require quite different recording methods. The lack of control on location, especially outside, can make shooting very demanding. The light changes. Weather changes. Jets fly over. People intrude. Only the director can decide if the outdoor shot is worth the trouble. Recording indoors allows more control but there still may be significant problems. It is often difficult to get the camera far enough back from the action. Ceilings may be too low for proper lighting or microphone placement. Sound has a different quality in every type of room. Any location should be carefully preselected to be sure the required shots are possible.

There is a reason that movie companies spend millions on huge soundproof sound stages: They provide control. The TV studio is a smaller, more reasonably priced version. It will contain all the needed lighting, sound equipment, multiple cameras, monitors, and soundproofing that make shooting much easier. This location will be the first choice, except that it is difficult to set up many different realistic interiors in a studio. Maximum realism in the production will probably require shooting on location.

Cost Estimation

Estimate the most it could possibly cost and then triple it. It is easy to spend a thousand dollars for each minute of finished videotape.

There is no way to estimate costs without knowing what a specific script calls for.

If equipment can be borrowed, friends do the acting, and the production is kept simple, costs may be as low as a few hundred dollars. The one area in which cost cutting is difficult is the editing phase, because it requires special machinery and expertise. Cost estimation is another place for expert consultation.

Direction

A director has many difficult and exciting jobs. The primary one is to see that the script is turned into the type of individual shots that an editor can piece together effectively.

If possible, responsibilities are delegated to helpers who will cover the various facets of preparation and production such as finding locations, obtaining props, and ensuring actors are ready. The director has to decide what and when to shoot, not necessarily in the sequence that will appear in the final product. Shots are set up in the most cost-effective sequence. The classic example is a dialogue between two lovers where all the shots of the actor are done, then the actress comes in and all her shots are made. Later, they are intermixed in editing to appear to be an interchange between the two. With only one camera it may be easier to shoot all close-ups and reaction shots of one actor at a time.

Perhaps the most important direction job is to ensure that the actors are prepared and motivated. Much time is spent by the actors and crew just waiting. Some scenes may have to be redone many times. This is taxing for everyone, so it is worth the effort to do everything within reason to keep up the morale of the people involved. Praise something at the end of every shot, even if there were problems with it.

Setting Up the Shot

Once the key grip and best boy have all the equipment brought in and set up in approximately the right places, the first step in setting up a shot is to "block" it—that is, getting the actors and props in place and running through the movement and dialogue for practice. When actors have to move to exact places, pieces of tape may be put down as markers. Backgrounds, often neglected, can be carefully assessed and set up as needed.

Although the camera, lighting, and sound must be set up simultaneously, these factors will be discussed separately. The camera angle is set up, on a tripod, according to the general video directions in the script. Generally, novices do not get in close enough. For an average close-up of a person speaking, the head and shoulders will fill the frame, and the camera is at least 5 feet away to avoid distortion. Also, novices often set the camera too high. The camera should generally be at the actor's eye level or slightly below. So, if the actor is sitting, the tripod is dropped accordingly. Another common error is not having the camera perfectly level.

Composition of the picture must be considered. Rarely should people be directly centered on the screen or placed with their body directly facing the camera. Usually the actors should be shot right or left of center and looking somewhat toward the middle, unless they are narrating and looking directly into the camera. Some space should show above their heads, but the middle of their faces should be above the center line of the screen. Two people in the same picture who are talking to each other usually should stand or sit close together. This will look strange in reality but good on the screen. Doing 20 quick drawings of composition from scenes of TV shows will demonstrate the basic idea of how professionals place the "masses" (people or forms) in the screen area to keep them balanced but rarely symmetrical. This helps keep the visuals interesting and adheres to the viewer's ingrained rules for picture framing. Certain types of shots and compositions can greatly affect the aesthetic and emotional quality of the production. For example, an emotional reaction is almost always shown with a close-up, and an important person is shot from below eye level.

Generally, the camera should be kept rock still with no zooming or panning. It is fine to track the action, but usually a fluid-head tripod is necessary to turn the camera smoothly. If the shot needs to be closer, the shot should be changed to a close-up rather than using the zoom on the lens. Accurate focus especially with telephoto shots is critical, and as people move, it may be difficult to keep them in focus. Fortunately, with video one can immediately see errors and correct them.

As the exact camera angle is established, the lighting will have to be worked out simultaneously. Natural room light is rarely bright enough. As a minimum, one good light flooding the area to be shot is needed, preferably placed high and off to one side of the camera. A better minimum lighting setup includes one main bright light off to the side of the camera and pointed so that it illuminates the front planes of the main actor's face, one dimmer fill-light placed near the camera to reduce the shadows, and one back-light that is high and behind the main actor to illuminate his or her hair and shoulders. Ideally, each person is illuminated with a separate set of lights. The background also has special lighting to keep it from being too dark and to help minimize shadows on the background. Good lighting can have a substantial effect on the quality and mood of the shot. But most viewers will accept simple lighting as long as there is enough of it on the faces of the actors.

Audio

Even if they are bothered by it, viewers will usually accept marginal image quality, poor lighting, or amateurish acting. However, they will not tolerate poor sound quality. They must be able to hear the actors clearly.

The primary solution is to cut out all unwanted background noise and put the microphone within about 2 feet of the actor. In most shots, getting the microphone close can be accomplished with any type of boom or long pole that allows the microphone to be placed above the actor and pointed toward his or her head. In some circumstances, specialized microphones may be necessary. It is best to monitor the sound with headphones as the scene is shot. If one is not experienced in controlling sound volume, an automatic device can be relied on. However, the best sound is accomplished by manual control.

The continuity of sound is as important as the continuity of visual shots. If scenes shot with different microphones or in different rooms are juxtaposed, the sound quality may change noticeably. Cameras with an automatic gain control on the audio will, when no one is speaking, pick up ambient sound and increase its volume. If one shot ends with a long pause and the next shot does not have the background sound at the same level, the sense of sound continuity will seem violated. Viewers will probably accept only minor variations.

Shooting the Shot

When all of the above is in order, it is finally time to shout "action." *Every* shot begins with a "slate" that includes the shot and take numbers. In the rush of production it is easy to forget to use the slate or to change the numbers—sure to be maddening during the editing phase.

Following the taping of the slate numbers there should be a pause of at least a few seconds before the action begins. Also, at the end of the shot the camera should continue to run for several seconds. The actors should learn not to look at the camera or move out of the shot when they finish. Instead, they should learn to finish the last line in the shot and hold still or stay in character while the camera runs. Ideally, there should be a checklist of what the shot is supposed to accomplish that the director can check before he or she sets up for the next shot.

Postproduction

Many editing decisions are made as an integral part of the script, primarily the sequencing of shots. Still, nothing works out exactly as planned, so some rearrangement may be necessary. As mentioned earlier, enough material must be shot so that ineffective shots or segments can be left out altogether.

Once all shots, including still shots, graphics, and credits, are on tape, the first editing step is to determine which of the takes from each shot was the best and to record that shot and take number. Then each shot/take is played in the final sequence in which it will appear and careful notes are made about how each shot will be used. It will help to develop an editing script using a 4 × 6 inch card for each separate shot. On this card will be written the shot and take number, exact point the edited shot is to begin, exact running time, and exact point to end. Also, where on each of the tapes the shot can be found is noted, along with other information. These cards will be extremely helpful while editing.

Editing

Editing is not just copying shot after shot. There is, for example, the timing and pacing of the edits. As an initial scene is presented the viewer expects a few moments to become visually oriented before anyone speaks. The viewer expects a certain amount of time when locations within the production change. Some action is best depicted by a lot of short, closely edited shots, and others need slow pacing. These creative dimensions are probably best learned from experience.

With every shot and edit predetermined, the tapes and editing script can be taken to the video editor. Editing machines are becoming simpler, but a professional is usually needed to make the edits as directed. A videotape, unlike a film, must be made by putting down sequentially the first shot, second, third, and so on. If there is any error, the process must be started over from a point before the error.

There are few things more creatively exciting than finishing the editing and running the production from beginning to end for the first time. All the meaningless pieces have been magically transformed into a new whole. Almost as much fun is the traditional cast party at which all those who helped are invited to view the final production and celebrate their achievement!

ASSESSMENT

Although video modeling tapes should be made according to good production principles, just following them does not ensure an effective product. The ability of the tape to produce real behavior change in the intended audience must be assessed empirically. Any of the methods of assessing behavior change might apply, depending on the type and purposes of the production. McMahon and Forehand (1982) have outlined principles for assessing parent training materials, although the suggestions are broadly applicable to video modeling tapes.

LEGAL AND ETHICAL ISSUES

Two legal or ethical issues may be of particular relevance. Model releases from the persons in the production will be needed. Also, most producers will probably want to copyright the videotape. This is a fairly easy and inexpensive process. Copyright guidelines are available from the Copyright Office, Library of Congress, Washington, DC 20559.

CONCLUSION

Like raising children, making videotapes is the best and worst of things. It is usually incredibly frustrating but, sometimes, when things go right, truly exhilarating. Hopefully, the seeming complexity of the task will not be too daunting. If one is willing to start with one or two short tapes, an immense amount can be learned quickly and subsequent productions can be significantly improved. The creative combination of modeling principles, visual literacy, instructional technology, effective production, and assessment of behavior change should lead to a successful product.

CHAPTER 13

Trigger Tapes and Training

SIMON J. BIGGS

OVERVIEW

The term trigger tapes (*or* triggers) *has been coined to refer to brief videos that provoke discussions as the basis for group learning experiences. Dr. Biggs presents promising examples of the systematic development and application of triggers for professional development in circumstances such as social work services for families at risk for child abuse. Some explanation of terminology and the evolution of trigger methodology from social skills training are presented. Triggers are characterized as a type of social interaction, allowing some inferences to be drawn concerning the production and use of the medium. (The medium draws out more involvement than passive observation or commentating.) Functions of triggers are elucidated, distinct from modeling films. The author describes general and specific principles for producing trigger vignettes including content, design, scripting, and recording considerations. Details are given on such aspects as the composition of project teams and curriculum elements. The trigger video called* Acceptable Risk, *the primary illustration throughout the chapter, contains 63 carefully designed vignettes for in-service training of providers and supervisors in social services. Dr. Biggs then elaborates on (with specific illustrations) the use of trigger tapes: setting up prior to viewing, viewing and training facilitation, and using multiple triggers.*

P.W.D.

WHAT ARE TRIGGER VIDEOTAPES?

Trigger videotapes (or triggers) present a problem, dilemma, or situation in a vignette that encapsulates an issue but does not resolve it. The main application of triggers has been in the training of caring professionals. A brief example best illustrates the use of triggers for those who may not be familiar with this video method. The following script comes from a series of triggers designed to explore questions about the supervision of British social workers working on child abuse cases (Ash, Biggs, & Mayhew, 1987). The tape shows an Afro-Caribbean female social worker sitting at a desk, writing.

> She looks at the viewer and says, "I think things were much better when I last visited, but the husband was asleep, so I didn't insist on seeing the baby. Do you think I should have?" The trigger finishes with the social worker looking directly at the camera.

Triggers are short self-contained scenes (30 to 45 seconds long) that are addressed directly to the viewer and are problem-centered. They aim to provoke a response that will make attitudes explicit, to bring feeling responses into the open, and to provide an opportunity for sharing those responses with others. The trainer can reframe an often routine situation so that participants are prompted to construct appropriate coping strategies for the situation they find themselves in. Trigger users are provided with a variety of vignettes and may choose the most appropriate scene for the context in which they are working. Once scenes have been selected, they are shown individually as each scene forms the basis for a training session.

The impact triggers can have comes from the relatively context-free nature of the scenes and their element of ambiguity. It is not clear what action the viewers should take, although it is clear that the person on tape expects a certain response. The direct and personal delivery of the video material invites viewers to behave as if they are in the situation being portrayed. They are thus given an active role in a dilemma that needs behavioral resolution.

This chapter examines the value of trigger videos in training that addresses social behavior and attitude change. Triggers may be added to existing methods to enhance behavioral change. The special quality that triggers can bring to training depends in part on how they are produced and on the training environment itself; both of these factors are examined in later sections of this chapter.

SOCIAL SKILLS TRAINING AND TRIGGER VIDEOS

Questions about motivation and attitude change have become a major problem for social skills training (SST). Spence and Shepherd (1983) proposed that behavioral performance and continued role performance are separate problems, each requiring a different treatment approach. The solution to the pattern of transferring skills to day-to-day life, they stated, "is not likely to be forthcoming until we accept cognitive and social role difficulties as separate problems in their own right, not as problems of generalization from behavior" (p. 12).

Trower and Kiely (1983) have argued that direct attempts to modify cognitions should be made. This perspective has been given impetus by cognitive-behavior therapists (Beck, Rush, Shaw, & Emery, 1979; Ellis, 1977; Meichenbaum, 1975) while others (Cooper, Biggs, & Bender, 1983) have extended the use of group work in social skills training to include techniques from drama therapy.

As questions about social role and motivation are central to trigger use in training, their relationship to social skills training would seem worthy of further investigation. Unfortunately, the literature on trigger video methodology and effectiveness is disappointingly sparse. Although searches of the MARIS (1988) and HELPIS (1988) databases for video material available in the United Kingdom reveal a significant increase in the number of trigger formats being used since 1983, a computer search of psychological abstracts for the same period revealed no mention of this approach. A more intensive, manual search of references to video in psychotherapy, group therapy, and behavioral psychology also yielded nothing regarding trigger formats. Education technologists have shown a greater interest in this than psychologists and social workers. The earliest reference in that literature (Boud & Pearson, 1979) refers to the use of trigger films. These writers discussed the value of triggers as a means of confounding inappropriate intellectualization and idealization of actual performances—observations that have recently been elaborated on by Weil and Schofield (1986). Both Powell (1977), who looked at the development of teaching skills, and Huczynski (1982), who examined management skills, commented on trigger methodology as instrumental in the development of both cognitive understanding and emotional insight into personal attitudes.

Weil and Schofield (1986) suggested a six-stage model for trigger use. First, trainees experience the trigger scene, followed by process-centered observation, reflection, listening, and discussion. A third stage includes reference to relevant theory, research, and practice issues; stage four employs role play for skill development, integrated with previous learning (stage five) and evaluated in the light of future planning (stage six).

However, these accounts describe characteristics of trigger video material in common with video methodologies such as video feedback (Biggs, 1980) and interpersonal process recall (Kagan, 1975). Distinguishing qualities of trigger tapes have not been examined in an empirically or theoretically satisfying manner. An attempt will be made to address these issues while examining the value of trigger tapes as a means of resolving motivational problems in training. Related techniques using video vignettes are described in Chapter 5 of this book.

TERMINOLOGY

To discuss watching video involves the consideration of a potentially confusing variety of viewpoints. In this chapter, *viewing* is used to describe only the watching of taped training material. *Participant* is used to refer to a person who takes part in a trigger-based training session. *Observers* are people who watch other persons and are not expected to interact with the material on tape. Watching TV would thus be called *observing*. Finally, *character* refers to a role within a videotaped vignette.

TRIGGERS AS TRAINING MATERIAL

Triggers and Social Interaction

The central distinguishing feature of trigger production is that the person watching is addressed directly by the material. Schutz (1967) proposed that gaining direct experience of another person depends on the perceiver having a community of space and of time with whomever is under scrutiny. The immediacy of such an experience would depend first on concreteness in terms of perceptual detail, and second on whether an observer can convert his or her role into that of a participant. Of course, with triggers, the person is not directly available except on tape, and it would be difficult to presume that the character on tape and the viewer have been mutually constructing the meaning of the social situation. However, perceptual detail is available and, by turning to those observing the tape and asking them a question, a character invites viewers to join in an illusion that something is being watched at the time that it actually is happening.

How far does this illusion draw the viewer into a participant role? Recent developments in social psychology (Mugny & Perez, 1988) have indicated that this mutual construction of social reality is only part of the information available to a participant in social interaction. One does not merely respond to a previously unmet person on the basis of his or her immediate characteristics, but also to complex associations with the groups the person is assumed to belong to and one's attitude to those groups. The point that social judgments do not depend entirely on direct experience of the other as an individual is particularly important for the illusion of interaction that triggers attempt to provide. Following are implications for the development and use of trigger videos:

1. The video producer needs to use techniques that facilitate the illusion of interaction and not use techniques that reinforce the feeling that one is an observer of filmed material.
2. The trainer needs to prepare participants with general information about the context of the vignette on tape in order to facilitate identification with the events portrayed.
3. The participant has to respond on the basis of a tremendous amount of assumed information about the general characteristics of the action taking place. There is thus a shift away from individual experience and what people learn about themselves toward the perception of others and the action one takes as a result.
4. The focal point for training moves toward the consequences of watching a vignette. The trainer should concentrate to a greater extent on attitudes evoked and the responses of the viewer/participant and to a lesser extent on particular insight from the content of the tape alone.

Triggers contrast with video self-confrontation and modeling tapes that are intended to provoke a close examination of the content of material (Who did what? Who responded? In what manner?—and so on). With most video methods, the tape content is a reference point for behavioral learning and change; with trigger tapes, the material is a catalyst that provokes certain responses that are themselves the primary focus of therapeutic change and subsequent development.

Therefore, the function of the trigger is:

1. To evoke feelings about a situation familiar to those watching, but with which

they have lost touch or may not be aware of now. For example, vignettes that portray difficult situations faced by care staff when working in residential settings with adolescents may be shown to decision makers and managers who do not work in that setting any more (Weil & Scofield, 1985).

2. To give participants insight into their response to challenging situations that they have not yet experienced. For example, trainee social workers may be shown vignettes about decision making in child abuse cases, which, in view of the gravity of such cases, they would be unable to experience directly until they were fully qualified (Ash, Biggs, & Mayhew, 1987).

3. To show participants material from familiar, everyday situations, thus providing (on video) a better opportunity for reflection and for sharing responses than would be possible if the event were actually taking place. An example would be vignettes giving evidence of institutional racism (Weil, Charles, & King, 1985).

Triggers and Modeling Tapes

Differences between trigger and modeling methodology have implications for the production of taped material and its subsequent use in training programs. Whereas modeling material shows instances of appropriate behavior, triggers often portray difficult situations in which inappropriate behavior is taking place. An example from triggers on antiracism titled *Through a Hundred Pairs of Eyes* succinctly illustrates this problem. In this vignette, management personnel are discussing job applicants.

> "Bartych. . . . I am afraid I cannot pronounce this one! (knowing laugh, with glance around table and at camera) but let me be honest. . . . a black person would never be accepted, so we might just as well cross this one off the list, don't you think?" (She looks around the table for agreement.)

Clearly, in this example the learning process would not include identifying with the actors, in the sense of basing one's behavior on theirs. By so doing, participants would be learning an inappropriate behavior while failing to reframe the situation. The aim when using this tape and triggers in general is to critically assess the performance and the viewer's response to it. It is important that the trigger is not so different from everyday situations that participants fail to identify with the dilemma that is presented. The exercise should promote recognition of the problem but not subsequently encourage participants to copy or to act out the scene.

TRIGGER PRODUCTION

Triggers and Televisual Material

In 1983, I described the use of video materials as a socially constructed phenomenon (Biggs, 1983). I made a comparison between material viewed for psychological or training reasons and what one normally sees on TV. Television acting is a highly stylized presentation of information with its own rules and conventional behavior. Further, the relationship between the viewer and the trainer contains implicit assumptions about power and authority that skews the resulting definition of "watching video." The first of these factors has a bearing on the production of triggers; the second is considered later in relation to trigger use.

Viewers have established expectations about what is good, believable televisual material (Gunter, 1987). These expectations may be learned at a very early age (Noble, 1975). To be believed, the trigger must conform to the norms associated with the medium of communication being used, as it will inevitably be compared with other products on TV. Lovell (1980) argued that "the critics' or the viewers' naive complaint that such and such is not realistic frequently masks a complaint that these rules have been broken" (p. 80).

So, to be believable, to come across "naturally" from the screen, the trigger may need to be "unnatural" with respect to everyday behavior, as the rules governing the two are not necessarily the same (Biggs, 1983; Gunter, 1987). This factor has practical implications for trigger production:

1. It implies the employment of professional actors whose use of voice (more lively and attention-getting, with pace and emphasis) and nonverbal manner-isms (fewer, more controlled) differ from those of nonactors.
2. Triggers are unlike research videos, where behavioral evidence is the primary goal and cutaways or head shots may lose valuable visual information (Summerfield, 1983); with some reservations, the filming of trigger material may use head and shoulder shots, parts of the body, or refer to persons and events not fully on screen.

However, the trigger also needs to build a bridge between the illusion of reality constructed according to the rules of televiewing and the "as-if" reality participants adopt when they are directly addressed by the actors on tape.

On TV we often see talking heads who address us by imparting information. A trigger is asking us a question both verbally, "what do you think?" and nonverbally, turning from the ongoing action toward the viewer, engaging in eye contact, and so on. It therefore breaks with the idea that the viewer is a passive information receiver, divorced from the material being watched. Once addressed, the viewer has to consider the question personally, not just what he or she thinks about an issue, but also what he or she would do in that situation. Such triggers invite those watching to participate in the social construction of events following those shown on tape.

Specific Techniques in Trigger Production

The conventions of televisual production rely on changes in viewpoint and scene to keep the viewer interested as the narrative is played out. Triggers are very short. Brevity is, in part, a means of achieving impact so that the viewer's emotional response is not lost, and viewing is not allowed to become a purely intellectual and externalized phenomenon. However, brevity also means that the illusion of watching a real event does not require the changes in scene and viewpoint that maintain suspension of belief during viewing of everyday televised material.

The trigger material needs to be of a quality that is not jarring to participants used to polished televisual production. However, when special effects such as freeze-frame or zoom are used they can make the viewer break with the illusion. The use of these techniques conveys a message: "This is seen through a camera" and "I am making a film." One becomes aware that one's view of the event is being mediated and, with such a short exposure as triggers provide, the option of examining the veracity of the material as *material* rather than being drawn into events on tape would detract from the particular illusion that trigger videos are attempting to create.

It is a paradox of trigger production that one uses the conventions of teleproduction to make it real in the sense of not being an unpolished televisual performance, while not breaking the illusion that one is part of, rather than apart from, the trigger scene. Implications for trigger video production are outlined in Table 13.1

Although triggers are not aimed at facilitating imitation but at promoting identification with the situation that is portrayed, some of the criteria for effective video modeling, as outlined by Hosford and Mills (1983; also Chapters 4 and 12), are nonetheless useful during video production. These guidelines include models similar to the client in terms of age, sex, racial attitudes, and background; presented as having similar problems and concerns as the client; generally high in prestige; relatively (not greatly) higher in competence; and presented as warm, friendly, and attractive. Some modeling criteria, such as "being observed to be rewarded for appropriate behavior," are not relevant to trigger production. Others, such as similarity to the client, could be rephrased when using or producing triggers to read "similar to the situation in which the client finds her or himself in terms of the age, sex, race, attitudes, and background of those with whom interaction generally takes place."

Viewers should be able to feel that the role that they are assigned is not particularly unfamiliar or implausible given the milieu within which they have to function. Normally, a wide variety of potential triggers are made available within one training tape to allow a trainer to choose the most appropriate vignette, given the past experience of a particular group of participants. Therefore, it is possible to look for a similar organizational culture and interactions arising that would be familiar to the target audience.

Design

Authenticity in setting is important if viewers are to be convinced of the validity of the material. Thus, those responsible for set design, costume, and the provision of props should be familiar with the environments being portrayed. In production this may be achieved by either (a) field trips, whereby the director and relevant personnel visit such environments, or (b) expert consultancy, whereby a person familiar with

TABLE 13.1 Trigger Production.

The following points may be thought of as rules of thumb in trigger video production, to deliver a convincing illusion of participation to the viewer. The camera at the point of production is the viewer's defining perspective on the final product.

	Ideal Conditions	Function	Possible Exceptions
Camera Position	At eye level with actor (even if looking away for part of shot). Actors should look directly at the midpoint of the camera lens. The video director should check this by looking through the camera lens to ensure that the actor is directly addressing the viewer and is not looking to the viewer's left or right	Enhances illusion of direct communication between viewer and actor.	When viewer is inevitably at a higher (or lower) level to the type of character portrayed. When actor is sitting and script necessitates a standing position of viewer, such as in cases of disability, or with children. The final product should give a realistic visual position from the viewer's perspective.
Camera Movement	The camera should not exhibit unnatural movement; panning in a sideways direction is less disturbing than vertical movement where movement is unavoidable. In such cases the camera should follow the actor's eye level as indicated above. Care should be taken that instructions to actors do not involve changes in vertical position (e.g., sitting to standing).	The final scene should not be unnatural for the static viewer, and should not contradict the bodily sensations and generally sedentary position of the viewer. In order to maintain the fiction of interaction, eye level contact should still be maintained even though viewers are free to move their heads from side to side and so on.	Movement may be necessary to follow a character whose role dictates movement within the scene itself. The vignette may make sense only if both character and viewer are "moving."

Camera Zoom	Zoom should not be used. The possibility can be avoided by sensitive set design.	Eyes cannot zoom in on distant objects. The illusion of participation would be replaced by a sense of watching a production through a camera.
Freeze-Frame, Fade-Out and Editing	None of these techniques should be used.	These techniques would destroy the illusion of participation in triggers, although they would be commonly accepted by passive observers of longer productions.

Note: A trainer's scene-setting instructions to the group would need to take account of any exceptions.

Time should be taken to explain these guidelines to professional camera users and editors, whose use of such aesthetic devices may be almost automatic. Similarly, actors should be encouraged to adopt a naturalistic style that is appropriate for televisual material. This is not the same as normal social behavior. However, overly stylized performances, such as evoked by stage craft or by newsreaders, may communicate an overly hysterical or patronizing attitude to the viewer.

the milieu to be recorded is available during filming to advise on the authenticity of each set.

For example, if settings included social work offices, as was the case with *Acceptable Risk,* the designer should pay particular attention to the nature of decoration, layout, use of space, and indicators of status (such as clothing) that are appropriate for helping agencies. For example, the conventions pertaining to public sector workers in the United Kingdom vary markedly from those in private sector organizations.

Prior consideration needs to be given to the target audience and the desired transferability of trigger material across user groups. In order to make a tape relevant to one group, the final product may be less applicable to other potential users. This question is particularly difficult to address satisfactorily when, as with the antiracism triggers, *Through a Hundred Pairs of Eyes,* the issues raised pertain to a wide variety of potential settings. In such circumstances, a decision prior to production should be made for either (a) "neutral" scenes with a minimum of contextually specific cues, or (b) a wide variety of specific contexts covering the same or similar problems.

The former decision may reduce contextual obsolescence, but care should be taken to include dialogue cues to compensate for a lack of relevant props. For example, a man dressed in a suit and tie standing against a neutral wall saying, "As director of this organization I think we should . . . do you?" sounds rather unnecessary but may work. The technique of a dialogue cue may be less convincing for the cleaner or tea-boy. The latter decision may significantly reduce the number of issues covered, especially when the budget is limited.

Scripts

The situations, turns of phrases, and problem areas covered will have a significant effect on the authenticity of the final trigger videos. Therefore, it is important to tap the knowledge of persons familiar with relevant environments and issues. Once scripts have been produced, information should be deleted concerning place names, references to particular documents and legislation that would anchor the final product too readily in time or space. The example of a script generation described next may serve as a useful model for other contexts.

Method of Script Generation Example

The trigger video *Acceptable Risk* addresses the problems facing social workers, supervisors, and senior managers in British social service departments. Its context is thus relatively specific in terms of problem area, personnel, and target audience.

A steering group was convened whose membership reflected awareness of characteristics that were thought relevant to the project. The issues included:

- Race and cultural background.
- Gender.

- Differing levels of status within relevant organizations.

- Membership in public and voluntary agencies.

- Specific training experience.

- Specific experience in the problem area.

The team of 12 met on three occasions. Only three team members had prior experience with video production or its use in training.

At the first meeting, team members learned about the purpose of the steering group and the boundaries defining what information would be relevant to the exercise. Examples of existing trigger material were shown. The meeting consisted of two sessions, totaling one full day. Members were given material on the subject area to read prior to the next meeting. Two weeks after the initial meeting, a second meeting took place; it lasted four sessions (half a day each) in a residential setting away from the working environment of all participants. The team was given a series of sequential tasks:

1. To identify general issues arising from their practice that were relevant to the project's defined problem area (in this case, child abuse). The group subdivided into three groups of four, each of which was asked to generate four key issues. These issues were pooled in a feedback session and six were agreed on for further elaboration. The nature of trigger formats was reviewed at this point.

2. Subgroups then attempted to operationalize the six issues. They were asked to use examples from their professional experience that could be said to encapsulate the defined problem areas. Each subgroup was asked to generate:

   - A description of a particular event.

   - Specific dialogue that took place.

   - A list of those present at the event and comments on their attitude response and demographic characteristics.

3. At this point, the particular structure of this series of videos necessitated that each example was paired with ones covering interactions at other levels of a fictional organization, so that trios covering client-social worker, social worker-supervisor, and supervisor-manager addressed the same issue.

The whole team considered examples individually in order to assess their generality, communicability, and authenticity. Where examples overlapped, decisions were made about which ones should go forward to the production stage. A resulting 60 examples became scenes for production purposes. Some scenes would be repeated in order to provide examples of women, men, and characters of different racial backgrounds performing the same scene. Decisions also were made about casting in order to ensure an equitable distribution of gender and race across characters of different status.

A third meeting was planned to coincide with the actual production of video material to safeguard its authenticity. However, this intention proved to be impractical, so the production team relied on the services of two professional trainers in the steering group, each of whom had prior experience working in relevant settings.

Production of 63 triggers took six working sessions and included the use of two locations. The first of these was a large residential house in the Brixton area of South London with a variety of rooms and external locations. The second included a single floor of an office building in Central London. The production team consisted of a producer/director, two training advisers, a camera operator, a sound engineer, a props and makeup assistant, and a lighting engineer.

USING TRIGGERS IN A TRAINING SESSION

This section contains guidelines for those intending to use trigger-video-assisted training. Stages that trainers need to address include preparing themselves and the participants before triggers are used, the environment in which viewing actually takes place, and follow-up exercises that exploit trigger impact. Some trainers have specific learning goals in mind that shape a framework for the trigger session; others may wish to develop these as part of ongoing group processes. Factors that influence learning goals are indicated throughout this section.

Prior to Viewing

Prior to showing trigger material, the trainer needs to take certain moderating factors into account. These factors are outlined in Figure 13.1 and address questions of trainee familiarity with trigger methodology, content, and the relationship between participants and the trainer.

Because of a tendency for video to be taken as empirically true, viewers may assume the tape shows them aspects of behavior, sometimes their own, that others are immediately aware of but they have not been. This is not the case in normal social behavior, because looking at video material is not subject to the same social sanctions that affect what can legitimately be looked at during face-to-face interaction.

A tendency previously noted (Biggs, 1983) for a trainer to take a directive role when using video in traditional social skills settings may also need modification when triggers are being used. The trainer has two options to consider. First, it is important that those watching are free to draw whatever conclusions they like from what they see within the general goals of the exercise being undertaken. This approach is more appropriate if triggers are used to evoke spontaneous responses, where learning goals have not been defined beforehand and, on balance, would be expected to emerge "experientially" as part of a group process of learning. Second, it

Have you an agreed *contract* with your group?

Who asked you 'in'?
  The group members
  Other (often senior) members of the same organization
  An external source

What is your position with respect to group members?
  Your place within the organization's hierarchy
  External status

Each of these factors will affect the nature of the contract with participants and the perceptions these group members have of your role.

Learning goals will vary depending on the nature of this contract.

Are viewers familiar with *trigger format?*

Yes	No
Briefly recap.	Are triggers the most appropriate method?

	Yes	No
	Show some examples in a preview session and explain how they are used.	What other methods could be used?

Are viewers familiar with the *general area and contexts* covered by particular trigger materials to be used?

Yes	No
	Is the trigger material appropriate for this group of participants?
	Look for more contextually appropriate material.

Select particular trigger vignettes to use with your group.

Are *learning goals* specific?

Yes	No
Provide information to induce perceptual set.	Encourage participants to focus on their spontaneous response to trigger vignette.

Prepare viewers by giving scene-setting information about their role and the vignette that they are about to see.

Figure 13.1. Trainer's considerations prior to viewing.

may be appropriate for the trainer to suggest a focus for viewing in order to sensitize participants to evoke a particular perceptual set. A perceptual set from instructions given to participants before they view may be used to sensitize a group to a particular issue, in the light of which the trigger would be expected to raise certain questions. Once a perceptual set has been evoked, the viewer's free response to the trigger within that framework should be encouraged. Its purpose may be to help highlight an alternative perception to the common sense reality that is the norm for a particular group of participants. Group members from different backgrounds and with different allegiances are expected to vary in their responses to the material.

Viewing and Training Exercises

It has been noted (Willener, Millard, & Ganty, 1976) that viewers "migrate" from the social role they usually play and, on seeing such a role on tape, have attempted to assert their individuality in relation to previous role expectations. When trigger tapes are sufficiently authentic in terms of the setting, roles, and expressed behavior and allow viewers to identify with what is being shown, a similar opportunity for critical analysis may arise. The desired effect is twofold: first, to create a breathing space from immersion in day-to-day behavior and second, to provide an opportunity to use a different conceptual framework from that generally applied.

Seeing taped material always includes an element of suspension of belief insofar as the events are not happening in real time. The trainer works with this situation, both to seduce those watching into an illusion that events are unfolding in real time and, because it is on tape, to reflect on their responses. Also, because the trigger session is not a real situation, as it would be if it occurred during one's everyday activities, its consequences do not have a direct impact on ongoing social relationships. However, as it has consequences within the learning group, which the trainer should ensure is a "safe" environment, it should be possible to test out a variety of opinions and coping strategies before using them in one's social network.

To watch triggers in a group setting allows a sharing of different perceptions of the same event. This is necessary with social interaction, particularly when it takes place in organized settings such as large bureaucratic agencies where the "common sense," the unspoken assumptions about a person's tasks and attitudes, is not readily availabile.

As noted earlier, a trigger favors identification with the situation that is portrayed, rather than with the focal character. Inevitably, however appropriate the series of triggers are and however careful the trainer is in setting the scene for viewing, some participants will identify with particular characters on tape. In this situation, the trainer may wish to explore why identification has occurred with particular characters, and what this says to those particular participants about their feelings toward the vignette. The trainer could then redirect the participant back on task and discuss the roles that would be potentially available if he or she were really in the situation being portrayed.

If a trainer finds participants repeatedly identifying with the actors on tape, it is possible that they are not fully inducted into their appropriate roles, and more care may be needed in preparing participants beforehand. For example, given the vignette presented, trainers should encourage participant-viewers to take a role appropriate to their position, vis-à-vis the interaction on tape. This may be done in the following manner.

> Imagine that you are part of an interview panel. You are sitting in a group meeting with three white people reviewing application forms. The meeting's purpose is obviously an informal and initial "sifting out" of applicants for a post within your organization. Think about the expectations you would have of your role in this situation. What sort of judgments would you use? What feelings would you have about an appropriate applicant?

The trainer would then pause for participants to contemplate their role. Just before starting the tape, the trainer makes the following remark:

> You are sitting in the room with the other interviewers. The person opposite you refers to an application form and makes some casual comments.

The trainer switches on the trigger and participants view the vignette. Figure 13.2 notes factors that influence the effectiveness of viewing, while Figures 13.3 and 13.4 give examples of exercises following presentation of trigger material.

Use of Multiple Triggers

Methods have recently been developed to group triggers into duos or trios. The following vignette was made twice with male and female clients in different triggers:

> A client addresses a social worker on a home visit: "You can't possibly imagine what it's like . . . shut up! (*to children*) . . . raising two kids on your own. . . . You just don't know what it's like. . . . Why don't you just fuck off and leave us alone!"

By comparing responses to both male and female characters, the trainer gains an

---

Setting. The trainer should ensure that participants are seated in a comfortable manner and have a clear view of the TV monitor. Participants should be seated in positions that optimize eye contact with the character on the screen. They should not, for example, be so far to the side of the monitor, or in such an elevated or low-level position that illusion of participation effects are minimized. With large groups, more than one monitor may be needed. Low-light conditions may improve impact as the tape is being viewed.

Showing the Tape. The appropriate point on the tape should be selected prior to the session. Nearly all tapes have color-coded gaps between trigger vignettes that contain reference numbers or headings to the particular vignette. This allows them to be easily found. These titles should be shown to allow participants to settle in to a viewing role.

Figure 13.2. Factors that influence the effectiveness of viewing.

Stage One

How do participants feel about the character, the situation portrayed, their own associations and evoked emotions?

Ask participants about *feelings* generated by the vignette. Appropriate responses would reflect the emotional impact and awareness of this effect. Responses that concentrate on evaluating the value or technical effectiveness of the vignette would not be appropriate at this stage and may evidence intellectualization or denial of emotional impact.

Stage Two

How have participants *understood* the vignette?

Did it evoke memories of similar incidents?
What effect would such behavior have on other persons present?
What effect would be generated within an organizational setting?
How does the character see her/himself and what effect is being consciously conveyed?
What are the differences between how participants would ideally like to respond and how they would be most likely to respond?

If the participant groups consist of recognizable subgroups according, for example, to gender, ethnic and cultural background, institutional status, and professional affiliation, trainers should expect associated differences to add a richness to the diversity of opinion shown that could be capitalized on depending on agreed learning goals.

Stage Three—Group Activity

Ideas for group work exercises may have arisen during stages one and two that would require flexibility of response from the trainer. Decisions about the general nature of exercises would depend upon whether learning goals center on coping strategies or insight. Although both approaches may be used over time, two examples are given in Figure 13.4 that illustrate methods of developing post-trigger training.

Stage Four

Action. At this point participants decide on a plan of action for execution in the outside world. Such a plan may include:

- The practice of certain social skills in real settings,
- Participant observation of processes that have been identified from the trigger exercise,
- Formation of peer-support groups to influence current practice, and
- A re-examination of current policies and procedures in the light of new insight.

If a series of trigger sessions have been planned, opportunity for feedback and discussion of these activities may be included at the beginning of the next session.

Figure 13.3. Training exercises.

TRIGGER EXAMPLE

You are an experienced social worker with a new, but difficult child care case and attempt to discuss this with your manager, who responds: "You mean we haven't seen this child yet? Aren't you aware of the procedures in these cases? We'll have the members* on our necks if they knew. When are you going to do something about it?"

SOCIAL SKILLS APPROACH

Goal: to examine skills needed by social worker to achieve a solution to problem.

Method:

1. Role play situation with two participants taking parts of manager and social worker, respectively. Other group members are asked to observe behavior according to defined nonverbal uses (eye contact, use of voice, verbal statements, etc.).
2. Discuss nonverbal and verbal behavior that perpetuates miscommunication.
3. Give examples of behavior associated with redefinition of social interaction as problem-solving. For example:

   • State reason for initiating interaction in a friendly manner.

   • Allow time for other to ventilate or let off steam.

   • Show that one understands the other's concerns.

   • Check that the other understands one's concerns.

   • Avoid behavior (aggression, defensiveness) that could escalate confrontation.

   • Suggest looking at objective evidence together—such as the case file.

4. Practice behaviors individually and in an appropriate order.
5. A second role play, starting at the same point as the first, but using the skills rehearsed above. Both role plays may be videotaped to compare behavior and results.
6. Repeat 3, 4, and 5 if learning is incomplete.
7. Show trigger video for second time and use it to discuss situations that new skills could be applied to.

*(Refers to elected members of local government councils in U.K.).

Figure 13.4. An example of group activity.

opportunity to explore the differing assumptions, pressures, and services that would be available to these two cases.

A number of studies (Lawrence, 1979; Menzies, 1970; Miller & Gwynne, 1972) have drawn attention to the role of institutional systems in defense against threat. The everyday behavior of staff has been shown to collude in the control of awareness of attitudes, although the workers who have been studied would not generally recognize the effect of their behavior.

We (Ash, Biggs, & Mayhew, 1987) have also attempted to use trios of triggers to examine the effects of an issue at different levels in an organizational hierarchy. The following three triggers were designed to address the way in which defenses against emotionally disturbing events are "mirrored" throughout an agency—in this case, as a response to evidence of child sexual abuse:

> Client to social worker: "She's such a little flirt you know. You should see her, she's all over him; she won't leave my husband alone. But it's all in fun, isn't it?"

> Social worker to supervisor: "I didn't take it too seriously. After all, all little girls have fantasies about their dads. Forgotten your Freud then?"

> Manager to supervisor: "Oh come off it. We'd have half the kids in the borough in care on that basis, wouldn't we?"

In this particular example, confronting the possibility of child sexual abuse is avoided by central figures in that child's life and at different points in a decision-making hierarchy.

CONCLUSION

Trigger videos can be used in training groups to stimulate both cognitive and affective responses. These responses facilitate the examination of social attitudes as a precursor to behavioral change. Successful trigger production depends on a coming together of norms for television watching and norms that reflect everyday social behavior to foster an illusion of participation between viewers and characters on tape. Effective trigger use capitalizes on this illusion to challenge existing attitudes and unspoken assumptions about social behavior and is becoming widely used as a method of staff training in the United Kingdom. Further research is needed on the specific changes that result from different applications, and the ways in which these methods may be generalized. In the meantime, the growth of trigger material bears witness to its flexibility as a training resource.

NOTES

The trigger videos referred to in this article are available for preview from the following addresses:

> *Acceptable Risk* from The Central Council for Education and Training in Social Work, St Chad's St., London WC1H 8AD, England.

> *Through a Hundred Pairs of Eyes* from the Open University Press, Walton Hall, Milton Keynes, MK7 6AA, England.

CHAPTER 14

Interpersonal Process Recall

NORMAN I. KAGAN
HENYA KAGAN

OVERVIEW

Interpersonal process recall (IPR) illustrates an exemplary packaged system using video self-review. It is based on video replay strategies to promote recollection of the internal processes (thoughts and feelings) that occur at great speed during personal interactions. The methodology makes contributions to research, training, and theory. The authors make the case that the inquirer's role is of paramount importance. They describe this role in some detail, giving examples of the expectations at the basis of IPR and instructions that an inquirer (who runs the IPR session) might give to a participant (who sees himself or herself on video). The training model is described conceptually and in practical detail in the context of interviewer training: facilitating communication, affect expression, interviewer recall, inquirer role, client recall, discussion, and mutual recall. The authors also describe training of IPR inquirers, with reference to available films and manuals. The chapter ends with a summary of training and research applications (e.g., medical interviewing, military personnel, and rehabilitation following brain injury).
P.W.D.

IPR DEFINED

What is interpersonal process recall (IPR)? Videotape playback? A human-interaction training model? A research tool? Stimulated recall applied to counseling relations?

IPR is the name given to a process developed at Michigan State University beginning in the early 1960s. At first, we conceptualized the process as stimulated recall enhanced by the power of videotape playback (Kagan, Krathwohl, & Miller, 1963). As we gained experience with the model we came to realize that IPR serves three interrelated purposes. As a research tool, it enables examination of psychological events in ways not previously possible. It is also the core of a training

222 Selected Applications

model for improving the interpersonal abilities of counselors, teachers, prison guards, medical students—nearly anyone who could benefit from improved competence in human interactions—practitioners or clients. IPR also contributes to theory and knowledge about human interaction that emerges from its applications in research, training, and therapy. These three facets, IPR the research method, IPR the training model, and IPR the interpersonal theory cannot be separated from one another.

The theories of human interaction that IPR has helped to formulate have, in turn, shaped and refined the IPR training and research process. For instance, we found in recall sessions that people have much more knowledge about their interactions than their overt behavior suggests. This simple truth should have surprised no one. However, the extent of the knowledge, the depth of understandings, the multiple layers of meanings that are known to people as they interact with each other and that could be nudged into conscious awareness and spoken language surprised us. We observed again and again that people have an uncanny awareness of each other's most subtle emotions, an awareness that was not apparent under ordinary circumstances, but that was acknowledged and described during IPR sessions.

The understandings made sense not only from a dynamic psychological perspective but also from an evolutionary perspective. Humans have survived and populated the earth because they came to live in a community bound by culture (Leaky, 1979). Successful communal life is dependent on communication—the ability to "read" each other's messages. It is not surprising, therefore, that everyone has a "third ear." This knowledge becomes an integral part of the inquirer's expectations in IPR, and hence an essential part of the model itself.

The most fundamental and unique characteristic of IPR is not the videotape or audiotape recording, its technology and most obvious structural feature, but rather *it is the inquirer role and function that is the heart and soul of IPR. It is the inquirer's expectation that people have encyclopedic knowledge of their interactions that can be brought to awareness that makes IPR the powerful tool it is for discovery and training.* The inquirer's behavior and expectations in an IPR session are what make IPR different from self-confrontation and more potent than stimulated recall.

For instance, we observed that people's anxieties about involvement in psychologically intimate human interactions are variations on a limited number of fundamental human interaction themes. The first was, "If I drop my guard the other person will hurt me." The fear was not based on the reality of the setting but rather on a vague potential sensed in the situation or, like an interpersonal allergy, stimulated by a mere hint of the situation's potential to cause harm. This fear and the others seemed to be primitive, childlike, or infantile in nature, vestiges of our earliest years when we were little people in a big people's world. These and the other fears were often expressed in terms reminiscent of the helplessness of a child; for instance, "I feel as if I'm going to be picked up and hurt physically," or, "It feels as if the other person will walk out and abandon me, and I won't be able to survive on my own; I'll die." A second concern was people's fears of harming the other. People seemed to expend considerable energy in protecting themselves from their own aggressive impulses. The theme was, "If I'm not careful, I'll hurt you." A third concern was that the other would engulf us, control us, or devour us. A fourth concern was that we might engulf or devour the other person. A fifth concern was of our sexual potential in the situation, and the sixth was our perception of the sexual potential of the other to act out on us.

We noted also that our fear of human interaction fosters an interpersonal dynamic in which we establish a psychological interpersonal distance, a boundary or limitation on the degree to which we will allow ourselves to reveal our intimate thoughts and feelings to another. If this distance is violated, and a person feels intruded upon, the person then experiences the discomfort of anxiety—a rapid, loud heartbeat, shallow breathing, and a vague feeling of vulnerability. If, on the other extreme, an individual finds himself or herself too far removed from human interaction and too remote from a "comfortable" interpersonal distance, then he or she experiences boredom and loneliness—the discomfort of sensory deprivation. The work of maintaining mutually acceptable degrees of intimacy in human interaction is a dynamic that is often made explicit to the inquirer during an IPR session. *An awareness that such material may exist becomes one more avenue of potential exploration for the inquirer.*

INQUIRER ROLE AND FUNCTION

The core of IPR, then, is the inquirer's role and function. The inquirer assumes that people perceive each other in depth and detail on numerous levels simultaneously, but ordinarily acknowledge little of what they do indeed know. *Feigning clinical naiveté* is assumed to be a fundamental characteristic of human interaction. The inquirer assumes that the persons reviewing their tapes have an immense wealth of information not obvious to an observer, and that the inquirer's task is to help the participants make explicit in language what they already know.

These assumptions shape the behavior of the inquirer. First, the expectation of the inquirer is shared with the participant at the beginning of the recall session. The inquirer gives the following instructions to each participant:

We know the mind works faster than the voice and so during the session you recorded there couldn't have been time to say all the things you thought or perceived. There also may have been thoughts and feelings you had which you chose not to share. When we interact with someone we have thoughts and feelings; we experience images or mental pictures. There are ways in which we do and do not want to be perceived by the other. We have feelings and sense the feelings of the other. At times we are tempted to say things that we hold back because we cannot think of a satisfactory way to say them. Often, we become aware of responses we anticipate from the other; sometimes these are responses we want, sometimes ones we fear.

If I asked you now to recall some of these thoughts or feelings or images you probably could remember some, but I think you'll find that the playback is a powerful stimulant for memory. You'll find that you're able to remember what your thoughts and feelings had been as well as images, thoughts, and feelings you sensed the other person had. Here is the control switch. As you review the tape, stop the playback whenever you remember any thought or feeling you had. My role will be to ask you to elaborate on your experience of those moments on the tape.

The inquirer then gives sole responsibility to the participant for stopping and starting the tape. However, the inquirer is not passive. Participants need guidance and encouragement to make their covert processes overt in language. The inquirer is guided by the assumptions just referred to and by a set of inquiries that emerge from those assumptions. To use an analogy, an anthropologist who studies a new culture does not debrief members of that culture by attempting to interpret their own culture to them, nor does the anthropologist ask only such vague nondirective questions as, "Tell me about your culture." Rather, the anthropologist knows that the character-istics of every culture can be understood around specific themes. Every culture has rites of passage. Every culture has some sort of sex-role differentiation. Every culture has taboos and every culture has a religion. The anthropologist's inquiries are designed to discover what is in each of these inevitable content areas. For instance, "What is your people's understanding of their origin—where do they believe they came from?"

What would be the interpersonal equivalent of the anthropologist's categories? When people interact they have thoughts and feelings, aspirations, and anticipations. They have visual images and memories. They have degrees to which they wish to reveal themselves and have others revealed to them. They sense these reactions in themselves and in others with whom they are interacting. In a recall session, when a person stops the tape to comment, the inquirer encourages elaboration through questions designed to open these categories of probable or inevitable content. For instance, if a participant stopped the playback and commented, "At that moment I was surprised by my own aggressiveness," the inquirer might ask, "What thoughts and feelings accompanied your behavior?"; or "Do you recall what impact you wanted your reaction to have?"; or "Do you recall how your behavior impacted the other?"; or "Do you recall any risks you imagined at the time of the behavior you referred to?" The instructor's manual that accompanies the IPR film series contains several pages of additional questions that are used to open up probable or inevitable content areas.

THE IPR TRAINING MODEL

Training Concepts

The remainder of this chapter focuses primarily on the training model that was developed from information learned from our early controlled studies of the use of IPR for the education of counselors (Kagan & Krathwohl, 1967; Kagan, 1978). We concluded that the education of a mental health professional is best achieved through a developmental series of educational experiences. Each experience is designed to focus on learning or refining a particular ability that would improve an individual's capacity to relate in a helpful way with another human being. The challenge is to conceptualize the learning tasks needed to be accomplished in order to be able to serve as a counselor.

We established a series of experiences beginning with instruction in fundamental skills, followed by analyses of client messages or behaviors especially difficult for a student to cope with, self-study, client feedback, and finally learning to cope with the mutual impact of counselor and client on each other. The experiences are thus graduated in degree of threat and complexity from least to most. The materials designed to support the units of instruction are also graduated from low- to high-fidelity simulation. In order to avoid the impossible job of identifying where each student might be placed on the continuum of tasks, each unit contains enough subtlety so that even the most advanced counselors will find challenges within the unit.

Description

The IPR training model was first developed to improve the training programs for mental health workers, but was later broadened to include teaching other professionals to achieve improved interpersonal relations. The training model consists of a series of films. The films contain lectures, demonstrations, exercises, and instructions. The model recall films are recordings of actual sessions from teaching, psychotherapy, medicine, and other arenas of human interaction to facilitate the application of IPR to a broader range of people. The program is not intended to be self-instructional, but rather the films and manual are intended to provide the necessary aids to a psychologically sophisticated instructor. The series consists of several units approximately 9.5 hours in length, and requires 30 to 60 hours of a person's time.

A 457-page instructor's manual accompanies the film series (Kagan, 1980). The bulk of the manual consists of complete typescripts that include suggestions to the instructor about when to stop each film and questions to ask the students. The manual also contains sections that can be copied and distributed as a student manual to participants.

The basic units of the IPR model are:

1. Elements of facilitating communication.
2. Affect simulation.
3. Interviewer recall.
4. Inquirer role and function.
5. Client recall.
6. Discussion.
7. Mutual recall.

Elements of facilitating communication. In this skill unit and throughout the entire program, students are reminded that we are attempting to add to their abilities rather than to dictate a new interpersonal life style. This emphasis on adding to one's repertoire is repeated throughout the entire training program.

The film that supports this unit is designed to help students expand their repertoire in responding to requests for help or understanding by another. Four skills are defined and illustrated:

1. Exploratory responses (i.e., ask open-ended questions and establish a relationship based on collaboration).
2. Listening responses (i.e., listen intently to the client and communicate your attempt to understand the client by asking for clarification or paraphrasing).
3. Affective responses (i.e., focus your attention on client's affect).
4. Honest labeling (i.e., focus your attention on the metacommunication between you and your client).

The student is shown vignettes in which a person makes a statement and an interviewer responds to the statement. In the next scene, the person repeats the statement to the interviewer who responds differently to the statement. Several occupational types are presented for each of the four sets of concepts. Usually, 4 to 6 hours are enough class time for this unit.

Affect simulation. This unit is based on an important discovery about human interaction using IPR. There are basic themes in human interaction that represent fundamental concerns. This discovery not only influenced the functioning of the inquirer (see previous section) but also led to the creation of film vignettes in which a viewer is engaged in a simulation experience designed to evoke one or more of the human fundamental fears. The unit was added to the model in order to help participants overcome their resistance to the often intense intimate communication that the use of interpersonal skills usually elicits. People often have "allergies" to certain types of communication/behaviors. For example; "If I drop my guard, if I become psychologically intimate," then "the other person will hurt me," or "I will engulf the other person." In this unit, participants watch brief film vignettes and are asked to imagine that the actor is talking directly to them. Participants are then encouraged to express their reactions to each vignette. For example, "What did you feel? What were your bodily reactions? What did you think?" "What did you really want to do?" There are more than 70 vignettes. Most are general, but some are designed for specific audiences, such as physicians, student counselors, teachers, supervisors, and military personnel. Specific themes such as racism, ageism, and sexism are also included.

Interviewer recall. The purpose of this unit is to help interviewers (student counselors, therapists, supervisors, colleagues, partners, or anyone in the "helper" role) learn to study themselves in action. The developmental task is to help the students learn to identify, organize, and put to use information they already possess. The process helps participants to become aware of messages that they denied or ignored and to identify their own unstated fears and imagined vulnerability in personal interactions. Interviewer recall also encourages change out of a sense of personal responsibility for one's own behavior and out of a feeling that one is capable of determining one's own direction. Interviewer recall usually increases participant confidence and risk-taking in interviews.

In interviewer recall, a video or audio tape is made of an interaction between an interviewer and a client; the tape is then reviewed with the interviewer. The review process is not a critique and not self-confrontation. It is a recall session in which the interviewer is given control of the playback switch and asked to stop the tape whenever he or she recalls any thoughts, feelings, goals, impressions, conflicts, confusions, images, internal dialogues, or any other covert processes that occurred during the session. Only the interviewer is allowed to stop the tape. However, the person who reviews the tape with the interviewer encourages the interviewer to elaborate whenever the tape is stopped and asks questions such as: "What were you thinking/feeling?"; "Do you recall how your body felt—can you recall any specific parts of your body reacting more than any other parts?"; and "What did you think the other person was feeling?"

Inquirer role and function. This unit is designed to enable students to understand the conceptual bases of the inquirer role and to permit students to safely practice the role for the first time. The person who reviews the videotape with an interviewer is called the *inquirer.* The inquirer assumes that the interviewer is the best authority on his or her own thoughts and feelings. The inquirer role requires nonjudgmental but assertive probing and consists entirely of asking exploratory questions. The inquirer facilitates learning by discovery and does not provide information, lectures, or observations. Some inquiry leads are: "What pictures, memories or words were going through your mind?"; "What did you think the other person wanted of you?; How did you want the other person to feel about you?"; "Was there anything you wanted to say but couldn't find the 'appropriate' words for?" In summary, the inquirer's approach should be of listening rather than interpreting, counseling, or teaching. It should focus on the videotape: then, rather than now.

Client recall. The purpose of this unit is to expand student knowledge of clients' (patients,' supervisees,' partners') wants, perceptions, aspirations, and how they learn and change. Students seem to gain more knowledge about client dynamics through discovery than through demonstrations or lectures. In this unit, the clients themselves become the student's instructor. A student interviews a person. At the end of the interview the student asks the person to review the videotape recording without the interviewer present but with one of the student's colleagues serving as inquirer. During the recall session, the client is encouraged to be as open as possible about aspirations, satisfactions, and dissatisfactions. Some leading exploratory questions might be: "What did she seem to you to want of you?"; "What did you want her to think or feel about you?". With the client's informed consent, the recall session, too, can be recorded or might be observed by the counselor through a one-way mirror. This experience provides a unique opportunity for the student to learn how the client reacts to him or her.

Discussion. This unit is designed to acquaint students with an interpersonal behavioral theory that summarizes some of the conclusions reached about human interaction. In each of the units of the IPR model, we have presented theoretical explanations appropriate to the unit. The decision to so emphasize theory is based on the concept stated at the beginning of this chapter, namely that IPR cannot be separated from its theories. Based on more pragmatic considerations, a study by Rowe (1972) concluded that adding interpersonal theories to IPR training resulted in significant improvement in counselor behavior. The Elements of Facilitating Communication unit contains concepts about decoding affect in interpersonal communication. The unit on inquirer role and function contains theory on interpersonal learning. In the unit on affect simulation, a theory of the subjective experience of interpersonal threat is presented. The discussion unit is devoted *entirely* to a description of fundamental interpersonal behavior patterns.

Our descriptions are similar in many ways to those developed by Karen Horney (1945). We describe three basic patterns of behavior, each of which is a continuum. First, as one perceives other people impinging, one can *attack* or strike out. On the most extreme end of the continuum, the word "attack" is appropriate. On the other end of the attack continuum is assertiveness. There are people who rely almost exclusively on an attacking posture as they relate to others. Another basic pattern is to *withdraw* or back off. One extreme is to withdraw; the other is to back out graciously. The third basic pattern is to *conform,* to go along with. On the extreme end is the conformist, and on the other end of the continuum is the agreeable person.

These three patterns often achieve long-term interpersonal postures or styles for people that are different from what the surface behavior appears designed to achieve. The person who attacks may achieve a lifetime style not of engagement, but of withdrawal. The person may attack not to engage people, but as a way of ultimately withdrawing from human contact. Another pattern is attack with conformity as a long-term achieved status. Withdrawal as a pattern can also be a way of achieving a long-term attack or hostile expression. Withdrawal can also serve as a way to conform in the long run—to maintain a belief system, a set of interpersonal relations unchallenged. Conforming as a pattern of behavior can serve a long-term posture of attack. Finally, a conforming pattern can be a vehicle for ultimate withdrawal.

Students are told how the typology can be useful in understanding what people have said during their recall sessions. The typology also suggests one more way of conceptualizing mental health. The more fully functioning person seems to be capable of any number of behaviors depending on the situation and the person's needs within the situation.

Mutual recall. The purpose of this unit is to help students learn to use the here-and-now, to bring them to act overtly on client behavior as it occurs, and most importantly, to make explicit in the interview the covert, often subtle metacommunication between themselves and their clients. This is one of the most powerful phases of IPR training.

An interview between the student and a client is videotaped. During the recall, *both* participants remain in the room to review the tape with the inquirer. Interviewer and client are each asked to share their recalled thoughts and feelings, paying particular attention to how they perceived each other and what meanings they ascribed to each other's behaviors. Some of the inquirer's questions to the interviewer might be: "What did you suspect (the client) thought/felt then?"; "What did you think she thought at that moment?"; "What were you yourself feeling?" (To the interviewer) "Were you aware of that?".

Mutual recall gives the student an opportunity to learn how to use the metacommunication of the ongoing interview as a vehicle for understanding the other and of helping toward better self-understanding.

Instructor Role

The films and manuals that support IPR training provide most of the instruction for students who are going through the IPR units just described. Nonetheless, the instructor plays an important role in providing structure, leadership, and protection for the participants. It is imperative that the instructor preview the entire series before attempting to use it with students. The instructor must understand not only the IPR process, but also the developmental training series as a stepwise, sequential progression beginning with a didactic presentation of concepts, then stimulation exercises, study of self, study of others, and, finally a study of relationships through mutual recall. General illustrations and simulations are selected to apply to a wide variety of groups. The manual and films are designed to train an instructor to teach IPR without additional training. The learning that occurs is based on discovery by the participants. As with the inquirer role, the experience can be equally satisfying for both instructor and participants.

The instructor needs to assess the population to engage in IPR training. No assumption should be made about people's knowledge of personality theory or about their previous experience. The series is intended to be as useful for the experienced clinician as it is for the uninitiated paraprofessional. The instructor would do well to check out in advance the kinds of expectations people bring to the class. The instructor should look for basic necessities in the physical environment in order to conduct the training. For example:

- Is a video playback unit or a 16mm projector available, with screen and replacement bulbs?
- What room size is available?
- Are videotape recorders available in a space that provides privacy for the IPR labs?
- Are there sufficient manuals and copies of the syllabus?
- Is there enough time available to conduct each session without being under pressure?
- Are inquirers available?
- Are classroom assistants available?

It is especially helpful when the content of much of the discussion in IPR instruction is highly personal that participants be given need to ask permission to take their time and to feel supported as they risk testing their ideas.

IPR training is dependent on active participation by the learner. Therefore, it is important that the instructor frequently stop each of the film playbacks to encourage discussion, to allow note taking, to stimulate debate, and to challenge the ideas presented. Participants should watch no more than 10 or 15 minutes of film without interruption by the instructor for discussion.

Throughout the films, there are questions raised by the film narrator and "fades" and "pauses" that lend themselves naturally to interruption of the playback for discussion. One activity that is especially useful for encouraging student classroom participation, improving the interactions between instructor and students, and providing students and instructor with additional experience with the recall process is to use classroom recalls (as illustrated in one of the films) in the IPR class itself.

The inquirer role is more difficult to enact than it appears to be. Instructors are encouraged to preview the film *Inquirer Role and Function* with one or more colleagues, then to look at the recall-sessions presented in the film series "A," "B," and "C." Some instructors have found it very useful to videotape or record themselves while conducting a recall session so they could study their own inquirer behavior.

TRAINING AND RESEARCH APPLICATIONS

The IPR model has been extensively used to train mental health workers, teachers, physicians, medical students, nurses, prison guards, prison inmates, undergraduate and graduate students in counseling, and military personnel (Kagan, 1984, 1988). IPR was also used in the training of newly brain-injured patients aged 17 to 35 years in remediation of interpersonal and communication skill defects (Helffenstein, 1981). In the 1970s, every drill sergeant in the U.S. Army completed an IPR course as part of basic drill sergeant training (Kagan, 1984). According to a national survey (Kahn, Cohen, & Jason, 1979), 27% of all medical training programs in the United States reported they were using IPR in their training. More recently, the model was used by Australian airlines to train cockpit crews. Another study is being conducted with lupus patients and their families (Barrand, 1989), and a third study is using the IPR model with 430 members of the emergency medical service of the Houston fire department.

The model has been translated into Swedish, Danish, Dutch, and German. It has been used not only in the English-speaking countries of Great Britain and Australia, but also in Israel, Japan, Malaysia, and New Guinea.

Some research claiming to be based on IPR unfortunately has sacrificed the real potency of IPR in order to increase the likelihood of obtaining quantifiable data. All too often, the kinds of questions asked during recall have been restricted to specific categories or parameters. Such applications of IPR limit the model's unique potential as a tool for discovery.

A current project of ours is to determine the impact of IPR on the behavior of emergency medical service personnel in combination with stress-reduction programs. Another current study is of the effectiveness of IPR training for teachers in a large urban elementary school experiencing rapid change in the racial composition of its student body. The model also has been proposed for training of police in hostage negotiation skills.

CHAPTER 15

The Use of Video in Sport Skill Acquisition

IAN M. FRANKS
LAWRENCE J. MAILE

Video is widely used in sport and other motor skill training but remarkably little has been written about it. The authors of this chapter bring together the perspectives of educator, scientist, coach, and athlete while linking feedback to video analysis and self-modeling to peer modeling. The principles of feedback as knowledge of performance are reviewed, including the implications for the coach who supervises video replay and the analysis of computer-aided video. Details are given on the computer-video interface, the use of criterion movement patterns, and management of the viewing situation. Modeling is described as it applies to motor skill acquisition, with particular emphasis on the qualities of the model relative to the observer and the development of personal, skill-related imagery. These notions are related to self-modeling and the authors' experiences in the diverse activities of beginning juggling and national class powerlifting. The authors provide procedural information from a number of sources and offer specific suggestions for the use of video in sport.

P. W.D.

The importance of using a pictorial representation of human skilled action for analysis was first emphasized by Marey's (1895) work with cyclophotography. This technique allowed Marey to study in detail the kinematic representation of such everyday movement skills as walking, running, and descending a staircase. His subjects wore black body-suits with phosphorescent markers or strips placed over the key link segments of the body. With the camera shutter open, a strobe light could project a point-light movement display on a single photographic plate. Marey's techniques were subsequently adopted in the early 1900s by the Russian physiologist Nicholia Bernstein (1967) who was instrumental in bringing into joint focus the areas of biomechanics and skill acquisition. The detailed analysis of human skills via film recording is now commonplace and is seen as an essential element in understanding how one learns and performs well-skilled motor acts.

Although *film* analysis is still used by many biomechanists, the introduction and development of the videotape recorder by Ampex in 1956 led to the establishment of video technology in a large number of skill-acquisition/motor-learning laboratories, as well as in many professional sports organizations. In fact, the use of videotape in the analysis of sport has now become a fundamental component in the process of coaching and instruction (McCallum, 1987). The benefits of using such a medium lie in the ability to preserve the audiovisual image of the skill in its entirety, to replay components of the skill at various speeds, and to "freeze" a particular visual image in time. This video technology has been used in two aspects of the skill-learning process. First, and most frequently, the videotape recording has been used as information *feedback* that depicts a performance just completed. Second, videotape has been used to display a *model* of the correct performance that is to be completed. General video strategies of relevance to this chapter are discussed in Chapters 4, 6, and 7.

FEEDBACK

Information provided to the athlete about action is one of the most important variables affecting the learning and subsequent performance of a skill. Knowledge about the proficiency with which athletes perform a skill is critical to the learning process and, in certain circumstances, a failure to provide such knowledge may even prevent learning from taking place. In addition, the nature of the information that is provided has been shown to be a strong determinant of skilled performance. That is, precise information about the produced action will yield significantly more benefits for the athletes than feedback that is imprecise (Newell, 1981).

How then does the athlete acquire this vital information about action? First, a major contributor to the athlete's knowledge base about skill performance is intrinsic feedback—information that is gained from the body's interceptors, such as muscle spindles, joint receptors, and so on. (For a more detailed description of this internal process, see Schmidt, 1988, Chapters 6, 7, and 8.) A second source of feedback is that which augments the feedback from within the individual. This can be thought of as extrinsic information or knowledge of results (KR). Knowledge of performance (KP) also has been used to differentiate between information about the outcome of the action (KR) and the patterns of actions used to complete the skill (KP). A full discussion of this issue is found in Gentile (1972) and Salmoni, Schmidt, and Walter (1984). However, for the purposes of this chapter, we shall use KR to denote both knowledge of results and knowledge of performance. Magill (1989) offered perhaps the best global definition of KR: ". . . information provided to an individual after the completion of a response that is related to either the outcome of the response or what performance characteristics produced that outcome."

Although intrinsic feedback is of vital importance to skill performance, there is very little that coaches and teachers can do to improve upon this "hard-wired" system. Therefore, it remains the responsibility of the coach to offer the best possible extrinsic feedback that will enable the athlete to accurately compare "what was done" with "what was intended." Clearly, the use of video or film has the potential to provide such feedback. The benefits of using such aids are intuitively obvious. In the case of video, the information can be played back on a TV screen only seconds after the event has taken place. There is no delay period that may hamper the comparison being made by the athlete. Also, the motivation to perform is enhanced by individuals wanting to see themselves on a TV screen. In addition, the whole performance can be stored, in its entirety or in edited form, for later analysis. The videotape can therefore provide error information, can be a reinforcer when performance is correct, and can be a strong motivating force.

Given the fact that video offers the potential to be an excellent source of information feedback, the research into the effects of video feedback upon the skill-learning process should show positive benefits. Surprisingly, however, there are few research studies that show video as a superior form of KR that will affect the learning of a skilled motor act. An excellent review of 51 studies using several sport-skill examples was completed by Rothstein and Arnold (1976). While the results of these studies did not offer unequivocal support for the use of video as an essential component in the process of coaching and instruction, there was uniform agreement on one aspect: the interaction of the level of skill at which the athlete was performing and the method of giving the video feedback. Athletes that are in the early stages of learning a skill cannot improve their performance by observing videotapes without the assistance of a coach who can draw their attention to the key elements of performance competency. Recent evidence (Ross, Bird, Doody, & Zoeller, 1985) shows that indiscriminate viewing of videotape by early learners may even retard the learning process. One possible explanation of this phenomenon may be that there is too much information for the beginner athlete to assimilate. Furthermore, these novice athletes have a good probability of paying attention to the noncritical elements of performance. The practical implication of this finding is that coaches should either edit the videotape before showing it to their athletes, or highlight, by instruction or slow motion, cues that are responsible for correct performance. It does appear, however, that the need for this type of intervention by the coach diminishes as the skill level of the performer improves.

Therefore, on a practical level two problems seem to arise for the coach when considering the use of video feedback. The first problem is that of identifying the "critical elements" of successful athletic performance. Having identified these elements, the second problem is a technological one. Can a system be developed that can provide fast and efficient feedback that pertains only to the critical elements of performance? These problems have been of central concern to the research group at the Centre for Sport Analysis (UBC) where one of us, Franks, and colleagues have been adopting a systems approach to the analysis of athletic performance (Franks & Goodman, 1986a). Several computer-aided sport-analysis systems have been developed (Franks, Goodman, & Paterson, 1986; Franks & Goodman, 1986b; Franks, Wilson, & Goodman, 1987) that capture the critical elements of competition, store these events in a computer's memory, compute specified analyses on these data, and print out the results immediately following competition. In developing these systems, it was necessary to define and identify the critical elements of performance and then devise an efficient data-entry method so that a trained observer could record these events in real time. The benefits of using computers to record human athletic behavior in this way can be summarized in terms of speed and efficiency.

A recent addition to these computer-analysis systems has been the inclusion of an interactive video component. Since considerable advances have been made in recent years in computer and video technology, it became apparent that computer-video interaction could add a new dimension to the quality of the feedback that was available to athletes following competition. The behavioral data from computer printouts can now be directly identified as an audio-visual image on the videotape. In essence, this new technology enables the computer to control the functions of the VCR. This is achieved by recording a time-code signal (supplied by the computer) onto an audio channel of the videotape, thus providing frame-accurate indexing of the video material. This time code is the key to efficient indexing and electronic control of the videotape, thus allowing computer software to control such functions as searching (fast forward and rewind) the tape for a point in time, playing (play) a particular video section of tape that has been temporally defined, and editing (edit) selected scenes of video.

Once the concept of interfacing video and computer technologies became a reality within the field of quantitative sport analysis, it was obvious that the data from athletic performance, stored in the computer, could be linked directly to the video image that corresponded to a particular coded athletic behavior. Video scenes of performance can be preselected and edited automatically. The advantages of using computer-video interactive systems in sport analysis has been detailed by Franks and Nagelkerke (1988); they outlined procedures and hardware needed to undertake such an analysis. Figure 15.1 illustrates an on-line, real-time method of using computer-interactive video in sport analysis. The observed athletic behavior is recorded and stored along with its corresponding time. A concurrent video recording of the performance is made, and a computer-produced time code is dubbed onto the second audio channel of the videotape, giving the computer data and video data a common time base. At the commencement of a competition, the coach (or analyst) can access via the computer not only a digital and graphic summary of athletic performance, but also a video scene that corresponds to one, or a classified group of, specified athletic behaviors.

The use of such computer-aided video analysis has expanded and elaborated the coaching process, especially for team sports. This process is illustrated in the flowchart in Figure 15.2. While a trained observer enters a sequential history of coded events into a computer, the VCR is used to record the pictorial image of the competition. Having made the comparison between the observed data and the expected data, the coach can then highlight several priority problems associated with the performance. These itemized problems are automatically edited from the tape and assembled for viewing by individuals or groups of athletes. After these video excerpts from competition have been discussed, the athletes engage in a practice session organized by the coach. Recently, several analytic techniques have been developed that examine in detail the behavioral interaction between the coach and athlete during this practice session (Franks, Johnson, & Sinclair, 1988). It is therefore now possible to have available feedback about athletic performance and coaching performance throughout this cyclical process of competition, observation, analysis, and practice.

The majority of computer-aided analysis systems that have been developed to date collect data on relatively gross behavioral measures of performance. These

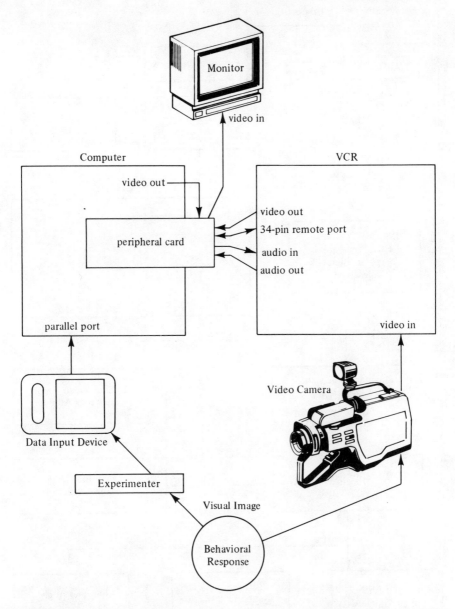

Figure 15.1. Schematic representation of the process involved in using interactive video technology while recording behavior in sporting environments.

measures include such elements as "a shot at goal" in soccer and the various descriptions of the results, a "check" in ice hockey and the results, a "possession change" in basketball, and a "penalty corner" in field hockey. Whereas this information, logged in the manner just mentioned, is extremely valuable to the overall improvement in performance of the various teams that use it, the need for

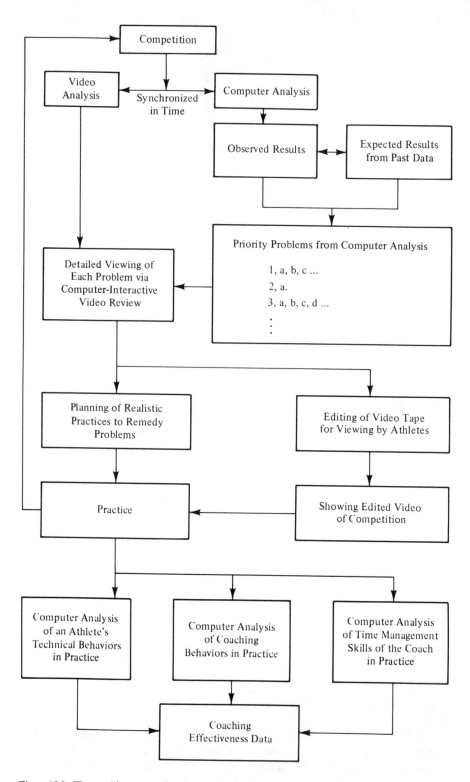

Figure 15.2. The coaching process involves a quantitative measurement of athlete and coach behaviors.

more precise and sophisticated analysis is evident when considering the individual closed-sport skills (environmental uncertainty is at a minimum) such as diving, gymnastics, and golf. In these skills the movement patterns themselves are fundamental to the overall performance. For that reason the athlete should be able to view the details of the pattern of movements that are used to produce the skill. It is also important for the athlete to be able to highlight the differences between a criterion movement pattern that is to be produced and the movement pattern that was actually completed. There are, however, several problems associated with this comparison process.

First, the criterion performance itself should be a model movement pattern. This will be discussed in detail later in this chapter. Second, the angle of viewing must be from a position that can pick up key points in the movement pattern. Several simultaneous recordings from various specified angles are preferable. Third, there should be a relatively short time delay between performing and viewing, and also between viewing and performing again. Fourth, the athletes should have control over the videotape's "slow motion," "pause," and "replay" functions to allow them to fully analyze their performance. Finally, the athletes must have some method of identifying the errors in their movement patterns so that changes can be made on subsequent attempts.

An interesting experiment by Hatze (1976) not only speaks to this final problem but also may point the way for future use of audiovisual feedback techniques. Hatze developed an optimum mathematical model for a simple skilled action (kicking a can with a weighted boot while being constrained to movements of the hip, knee, and ankle). From this model he determined the shortest possible time that was needed to complete the act (less than 2 seconds). The subject, upon whom the model was based, was asked to complete the task in as short a time as possible and was also told the optimum performance time. During the first series of trials, in which the only feedback given to the subject was the time of the attempted skill, the subject improved (reduced the time to complete the skill) only marginally. In the second phase of the study, the subject was shown his own performance superimposed upon the optimum performance of the model (a specially constructed manikin). The improvement in performance was dramatic. After only three trials, the subject's performance had reached the criterion time, hence the optimum movement pattern. It was evident when viewing the subject's earlier attempts that, before a model was available, several ineffective strategies were being tested. These strategies involved varying the joint angles that were free to move. Once a model was used to highlight the errors in the movement pattern for the subject, the correct movement pattern was achieved.

These methods of giving comparative feedback have not been studied extensively, mainly because of the problems associated with developing the mathematical model and the technique of video superimposition. Whereas the latter of these two problems is now easily overcome (there are several "special effects generators" that allow one to superimpose images and also to split the screen into two images), the former still presents practical problems. In Hatze's study, the motor task was simple and involved few degrees of freedom (the task constrained the number of usable joints). However, in real-world sports skills such as diving, gymnastics, or golf the number of degrees of freedom associated with a pattern of multijoint coordination is extremely large and would cause many problems for the mathematician and biomechanist if they were to try to model the optimum performance. Also, the optimum performance can only be calculated for each individual and his or her own body type at that particular time. Changes in body type (muscle development) due to training would require a further recalculation and a new optimum performance. The problems associated with the determination of this optimum performance are at the present time prohibitive, making the construction of a model similar to that used by Hatze impractical. Despite these problems, there has been considerable research and practical use made of alternative models of performance. This will be the focus of the next section of the chapter.

MODELING AND SELF-MODELING

The operational definition of *modeling* was first outlined to describe the demonstration of performance behaviors by one individual for the purpose of enhancing the skill acquisition of another (Bandura, 1969). It is now frequently used to refer to a technique widely used for teaching motor behaviors as well as honing skills and strengthening abilities once present. Indeed, Gould and Roberts, in their review of the role of modeling in the acquisition of motor skills, stated that modeling is "the most widely used teaching technique employed in physical education and sports" (1982, p. 222). Modeling has proven useful in the area of sport and sport-related performance improvement in a variety of settings, including the acquisition of a gymnastic skill (McAuley, 1985), the Bachman ladder task (Landers & Landers, 1973; McCullagh, 1986), as well as other areas of athletic endeavor (Gould & Weiss, 1981; Landers, 1975; Martens, Burwitz, & Zuckerman, 1976). In addition to the significant number of examples reported in the literature, examination of personal experience illustrates the ubiquity of demonstrations of skilled performance by others. Modeling is a vital component in the process of coaching and teaching motor skills and is used freely today in both these professions.

Given the almost universal use of modeling in the acquisition of motor skills, it is necessary to examine the applications in which optimal results may be obtained. The knowledge gleaned from such an examination will have important implications for the use of modeling as a process of self-review using the feedforward technique, specifically, self-modeling. This investigation will be facilitated by a review of the contexts in which modeling has been shown to be effective, the characteristics of models associated with superior performance, and the specific characteristics of tasks to which modeling may be applied.

Use of Modeling in Motor-Skill Acquisition

While modeling has been shown to be effective across a range of motor skills, its application has not been universally successful. Doody, Bird, and Ross (1985) did not find a significant improvement through the use of a model in the visual medium in a sequential, barrier-knockdown timing task. The experimental condition—which used videotaped modeling with knowledge of results during a 10-trial acquisition period and an 18-trial measure of retention without knowledge of results—was not found to be significantly more effective than the control condition in which no modeling took place. The findings of this study suggest that modeling does not increase the observer's ability to complete a complex response in a specified period of time. Supportive results were reported by Burwitz (1975) and Kelly (1986) who attempted to use models to improve performance on a pursuit-rotor task. Kelly's use of videotaped models did not significantly improve accuracy as measured by the time the subject was able to maintain a photosensitive stylus on an illuminated target when compared with use of guided imagery and physical practice. The results of Whiting, Bijlard, and den Brinker (1987), which demonstrated no improvement in distance of movement of the "sled" in a slalom skiing simulator, show a similar failure of modeling effects in the improvement of skills relative to some established criterion. However, in this particular task, improvement was seen in the subjects' ability to increase frequency of side-to-side motion—a critical factor in the shifts of the body necessary to clear the "gates" in competitive skiing situations. "Fluency," or the smoothness of the overall motion, showed improvement as well, but unfortunately, as noted previously, not all of the criteria for better performance followed this trend.

These seemingly negative results taken alone may appear to demonstrate the limited efficacy of modeling procedures in the acquisition of skills related to sports. However, within the field of physical education, coaching, and beyond, modeling has proven to be a useful and successful tool in the teaching of motor skills. Landers (1975) used live models to convey the performance of the Bachman ladder task (Bachman, 1961) to girls between 11 and 13 years old. Subjects in the groups who received modeling performed substantially better than control subjects. Hall and Erffmeyer (1983) used modeling procedures through the medium of videotape to improve female intercollegiate athletes' ability to use visual imagery. Also, Martens et al. (1976) found the demonstration of correct performance and modeling of a learning sequence to be effective in lowering scores on a "rollup" task (for a description, see Martens, 1970). Additional findings by Martens et al. (1976) lend support to the hypothesis that the efficacy of modeled demonstrations relates to the information-conveying properties of such communications (Newell, 1981). To be effective, the model must convey information that the person observing may use to learn behaviors necessary for improved performance. The absence of such information negates the utility of a model during the acquisition of a motor task.

Gentile (1972) stated that the goal of the first stage of learning was to "get the hang of the movement." Modeling may allow the observer to create an image or some other form of internal representation, a code, that will allow a subject to learn the task. It has been suggested that increasing the information capacity of the demonstration facilitates the learning, retention, and reproduction of a motor task (Gould & Roberts, 1982). It may be that through the systematic viewing of videotaped representations of desired behavior, subjects improve their ability to generate internal representations. If supported by empirical investigations, this area would provide further impetus to the use of modeling.

Status of the Model

When considering the status of the model, the observer's perspective must be kept in mind. Failure to do so, as is often done when "experts" such as coaches or teachers select the performances to be observed, may result in attenuation of the desired positive effects. Past investigations (Landers & Landers, 1973; McCullagh, 1986) have used face-valid means of selecting high- and low-status models for subjects to observe. High-status models appropriate for the target tasks have included teachers, coaches, university cheerleaders, and professional athletes or comparably skilled performers. Low-status models were those accorded lower esteem by subjects, such as moderately skilled or unskilled performers. Results unequivocally demonstrated the superiority of using high-status models. High status may be the result of several different attributions made to the model including competence (Baron, 1970; Gelfand, 1962), prestige (Mauser, 1953), age (Bandura & Krupers, 1964), social power (Mischel & Grusec, 1966), and similarity (Gould & Weiss, 1981). For a brief review of the relevant literature, see McCullagh (1986).

   With these considerations in mind, one of us (Maile, 1985) invited subject input into content and presentation of videotapes for the training of powerlifting, in which subjects served as their own models. Each subject was allowed to select the backdrop and attire to be worn, as well as providing input into camera angles, examples of performance, and appearance during practice—all to represent them in the best possible light. The subjects' level of attention to the salient facets of the task being performed was affected either positively or negatively by the regard subjects had for themselves and the degree of comfort they experienced while viewing themselves. While some subjects were able to observe themselves calmly, others experienced such a degree of distress that the modeling session was terminated. According to Danet (1968), self-images are inherently anxiety-invoking. This potential problem was alleviated by allowing subjects to select the environment in which they felt the most comfortable.

   Some caution should be exercised when considering the use of demonstrations in which the model is far superior in performance competency to the observer. Those who have a less-than-positive perception of themselves may "trap themselves" in an ever-increasing negative spiral (Trower & Kiely, 1983). While these conclusions have not been fully substantiated in the area of sports, results from manipulations of model correctness within this field have shown that models who are less similar to the observer make a less significant impact on those trying to imitate the modeling performance than more similar models (Gould & Weiss, 1981). An important dimension of model similarity is performance ability. The disparity of performance abilities between the subject and the model (or self-model) can be mediated by the explanation that the superior performance seen in the demonstration represents future behavior rather than present abilities.

Self-Modeling: A Feedforward Technique

We argue here (as elsewhere, see Chapter 7) that rapid acquisition of a sport skill can sometimes be achieved by video self-modeling, in which subjects are shown images of themselves, not as they have performed in the past (including errors), but as they will perform (correctly) in the future. Self-modeling is implemented in consideration of apparently antipodal aspects of modeling effectiveness—those of graduated practice and modeling of mastery. Graduated self-model tapes in which the subject's skills appear to improve over time have been used in self-modeling to enhance the locomotion abilities and swimming skills of physically disabled children (Dowrick, 1976; Dowrick & Dove, 1980). It is important to note that these behaviors were portrayed on video in correct form and with relatively lower anxiety than the subjects experienced when attempting the target behaviors. This technique, which embodied both a coping and mastery model simultaneously, is not possible using a feedback model.

One of us (Maile, 1985) worked with a nationally ranked U.S. athlete to improve her powerlifting performance. Several self-modeling videotapes were constructed that showed the subject lifting more weights than she had previously achieved, and doing so in perfect form. This was accomplished by following these steps:

1. A significant quantity of videotaped scenes were accumulated of the subject during training sessions. During these sessions, the subject performed the lifts she would later complete in competition. Each lift was performed consistent with competition rules and in attire worn by the competitor during meets.
2. These scenes were reviewed by the researchers and the subject to determine which examples of performance were most representative of correct competition performance. As noted, the subject was allowed to determine which scenes were most aesthetically pleasing to her.
3. These scenes were inserted into sequences involving the initiation and completion of each competition lift, but in these surrounding sequences the subject was using more weight than she had previously attempted.
4. The completed sequences were shown to the subject in the weeks immediately prior to the measurement of performance. Objective criteria were employed in determination of correct performance as specified in the rules of the International Powerlifting Federation (IPF, 1982).

Through this technique, the subject witnessed visual evidence that she was capable of lifting amounts previously untried. All lifts were performed in apparent comfort and in the absence of anxiety.

With selective application of self-modeling to the squat, bench press, and deadlift, an improvement of 26% was achieved over the course of 25 weeks of intervention. An improvement of not more than 10% was expected on the basis of weights used in training. John Kuc, a former American and world powerlifting champion, and among the most successful coaches involved in powerlifting, characterized improvement of more than 10% in less than a 1-year period as "remarkable," especially when considering the elite level of the athlete prior to the intervention (J. Kuc, 1985, personal communication).

Considerations in the Use of Video in Sport Settings

When deciding to use recorded media such as videotapes, the potential educator or coach must consider a number of factors. The advantages of using videotape demonstrations have been succinctly summarized by Christina and Corcos (1988):

- Athletes can review the demonstration as often as desired.

- The skill can be demonstrated from many angles.

- The videotaped demonstration can be either speeded up or slowed down consistent with the needs of the subject.

- The demonstrated task may be examined as a whole or in parts, allowing a focus on specific aspects of the skill to be acquired.

Overall, the use of video in modeling offers resources not otherwise available. However, there are several drawbacks in the use of video to convey modeled information (Christina & Corcos, 1988):

- Equipment is expensive and requires a knowledgeable operator.

- Much of the hardware necessary in editing videotapes is not portable.

- Video does not utilize three dimensions.

- Limitations exist in terms of demonstrating the skills from all possible angles.

Because equipment must be portable enough to capture images of the potential models in the performance environment, researchers must be willing and able to go to the athlete. This has been an important consideration in recording the behavior of those involved in outdoor sports such as skiing or running (see Dowrick, 1983).

The time-intensive process of manufacturing an adequate model tape must be considered. Subjects must be involved in selection of the correctly performed behavior, as noted earlier. If editing is to be used, the potential observer should be present while the tape is being constructed. If the behavior to be demonstrated is complex, more demonstrations may be required to convey maximum information value with the material. This may require time that is usually taken up by physical practice. Videotraining is no substitute for the physical practice necessary to acquire skills such as pitching a baseball, performing a gymnastic routine, or kicking a football. It is estimated that many thousands of repetitions are necessary to develop the required physical skills for competent performance (Christina & Corcos, 1988). Without the abilities acquired from extensive training, performance cannot and will not occur despite the subject having learned the desired target behaviors (Bandura, 1977). A balance must be struck between physical practice and modeling.

Finally, it is important to consider the interest of the observer. Some studies (e.g., Maile, 1985) have found, through self-reports of the subjects, that they tired of repeated demonstrations after a handful of sessions. It is hypothesized that with simple tasks or those with which the subject is familiar, sufficient information is assimilated to form a workable internal representation (image) in only a few viewing sessions. To maintain the interest of observers, tapes or other demonstrations should evolve so they remain engaging to the subject. In videotraining for the powerlifter reported earlier, interest was maintained by increasing the amount of weight the subject lifted successfully over the course of the intervention. The decision to change tapes was made on the basis of reported subject boredom and achievement of a ceiling in self-efficacy scores found to be predictive of actual weightlifting performance.

Developments of Self-Modeling in Sport

I (Maile) am now investigating the use of differing camera perspectives and its effect on skill acquisition in the sport of powerlifting. This course of investigation is possible with the development of split-screen technology in videotape. Two images may be shown simultaneously to subjects. This allows comparison of the efficacy of using an internal perspective, an external perspective (what another individual would see watching the subject performing the task), and both perspectives at once. The effectiveness of internal perspective is thought to be a result of motivational factors, while external perspective primarily reflects delivery of information to the subject. Both processes would be utilized in the dual-perspective condition.

Self-modeling is currently being used to lift athletes "off a plateau" in some sports at the University of Alaska, Anchorage, under the direction of Peter W. Dowrick. Examples include the triple lutz in figure skating, a flip and twist in gymnastics, and the Eskimo roll in kayaking. The use of self-model tapes also has proven effective in the teaching of juggling skills, in which one of us (Franks, 1988) found that the most positive results are achieved early in the acquisition phase of the skill and that the subject's interest wanes following the initial intervention period. Self-modeling was also used successfully by U.S. Olympic volleyball players in 1988 (Frank Gipson, personal communication). Several commercial video production companies are currently using self-modeling applications with high-level athletes, including tennis players and figure skaters. Even if no data are gathered by these commercial companies, it will, however, increase the attention to feedforward applications. While applications of self-modeling to sport and sport-related behavior have shown remarkable results, surprisingly little research can be reported. We hope that this chapter has conveyed the nature of this technique, and the potential for contributions to the literature on its application and the illumination of the theoretical underpinnings governing its use.

CHAPTER 16

Self-Modeling for Children's Emotional and Social Concerns

THOMAS J. KEHLE
FRANK GONZALES

This chapter elaborates with procedural detail on (primarily) the authors' self-modeling applications. It begins with descriptions of internalizing disturbances (e.g., social withdrawal) and externalizing disturbances (e.g., aggression) in the context of child development. The authors then describe, with useful detail, several self-modeling interventions for children with externalizing social disorders: hospitalized children with severe conduct disorders, an aggressive 11-year-old special education student, children with attention deficits in a special classroom, a 2-year-old acting-out child with Down syndrome, and a 7-year-old girl with psychosis. They also describe interventions with internalizing disorders, including selective mutism, shyness, and a particular reference to adolescent depression. In the application to depression (in which the efficacy of three different interventions are compared), they offer information about how they planned and produced the videotape content, viewing schedules, and so on, with suggestions for variations on these procedures based on their experiences.

P.W.D.

This chapter introduces procedures involved in the implementation of self-modeling interventions designed for children exhibiting social-emotional problem behavior. The goal is to present the procedures in enough detail so that the chapter serves as an introductory guide to self-modeling with this population. The chapter is organized in three primary sections, including:

1. A brief overview of social and emotional disturbances in childhood with emphasis on the broad-band groupings of internalizing and externalizing problem behaviors.
2. A discussion of a rationale and specific applications of self-modeling as an intervention for children exhibiting externalizing problem behaviors such as fighting, inappropriate and disruptive classroom behavior, hyperactivity, inattentiveness, tantrumming, and aggressiveness.

3. A presentation of specific applications of self-modeling with children exhibiting internalizing problems such as elective mutism, poor socialization skills, and depression.

INTERNALIZING AND EXTERNALIZING DISTURBANCES IN CHILDHOOD

With respect to childhood social-emotional problem behavior, there is a need to be sensitive to the child's current level of cognitive and developmental functioning. Behaviors that could be classified as expected and normal during one stage of development may be significant symptoms of maladjustment at a subsequent stage of development. Further, because social-emotional difficulties in adjustment are often transitory and occur in the majority of children at some time during their development (Gelfand, Jenson, & Drew, 1982), it is necessary to ascertain the extent to which these difficulties are characteristic of the child's everyday functioning. Social-emotional difficulties involve a wide range of inappropriate, maladaptive behaviors, including noncompliance with school routines or rules, inappropriate classroom behavior, peer conflicts, fighting, fears associated with personal or school issues, social withdrawal, shyness, lack of ability to initiate and maintain friendships, and depression. If these difficulties are transitory, they do not appear to have long-term negative effects for most children; however, children who persist in exhibiting these maladaptive behaviors, could be considered as socially or emotionally disturbed, behavior disordered, or emotionally handicapped. In concert with Bower's (1982) definition of emotionally handicapped students (see U.S. Public Law 94-142 as the basis for the definition of seriously emotionally disturbed children; *Federal Register*, 1977, and its 1981 revision), these children exhibit social-emotional problems over a relatively long period of time to the degree that they adversely affect their academic performance and ability to initiate and maintain friendships. Further, these children also tend to exhibit fear or anxiety with regard to personal and school-related issues and display a pervasive mood of unhappiness or depression. Generally, the inappropriate social-emotional behaviors exhibited by these children can be used to classify them into two broad-band groupings that have received support from numerous investigations. (For reviews, see Achenbach & Edelbrock, 1978; Quay & Werry, 1986.) These two groupings reflect a distinction between children exhibiting undercontrolled, externalizing behaviors such as those classified as verbally or physically aggressive, disruptive, hyperactive, antisocial, destructive, and noncompliant; and those children exhibiting overcontrolled, internalizing behaviors such as those classified as fearful, inhibited, withdrawn, socially inhibited, and depressed.

The prevalence estimates of children experiencing social-emotional problems are quite varied depending on whether there is more emphasis placed on externalizing or internalizing problems. Variability in prevalence estimates is also exacerbated by a lack of standardized measures to assess characteristics indicative of serious social-emotional impairment, differences in the methodology employed, as well as social policy and economic variables that may influence identification procedures (Kauffman, 1985). In addition, attitudes, expectations, and biases of school personnel influence prevalence estimates (Ysseldyke, Algozzine, & Richey, 1982). With respect to the externalizing type of emotionally disturbed children, Walker et al. (1987), on the basis of their review of numerous studies, stated that approximately 2% of students are identified as having serious behavior disorders. However, Wood and Larkin (1979) claimed that this frequently cited 2% prevalence estimate is based more on tradition and myth than on actual data. Achenbach and Edelbrock (1978) reported a prevalence estimate for externalizing behavior disorders at a substantially higher 6–10%. Children who exhibit social and emotional problems that are externalizing, such as noncompliance and aggression, have the highest probability of being referred to a professional for help and intervention (Walker, Reavis, Rhode, & Jenson, 1985)—at about the rate of one child per classroom. According to Achenbach (1966), externalizers outnumber internalizers by a two to one margin in boys, while the converse is apparent for girls. Children who exhibit emotional or social problems characterized as internalizing in nature, such as depression, social withdrawal, and isolation, are usually perceived as having problems that are the result of self-owned deficiencies rather than environmental deficiencies (Brophy & Rohrkemper, 1981). These internalizing children are less likely to be referred for special education services (Walker et al., 1985). Investigations employing peer group norms in attempts to identify seriously emotionally disturbed children who could be classified as the internalizing type suggested a prevalence rate of 1–3% of the school-age population (Walker et al., 1985). That is equivalent to approximately one child in every two classrooms.

Children exhibiting social-emotional problem behavior, irrespective of whether they are internalizers or externalizers, are typically referred for professional help that may employ any number of interventions (with varied results) ranging from counseling to exclusion from classroom activities to medication. The internalizers, depending on their age and developmental status, are the most likely candidates to receive either no help or some sort of individual or group counseling.

For the externalizers, almost all the school-based interventions, irrespective of their theoretical underpinnings, involve some degree of exclusion from regular classroom activities. This exclusion from the regular classroom activities appears to be most appreciated by teachers—as may be quite understandable. If a child exhibits disruptive behavior to the extent it interferes with a teacher's instructional efforts, the easiest and quickest way to deal with the problem behavior is to exclude the child from the classroom. Further, many externalizing children are excluded not only from regular education, but also from special education. Safer (1982) suggested that after the externalizing problem child reaches the age of 16, the educational system covertly encourages the child to drop out. Safer believes that these "pushed-out" externalizing children comprise 17–24% of the population of students who withdraw from public education prior to finishing high school.

SELF-MODELING FOR CHILDREN WITH
SOCIAL-EMOTIONAL PROBLEMS

Self-modeling is defined as the process of repeated observation of oneself on videotapes (usually edited) that depict only appropriate or desired behaviors (cf., Dowrick & Dove, 1980; see Chapter 7 for a more thorough presentation of the rationale and theoretical assumptions underlying self-modeling). Because socially and emotionally disturbed children tend to be deficient in self-esteem and self-efficacy, one would expect that interventions based on modeling would not be very effective. Although social learning theory postulates that the greater the similarities between the model and the observer, the greater the potency of the model (Kagan, 1958; Kazdin, 1974a), it also postulates that the higher the level of esteem in which the model is held, the more potent the model (Bandura & Huston, 1961; Bandura, Ross, & Ross, 1961; Hosford & Krumboltz, 1969; Eisler & Hersen, 1973). Therefore, one would not expect the self-esteem of these children to be high enough to make the models (i.e., themselves) potent to the observer. Nevertheless, self-modeling has been shown to be an effective intervention with children exhibiting social-emotional problem behaviors (Dowrick, 1986). Furthermore, there is some evidence to suggest that the self-modeling intervention enhances self-esteem. For example, Germaine and Dowrick (1985), in a study that targeted public-speaking skills, found that subjects who profited most were those who evidenced the lowest levels of self-esteem prior to intervention.

One possible explanation for why self-modeling is an effective intervention for children with relatively low self-esteem may be that, in addition to imitative learning, the self-observer may also be influenced by self-efficacy. That is, in addition to being influenced by imitating the self-model, the child's behavior may also be influenced by seeing himself or herself perform a task successfully and therefore seeing the evidence that he or she can indeed perform the target behavior appropriately. The child's level of self-efficacy is enhanced to the degree that there is a consequent change in behavior.

When there is need for individualized treatment for children exhibiting social-emotional behavior problems with the concomitant deficits in self-esteem and self-efficacy, the selection of self-modeling as an intervention may be warranted. Furthermore, self-modeling clearly meets the criteria for the least restrictive intervention available to many of these children. There is an increasing amount of evidence to support the use of self-modeling as an effective intervention over the wide range of target behaviors characteristic of these children.

SELF-MODELING FOR EXTERNALIZING CHILDREN

A study that illustrates the efficacy of self-modeling across several externalizing problem behaviors was conducted by Gonzales (1988). He employed self-modeling with four children who were inpatients in a child psychiatric hospital ward. These children, who ranged from 8 to 11 years old, were diagnosed as having "severe conduct disorder." Each child was videotaped attempting four target behaviors: bed making, saying "thank you" in response to appropriate social cues, playing and interacting appropriately with peers, and eating appropriately. These videotapes were then edited to create four self-modeling tapes for each child, one for each of the four target behaviors. After baseline data were collected, the children then viewed one of their edited videotapes per week during the 4-week multiple-baseline treatment phase of the study. The sequence of presentation of each child's four videotapes was varied according to a Latin square design. All subjects evidenced significant improvement in their performance over baseline for all four target behaviors. The results support the use of the self-modeling intervention as a behavioral treatment modality with a severely behaviorally disturbed, hospitalized population.

One of the earliest studies employing self-modeling with externalizing children was conducted by Davis (1979) to reduce fighting behaviors and noncompliant responses in an 11-year-old special education student. Previous attempts to alter the child's behavior using a contingency management program and a token economy were not appreciably successful. With respect to the fighting behavior, Davis engaged the child's peers as confederates in order to assist in the construction of the self-modeling videotape. The peer-confederates role played aggressive and abusive behavior toward the subject—behavior that would typically provoke the subject into a fight. The subject role played resisting the urge to respond by fighting, and instead stated, "I don't fight anymore." This videotape, constructed through role playing, was then employed as the self-modeling intervention. The noncompliant responses to teacher requests were also addressed by having the child role play appropriate responses to the teacher's efforts to control his behavior. The result of the intervention designed to reduce fighting was the occurrence of only one episode during the 4th day of intervention. Fighting did not occur again during the remainder of the intervention phase or during the follow-up observation. The second target behavior, the child's inappropriate responses to teacher attempts to control his classroom behavior, was reduced from a baseline average of five per day to no occurrences for 6 of the 10 days of intervention. During the other 4 days, inappropriate responses were recorded at a maximum rate of only twice a day, and then only in the presence of a substitute teacher.

As previously mentioned, children who exhibit severe social-emotional problems, particularly externalizing behavior problems, are usually excluded, to some degree, from regular classroom activities and placed in self-contained special education classes. These settings almost always employ, with varying degrees of success, some form of token economy as the primary means of controlling the children's behavior. Consequently, if self-modeling is going to be used as an intervention for children within these settings, it may be advantageous to implement it "on top of" the token economy. In one of our studies (Kehle, Clark, Jenson, & Wampold, 1986) we used self-modeling to reduce disruptive classroom behaviors of four externalizing, behavior disordered children. We employed the procedure in an ongoing, self-contained, special education classroom of 12 children, where the teacher used a token economy that consisted of both positive reinforcements for nondisruptive behaviors and response cost for disruptive classroom behaviors. Although the token economy was in place, the level of disruption in the classroom still remained quite high. The teacher report indicated that the four children who were selected to be involved in the study were the most disruptive and inattentive (46% of the time) in the class. Furthermore, three of the children, on the basis of the Revised Connor's Questionnaire, Teacher Form (Connor, 1973), were judged to be hyperactive. Maladaptive behavior was defined, in accordance with O'Leary et al. (1979), as instances of touching, vocalizing, aggression, playing, orienting (head turned at least 90 degrees from point of reference), making noise, and being either completely or partially out of one's seat.

We used an ABA withdrawal design replicated three times, with a control subject and a follow-up phase. The procedure consequently involved four phases: a baseline, an edited-tape intervention, a withdrawal of intervention, and follow-up observation. During the baseline phase the observers sat at a table to one side of the classroom. No special instructions, other than those needed to produce the individual videotapes, were given to the teacher, the teacher's aide, the four subjects, or any other child in the classroom. All data-collection sessions occurred during regularly scheduled afternoon class lessons, which typically involved the academic subjects of history, reading, and science. Whenever possible, data were collected concurrently on all subjects. Baseline data were collected for 4 to 6 days. During the baseline, disruptive behaviors were recorded for all subjects.

The intervention phase began immediately following baseline. The subjects were videotaped during regular classroom activities for a period of approximately 25 to 30 minutes. Three of the children (the fourth served as a control) were instructed to behave in a manner that was incompatible with their typically disruptive classroom behavior for the entire taping session. This instruction was intended to reduce the actual amount of editing. However, as should have been expected, asking the children to be good was not very effective. The percentage of time the children were disruptive remained quite high; therefore, it was necessary to substantially edit the tapes to remove all occurrences of the seven disruptive behaviors described by O'Leary et al. (1979). To eliminate the possibility that the children would view themselves receiving rewards and therefore confound the treatment effects of the tape, the administration of tokens was also deleted from the tapes. After editing, each of the three children, accompanied by an adult, individually viewed their 11-minute edited videotape of appropriate-only classroom behavior. There was no substantial time delay between the baseline videotaping, editing, and the children viewing their edited videotapes. The three experimental children were videotaped on one day, the videotape was edited that evening, and the children were shown their edited videotape of appropriate-only behavior the next day that they were present in class. Similarly, the control child viewed an 11-minute videotape; however, this videotape was not edited and depicted his typically disruptive and inappropriate classroom behavior. He viewed his unedited tape for 3 days, then for 1 day did not view any videotape, and finally viewed an edited videotape for 2 days. After the children viewed their respective videotapes, they returned to their regularly scheduled classroom activities where their behavior was observed and recorded.

During the withdrawal phase, which immediately followed the intervention phase, the observers simply recorded the classroom behavior of the children. They did not remove children from the classroom to view their edited videotapes. For the three experimental children, data were collected for a period of 6 to 7 days.

Finally, the procedure employed a follow-up phase that was conducted 6 weeks after the termination of the withdrawal phase. Classroom behavioral data were collected on all four children for a period of 3 days. During this follow-up, no tapes were presented to the children.

The results of the Kehle et al. study indicated clear and dramatic effects for the three experimental subjects and for the control child after introduction of the self-modeling condition. As stated previously, during baseline, the four children involved in the study displayed inappropriate and disruptive classroom behavior approximately 46% of the time. During the intervention phase of the study, the disruption rate for the children in treatment was reduced to an average of 11%. The control child, as previously mentioned, was initially shown an unedited 11-minute videotape that essentially depicted his gross inappropriate and disruptive classroom behavior; consequently, his behavior worsened. After introduction of the unedited videotape, his inappropriate behavior increased from 48% at baseline to 57%. An edited, self-modeling videotape was presented after the control condition, and his behavior improved markedly to the extent that his inappropriate behavior occurred only 14% of the time. Six weeks after the termination of the study, follow-up observations indicated that the positive treatment effects were maintained. The children exhibited disruptive and inappropriate classroom behaviors on an average of only 8% of the time. The teacher's perceptions of the children's behavior were also substantially improved, relative to her prestudy Connor's scores, indicating that none of the four children involved in the study exhibited hyperactive behaviors.

In the Kehle et al. study, the subjects' behavior did not return to baseline after withdrawal of treatment. It is difficult to state with confidence exactly why the children's behavior did not reverse. The self-modeling intervention was implemented "on top of" the ongoing token economy. A possible explanation is that a "behavior trap" occurred where the children's improved behavior was maintained by increased rewards received through the token system. Also, it is reasonable to assume that the token points dispensed by the teacher and aides increased in salience, and, possibly, the effect of observing peers that were also subjects may have been influential. Irrespective of these possible alternative hypotheses, the self-modeling intervention was impressive. Further, the technique was employed in an ongoing self-contained classroom and proved to be relatively simple to implement, requiring little time. Perhaps most significantly, the intervention was relatively unobtrusive and therefore in concert with the notion of employing the least intrusive intervention to ensure positive gain.

In another study conducted in a school setting, Gonzales and Pigott (1986) used a self-modeling intervention with a 2-year-old Down syndrome child who exhibited severe externalizing or disruptive classroom behavior. During classroom activities, this child would typically run and hide from his teachers. He would also engage other children in play during inappropriate times, strike other children, and, on occasion, purposely fall out of his chair. In this study, baseline data were obtained prior to the filming and construction of a self-modeling videotape. During the baseline phase of the study, mean percentage of appropriate behavior was determined to be 46%. The self-modeling videotape, in which all inappropriate or "off-task" behaviors were edited out, was then introduced to the child, who viewed it twice per day for a period of 3 to 5 minutes. The child's percentage of appropriate behavior increased from a baseline mean of 46% to a posttreatment mean of 96%.

In a study dealing with an externalizing 7-year-old female special education child who was also diagnosed as having schizophrenia, Greelis and Kazaoka (1979) employed a novel variation on self-modeling using cartoons as a reinforcer. The primary purpose of the intervention was to attempt to increase on-task school-related behaviors, decrease temper tantrums, and decrease "turnovers" (instances of moving from on-task to off-task behaviors). The first phase of the study involved the recording of baseline frequencies of on-task/off-task behavior, tantrumming, and turnovers. During this condition, the child was placed in a training room that had a one-way mirror, but taught by her regular teacher. The teaching sessions were videotaped and eventually an edited videotape was constructed. This edited videotape began with a 30-second segment in which the child was engaged in on-task behavior. This was followed by a 30-second segment of the child's favorite cartoon (*Popeye*). This sequence was repeated and then followed by a 30-second segment of the child tantrumming and a 60-second segment of blank screen. The sequencing was designed so that apppropriate behavior was followed by the cartoon reinforcer, while inappropriate behavior was paired with an absence of the reinforcer. This videotape intervention resulted in a decrease in tantrums from a baseline frequency of 6 per day to an intervention frequency of 0.6 per day. Turnovers also decreased substantially, although levels of on-task behavior increased only slightly (54.8% during baseline to 57.8% during the intervention). The result that tantrumming, paired with punishment (i.e., a blank screen), decreased in frequency, while on-task behavior paired with a reinforcer (i.e., cartoon) did not substantially improve was explained with reference to research conducted by Gunderson, Autry, and Mosher (1974), who maintained that schizophrenics are more responsive to punishment than positive reinforcement. (For a closer examination of related issues, see Chapter 17.)

SELF-MODELING FOR INTERNALIZING CHILDREN

Dowrick and Hood (1978) used a self-modeling intervention to increase the classroom conversational skills of two electively mute 5-year-old children. These two children conversed freely in the home environment but elected to remain completely silent in the school setting. Dowrick and Hood experimented with constructing an appropriate self-modeling videotape. They first attempted to combine talking scenes taken in the home situation with different scenes from the school setting to give the impression that the two environments were somehow compatible, if not contiguous; however, this strategy proved to be ineffective. The tapes that finally were successful were designed to duplicate the classroom environment in the home setting; they combined carefully scripted footage from both situations. Dowrick and Hood included props such as wall charts and books to help create the illusion that the home setting was the classroom. The self-modeling intervention produced dramatic results; the frequency of classroom verbal expression increased to appropriate levels and was maintained at a 6-month follow-up.

In another study involving elective mutism, we used self-modeling in the treatment of a 3rd-grade boy in a regular classroom setting (Pigott & Gonzales, 1987). Apparently, the child had evidenced periods of elective mutism for over 4 years. The child was academically above average. Nevertheless, his behavior was characterized as extremely shy and so socially withdrawn that he would not answer direct questions from teachers or peers, would not initiate interactions or volunteer to answer questions, and would evidence severe psychomotor retardation when called upon to assist the teacher in distributing papers or other tasks. Behavioral observations in a clinic setting revealed that the child was completely mute and simply would not play or talk with the therapist in this situation. When asked a direct question, he typically would respond by curling up into a fetal position in the corner of the room. However, when his mother or younger brother were present in the room, he would respond to the therapist's questions in a normal voice and also would play normally. Videotapes were constructed of him in his reading class while his mother and younger brother were present and by staging scenes after class. The videotapes were edited into two self-modeling tapes of approximately 3 minutes in duration. The first tape depicted the child responding to direct questions, and the second tape showed the child raising his hand to volunteer to answer various questions that were asked to the class as a whole. The tapes were then viewed by the child, approximately 8 to 10 times, while in his home setting over a period of 2 weeks. The results indicated that both behaviors, answering direct questions and volunteering to answer questions, increased. Further, these marked improvements in appropriate behavior were maintained until the end of the academic year.

In a study involving the treatment of a 5-year-old internalizing child, Dowrick (1979) used self-modeling to improve the child's socialization skills. Specifically, the target behaviors included increasing the child's willingness to participate in group activities, increasing nonverbal interactions in peer play activities, and increasing the number of verbal interactions. The child did not emit enough appropriate responses to allow the construction of an intervention tape. Consequently, to facilitate making the videotape, the child was administered a single dose of Valium. Dowrick reported that the target behaviors were substantially increased and were maintained at 3-, 4-, and 12-month follow-ups.

Self-modeling has also been shown to be an effective intervention to improve the personal safety of developmentally disabled young adults (Dowrick, 1986). Videotapes were used to create role plays showing the subjects responding to risky social situations with appropriate "safe" choices. There were some unanticipated interesting and socially relevant results. An assessment of the intervention indicated that the majority of new learning occurred during the self-modeling phase of training. The subjects tended to view their self-modeling videotapes intermittently as a "review" in order to enhance memory of their newly acquired social skills, and, as a result of learning new choices in socially risky situations, one subject was able to appropriately assert herself to prevent potentially harmful harassment by a man in a grocery store, about a year after the training.

SELF-MODELING FOR DEPRESSED CHILDREN

There is a dearth of literature on effective interventions for children who are diagnosed as depressed. One of the few recently completed experimental studies was conducted by Kahn, Kehle, Jenson, and Clark (1990), who reported that self-modeling can be successfully employed as an intervention to deal with adolescent depression. Their extensive study consisted of two comprehensive phases. The first phase was designed to assess the prevalence of depressive symptomatology among middle-school students, aged 13–15; the second phase was designed to test the efficacy of self-modeling, along with two other more traditional treatments, in decreasing depressive symptomatology. The first phase employed a three-stage, multimethod assessment model for the screening of an entire middle-school population of 1,293 sixth-, seventh-, and eighth-graders. The results of the prevalence study indicated that between 6 and 14% of middle-school adolescents were identified as depressed at various stages of the multistage-multimethod assessment model. The second phase of the study employed a pretest-posttest control group design to compare the efficacy of self-modeling with cognitive-behavioral and relaxation therapy interventions. All three active treatment groups were compared to a wait-list control group. Students identified in the initial prevalence phase as meeting the clinical criteria for depression were randomly assigned to one of the four groups. Depressed students who were assigned to the cognitive-behavioral or the relaxation therapy conditions were seen in small groups. In total, both of these treatment conditions consisted of twelve 50-minute sessions over an 8-week period.

The cognitive-behavioral and relaxation treatment strategies have been previously validated as effective interventions for adult depression (Beck, Rush, Shaw, & Emery, 1979; Kazdin, Esveldt-Dawson, Sherick, & Colbus, 1985; Lewinsohn & Clarke, 1984), and Prince and Dowrick (1984) have employed self-modeling to treat adult depression. The use of self-modeling as an intervention for depression assumes that internal events, such as cognitions and feelings, function as covert behaviors that are subject to the same laws of learning as overt behavioral responses (Lewinsohn et al., 1984). Consequently, we assumed in the Kahn et al. study that the targeting, videotaping, and self-modeling of covert and overt behavior responses incompatible with covert processes of depression, such as smiling, verbalizing positive self-statements, and attributions, would facilitate both behavioral and affective gains.

The students who were randomly assigned to the self-modeling treatment condition initially received a brief explanation by the senior author of intervention procedures and rationale. Target behaviors were selected from the depression and social skills literature (Kazdin et al., 1985; Lewinsohn & Clarke, 1984; Prince & Dowrick, 1984). These target behaviors included appropriate eye contact; body posture; positive affect-related expressions such as smiling, gesturing, and the use of a pleasant tone of voice; verbalizations of positive, prosocial self-attributions regarding personal, family, school, and social functioning and pleasant events. The construction of the edited videotapes involved the subjects role playing not being depressed. Consequently, in order to construct the tapes, subjects were given instructions on how to act and opportunities to model and rehearse these behaviors. This procedure not only substantially reduced the amount of editing needed, but also greatly increased the quality of the videotapes. The self-modeling treatment condition involved each student viewing his or her own edited intervention videotape 12 times during the same 8-week period that the other two treatment conditions were implemented. The videotapes were approximately 10 minutes in length. During the student's viewing of his or her videotape, no critique or social reinforcement was provided.

Posttesting and a 1-month follow-up indicated that the self-modeling, cognitive-behavioral, and relaxation treatment groups all produced substantial and significant results relative to the control group. The students who were involved with the cognitive-behavioral treatment evidenced the most pronounced attenuation of depression; however, both the relaxation and self-modeling treatment groups also evidenced substantial improvement to the degree that there was an absence of clinically significant depressive symptomatology. The results also indicated that students in all three treatment groups clearly evidenced significant and substantial improvement in their self-concepts over the control students. Parent and consumer report data added further support for the efficacy of the active treatment conditions. The results support the contention that effective interventions designed to attenuate adolescent depression can be implemented in regular educational settings. Further, all three interventions were short term and did not involve an inordinate amount of staff time or expense. This is particularly true for the self-modeling intervention that, in total, involved only 120 minutes of the students' time. Consequently, the self-modeling procedure, relative to the other two treatment conditions, may be most in concert with the notion of employing the least restrictive intervention that ensures positive gain.

The Kahn et al. (1990) study was an interesting experimental test for the efficacy and applicability of the self-modeling intervention. In comparison with two established interventions designed to attenuate depression, self-modeling proved to be comparable in promoting the psychological health of adolescent students. In the majority of the previous studies reviewed in this chapter, the primary foci were on the modification of behavior. In the Kahn et al. study, self-modeling was employed to change the students' attitudes toward themselves resulting in increased positive self-concepts and decreased depressive symptomatology. Close inspection of the results of this study, along with anecdotal data gleaned from discussions with the students following the termination of the experimental procedures, would argue for the design of an intervention for adolescent depression that incorporated aspects of all three treatments. Further, it seems reasonable that the potency of the self-modeling intervention with depressed adolescents could be enhanced by presenting two or three times, three or four different edited treatment videotapes to the students, rather than the same tape 12 times. Another possible refinement of the self-modeling procedure with this type of population is to socially reinforce the students while they view their respective videotapes.

CONCLUSION

The majority of studies examining the efficacy of self-modeling videotapes as an intervention to enhance children's emotional and social functioning indicate positive results. The intervention is relatively simple to use, requires little time to implement, and is unobtrusive. Also self-modeling can be employed in a variety of settings with both externalizing and internalizing children who exhibit diverse social and emotional problems.

With the presentation of a videotaped self-model to a child, one can expect the target behavior to increase. Care must be taken to ensure that the constructed edited videotape shows only the targeted behavior. Often the construction of videotape is such that scenes depicting irrelevant behaviors are left on the edited videotape. If such does occur, one can expect that, in addition to the target behavior, the irrelevant behavior will also be modeled and will increase in frequency relative to baseline. In the Kehle et al. study, showing an unedited videotape of inappropriate and disruptive classroom behavior to the control child produced immediate and dramatic gains in inappropriate and disruptive classroom behavior. Also, during that particular study, we inadvertently left in some footage on one child's edited intervention tape that depicted him with his hand at his mouth. This behavior was not one of the seven disruptive classroom behaviors that were targeted to be edited out of the intervention tapes. Although no systematic data were collected on the frequency of the child holding his hand to his mouth, the increase of this behavior was substantial and salient enough that we reedited the videotape to exclude this behavior.

CHAPTER 17

Using Video with Developmentally Disabled Learners

PATRICIA J. KRANTZ
GREGORY S. MacDUFF
OLLE WADSTROM
LYNN E. McCLANNAHAN

In this chapter, Dr. Krantz and her colleagues explore variations on the established ways of using video for the benefit of children and adults who have very challenging disabilities. First, they briefly enumerate several arguments for using video where other methods have failed (e.g., video eschews reliance on language; video readily enables repeated exposure). They then describe self-modeling procedures for deaf, mentally retarded adults. Five case studies are described in some detail to indicate when and under what circumstances success was achieved (or not achieved) in attempts to teach sign language and self-care skills. The remainder of the chapter concerns children and teenagers with autism. One case (a 7-year-old girl with high rates of self-injury) is particularly instructive because: (a) they were eventually successful with a generalization issue previously resistant to other efforts, (b) a succession of techniques and combined approaches is described in a multistage solution, and (c) through this sequence of techniques they effectively taught the girl how to learn from her own adaptive (edited) video image. Other cases (precursors to self-injury, conversational skills, and noncontextual vocalizations) are described in detail to offer some insight into the procedural elements contributing to these developing techniques. Based on these experiences, the authors end with a list of recommendations and suggestions for further exploration.

P.W.D.

Teaching everyday living skills and management of difficult behavior problems to children and adults with severe developmental disabilities presents many challenges. This chapter examines the potential of video in helping to meet these challenges. The section that follows provides a selective review of other investigators' experiences with video-intervention strategies. Subsequently, our own experiences in exploring the promise (and the limitations) of video self-modeling are described in some detail. The chapter concludes with some methodological considerations that appear to preface a more systematic and informed approach to the use of video technology with learners who are severely handicapped.

SOME POTENTIAL ADVANTAGES OF VIDEO

Video appears to offer many advantages to learners with developmental disabilities. First, for those who have acquired "TV-watching" skills, video can sometimes capture the attention of people who, in other contexts, display extreme attentional deficits. We first noted this some years ago, after videotaping children with autism while they performed in a holiday program for their parents. After a first viewing of the tape, some of the children repeatedly requested it; we made copies of the original tape, because of its frequent use.

Second, video offers an alternative instructional medium for students who cannot read or who do not have complex language repertoires (Browning & White, 1986). Indeed, a well-constructed video may circumvent many symbol interpretation requirements by presenting learners with straightforward imitation tasks.

Third, for people whose observational learning skills are not well developed, video creates opportunities for repeated viewings of target performances. Charlop and Milstein (1989), for example, reported that three high-functioning children with autism met criterion on a brief conversation after 3 to 20 presentations of the videotaped conversation. (People with more severe skill deficits might require more viewings.)

Fourth, the video medium can display target skills in the settings where they must ultimately be displayed, for example, at home, at school, in the community, or in the workplace. Haring, Kennedy, Adams, and Pitts-Conway (1987) questioned partic-ipants about videotaped models' performances in order to promote generalization of shopping skills from training settings to probe settings. The three participants with autism did not generalize to community stores until video training was provided. DeRoo and Haralson (1971) used video to increase the work rates of educable mentally retarded adults in a vocational evaluation center. Videotapes were presented individually to each participant; the tapes were stopped when off-task behavior occurred; and workers were asked how those behaviors affected their work. All individuals in the experimental group made at least 50% gains in productivity, while none of the control group members achieved this criterion.

Fifth, video may lead to new intervention strategies that help disabled learners control severe behavior problems. For example, Greelis and Kazaoka (1979) obtained videotapes of a 7-year-old retarded girl's tantrums and on-task behaviors in the classroom. After baseline, the child viewed 30-second segments of her on-task performance, followed by 60 seconds of cartoons, and 30-second segments of her tantrums, followed by 60 seconds of a blank screen. Tantrums decreased and remained low after the intervention was withdrawn.

Sixth, video promises augmented behavioral measurement, such as recording of complete response chains and assessment of complex behavior. Video also can enhance data analysis and estimates of the reliability of measurement (Powers & Handelman, 1984).

Seventh, the video medium offers new opportunities to address the generalization deficits displayed by people with severe developmental disabilities. Although clients may acquire many new skills and learn to control inappropriate responses, these accomplishments are of limited value unless the new repertoires transfer to extra-treatment settings. Daoust, Williams, and Rolider (1987) successfully employed audiotapes and videotapes to mediate delayed consequences for the aggressive and self-injurious responses of an adolescent girl with severe retardation. Delayed consequences (rewards, compliance training, momentary manual restraint, and timeout) were first delivered in the clinic to decrease target responses at home; later, the parents used audiotape-mediated delayed consequences to alter their daughter's school performance.

Traditionally, many strategies for promoting transfer of skills from treatment to nontreatment settings have depended upon clients' verbal reports. Thus, training to achieve isomorphic relationships between verbal and nonverbal behavior, or between "saying" and "doing," is of particular interest because it appears to offer a means of programming generalization across settings and time. By reinforcing *accurate* verbal reports of nonverbal behavior, investigators have increased children's prosocial responses (Rogers-Warren & Baer, 1976) and their use of specific leisure materials (Israel & Brown, 1977) and have decreased hyperactivity and inattention (Paniagua, 1987) at different times and in different settings than those in which the verbal reports were made. Risley and Hart (1968) noted that their training procedures "developed a generalized correspondence between the verbal and non-verbal behaviors of these children such that their temporally remote non-verbal behavior could be modified by simply reinforcing their verbal behavior" (p. 280).

Perhaps partly as a result of requirements for verbal reports of temporally remote events, research that addresses verbal-nonverbal correspondence training with severely developmentally disabled learners is virtually nonexistent. It is precisely in this area, however, that video may hold special promise. For people with minimal language repertoires, videotapes may bridge the gaps between different settings and times, enabling them to report on their previously occurring (but presently visible) nonverbal behavior. The establishment of verbal control over nonverbal behavior, or the development of functional say-do relationships, could have an important impact on treatment efficacy for persons with severe handicaps.

SELF-MODELING FOR ADULTS WITH SEVERE HANDICAPS

There is a logical connection between deafness and visual media. Video self-modeling procedures appear especially appropriate for people who are hearing impaired. As early as 1976, Dowrick described techniques for editing videotapes that displayed the subject as model; in subsequent years, he documented the salutary effects of self-modeling for children with physical disabilities such as cerebral palsy (Dowrick, 1983) and spina bifida (Dowrick & Dove, 1980). To date, however, only a handful of studies have examined videotaped "self as a model" procedures with persons who are severely developmentally disabled, and none have described the use of these procedures to teach sign language. The pilot studies described next were carefully monitored to determine how to revise, redevelop, and refine procedures.

The participants in these studies resided in an habilitation center for deaf, mentally retarded adults in Sweden. They viewed themselves on videotapes that consisted of three brief segments: (a) an "interest catcher" showing the person engaging in some nontarget activity in a familiar setting (providing an opportunity for the subject to identify himself or herself), (b) footage showing the participant modeling a target response (the duration of which was extended during editing), and (c) a segment showing the participant enjoying a natural consequence of the target behavior. For example, the subject might first see himself seated at the kitchen table, then see himself using the manual sign for coffee, and finally, see himself getting a cup of coffee and drinking it.

Self-Modeling of Manual Signs

T.H., a 39-year-old deaf and moderately retarded man, had learned to use some manual signs (nouns); his receptive vocabulary of signs appeared to be larger than his signing repertoire. A self-modeling videotape targeted his use of the sign "I do not want to. . . ." T.H. was able to imitate a staff member who modeled the sign off camera during videotaping. He watched his tape once a day and frequently imitated the video model. On day 40, he used the sign contextually at a time when he was *not* watching the tape, and subsequently continued to use the sign spontaneously and appropriately.

Similar procedures were used with L.P., a 43-year-old woman with mild retardation who engaged in self-injurious and destructive behaviors. At mealtimes, L.P. used a few manual signs (e.g., "eat," "cheese," "coffee," and "butter"). Her self-modeling tape featured the target sign for milk, which she used in her coffee. L.P. watched her videotape once a day for 30 days. Fifteen days after her last exposure to the self-modeling tape, she began to use the sign for milk at mealtimes, but she did not use the sign in any other relevant context.

A third participant, T.P., age 25, was deaf and moderately retarded. She had a lengthy history of self-injury (biting her wrists). She used approximately 10 signs, all of which were nouns. The target sign, "I do not want . . . ," was viewed on a self-modeling tape once a day for 51 days. T.P. used the sign immediately before or during her reviews of the videotape, but never used it functionally in other situations or at other times of day.

Finally, O.S., age 38, who was deaf and moderately retarded, had not acquired any signs. He communicated with staff members by taking their hands and leading them to objects that he wanted or to situations with which he needed assistance. When his videotape was prepared, O.S. was able to imitate a staff member who stood off camera and modeled the signs for apple and coffee. O.S. viewed his videotape twice a day for 63 days; he imitated the signs for apple and coffee while he watched the tape, but he never used these signs at other times of day or in other settings. A fortnight after he had ceased to review his videotape, a staff member reported that he had spontaneously signed "apple." He immediately received the apple, but there were no further reports of unprompted signing.

These projects suggest that subjects' extant expressive and receptive signing vocabularies may be predictors of the effects of video self-modeling procedures; to date, attempts to use self-modeling to teach a *first* manual sign have not been successful (cf., O.S.). It may also be noteworthy that T.P., who used only a small vocabulary of nouns, did not achieve functional use of a simple communication that included a verb.

Video Modeling of Toileting Skills

B.C., age 45, deaf and mildly retarded, had spent most of his life in an institution and had not yet learned how to clean himself after a bowel movement. When a videotape was prepared, a staff member modeled the relevant toileting skills, but the tape was edited to make it appear that B.C. was engaging in these behaviors. When B.C. first watched his tape, he appeared very confused; a week later, however, he approached the experimenter and signed, "You sly fox." B.C.'s underwear offered evidence that he was able to imitate "himself" after seeing the videotape. In evaluating this self-modeling procedure, it appears noteworthy that B.C. had an extensive signing vocabulary.

USING VIDEO WITH CHILDREN WITH AUTISM

On the other side of the Atlantic, other authors of this chapter were assessing video intervention strategies in a community-based treatment program for children, youth, and young adults with autism. Although these investigations varied with regard to settings, target responses, and characteristics of participants, all used videotaped models of the subjects themselves.

Videotapes in Intervention for Self-Injury

When first seen at age 4 years, Casey's head hitting had altered the configuration of her skull. She presented with multiple bruises, wearing a protective helmet. At school, an intervention package that included a rich differential reinforcement of other behavior (DRO) schedule, gradual fading of restraints, and a delayed reporting system ("notes" from her teachers that determined later access to special rewards) eventually eliminated self-injury. She began to acquire expressive language and academic skills.

At age 7, however, Casey continued to self-injure at home and on rides to and from school, at rates as high as 660 head hits per hour. Head hitting was usually accompanied by loud crying and screaming, kicking and tapping on objects, and "picking" with her fingernails at various parts of her body, causing bruises and contusions. Many hours of parent training and home programming did not alter these dysfunctional responses. Because Casey's treatment-setting repertoire was very different from her behavior in the presence of family members, self-modeling appeared to be a promising intervention. Thus, videotapes were made using Casey herself as a model of noninjury.

Videotapes of appropriate car ridership were made in the school driveway, with a therapist running beside the slow-moving vehicle to help Casey refrain from self-injury. The home-to-school tape showed Casey and her mother leaving the house and getting into the family automobile and then showed Casey (with hands in lap) talking to her mother. The school-to-home tape was the same, except that it began with a scene in which Casey and her mother left school. Videotapes of appropriate activities at home (e.g., playing the piano, playing with toys and siblings, eating meals, and preparing for bed) were also made with a therapist present and, like the ridership tapes, were edited to present only good performances.

At school, Casey began daily reviews of a 2-minute tape of her car ride from home to school. Although she visually attended to the video screen, self-injury continued during rides. Therefore, her parents were given a video camcorder and were asked to tape occurrences of self-injury while Casey was sitting in the car before the ride to school began. When Casey arrived at school, she and her mother were met by a therapist who obtained the parents' data and the videotape. Subsequently, Casey saw a tape of her self-injurious behavior and received a 30-second overcorrection procedure (Foxx & Azrin, 1973) consisting of rapid, guided hand movements; if no self-injury was reported, she reviewed a tape showing an appropriate ride from home to school and subsequently selected preferred activities or snacks. By day 18, self-injury was eliminated on the way to school, but continued to occur regularly during the ride from school to home and at home with her family. When the school-to-home videotape was scheduled for daily review, it had no impact on self-injury. But again, the differential consequences (overcorrection or special activities immediately following viewings) were applied. After day 24, parents' reports indicated that self-injury had ceased on rides from school to home.

Casey then began to review self-modeling tapes of her appropriate performances at home, and on this third intervention video self-modeling decreased self-injury at home without the addition of the overcorrection procedure. On those few occasions when she did self-injure, Casey attempted to negotiate with her parents to prevent them from getting the camera. The parents reported isolated episodes of self-injury over a 3-month period; then these reports ceased. A follow-up interview with the parents confirmed that self-injury was no longer observed at home.

This important therapeutic outcome encouraged us to undertake a controlled investigation of video self-modeling. Casey was again selected as the participant. It was noted that she sometimes exhibited certain responses—foot stomping, bruxism, pinching and scratching herself, tapping on objects, and "fussing"—that had been part of her earlier repertoire of self-injury. Continued practice of these behaviors seemed to enhance the possibility that head hitting could be reinstated.

Three classes (math, reading, and spelling) were selected for investigation because preliminary data showed that levels of potentially self-injurious behaviors were highest in these sessions. Three different teachers conducted these learning activities, which were scheduled Monday through Friday at 9:00, 10:30, and 11:30 A.M., respectively. Before research began, videotapes were obtained in each class and were edited to show only good performances. Throughout the study, camera operators (nonclinicians unfamiliar to Casey) taped 15 minutes of each class; observers later retrieved data on potentially self-injurious behaviors from the videotapes using a procedure of time sampling within 15-second intervals. A multiple-baseline design (Baer, Wolf, & Risley, 1968) across classes was used to assess the effects of self-modeling and video-mediated consequences.

During baseline (self-modeling), Casey watched 2-minute tapes of her own appropriate performances immediately before each class. The data showed that self-modeling tapes alone did not result in socially significant decreases in potentially self-injurious behavior.

When delayed consequences were added, Casey continued to view her good performance prior to each class, but also was taken to a nonacademic setting (a conference room) 20 minutes after each class; the 20-minute delay was used to review classroom tapes and to flag relevant segments. A therapist showed Casey 2 minutes of selected footage of the most recent videotape of her classroom performance. The absence of potentially self-injurious behaviors resulted in preferred activities, while the presence of tapping, stomping, bruxism, or other target responses produced the previously described overcorrection procedure. This treatment package was successively introduced in each of the three class sessions, producing rapid and robust changes in the levels of target responses.

It is noteworthy that Casey initially responded to the overcorrection contingency in two ways: (a) she ceased to exhibit target responses that had been followed by overcorrection, but during the next class sessions displayed different target responses, and (b) she began to close her eyes during video segments that showed target responses. When the latter behavior occurred, the videotape was placed on pause until she opened her eyes.

This successful intervention package is of special interest because video-mediated delayed consequences, delivered in a nonacademic setting, effected changes in Casey's behavior in three different classes, at different times of the day. It has been suggested that this generalization across persons, settings, and times (a central issue in autism treatment) might, in the context of video research, be dubbed "remote control."

Self-Modeling of Conversational Skills

Two youths with autism, Rory and Don, ages 19 and 15, had been in treatment for 12 years; in intervention settings, Rory's aggressive and disruptive behavior and Don's self-injury had decreased to low levels. Both youths were established "TV watchers," that is, they had been taught to visually attend to the screen and to answer questions about visual stimuli presented on video. In addition, clinical data indicated that both boys could imitate motor and verbal behavior modeled in vivo. Although they had acquired functional expressive language and frequently used phrases and simple sentences when interacting with treatment agents, they rarely conversed with peers. Their social interaction repertoires with adults suggested that self-modeling tapes of peer interaction could be obtained readily; this was not the case.

A month of training was necessary in order to tape self-modeling of peer interaction. Rory, who had some reading skills, eventually learned to use a script presented on a large, off-camera easel. Don used an audio headset and learned to repeat verbal prompts from a therapist who stood outside the classroom and observed via sound system and one-way window. Throughout training, neither youth responded to the other; both were dependent upon off-camera prompts.

After baseline measures documented negligible levels of peer conversation, the two youths watched their self-modeling tapes for 5 minutes three times per day but failed to interact during observation periods. Rewards for visually attending to the monitor did not increase peer conversation. Subsequently, simplified self-modeling tapes were made and the youths were rewarded for imitating their own videotaped behavior (e.g., standing up, sitting down, and saying one- to six-word utterances). During training, they met criterion on imitation of the simplified tapes, but they still failed to interact at scheduled observation times, even after three daily viewings of the peer-interaction tapes and the simplified tapes.

Finally, a therapist prompted and rewarded imitations of the peer-interaction tapes as the youths viewed them. Peer interactions during probes continued to be minimal.

The length of training time required to obtain self-modeling tapes may have been a predictor of outcome. Retrospectively, it appeared that we may have erred in targeting peer-interaction responses that were totally absent from the subjects' repertoires. Although following training the videotapes cued imitation, the presence of a peer in the environment did not evoke conversation.

Self-Modeling and Delayed Consequences to Decrease Noncontextual Laughing, Crying, and Vocal Noise

Scott entered a group home and school program at age 7. When first seen, he was mute, not toilet trained, and spent most of his waking hours attempting to shred clothing, linens, house plants, and other available materials and engaging in noncontextual laughing, crying, and noisemaking.

By age 11, he had acquired a small expressive language vocabulary, as well as many self-care, leisure, and home-living skills, but continued to display inappropriate laughing, crying, and vocal noise. For purposes of data collection, these three response classes were lumped together under the heading of "disruptive behavior."

A multiple-baseline design across three school sessions (verbal imitation, receptive language, and leisure skills) was used to assess the effects of self-modeling and video-mediated delayed consequences. These sessions were scheduled at 9:30 A.M., 11:00 A.M., and 12:00 noon, respectively, and were conducted by three different teachers, all of whom were uninformed about the purposes of the study. Videotaping began 60 seconds after Scott was seated in a classroom, and continued for the next 17 minutes. Data were later collected from videotapes by independent observers who scored the occurrence/nonoccurrence of disruptive behavior in 15-second intervals for 15 consecutive minutes, beginning after the first 60 seconds of videotape.

Prior to baseline, Scott was taught to identify himself in videotapes of his usual activities. When a trainer pointed to his image and asked, "Who is this?," he learned to respond "Scott" or "me." Training continued until he achieved criterion—8 of 10 correct responses in three consecutive session.

During baseline, Scott viewed no videotapes, with the exception that, after the last baseline session in his 12:00 P.M. class, he saw six taped segments, each 10 seconds in length. During each of these screenings, he was asked, "Who is this?," and he correctly responded. Footage of appropriate performances alternated with segments showing disruptive behaviors. After viewing appropriate performances, Scott received praise, tickles, and preferred snacks; after viewing disruptive segments, he engaged in contingent exercise (running in place). This "preview" of positive and corrective consequences occurred the day before treatment began in his 12:00 P.M. session.

During treatment, an experimenter scanned the videotapes immediately after they were made and selected three 10-second episodes of disruptive behavior or three 10-second segments of appropriate behavior. If less than three examples of disruptive behavior had been taped, one or more segments was repeated. If no disruptive behavior was taped, three examples of appropriate behavior were chosen. No later than 15 minutes after the end of a class, Scott and the experimenter went to a meeting room where he either (a) viewed three exemplars of his appropriate behavior and received three periods of preferred activities or (b) viewed three illustrations of his disruptive behavior and engaged in contingent exercise after each screening. During each 10-second videotape, the experimenter pointed to the screen and asked, "Who is this?"

Scott's levels of disruptive behavior dropped considerably when self-modeling tapes and delayed consequences were sequentially introduced. In his 12:00 noon, 11:00 A.M., and 9:30 A.M. classes respectively, mean percentages of 15-second intervals scored for disruptive behavior were 65%, 51%, and 60% during baseline and 15%, 17%, and 16% during treatment. Interval-by-interval interobserver agreement was calculated by dividing the number of agreements by the number of agreements plus disagreements and multiplying by 100 (Sulzer-Azaroff & Mayer, 1977). The means and ranges of interobserver agreement for each class were: 12:00, mean = 94% (range = 77% to 100%); 11:00, mean = 93% (range = 78% to 100%); and 9:30, mean = 94% (range = 75% to 100%).

Although Scott's classroom performance was variable, teachers perceived reductions in his disruptive behaviors as significant. After treatment began in his 12:00 class, the teacher spontaneously reported that she was becoming more skilled in working with Scott; similarly, after intervention began in the 11:00 session, that teacher also reported improvement in classroom behavior. In reviewing videotapes, the experimenters noted changes in the topography of Scott's behavior in all three classes after treatment began; loud screams and ongoing vocal noise were replaced by brief, low-volume vocalizations.

Ten months later, Scott was taken to the setting in which video reviews had occurred, and with "snow" on the monitor, he was asked, "Who is this?" On 10 consecutive trials, he replied, "Scott," or "me." His responses to snow on the monitor pose several possibilities. Perhaps he never recognized his own image on videotape, but learned that the question, "Who is this?," when paired with the monitor and/or the experimenter, required the responses "Scott" or "me." Or perhaps this severely language-delayed youth *did* recognize himself on videotape, but had no language to describe snow on the monitor. This dilemma illustrates one of the many methodological considerations that will be important in exploring, specifying, and enhancing the effectiveness of video self-modeling procedures for people with severe developmental disabilities.

SOME RECOMMENDATIONS ON METHODOLOGY

Developmentally disabled subjects vary widely in observation and imitation skills, language repertoires, and prompt dependency. Self-modeling procedures often include a large number of variables in addition to those identified as the primary independent variables (i.e., observation of video images of oneself). Our early incursions into video self-modeling have raised many questions and have suggested a number of methodological considerations that appear relevant to future investigations.

1. Detailed descriptions of subjects aid in determining when self-modeling procedures may be viable. Self-modeling was effective when a deaf learner had previously acquired manual signs, but was not effective in teaching a first sign. And there were major differences in the performances of high-functioning children with autism (cf., Charlop & Milstein, 1989) and low-functioning participants such as Rory and Don.
2. Preinvestigation assessment of subjects' skills may help to avoid underestimates of the potential of self-modeling procedures. Does the participant visually attend to the monitor? Can she label stimuli presented on the monitor? Can he discriminate images of himself from other persons or objects presented on the screen? Can she imitate responses that are modeled on video? These assessments are needed in order to identify behavioral repertoires that are prerequisite to participation in video modeling studies.
3. Isolation of relevant videotaped stimuli can rule out confounding variables. Typically, videotapes present multiple cues. Auditory stimuli could include treatment agents' voices and/or instructions, as well as other sounds embedded in the environment used for taping. Similarly, visual stimuli may encompass many aspects of the setting, for example, equipment and materials, caregivers, and other clients. Depending upon the purposes of a given investigation, it may be useful to turn off the sound, to display target video images against a plain background, or to edit out auditory and visual cues that are not necessary to the study.
4. The identity of the camera operator is important. If the camera operator also screens the resulting videotapes, this individual's presence may promote generalization across settings and times. This appears most likely when there is regular, ongoing taping and review of tapes (cf., the 1971 investigation of workers in a vocational evaluation center by DeRoo & Haralson) and perhaps less likely when a single videotape is created (cf., the manual signing tapes discussed earlier). In the studies of Casey and Scott described earlier, camera

operators were unfamiliar persons who were never present during videotape reviews.

5. The learner's history with the person who presents videotapes for review may impact on the results of the investigation. If this person is present in settings where new repertoires are ultimately to be displayed, the possibility remains that the treatment agent, rather than the videotapes, may mediate generalization across settings and times. Indeed, in some interventions, this possibility has been intentionally exploited for the purpose of transferring stimulus control from primary treatment agents to family members (cf., Daoust, et al., 1987).

6. The use of delayed contingencies can be preceded by video self-modeling to establish if videotapes alone may result in behavior change. Casey, for example, reviewed self-modeling tapes throughout each successive baseline condition before delayed contingencies were introduced, providing a demonstration that self-modeling alone was not sufficient to alter her potentially self-injurious behavior. In the absence of self-modeling baselines, it is impossible to determine whether video models, delayed consequences, or a combination of these is responsible for behavior change.

7. The use of video self-modeling procedures to achieve verbal-nonverbal correspondence across treatment and nontreatment settings has not yet been explored, but appears enticing. Such studies will be expensive, since they will require camera operators to regularly visit extratreatment environments.

8. Comparative analyses of video modeling and video self-modeling are needed. An extensive literature documents the effectiveness of video modeling across a variety of subject populations and target responses. Do video modeling and video self-modeling procedures produce differential effects? This important question has not yet been addressed.

A FINAL NOTE

Bud was a 5-year-old youngster with autism; his lengthy history of toe walking resulted in shortened tendons. Thus, he began to wear ankle weights and his therapists frequently reminded him, "Heels down." Some weeks later, Bud was asked to "point to heels"; he was unable to do so. When applied to video self-modeling, this anecdote can be viewed as a warning or an enticement. Can video images assist severely language-delayed people who cannot yet identify the referents for words such as "heels"? Is complex language a prerequisite for video playback procedures, or do video images supply useful feedback to people who cannot benefit from verbal descriptions of behavior?

Epilogue

SIMON J. BIGGS

The initial use of video by behavioral scientists, in the broadest sense of the name, seems at first glance to have been extremely optimistic. Here was a medium that provided quick and easy access to human activity. In therapy, unlike film, it could be fed back almost immediately, while in research video presented the opportunity for repeated exposures of identical events. However, 20 years after an edition of the *Journal of Mental and Nervous Disease* (Geerstma, 1969) was devoted solely to video, much of the promise of that initial work has yet to be fulfilled. This may be partly because video use fell between different existing fields of work. Although video users spanned a variety of disciplines and contexts (see Dowrick & Biggs, 1983), the concept of "videologist" first advanced by Willener, Millard, and Ganty (1976) has failed to take root. Instead, an alternative view that this technology is just another method (Alger & Hogan, 1967)—a tool in the hands of skilled practitioners in their parent fields—seems to have become the dominant understanding of how video should be used. Changes in methodology rarely have the moral or social impetus of innovation that accompanies the particular problems or needs of client or patient groups, unless they are closely identified with a single, high-profile issue. It may have been a singular act of hubris to expect anything more.

There is, as Shotter (1983) pointed out, something alienating about an overdependency on the external image that obscures human agency. Video comes between the investigator and the active subject (and not only when the equipment will not work properly), presenting humans as objects within a social context already suffused with preexisting constraints to self-activity. Video users often find that people are reluctant to appear on video; they dislike the image they see of themselves and are suspicious about how the taped material might be used. A second factor, however, may be more helpful to understand this fragmentation of video study. Television carries associations that influence what is seen on it. Outside the therapy room and research laboratory, TV monitors convey information that is both socially important and highly manicured. Images are presented following extensive editing, the telescoping of time, and the conscious self-presentation of those conveying "bites" of pithy and encapsulating information. It is difficult to argue that video's crude records of unguarded behavior are viewed as objective, real, and scientifically sound—outside, that is, the purest of settings. In short, the medium influences the data collected from viewing subjects in a reflective manner; that does not sit well with empiricist notions of direct apprehension by the scientist of social behavior. It is not at all clear to me that behavioral science has a paradigm that can both absorb this reflexivity and maintain existing investigative methodologies.

Against and perhaps in spite of such a background, the current compendium evidences a steady swell in video use on a wide variety of fronts; an increased depth in understanding for specific uses and breadth of application of video has been achieved. Video *does* make content available that cannot be found elsewhere. Material *can* be organized and presented in a variety of ways to enhance learning and inquiry, and the extent of viewing can be manipulated to facilitate different responses. There is growing attention to detail that maximizes the benefits and minimizes the negative effects of video use, often involving techniques that previously had been thought to contaminate the raw data of real-time recording. Examples include the use of computerized search and recall, self-modeling (democratic editing?), and triggers (video bites?) that, although described within a scientific or training paradigm, use techniques that would be familiar to any professional in the mass media. In harness with televisual literacy, video users have become more specific in the problems they are trying to address and less wary of using one method or technique as an integrated package in the service of functional goals.

The emerging result is one of a powerful medium with an identifiable record of achieving positive change in specialized areas. Video also can be used to reveal micro- and macropatterns of behavior and thus increase our understanding of human activity. Is video coming of age? It could be argued that in certain fields of inquiry a healthy and mature body is already evident. However, not wishing to stretch this analogy to incredulity, it would be foolish to assume that maturity is without its own tensions. Of the many possibilities, two warrant further consideration. First, video training material is increasingly prepackaged while much of its value depends upon spontaneity of response and impact. This is largely a product of its flexibility, which could be lost if enchantment with technology triumphs at the expense of involved consumers planning collaborative progress with video practitioners themselves. A second tension involves the manipulation of time. If there is a temptation in video research to repeat analysis of single incidents, revealing ever finer detail of the same, the representativeness of that incident becomes highly important. This is true not only for a population at one moment in time but also for comparative analysis among different time periods, decades, and generations. While at the same time subjecting the objectivity of any one incident to increased critical scrutiny, the use of comparative time data opens up fascinating research possibilities, such as the study of nonverbal gerontology and ideographic analysis at different points in the life cycle.

In conclusion, current developments in practical video could be characterized by optimism tempered by pragmatism. No videology has emerged with fanfare and grand gesture; in fact, there is not even an agreed upon vocabulary. However, neither has video become the passive tool of blinkered scientism. It is hoped that video use will continue to evolve where it is valuable and most effective.

Glossary of Technical Terms

Most of the terms listed here are more technical than those used (and defined) elsewhere in this book. The list is not intended to be a technical dictionary, but to provide explanations likely to be useful for behavioral scientists and practitioners working with the video medium. Italics are used to indicate cross-referenced definitions, where it seems useful to do so.

adaptors: metal units used to connect a *plug* with a nonmatching *jack* (e.g., stereo to mono, mini to RCA).

address code: usually a time code (hour, minute, second, frame) associated with a specific *frame* of recorded tape.

ambient: in the environment, such that it is often unnoticed until replay, as in **ambient sound, ambient light.**

amplifier: an electronic unit that boosts a signal (video or audio). **Pre amps** are used to boost camera signals; **distribution amps** are used to increase signal strength enough to serve multiple monitors or VCRS; **processor amps** are used to manipulate composite video signals (e.g., to correct color).

analog: an electrical signal representing light or sound qualities (brightness, volume, etc.) by variations in the strength of the current.

aperture: the lens opening; the width of the aperture in proportion to the lens's focal length is termed **f-stop.** A small f-stop (e.g., f/1.2) maximizes the use of available light.

aspect ratio: picture width to height; in television currently 4:3; planned for *HDTV,* 16:9, similar to 35mm film.

assembly editing: see *edit.*

audio level: amplitude of sound signal, which distorts in the upper ranges and typically cannot be boosted from low levels without increasing tape hiss; monitored by headphones or *VU* meters, or controlled by *automatic gain* circuitry.

audio mix: combined sound sources (e.g., previously recorded tapes) on a single track.

audio track: on most video systems of the 1980s, a **linear** magnetic code along the edge of the tape; newer systems (VHS and Beta *Hi-fi,* 8mm *PCM*) code audio diagonally across the tape with the video signal.

authoring: programming interactive video, or a computer system (e.g., authoring language) designed to assist that purpose.

auto iris: see *iris.*

auto focus: motor-driven focus, responding to picture sharpness or an infrared beam bounced off the center of the subject, or other system; often "confused" by very bright or dark objects and when primary subject is off center.

automatic gain control (AGC): circuitry (audio or video) to boost low signals and to prevent distortion of high-amplitude signals.

backlight: more light behind than in front of subject—may create exposure problems or may be used deliberately (e.g., disguise identity, glow around a person's head).

backtime: time remaining on a recording or in an editing interval.

balanced line: audio connection that induces no hum or random noise; requires XLR *connectors.*

band: range of frequencies. Also see *high band* and *format.*

Beta(max): see *format.*

black body: in theory, a completely nonreflective object used as a basis for calculations such as *color temperature.*

black box: in interactive video, a unit that interfaces the video and computer systems.

black level: video signal (approx. 7.5 *IRE*) too low to show on the picture tube; **black-level retention** is the quality of a TV screen that maintains subjective black color.

blanking: breaks during picture formation at the end of a line or a frame, like lifting the pen off the paper between words.

bleed: a tendency for colors (especially red) to spread, depending on picture-tube quality.

blocking: the director's plan for movement of subjects (*talent*) and camera.

BNC: see *connectors.*

boom: a pole, usually to position a microphone close to the action, above the view of the camera.

bridge: scaffolding for setting up lights.

broadcast mic: see *mic.*

broadcast quality: recording or receiving equipment meeting the current standards for broadcast TV (e.g., 330 lines of horizontal *resolution* in effect in most countries). See also *industrial* and *consumer quality.*

burn: damage done to a camera pickup tube by excessively bright, direct light; the resulting black spots can sometimes be repaired by recording several minutes of a uniform, white wall. Not to be confused with **burn-in,** which refers to a time code superimposed on a rough edit.

bus: usually a group of contacts related to a specific function.

busy: a scene in which some of the action or visual effect distracts from the main intent (calls for the direction, "don't just do something, stand there").

C: symbol for *chrominance.*

C-mount: a standard lens mount, interchangeable with most 35mm cameras.

cable compensation: electronic adjustment necessary with very long video (camera to recorder) cables.

CAI: computer-aided instruction, from which interactive video is a natural development.

cameo: a subject lit against a dark background (see also *limbo*).

camera: transmits the picture to a recorder or a monitor; a **camcorder** combines the camera and recorder in one unit.

capstan: a revolving shaft that controls tape speed (tape is pressed against capstan by a soft roller).

capture: original video footage as recorded through a camera.

cardioid: see *mic.*

cassette: self-loading videotape, including take-up reel in one housing; a **cartridge** loads onto a take-up reel inside the recorder or player.

cathode ray tube (CRT): the most common device used to project video signals, providing the screen in monitors and TVs; also used in video camera viewfinders, computer monitors, and oscilliscopes (see also *LED*).

CAV: see *disc.*

CCD: a tubeless video camera *pickup* device, popular because it is small and requires no time to warm up.

CCTV: closed-circuit television, mostly refers to video monitoring of another location without necessarily recording.

chapter: a division of a videodisc (not physical but set up by an address code) making direct access easy, sometimes incorporating an automatic pause.

character generator: circuitry for creating titles, sometimes a separate unit or built into a recorder or editing controller; usually operated through an alphabetic or typewriter-style keyboard.

chroma or **chrominance:** color signals, including the three primaries (red, green, blue) or **hue,** and their intensity, called saturation.

chromakey: a color (usually blue) that when used as a background in one recording can be replaced (overlayed) by another source.

cine film: celluloid (photographic) movie film (as used in cinemas).

CD: see *disc;* **CD-ROM,** see *ROM.*

CLV: see *disc.*

coax: see *connectors.*

color bars: standard rainbow signal with which to check color response (see *chroma*) of cameras and monitors.

color correction: limited adjustment to color may be achieved by controls on a monitor during replay; correction of the recording can be made only through editing, see *amp.*

color lock: a circuit to stabilize color during replay.

color matte: usually a border of adjustable width that can be superimposed on a recording during editing (*special effects*).

color temperature: indication of a color, usually the "whiteness" of a light; based on the degrees Kelvin of a *black body* that radiates the same hue (e.g., a tungsten light is about 3200° K).

colorizer: circuitry that provides editing control over color components of the video signal.

comb filter: circuitry to improve picture clarity (*resolution*) during replay or editing.

comet-trailing: effect of a bright object's movement on a dark background, occurring more with some types of *pickup* devices than others; see also *lag.*

compatibility: ability of a system to process recordings made in another system. There is no compatibility between *U-matic, Beta, VHS,* and *8mm;* there is no compatibility between *NTSC, PAL,* and *SECAM* (but some switchable machines are available); there is limited compatibility between different versions of the same format (newer versions often have **downward compatibility;** e.g., S-VHS machines can read VHS tapes, but not vice versa).

condenser: see *mic.*

connectors: to make a connection, a *plug* and a *jack* must be of the same type, and unfortunately there are myriads, the most common of which include:

  BNC: self-locking connector for video line.

  coax: coaxial (concentric conductors) video line, now usually with BNC or RCA connectors.

  mini: plug with a small, single pin with no sleeve, usually for audio (there are mono and stereo versions); also called **Japanese.**

  phono: bigger, heavyweight version of the mini.

  RCA: plug with a medium pin and a sleeve; also, confusingly, called a **phone** (plug).

  RF: plug with a very thin pin and a sleeve, sometimes threaded (receptacle usually sticks out, with thread visible); lugs and a screwdriver are also sometimes used for RF connection.

S: video line connector that keeps *chroma* (C) and *luminance* (Y) separate (see *high band* and *format*—Hi-8, S-VHS, etc.); also called **Y/C** connector.

VTR: various specialized heavy duty connectors carrying all video/audio signals, usually 1 1/2 inches wide, about eight pins, rectangular sleeve, used on professional equipment.

XLR: three-pin, locking audio connector used on professional equipment.

Y/C: same as *S.*

consumer quality: historically, off-the-shelf equipment from retail stores has been much inferior to *industrial* and *broadcast* quality; recently available consumer equipment often differs (from industrial) only in its more fragile components, fiddly controls, and automatic features.

contrast: the difference between black and white (10 steps between the extremes of brightness on the standard **gray scale**).

control track: a recorded pulse per frame on the edge of videotape, used to control speed.

conversion: usually a copy of a recording from one *format* into another (e.g., 8mm to VHS), or one national standard to another (e.g., PAL to NTSC).

cover shot: a shot from a quite different angle or one of related material (e.g., the faces of onlookers) recorded in case a **cutaway** is necessary (inserted to prevent jolts in subjective continuity of the edited product; see also *jump cut*).

crawl: see *titles.*

cross-fade: picture fades to black, new scene immediately fades in; similar for audio (see also *cut, dissolve,* and *wipe*).

crosstalk: interference on one track from a neighboring track (video or audio).

cue: distinctive sound or picture quality to indicate the beginning of a production step (record, edit, etc.); **cue track,** alternative name for an *address track.*

cut: sharp transition between edited or recorded scenes (see also *cross fade, dissolve,* and *wipe*).

cutaway: see *cover shot.*

cyc: cyclorama, a backcloth in a studio.

DAT: *digital* audiotape (tradename, there are other digital systems), the highest quality sound reproduction on tape currently available in retail stores.

dB or decibel: the measure used in signal-to-noise ratios (among other things); look for analog sound S/N more than 50 dB, digital sound about 100 dB, luminance and chroma, over 40 dB.

degausser: electromagnetic device for erasing tapes.

depth of field: the amount of the scene in focus; the wider the angle of the lens, the greater the depth of field.

dichroic: usually a type of one-way mirror that passes only one color.

digital: encoding by numerical values (rather than strength of a signal, see *analog*), providing stability and manipulability; used in discs (and some audiotapes), in picture information storage, and in some kinds of special effects.

dimmer board: system for controlling studio-lighting intensities.

disc: video discs, have picture information coding in refraction patterns, read by lasers (very stable, but unlike magnetic coding on tapes, cannot be readily erased and rewritten); two types: **CAV,** constant angular velocity; **CLV,** constant linear velocity, which fits more frames to a disc. Audio-only versions usually 4 1/2 inches (120cm) **CDs** (compact discs).

display: usually a video screen or the picture on it.

dissolve: picture "disintegrates" as new picture appears in its place (see also *cross fade, cut,* and *wipe*).

dolly: a platform (for a tripod) that rolls on wheels.

dropout: deterioration in magnetic coating of a videotape, evidenced by white flecks in the picture.

drum: cylinder around which tape moves, containing video *heads* (sometimes audio also).

dub: to copy recorded material. **Audio/video dub** refers to adding sound/picture to a recording, leaving the rest of the recording (video/audio) intact. **Dub up/down** refers to copying onto a better/worse format (if, say, 8mm is used for capture and replay, quality can be maximized by dubbing up to Hi-8 for editing, and dubbing down afterwards).

dubmaster: same as *submaster.*

edging: border effects on characters in *titles.*

edit: the process of copying *selected* excerpts from recordings to produce a new, electronically coherent recording. **Assembly** refers to editing in which each scene is added in sequence from beginning to end; **insert** editing, replacing a scene in the middle of a sequence, is more complicated because of timing and framing.

EFP: see *ENG.*

EIA: Electronics Industries Association (USA), sets national standards for equipment and cooperates with associations in other countries attempting to set international standards.

8mm: see *format.*

electret: see *mic.*

encoder: camera circuitry that codes *luminance* and *chrominance* (brightness and color).

ENG: electronic news gathering, production on location using portable recording equipment; when intended to go live, with in-field capability to switch between multiple cameras, it is called **EFP,** electronic field production.

enhancement: usually refers to contour sharpening during replay or editing.

erase: to scramble magnetic code on tape so that it appears (or sounds) blank; when a **stationary** erase head is used on a videorecorder, it leaves partial frames because the erase head is vertical and the picture coding is diagonal (see also *degausser* and *flying erase heads*).

establishing shot: picture, usually a long shot or wide angle, to show the context of the action.

fade: see *cross-fade.*

feedback: part of a signal bounced back to its source; can be used to improve the signal or may cause distortion (as when a microphone is pointed at a monitor); for use of the term psychologically, see Chapter 6 (feedforward, see Chapter 7).

field: half a video *frame.*

fill: lighting to reduce shadows.

film chain: projection and recording system to copy *cine film* onto videotape.

flying erase head: positioned in front of the moving *record head* to erase other recorded material line by line; facilitates glitch-free recording and editing.

format: a reference to the type of recording system used (see Chapter 1), the most common of which are:

Betamax: 1/2-inch cassette type; also **Super Beta,** a similar, slightly superior system.

ED-Beta: "extended definition," physically similar to Beta, uses superior high band electronics—as in *Hi-8.*

8mm: videotape is 8mm wide, packaged in a cassette (similar size to an audio cassette).

Hi-8: "*high band* 8mm" physically similar to 8mm, uses effectively superior electronics to separate and improve *luminance* and *chrominance* signals.

S-VHS: "super" VHS, physically similar to VHS, uses superior high-band electronics—as in *Hi-8.*

U-matic: 3/4-inch large cassette type (originally a Sony trademark).

VHS: "video home system," 1/2-inch cassette type (**VHS-C** is the same format in a smaller cassette).

frame: one screenful of picture; in the American *NTSC* standard, 525 lines of picture code, exposed for 1/30 sec.; in *PAL* and *SECAM,* 625 lines, 1/25 sec.

freeze frame: (also **still frame**) a still picture created from a single frame; quality greatly facilitated by multiple video *heads* (three or more) on tape machines, *CAV* on discs, or *digital* capability of the player (displays a stored picture).

FM (frequency modulation): a system for sending a signal in which frequency is used as the code for other properties (e.g., amplitude). Video recordings use *high-band* and *low-band* frequency modulation.

f-stop: see *aperture.*

fuzzy logic: microchip circuitry that attempts to improve a picture (during recording or display), based on information about probable patterns of light and color.

F/X: shorthand for special effects, especially of the type used in fantasy sequences.

gaffer: chief lighting technician and operator.

gain: increase in signal, often in reference to a boost in picture under low-light conditions.

gel: colored filter, usually heat-resistant plastic, for a lamp.

generation: a copy (or subsequent copy) of a tape. Note each *dub* (e.g., from capture to edit master to distribution copy) takes another generation, inevitably with some loss of quality.

genlock: component for synchronizing recording sources, essential to exact editing or combining multiple cameras.

ghosting: a double image in which the unintended version is relatively faint, usually a result of an unclear signal.

graphic: a drawing, usually electronically generated rather than "photographed."

gray scale: see *contrast.*

HDTV: high definition television, with more lines to the frame, international standards for which are currently being negotiated. (A European version will probably be commercially available by the time this book is published.)

head: electromagnet for recording or erasing.

head shot: recording in which head and shoulders of subject fills most of the frame; also **very close up.**

helical scan: the process of recording with *heads* that rotate in a *drum* around which the tape is moving; resultant recordings are laid diagonally across the tape.

hertz: cycles per second.

Hi-8: see *format.*

high band: a recording in which coding for brightness and color is much more precise than **low band** (using *FM* for *luminance* and *chrominance* over greater bandwidths). See *format.*

hi-fi: in video systems, usually reserved for audio recordings that use *helical scan,* producing much better quality sound than those using linear *tracks.* See also *PCM.*

high gain: descriptor of a component (e.g., screen) or a switch setting that enhances apparent brightness (may result in a grainier picture).

hold: **horizontal** and **vertical** hold refers to systems for adjusting the top of a frame or the ends of lines to match the edge of the cathode ray tube in the screen; manually adjustable on some monitors.

hue: see *chroma.*

hunting: unwanted movement of a camera's automatic focusing system, usually the unstable response to too much or too little light on the main picture subject.

illumination, minimum: the least amount of light, usually stated in *lux,* for a given camera to operate to capacity. (Manufacturers specifications serve as a rough guide, compared with independent lab measurements.)

image enhancement: system to improve picture detail, usually by sharpening brightness or color contours.

image retention: tendency of picture elements to fade too slowly after removal of light or electronic stimulus; similar to *lag.*

impedance: resistance to an electrical current, often important in audio con-figurations (e.g., microphones have different, relatively low impedances; "line" inputs have high impedance).

indexing: ability of a player or recorder to mark and find a recorded element, usually a frame.

industrial: term used to refer to **quality** of equipment (see also *broadcast quality*), usually distinguished from *consumer quality* by durability of components and minor design attributes relative to purpose (e.g., may have no extended or slow recording speeds).

insert: see *edit.*

interactive: automated ability of a video system to stop and proceed at different choice points, usually with "branching" (restarting at different places) depending on the user's response. (See Chapter 9 for conventional distinctions between different "levels" of interactivity.)

interlace: a system of fitting two fields (half-frames) into a *frame.* For example, in NTSC, a picture is displayed as one field of even-numbered lines (for 1/60 sec) followed by a field of odd lines; perfect interlace is necessary for the proper alignment of the picture elements.

iris: variable diameter hole behind a lens affecting the amount of light in the picture. Most cameras have an **auto**(matic) **iris;** being able to override with a **manual iris** is desirable in unevenly lit conditions (especially *backlight*).

jack: common term for the receptacle of a *plug.* For types, see *connectors.*

jog/shuttle: control (dial) on a player that allows convenient frame-by-frame (jog) and variable-speed (shuttle) forward and reverse tape movement; very useful in editing and for informal video analysis.

joystick: control device for computer-generated pictures, used in computer games and some interactive video.

key: see *chromakey.*

lag: an effect in which moving-picture elements leave an image momentarily behind themselves, usually a result of weak signal relative to screen or pickup device quality.

lavalier: see *mic.*

LED: light-emitting diode, commonly used for counters on portable equipment, because it uses very little power.

light pen: penlike device, capable of interacting with computer-based video systems through the screen.

limbo: subject visible against a white or neutral background apparently of no substance (see also *cameo*).

line: screen-width component of a picture (see *frame*) made up of points of light, coded for brightness and hue. Also a term for video and audio transmission (via patch cords) between recorders and some monitors; hence **line in/out** receptacles on equipment.

linear: a recording designed to play without interruption (contrast with *interactive*).

lip sync: see *sync sound.*

location: productions making use of natural settings (not a studio) are said to be "on location."

looping: taking a video/audio signal out of one device into another; special switch settings or *distribution amps* may be necessary if several devices are linked to one source.

low band: see *high band.*

lumen: a measurement unit used in reference to the amount of light emitted by a source (e.g., lamp).

luminance: the video signal information concerning brightness.

lux: a measurement unit of illumination, used in reference to the amount of light available to the camera.

master: the videotape (usually the final product of editing) from which copies (sometimes *submasters*) are made.

matte: a solid color used as a border, a background, or a *chromakey.*

menu: a list, usually on a screen, from which to choose operations or program continuation points.

mic: microphones convert sound vibrations into electrical impulses; types are distinguished by their use or design, including:

> **broadcast,** clip-on or directional type, using restricted radio frequencies to transmit to a receiver connected to camera or recorder.

> **cardioid** and **spherical,** receptive to a sphere-shaped, relatively close field in front of the mic.

condenser, electrical condenser component improves sensitivity to sound, but also to damage.

dynamic, mechanical diaphragm less sensitive but more robust than condenser type.

eight-characteristics, most receptive to two spherical fields either side of the mic.

electret, a condenser type, using less power to operate.

lavalier, small clip-on or "collar" type.

wireless, same as "broadcast."

mini: see *connectors*.

mixer: a component that creates a single signal from multiple sources.

modulation: see *FM*.

monitor: a screen set that accepts *line* signals (in contrast to a television that accepts broadcast signals, including those from a VCR using an *RF* converter); the majority of quality TV sets also function as monitors.

NAB: National Association of Broadcasters (USA, radio and television), another standards-setting organization.

Nebraska scale: original term for the description of "levels" of *interactivity* in video and computer assisted applications (see Chapter 1).

newvicon: a type of camera *pickup tube* (quite sensitive in low light).

noise: unwanted signal, video or audio, hence *signal-to-noise ratio*.

NTSC: National Television Standards Committee, sets technical standards for recording and broadcasting (see *frame*) adopted in North America and Japan. Incompatible with *PAL* and *SECAM,* although some "switchable" equipment is available.

oversampling: essentially the rate (2x, 4x, 8x the standard) of reading discs, in which code is read multiple times for slightly improved quality (higher rates of oversampling actually make the conversion of digital back to analog cheaper— beware of marketing enthusiasm).

overscan: the amount of the picture that gets trimmed off the edges when projected on a monitor or TV screen (from less than 1% up to 10%, hence the central 90% called "safe area").

package: system of diverse components capable of accomplishing a set task without supplement; hence video or "equipment packages," also "intervention packages" possibly incorporating multiple uses of video.

PAL: Phase Alternation Line; standards adopted in most European countries and their trading partners for recording and TV broadcasting (see *frame*). Incompatible with *NTSC* and *SECAM,* although some "switchable" equipment is available (more complex, but better definition and color than NTSC).

patch: a connection between one system component and other, as in **patch cord** and **patch board.**

PCM: pulse code modulation, a superior sound-recording system (digital, not to be confused with *DAT*) often available with top-end 8mm video equipment.

phase: a complete unit in a repeated pattern (usually a frequency cycle), hence the need for phase **correctors** to merge some kinds of signals.

phone plug: see *connectors.*

phosphor: the coating inside a cathode ray tube that responds to electron beams, producing the screen picture.

pickup tube: video camera cathode ray tube, for converting light into a TV picture or a recording. See also *CCD,* a newer device with similar function.

picture tube: see *cathode ray tube.*

PIP: picture-in-picture; capability of a television or a VCR to display a picture with one or more other pictures superimposed on segments of the screen (made possible by *digital* technology).

pixel: discrete (individual) picture element; the more pixels, the better the picture quality (potentially).

plug: the "male" end of a connector or patch cord; for types, see *connectors.*

plumbicon: type of camera *pickup tube* (popular industrially for its minimal *lag*).

polarity reversal: reversing brightness values, to produce an image that looks like a "negative"; some cameras and special effects components have a switch for this purpose.

portapak: small portable recorder with separate camera (originally an early Sony trademark).

postproduction: mostly refers to postrecording, as in editing, etc.

preroll: pre-edit tape movement (usually 5 sec.) to bring two machines up to full speed before copying (editing) one recording onto another.

processing amplifier: a component to electronically correct identifiable anomalies (e.g., framing errors) in a recording.

pulse: a code added to each video frame to facilitate editing.

quad: quadraplex; a 2-inch videotape system, for a long time the standard in broadcast television (common *tungsten* type).

quartz lamp: popular lighting, because it maintains even *color temperature* through most of its life.

rack focus: a change of focus (camera otherwise unmoved) to shift viewer's attention (e.g., to a more distant person).

RCA: see *connectors.*

reaction shot: usually a close up of an observer's emotional reaction (useful as a cutaway; cf. *cover shot*).

real estate: available space on disc or tape.

real time: a sequence that does not abbreviate or expand elapsed (actual) time.

rear-screen projection: still or moving scene, often used as a studio backdrop, on a translucent screen with projector behind it.

record head: electromagnet for coding signals on tape; may be in a fixed position (most audio) or rotating in a drum for video or *hi-fi* and *PCM* audio.

registration: bringing together the three primaries in a color picture element.

remote: a wireless control unit. Also a term for on *location* production.

resolution: picture clarity, based on the number of elements in a picture (*pixels*), confusingly referred to as "lines." See Chapter 1 for resolution capacities of different *formats* (also limited by TV/monitor capacity).

RF: radio frequencies, including TV frequencies, for broadcast purposes; an **RF converter** translates a video/audio signal into a broadcast frequency so it can be fed into an antenna (usually via channel 3 or 4)—results in a slight loss of quality compared with a *line* connection to a *monitor*.

RGB input: indicates a capability to accept this type of computer screen (color) signal; some monitors can carry both RGB and television/VCR images.

roll: see *titles*.

ROM: read-only memory; picture and data on compact discs as **CD-ROM** are becoming common to interactive video.

room noise: recordings on *location* to provide background in later editing.

safe area: see *overscan*.

saticon: type of camera *pickup tube*, with good response and reasonable cost, used in consumer and industrial products.

saturation: see *chroma*.

scan: fast forward or fast reverse while displaying picture or sound. See also *search*.

S-connector: see *connectors*.

search: fast forward or reverse (video or audio), programmed to stop at blank intervals or other conditions; does not usually display picture or sound while searching. See also *scan*.

SECAM: Sequential Couleur a Memoire, standards adopted in France, USSR, and many of their trading partners for recording and TV broadcasting (see *frame* for specifications). Incompatible with *NTSC* and *PAL,* although some "switchable" equipment is available (less complex than PAL, and best color stability of all three).

SelectaVision: a type of videodisc system (developed by RCA), no longer manufactured.

sequence: one or more video shots expressing a single thought (cf., a written paragraph).

shot sheet: list of shots in order of production (usually different order from script).

signal-to-noise ratio: measure of wanted signal level relative to unwanted signal generated by the circuitry (units in *dBs*).

skew: tension of videotape during recording or replay.

small-format video: currently anything with 3/4-inch or narrower tape width (use likely to change).

SMPTE time code: Society of Motion Picture and Television Engineers, widely adopted address code: hour, minute, second, frame (two digits each).

softlight: provides diffuse, even light over the whole scene.

special effects generator (SEG):   editing component that creates special transitions (e.g., *cross-fades*) and interfaces multiple sources (**switcher**). May also add effects, such as borders, titles.

splice: method of cutting and joining, common with *cine* film but used with video or audiotape only in emergencies such as preserving an original too poor to be copied.

split screen: capability of showing two half-pictures on the screen simultaneously.

stabilizer: device for absorbing vibrations and jolts during camera movement (enables smooth pictures from hand held and vehicle mounted cameras—trade name **Steadicam**).

still frame: same as *freeze frame.*

storyboard: a script incorporating cartoon-like drawings of each scene.

strobe: a flickering light with black intervals (1/10 to 1/2 sec), creates the impression of jerking movements; or an imitation of the effect on screen.

submaster: or dubmaster, direct copy of *master,* used to make distribution copies (adds a *generation,* but saves wear on the master).

superimposition: combination of two images, usually title or text over picture.

switcher: see *special effects generator.*

sync: a component to generate or read the timing pulse on the *control track.*

sync sound: use of original sound from a scene, especially speech (called **lip sync**), i.e., not dubbed or added sound.

take: recorded material from a single camera "roll" (start to stop or pause); directors frequently produce multiple takes of a scene and select the best one during editing.

talent: filmakers' term for actors, subjects, or anyone else who is to appear in the recording.

tape: videotape of different *formats* (VHS, 8mm, etc.) is essentially the same material (metal oxide or particle-coated plastic, capable of maintaining electro-magnetic fields), but packaged in physically incompatible cassettes; recording incompatiblity may exist between *high-band* and low-band tapes, which use different coatings.

tearing: horizontal sliding within the picture.

technical director: second in command to "the" director, responsible for equipment operation and sets.

telecine: same as *film chain.*

teleprompter: display of text for actors to read while on camera (originally a trademark).

termination: a resistance setting (usually 75 ohms) for the last unit when several monitors are linked (*looped*) together.

tight shot: close-up in which very little background is visible, often used to surprise the viewer with a change of setting, conceal the presence of a threat, etc.

time base corrector: component, essential to some forms of editing, to synchronize video signals (frame onset, line duration, etc).

time code: see *address code* and *SMPTE.*

time-lapse recording: product of a system that records short sequences at specified intervals only, featured as an automatic control on some cameras.

titles: may be captured from mockups or generated from keyboards on cameras or *SEG*s; some systems allow titles (or other images) to **crawl** across the screen or to **roll** up it.

track: linear or diagonal (on tape) or circular (on disc) coding of video, audio, address, or control information.

tracking: extent to which tracks on a recording match the read heads of a player; most VCRs automatically adjust the thread of a tape to maximize tracking, but some machines have manual controls.

tracking shot: one in which the camera moves to match the subject's movement.

treatment: summary of a production proposal.

triaxial cable: an efficient, lightweight cable, useful when video components (especially camera and recorder) are separated by distances of several meters.

tungsten light: a studio favorite for general lighting because it maintains relatively uniform *color temperature* throughout its lifetime.

two-shot: two people in the picture.

UHF: ultra-high frequency, an inferior band of broadcast frequencies, usually to be ignored in video configurations (see *VHF*), but, confusingly, may also be used to refer to cables and *connectors.*

U-matic: see *format.*

VCR: video cassette recorder, now more common than **VTR,** video tape recorder.

VDU: visual display unit, includes video monitors and computer screens.

VHF: very high frequency, band of broadcast frequencies used by most major networks and the usual antenna marker for connecting a VCR with *RF converter*.

VHS: see *format*.

video level: strength of video signal, from *black level* to white (7.5–100 *IRE*), displayed on *VU* meters on sophisticated equipment only.

viewfinder: actually a miniature monitor built into the camera, shows almost exactly what the recorded image will look like, except it is usually monochrome.

voice-over: narration or other speech added to a video recording (usually via audio *dub*).

VU: volume units, meter to indicate signal strength (audio or video).

white balance: a camera circuit that adjusts the mix of primaries (analogous to human perception) for white and other colors to appear stable under different lights, such as fluorescent versus daylight. Usually automatic, older systems require resetting using a white card.

window: an area on screen in which images may be inserted (or in the recorded picture—see *chromakey*).

windscreen: usually foam plastic covering for a mic to prevent recording of wind noises without interfering with recording of voices and other sounds.

wipe: a transition (using an *SEG*) in which the new picture starts as a point or a line on the screen and expands behind a leading edge (straight line or a circle) to "wipe" out the previous picture.

workprint: a roughly edited copy from original capture used to establish sequences, timing, and transitions.

XLR: see *connectors*.

Y: symbol for *luminance*.

zoom: a lens that is variably adjusted from wide angle (zoom **out**) to telescope (close up or zoom **in**), or the recorded effect of using one; most camcorders have zoom lenses with **ratios** 6:1, 8:1, or 10:1 (ratio of the widest visual angle to the narrowest); sometimes with motors (that can be heard faintly when using a built-in mic).

References

Abkarian, G. G., King, P., & Krappes, T. L. (1987). Enhancing interaction in a difficult-to-test child: The PPVT-TV technique. *Journal of Learning Disabilities, 20,* 268–269.

Achenbach, T. M. (1966). The classification of children's psychiatric symptoms: A factor-analytic study. *Psychological Monographs, 80,* (7, Whole No. 615).

Achenbach, T. M., & Edelbrock, C. (1978). The classification of child psychopathology: A review and analysis of empirical efforts. *Psychological Bulletin, 85,* 1275–1301.

Acker, S. R., & Levitt, S. R. (1987). Designing videoconference facilities for improved eye contact. *Journal of Broadcasting & Electronic Media, 31,* 181–191.

Adamson, L. B., Bakeman, R., Smith, C. B., & Walters, A. S. (1987). Adults' interpretation of infants' acts. *Developmental Psychology, 23,* 383–387.

Aguirre, B. E., & Marshall, M. G. (1988). Training family day care providers using self-study written and video materials. *Child & Youth Care Quarterly, 17,* 115–127.

Alger, I. (1969). Therapeutic use of videotape playback. *Journal of Nervous and Mental Diseases, 148,* 430–436.

Alger, I. (1978). Freeze-frame video in psychotherapy. In M. M. Berger (Ed.), *Videotape techniques in psychiatric training and treatment* (2nd ed.). (pp. 244–257). New York: Brunner/Mazel.

Alger, I. (1984). Stimulus tapes on attitudes, supervision, and stereotypes. *Hospital & Community Psychiatry, 35,* 984–985.

Alger, I., & Hogan, P. (1967). The use of videotape recording in conjoint marital therapy. *American Journal of Psychiatry, 123,* 1425–1430.

Alkire, A. A., & Brunse, A. J. (1974). Impact and possible casualty from videotape feedback in marital therapy. *Journal of Consulting and Clinical Psychology, 39,* 203–210.

Alloy, L. B., & Abramson, L. Y. (1979). Judgment of contingency in depressed and nondepressed students: Sadder but wiser? *Journal of Experimental Psychology, 108,* 441–487.

American Medical Association. (1980). *Principles of medical ethics.* Chicago: Author.

American Nurses' Association. (1976). *Code for nurses with interpretative statements.* Kansas City, MO: Author.

American Psychiatric Association. (1968). *Diagnostic and statistical manual of mental disorders* (2nd ed.). Washington, DC: Author.

American Psychological Association. (1981). Ethical principles of psychologists (rev. ed.). *American Psychologist, 36,* 633–638.

Anderson, J. R. (1984). The development of self-recognition: A review. *Developmental Psychobiology, 17*, 35–49.

Anholt, R. E. (1987). The effectiveness of relaxation training in reducing the anxiety level of vocational rehabilitation clients prior to an audio-videotaped simulation of a job interview. *Dissertation Abstracts International, 48*, 5A.

Annon, J. S., & Robinson, C. H. (1981). Video in sex therapy. In J. L. Fryrear & B. Fleshman (Eds.), *Videotherapy in mental health* (pp. 163–179). Springfield, IL: Charles C. Thomas.

Asendorpf, J. B. (1987). Videotape reconstruction of emotions and cognitions related to shyness. *Journal of Personality and Social Psychology, 53*, 542–549.

Ash, E., Biggs, S. J., & Mayhew, R. (1987). *Acceptable risk? Supervision in child abuse cases.* [Video]. London: Central Council for Education and Training in Social Work.

Bachman, J. C. (1961). Specificity vs. generality in learning and performing two large muscle motor tasks. *Research Quarterly, 32*, 3–11.

Badura, H. O., & Steinmeyer, E. M. (1984). Psychotherapeutic effects by audiovisual heteroconfrontation in a case of anorexia nervosa. *Psychotherapy and Psychosomatics, 41*, 1–6.

Baer, D. M., Wolf, M. M., & Risley, T. R. (1968). Some current dimensions of applied behavior analysis. *Journal of Applied Behavior Analysis, 1*, 91–97.

Bailey, D. C., Deni, R., & Finn-O'Connor, A. R. C. (1988). Operant response requirements affect touching of visual reinforcement by infants. *Bulletin of the Psychonomic Society, 26*, 118–119.

Bailey, G. D., & Scott, R. E. (1982). Studying nonverbal cues to improve trainer behavior. *Performance and Instruction, 21*, 24–25.

Bailey, K. G., Deardorff, P., & Nay, W. R. (1977). Students play therapist: Relative effects of role playing, videotape feedback, and modeling in a simulated interview. *Journal of Consulting and Clinical Psychology, 45*, 257–266.

Bailey, K. G., & Sowder, W. T. (1970). Audiotape and videotape self-confrontation in psychotherapy. *Psychological Bulletin, 74*, 127–137.

Balamore, U. (1987). Moral decision making in adolescence: A process oriented investigation. *Dissertation Abstracts International, 48*, 1526B.

Balzer, W. K., Doherty, M. E., & O'Connor, R., Jr. (1989). Effects of cognitive feedback on performance. *Psychological Bulletin, 106*, 410–433.

Bandura, A. (1969). *Principles of behavior modification.* New York: Holt, Rinehart, and Winston.

Bandura, A. (1972). *Who did what to whom?* [Film]. Champaign, IL: Research Press/Mager Associates.

Bandura, A. (1977). *Social learning theory.* Englewood Cliffs, NJ: Prentice-Hall.

Bandura, A. (1986). *Social foundations of thought and action: A social cognitive theory.* Englewood Cliffs, NJ: Prentice-Hall.

Bandura, A., Blanchard, E. B., & Ritter, R. (1969). The relative efficacy of desensitization and modeling approaches for inducing behavioral, affective, and attitudinal changes. *Journal of Personality and Social Psychology, 13*, 173–199.

Bandura, A., & Huston, A. (1961). Transmission of aggression through imitation of aggressive models. *Journal of Abnormal and Social Psychology, 63*, 575–582.

Bandura, A., & Krupers, C. J. (1964). Transmission of patterns of self-reinforcement through modeling. *Journal of Abnormal and Social Psychology, 69*, 1–9.

Bandura, A., Ross, D., & Ross, S. (1961). Vicarious reinforcement and imitative learning. *Journal of Abnormal and Social Psychology, 67,* 601–607.

Barmann, B. (1982). *The relative efficacy of peer versus self-modeling procedures for training abusive parents in positive child management techniques: Analysis of applied behavioral research using randomization test procedures.* Unpublished doctoral dissertation, University of California, Santa Barbara.

Barnes, O., Haith, M. M., & Roberts, R. J. (1988). Simultaneous electronic recording of video and digital information on the video channel of a VTR or VCR. *Behavior Research Methods, Instruments, and Computers, 20,* 32–36.

Barnett, M. A., Tetreault, P. A., & Masbad, I. (1987). Empathy with a rape victim: The role of similarity of experience. *Violence & Victims, 2,* 255–262.

Baron, R. A. (1970). Attraction toward the model and model's competence as determinants of adult imitative behavior. *Journal of Personality and Social Psychology, 14,* 345–351.

Barrand, J. (1989). Interpersonal process recall in the management of lupus erythematosis. *The University of Sydney Annual Report 1989.* Sydney: The University of Sydney.

Bass, R. F. (1987). Computer-assisted observer training. *Journal of Applied Behavior Analysis, 20,* 83–88.

Batts, C. L. (1978). The effects of modeling with contingent reinforcement, self-modeling, and role playing on developing interviewee skills in ex-offenders with the employment interview. *Dissertation Abstracts International, 89,* 2487–2488.

Beck, A. T., Rush, A. J., Shaw, B. F., & Emery, G. (1979). *Cognitive therapy for depression: A treatment manual.* New York: Guilford.

Beckner, S. (1990, July). Product probe: Bridging the chasm, with fancy features. *Videomaker,* pp. 17–20, 119, 121.

Begali, V. (1988). *Head injury in children and adolescents: A resource for school and allied professionals.* Brandon, VT: Clinical Psychology Publishing.

Beidel, D. C., Turner, S. M., & Allgood-Hill, B. (1989). *The use of videotape exposure sessions in the treatment of obsessive-compulsive disorder.* Paper presented at the annual conference of the Association for the Advancement of Behavior Therapy, Washington, DC.

Bensinger, C. (1981). *The video guide* (2nd ed.). Santa Barbara, CA: Video Info Publications.

Benton, D., Brett, V., & Brain, P. F. (1987). Glucose improves attention and reaction to frustration in children. *Biological Psychology, 24,* 95–100.

Berger, J. L. (Ed.). (1989). *Educators guide to free audio and video materials.* Randolph, WI: Educators Progress Service, Inc.

Berger, M. M. (Ed.). (1970). *Videotape techniques in psychiatric training and treatment.* New York: Brunner/Mazel.

Berger, M. M. (Ed.). (1978). *Videotape techniques in psychiatric training and treatment* (2nd. ed.). New York: Brunner/Mazel.

Bernstein, N. (1967). *The coordination and regulation of movements.* Oxford: Pergamon Press.

Berrenberg, J. L., & Weaver, C. A. (1989, August). *Teaching scientific method using self-produced videos of faculty research.* Paper presented at the annual meeting of the American Psychological Association, New Orleans, LA.

Betts, T. (1983). Developing a videotape library. In P. W. Dowrick & S. J. Biggs (Eds.), *Using video: Psychological and social applications.* Chichester, UK: Wiley.

Bigelow, A. E. (1981). The correspondence between self and image movement as a cue to self-recognition for young children. *The Journal of Genetic Psychology, 139,* 11-26.

Biggs, S. J. (1980). The me I see: Acting, participating, observing and viewing and their implications for video feedback. *Human Relations, 33,* 575-588.

Biggs, S. J. (1983). Choosing to change in video feedback. In P. W. Dowrick & S. J. Biggs (Eds.), *Using video: Psychological and social applications* (pp. 211-226). Chichester, UK: Wiley.

Blanchard, E. B., Kolb, L. C., Taylor, A. E., & Wittrock, D. A. (1989). Cardiac response to relevant stimuli as an adjunct in diagnosing post-traumatic stress disorder: Replication and extension. *Behavior Therapy, 20,* 535-543.

Boggs, J. E. (1989). *Videotaped self-observation: A method for reducing disruptive behavior in the classroom.* Unpublished master's thesis, Purdue University, West Lafayette, IN.

Booth, F. R., & Fairbank, D. W. (1983). Videotape feedback as a behavior management technique. *Behavior Disorders, 9,* 55-59.

Borgeaud, P., & Abernethy, B. (1987). Skilled perception in volleyball defense. *Journal of Sport Psychology, 9,* 400-406.

Borgenicht, L. (1985). Threat in the nuclear age: Children's responses to the nuclear arms debate. *School Psychology International, 6,* 187-193.

Borod, J. C., Lorch, M. P., Koff, E., & Nicholas, M. (1987). Effect of emotional context on bucco-facial apraxia. *Journal of Clinical and Experimental Neuropsychology, 9,* 155-161.

Boud, D., & Pearson, M. (1979). The trigger film: A stimulus for affective learning. *Programmed Learning and Education Technology, 16*(1).

Bower, E. M. (1982). Defining emotional disturbance: Public policy and research. *Psychology in the Schools, 19,* 55-60.

Bowker Company. (1986). *Educational film/video locator* (3rd ed.). New York: Author.

Brand, S. (1987). *The media lab: Inventing the future at MIT.* New York: Penguin.

Brooke, N. M., & Summerfield, Q. (1983). Analysis, synthesis, and perception of visible articulatory movements. *Journal of Phonetics, 11,* 63-76.

Brophy, J. E., & Rohrkemper, M. M. (1981). The influence of problem ownership on teachers' perceptions of and strategies for coping with problem students. *Journal of Educational Psychology, 73,* 295-311.

Brown, A. (1987). Using videotape feedback in a day treatment program. *Dissertation Abstracts International, 48,* 871B.

Browning, P., Nave, G., White, W. A., & Barkin, P. Z. (1985). Interactive video as an instructional technology for handicapped learners: A developmental and research program. *Australia & New Zealand Journal of Developmental Disabilities, 11,* 123-128.

Browning, P., & White, W. A. T. (1986). Teaching life enhancement skills with interactive video-based curricula. *Education and Training of the Mentally Retarded, 21,* 236-244.

Burch, M. R., Reiss, M. L., & Bailey, J. S. (1987). A competency-based "hands-on" training package for direct-care staff. *Journal of the Association for Persons with Severe Handicaps, 12,* 67-71.

Burkle, W. S., & Lucarotti, R. L. (1984). Videotaped patient medication instruction program using closed-circuit television. *American Journal of Hospital Pharmacy, 41,* 105-107.

Burwitz, L. (1975, September). *Observational learning and motor performance.* Paper presented at the IV Congress of the Federation Europeanne de Psychologie des Sports et des Activites Corporelles, Edinburgh, Scotland.

Buschbaum, D. G. (1986). Reassurance reconsidered. *Social Science & Medicine, 23,* 423–427.

Cacioppo, J. T., & Petty, R. E. (1979). Attitudes and cognitive response: An electrophysiological approach. *Journal of Personality and Social Psychology, 37,* 2181–2199.

Calvert, S. L., & Gersh, T. L. (1987). The selective use of sound effects and visual inserts for children's television story comprehension. *Journal of Applied Developmental Psychology, 8,* 363–375.

Campanelli, L. C. (1988). The effects of a didactic and guided imagery intervention regarding horrendous death by nuclear war upon fear of death, health locus of control, and social responsibility in health education college students. *Dissertation Abstracts International, 49,* 438A.

Carney, R. M., Hong, B. A., O'Connell, M. F., & Amado, H. (1981). Facial electromyography as a predictor of treatment outcome in depression. *British Journal of Psychiatry, 138,* 454–459.

Carr, E. G. (1985). Behavioral approaches to language and communication. In E. Schopter & G. Mesibov (Eds.), *Current issues in autism: Vol. III. Communication problems in autism* (pp. 37–57). New York: Plenum Press.

Carroll, W. R., & Bandura, A. (1982). The role of visual monitoring in observational learning of action patterns: Making the unobservable observable. *Journal of Motor Behavior, 14,* 153–167.

Cash, T. F., & Brown, T. A. (1987). Body image in anorexia nervosa and bulimia nervosa: A review of the literature. *Behavior Modification, 11,* 487–521.

Casswell, S. (1983). Applications of recording human performance. In P. W. Dowrick & S. J. Biggs (Eds.), *Using video: Psychological and social applications* (pp. 13–21). Chichester, UK: Wiley.

Caul, D. (1984). Group and videotape techniques for multiple personality disorder. *Psychiatric Annals, 14,* 43–50.

Channeling children's anger. (1988, Summer). *Amplifier,* pp. 3–4.

Charlop, M. H., & Milstein, J. P. (1989). Teaching autistic children conversational speech using video modeling. *Journal of Applied Behavior Analysis, 22,* 275–285.

Childress, A. R., McLellan, A. T., Ehrman, R., & O'Brien, C. P. (1988). Classically conditioned responses in opioid and cocaine dependence: A role in relapse? *National Institute on Drug Abuse: Research Monograph Series, 84,* 25–43.

Christina, R. W., & Corcos, D. M. (1988). *Coaches guide to teaching sport skills.* Champaign, IL: Human Kinetics Books.

Clark, H. B. (1988). *The GUIDE process: Guiding staff participation and performance.* [Videotape]. Tampa, FL: Florida Mental Health Institute.

Clark, R. E. (1983). Reconsidering research on learning from media. *Review of Educational Research, 53,* 445–459.

Clarke, A. H., & Ellgring, J. H. (1983). Computer-aided video. In P. W. Dowrick & S. J. Biggs (Eds.), *Using video: Psychological and social applications* (pp. 47–60). Chichester, UK: Wiley.

Cohen, H. (1980). *Equal rights for children.* Totowa, NJ: Rowman and Littlefield.

Colby, I. C., & Colby, D. (1987). Child sexual abuse: Videotaping the child sexual-abuse victim. [Special issue]. *Social Casework: The Journal of Contemporary Social Work, 68,* 117–121.

Collett, P. (1987). The viewers viewed. *Etc., 44,* 245–251.

Connor, C. (1973). Rating scales for use in drug studies in children. *Psychopharmacology Bulletin, 9,* 24–84.

Consolvo, C. A. (1988). *The influence of cognitive style on autobiographical memory in a brief videotape counseling interview.* Unpublished doctoral dissertation, Florida State University.

Cook, T. D., & Campbell, D. T. (1979). *Quasi-experimentation: Design and analysis issues for field settings.* Boston: Houghton Mifflin.

Cooker, P. G., & Nero, R. S. (1987). Effects of videotaped feedback on self-concept of patients in group psychotherapy. *Journal for Specialists in Group Work, 12,* 112–117.

Cooper, A. C., Biggs, S. J., & Bender, M. P. (1983). Social skills training with long-term clients in the community. In S. Spence & G. Shepherd (Eds.), *Developments in social skills training* (pp. 81–102). London: Academic Press.

Corder, B. F., Whiteside, R., Koehne, P., & Hortman, R. (1981). Structured techniques for handling loss and addition of members in adolescent psychotherapy groups. *Journal of Early Adolescence, 1,* 413–421.

Corder, B. F., Whiteside, R., McNeill, M., Brown, T., & Corder, R. F. (1981). An experimental study of the effect of structured videotape feedback on adolescent group psychotherapy process. *Journal of Youth and Adolescence, 10,* 255–262.

Cornelison, F. S., & Arsenian, J. (1960). A study of the response of psychotic patients to photographic self-image experience. *Psychiatric Quarterly, 34*(Suppl.), 1–8.

Costello, M. B., & Fragaszy, D. M. (1988). Prehension in Cebus and Saimiri: I. Grip type and hand preference. *American Journal of Primatology, 15,* 235–245.

Creer, T. L., & Miklich, D. R. (1970). The application of a self-modeling procedure to modify inappropriate behavior: A preliminary report. *Behaviour Research and Therapy, 8,* 91–92.

Crowell, J. A., & Anders, T. F. (1985). Case reports: Hypnogenic paroxysmal dystonia. *Journal of the American Academy of Child Psychiatry, 24,* 353–358.

Croyle, R. T., & Uretsky, M. B. (1987). Effects of mood on self-appraisal of health status. *Health Psychology, 6,* 239–253.

Czajka, J. M., & DeNisi, A. S. (1988). Effects of emotional disability and clear performance standards on performance ratings. *Academy of Management Journal, 31,* 394–404.

Dalton, D. W., & Hannafin, M. J. (1987). The effects of knowledge- versus context-based design strategies on information and application learning from interactive video. *Journal of Computer-Based Instruction, 14,* 138–141.

Daly, D. A. (1987). Use of the home VCR to facilitate transfer of fluency. *Journal of Fluency Disorders, 12,* 103–106.

Danet, B. N. (1968). Self-confrontation in psychotherapy reviewed. *American Journal of Psychotherapy, 22,* 245–258.

Daoust, P. M., Williams, W. L., & Rolider, A. (1987, May). *Eliminating aggression and SIB through audio/video mediated delayed consequences.* Paper presented at the meeting of the Association for Behavior Analysis, Nashville, TN.

Darrow, N. R., & Lynch, M. T. (1983). The use of photography activities with adolescent groups. In R. Middleman (Ed.), *Activities and action in groupwork* (pp. 77–83). New York: Haworth Press.

Dauw, D. C. (1988). Evaluating the effectiveness of the SECS' surrogate-assisted sex therapy model. *Journal of Sex Research, 24,* 269–275.

Davies, R. R., & Rogers, E. S. (1985). Social skills training with persons who are mentally retarded. *Mental Retardation, 23,* 186–196.

Davis, R. A. (1979). The impact of self-modeling on problem behaviors in school age children. *School Psychology Digest, 8,* 128–132.

DeAngelis, T. (1988, July). Family "thought units" clues to kids' coping. *APA Monitor,* p. 12.

DeBloois, M. (1988). *Use and effectiveness of videodisc training: A status report.* Falls Church, VA: Future Systems.

Denton, L. (1988, February). Mental health field begins to interact with new technology. *APA Monitor,* pp. 20–21.

DeRoo, W. M., & Haralson, H. L. (1971). Increasing workshop production through self-visualization on videotape. *Mental Retardation,* 22–25.

Dillingham, L. M., Roe, J. J., & Roe, M. D. (1982). Selected applications of computer-assisted video instruction in the education of hearing-impaired students. *American Annals of the Deaf, 127,* 652–658.

Dispezio, M. (1990, July). Digitizers: Importing the real life. *Videomaker,* pp. 15–16.

Dodge, K. A., & Cole, J. D. (1987). Social-information-processing factors in reactive and proactive aggression in children's peer groups. [Special issue: Integrating personality and social psychology.] *Journal of Personality & Social Psychology, 53,* 1146–1158.

Dodge, K. A., & Somberg, D. R. (1987). Hostile attributional biases among aggressive boys are exacerbated under conditions of threats to the self. *Child Development, 58,* 213–224.

Doody, S. G., Bird, A. M., & Ross, D. (1985). The effect of auditory and visual models on acquisition of a timing task. *Human Movement Science, 4,* 271–281.

Douglis, C. (1987, November). The beat goes on. *Psychology Today,* pp. 37–42.

Downs, S. (1985). Retraining for new skills. *Ergonomics, 28,* 1205–1211.

Dowrick, P. W. (1976). *Self-modeling: A videotape technique for disturbed and disabled children.* Unpublished doctoral dissertation, University of Auckland, New Zealand.

Dowrick, P. W. (1977). *Videotape replay as observational learning from oneself.* Unpublished manuscript, University of Auckland, New Zealand.

Dowrick, P. W. (Producer). (1978a). *How to make a self-model film.* [Film]. Auckland: New Zealand Crippled Children Society.

Dowrick, P. W. (1978b). Suggestions for the use of edited video replay in training behavioral skills. *Journal of Practical Approaches to Developmental Handicap, 2,* 21–24.

Dowrick, P. W. (1979). Single dose medication to create a self-model film. *Child Behavior Therapy, 1,* 193–198.

Dowrick, P. W. (1983). Self-modelling. In P. W. Dowrick & S. J. Biggs (Eds.), *Using video: Psychological and social applications* (pp. 105–124). Chichester, UK: Wiley.

Dowrick, P. W. (1986). *Social survival for children: A trainer's resource book.* New York: Brunner/Mazel.

Dowrick, P. W., & Biggs, S. J. (Eds.). (1983). *Using video: Psychological and social applications.* Chichester, UK: Wiley.

Dowrick, P. W., & Dove, C. (1980). The use of self-modeling to improve the swimming skills of spina bifida children. *Journal of Applied Behavior Analysis, 13,* 51–56.

Dowrick, P. W., & Hood, M. (1978). Transfer of talking behaviors across settings using faked films. In E. L. Glynn & S. S. McNaughton (Eds.), *Proceedings of the New Zealand conference for research in applied behaviour analysis.* Auckland: University of Auckland Press.

Dowrick, P. W., & Hood, M. (1981). A comparison of self-modeling and small cash incentives in a sheltered workshop. *Journal of Applied Psychology, 66,* 394–397.

Dowrick, P. W., & Jesdale, D. C. (1990). Effets de la retransmission vidéo structurée sur l'émotion: Implication thérapeutiques. (Effects on emotion of structured video replay: Implications for therapy). *Bulletin de Psychologie, 43,* 512–517.

Dowrick, P. W., McManus, M., Germaine, K. A., & Flarity-White, L. (1985, August). *Using video for personal safety with the developmentally disabled.* Video presentation at 15th Annual Conference of European Association for Behaviour Therapy, Munich.

Dowrick, P. W., Orth, C., & Chandler, J. (1988). *The outpatient surgery experience.* [Videotape]. Anchorage: Alaska Surgery Center.

Dowrick, P. W., Orth, C., & Ward, K. (1988). *The supported work advantage.* [Videotape]. Anchorage, AK: Alaska Specialized Employment and Training Services.

Dowrick, P. W., & Raeburn, J. M. (1977). Video editing and medication to produce a therapeutic self model. *Journal of Consulting and Clinical Psychology, 45,* 1156–1158.

Doyle, P. (1981). Behavior rehearsal to videotape simulations: Applications, techniques, and outcomes. In J. L. Fryrear & B. Fleshman (Eds.), *Videotherapy in mental health* (pp. 180–208). Springfield, IL: Charles C. Thomas.

Dozier, M. (1988). Rejected children's processing of interpersonal information. *Journal of Abnormal Child Psychology, 16,* 141–149.

Duehn, W. D., & Mayadas, N. S. (1976). The use of stimulus/modeling videotapes in assertive training for homosexuals. *Journal of Homosexuality, 1,* 373–381.

Durham, R. L., Fairchild, J. M., Ehrhart, L., Emilio, C., Andrews, L., Bonds, M., & Brookman, S. (1981). Teaching recreational skills to handicapped youths with video modeling and peer tutoring. *Journal of Special Education Technology, 4,* 13–21.

Effortless computing: The eyes have it. (1986, April). *Science,* p. 12.

Efron, D., & Veenendaal, K. (1987). Videotaping in groups for children of substance abusers: A strategy for emotionally disturbed, acting out children. *Alcoholism Treatment Quarterly, 4,* 71–85.

Eiser, C., & Eiser, J. R. (1987). Implementing a "life-skills" approach to drug education: A preliminary evaluation. *Health Education Research, 2,* 319–327.

Eisler, R. M., & Hersen, M. (1973). Behavioral techniques in family oriented crisis intervention. *Archives of General Psychiatry, 28,* 111–115.

Ekman, P. (1973). Cross cultural studies of facial expressions. In P. Ekman (Ed.), *Darwin and facial expression* (pp. 169–229). New York: Academic Press.

Ekman, P. (1977). Biological and cultural contributions to body and facial movement. In J. Blacking (Ed.), *Anthropology of the body* (pp. 34–84). London: Academic Press.

Ekman, P. (1979). About brows: Emotional and conversational signals. In J. Aschoff, M. von Cranach, K. Foppa, W. Lepenies, & D. Ploog (Eds.), *Human ethology.* Cambridge: Cambridge University Press.

Ekman, P. (1982). Methods for measuring facial action. In K. R. Scherer & P. Ekman (Eds.),

Handbook on methods of nonverbal behavior research (pp. 45–90). New York: Cambridge University Press.

Ekman, P. (1984). Expression and the nature of emotion. In K. R. Scherer & P. Ekman (Eds.), *Approaches to emotion* (pp. 319–344). Hillsdale, NJ: Erlbaum.

Ekman, P., & Fridlund, A. (1987). Assessment of facial behavior in affective disorders. In J. D. Maser (Ed.), *Depression and expressive behavior*. Hillsdale, NJ: Erlbaum.

Ekman, P., & Friesen, W. V. (1976). Measuring facial movement. *Journal of Environmental Psychology and Nonverbal Behavior, 1,* 56–75.

Ekman, P., & Friesen, W. V. (1978). *The facial action coding system.* Palo Alto, CA: Consulting Psychologists Press.

Ekman, P., & Friesen, W. V. (1981). *Collaborative studies on depression* (Contract No. HSM 42-72-213 [er]). Washington, DC: National Institute of Mental Health.

Ekman, P., & Friesen, W. V. (1982). Felt, false, and miserable smiles. *Journal of Nonverbal Behavior, 6,* 238–252.

Ekman, P., & Friesen, W. V. (1986). A new pancultural expression of emotion. *Motivation and Emotion, 10,* 159–168.

Ekman, P., Friesen, W. V., & Ancoli, S. (1980). Facial signs of emotional experience. *Journal of Personality and Social Psychology, 39,* 1125–1134.

Ekman, P., Friesen, W. V., & Ellsworth, P. (1982). What emotion categories or dimensions can observers judge from facial behavior? In P. Ekman (Ed.), *Emotion in the human face* (2nd ed.) (pp. 39–55). Cambridge: Cambridge University Press.

Ekman, P., Hager, J. C., & Friesen, W. V. (1981). The symmetry of emotional and deliberate facial actions. *Psychophysiology, 18,* 101–106.

Ekman, P., & Heider, K. G. (1989). The universality of a contempt expression: A replication. *Motivation and Emotion, 12,* 303–308.

Ekman, P., Levenson, R. W., & Friesen, W. V. (1983). Autonomic nervous system activity distinguishes between emotions. *Science, 221,* 1208–1210.

Ekman, P., & Matsumoto, D. (1986). *Depression and facial expression.* Unpublished manuscript.

Ellis, A. (1977). Basic clinical theory of a rational-emotive therapy. In A. Ellis & R. Greiger (Eds.), *Handbook of rational emotive therapy.* New York: Springer.

Erbaugh, S. J. (1985). Role of visual feedback in observational motor learning of primary-grade children. *Perceptual and Motor Skills, 60,* 755–762.

Eron, L. D. (1987). The development of aggressive behavior from the perspective of a developing behaviorism. *American Psychologist, 42,* 435–442.

Ethics Committee of the American Psychological Association. (1990). *American Psychologist, 45,* 390–395.

Eubanks, G. E. (1988). Effectiveness of message presentation format on consumer opinions, attitudes and behavioral intentions toward the domestic textile and apparel industry (Doctoral dissertation, Oklahoma State University, 1987). *Dissertation Abstracts International, 48,* 2946B.

Evans, R. I., Rozelle, R. M., Maxwell, S. E., Raines, B. E., Dill, C. A., Guthrie, T. J., Henderson, A. H., & Hill, P. C. (1981). Social modeling films to deter smoking in adolescents: Results of a three-year field investigation. *Journal of Applied Psychology, 66,* 399–414.

Farmer, S. S. (1987). Visual literacy and the clinical supervisor. *The Clinical Supervisor, 5,* 45–71.

Faust, J., & Melamed, B. G. (1984). Influence of arousal, previous experience, and age on surgery preparation of same day of surgery and in-hospital pediatric patients. *Journal of Consulting and Clinical Psychology, 52,* 359–365.

Federal Register: Education of handicapped children. (1977, August). Washington, DC: Department of Health Education and Welfare.

Feldman. L. (1988, April). Sony VCR ED-V9000. *Video Review,* pp. 66–67.

Feldman, L. (1989, September). JVC VCR HR-S1000U. *Video Review,* pp. 84–85.

Fidler, D. C. (1990). *Catalogue of medical educational videotapes.* Morgantown: West Virginia University, Department of Behavioral Medicine and Psychiatry.

Fischler, R. S. (1983). Teaching child development and behavior to family practice residents. *Journal of Family Practice, 16,* 571–579.

Flarity-White, L. A. (1988). *Behavioral role-play and cognitive measures of women's ability to refuse unwanted sexual advances.* Unpublished master's thesis, Texas A & M University, College Station.

Fleig, G. S. (1983). Media basics: A bridge to successful mainstreaming. *Educational Technology, 23,* 9–12.

Follick, M. J., Ahern, D. K., & Aberger, E. W. (1985). Development of an audiovisual taxonomy of pain behavior: Reliability and discriminant validity. *Health Psychology, 4,* 555–568.

Fortenberry, J. D., Kaplan, D. W., & Hill, R. F. (1988). Physicians' values and experience during adolescence: Their effect on adolescent health care. *Journal of Adolescent Health Care, 9,* 46–51.

Fosnot, C. T., Forman, G. E., Edwards, C. P., & Goldhaber, J. (1988). The development of an understanding of balance and the effect of training via stop-action video. *Journal of Applied Developmental Psychology, 9,* 1–26.

Foti, R. J., & Lord, R. G. (1987). Prototypes and scripts: The effects of alternative methods of processing information on rating accuracy. *Organizational Behavior & Human Decision Processes, 39,* 318–340.

Foxx, R. M., & Azrin, N. H. (1973). The elimination of autistic self-stimulatory behavior by overcorrection. *Journal of Applied Behavior Analysis, 6,* 1–14.

Franks, I. M., & Goodman, D. (1986a). A systematic approach to analysing sports performance. *Journal Sports Sciences, 4,* 49–59.

Franks, I. M., & Goodman, D. (1986b, May-June). Computer-assisted technical analysis of sport. *Coaching Review,* pp. 58–64.

Franks, I. M., Goodman, D., & Paterson, G. (1986). The real time analysis of sport: An overview. *Canadian Journal of Applied Sport Sciences, 11,* 55–57.

Franks, I. M., Johnson, R., & Sinclair, G. (1988). The development of a computerized coaching analysis system for recording behaviour in sporting environments. *Journal of Teaching in Physical Education, 8,* 23–33.

Franks, I. M., & Nagelkerke, P. (1988). The use of computer interactive video technology in sport analysis. *Ergonomics, 31,* 1593–1603.

Franks, I. M., Wilson, G. E., & Goodman, D. (1987). Analyzing a team sport with the aid of computers. *Canadian Journal of Sport Science, 12,* 120–125.

Fraser, I. H., Lishman, J. R., & Parker, D. M. (1987). Temporal manipulation of stimulus patterns using the Apple II: Tachistoscopic and part presentation. *Behavior Research Methods, Instruments, & Computers, 19,* 315-318.

Freedman, C. (1984). Study group I: A tale of three therapists. *Journal of Strategic & Systemic Therapies, 3,* 63-65.

Fridlund, A. J. (1979). Contour-following integrator for dynamic tracking of electromyographic data. *Psychophysiology, 16,* 491-493.

Fridlund, A. J. (1988). What can asymmetry and lateralization in EMG tell us about the face and brain? *International Journal of Neuroscience, 39,* 53-69.

Fridlund, A. J. (in press). Evolution and facial action in reflex, emotion, and paralanguage. In P. K. Ackles, J. R. Jennings, & M. G. H. Coles (Eds.), *Advances in psychophysiology* (Vol. 4). Greenwich, CT: JAI Press.

Fridlund, A. J., Ekman, P., & Oster, H. (1986). Facial expressions of emotion: Review of literature, 1970-1983. In A. Siegman & S. Feldstein (Eds.), *Nonverbal behavior and communication* (2nd ed.). Hillsdale, NJ: Erlbaum.

Fridlund, A. J., & Izard, C. E. (1983). Electromyographic studies of facial expressions of emotions and patterns of emotions. In J. T. Cacioppo & R. E. Petty (Eds.), *Social psychophysiology: A sourcebook* (pp. 243-286). New York: Guilford Press.

Fridlund, A. J., Schwartz, G. E., & Fowler, S. C. (1984). Pattern recognition of self-reported emotional state from multiple-site facial EMG activity during affective imagery. *Psychophysiology, 21,* 622-637.

Friesen, W. V. (1972). *Cultural differences in facial expressions in a social situation: An experimental test of the concept of display rules.* Unpublished doctoral dissertation, University of California, San Francisco.

Friesen, W. V., & Ekman, P. (1983). *EMFACS.* Mimeographed document. San Francisco: Human Interaction Laboratory.

Frisch, M. B., & Froberg, W. (1987). Social validation of assertion strategies for handling aggressive criticism: Evidence for consistency across situations. *Behavior Therapy, 2,* 181-191.

Frost, R. O., Benton, N., & Dowrick, P. W. (in press). Self-evaluation, videotape review, and dysphoria. *Journal of Social and Clinical Psychology.*

Fryrear, J. L., & Fleshman, B. (Eds.). (1981). *Videotherapy in mental health.* Springfield, IL: Charles C. Thomas.

Fuller, B. J. (1982). *Single camera video production: Techniques, equipment, and resources for producing quality video programs.* Englewood Cliffs, NJ: Prentice-Hall.

Fuller, F. F., & Manning, B. A. (1973). Self-confrontation reviewed: A conceptualization for video playback in teacher education. *Review of Educational Research, 43,* 469-528.

Gallup, G. G. (1987). Self-awareness. In G. Mitchell & J. Erwin (Eds.), *Comparative primate biology: Behavior cognition, and motivation* (Vol. 2, Pt. B) (pp. 3-16). New York: Alan R. Liss.

Garb, H. N. (1984). The incremental validity of information used in personality assessment. *Clinical Psychology Review, 4,* 641-655.

Gardner, R. M., & Moncrieff, C. (1988). Body image distortion in anorexics as a non-sensory phenomenon: A signal detection approach. *Journal of Clinical Psychology, 44,* 101-107.

Gaskill, A. L., & Englander, D. A. (1985). *How to shoot a movie and videostory.* Dobbs Ferry, NY: Morgan & Morgan.

Geerstma, R. H. (Ed.). (1969). *Studies in self-cognition: Techniques of videotape self-observation in the behavioral sciences.* Baltimore, MD: Williams & Wilkins.

Gelfand, D. M. (1962). The influence of self-esteem on rate of verbal conditioning and social matching behavior. *Journal of Abnormal and Social Psychology, 65,* 259–265.

Gelfand, D. M., Jenson, W. R., & Drew, C. J. (1982). *Understanding childhood behavior disorders.* New York: Holt, Rinehart, and Winston.

Gentile, A. M. (1972). A working model of skill acquisition with application to teaching. *Quest, 17,* 3–23.

Gerber, D. E. (Producer, Director). (1989). *Camera magic: Images of nature.* [Film]. Pittsburgh, PA: WQED/Pittsburgh in association with Oxford Scientific Films.

Germaine, K. A. (1983). *Self-esteem as a variable in the efficacy of self-modeling.* Unpublished master's thesis, University of Alaska, Anchorage.

Germaine, K. A., & Dowrick, P. W. (1985, August). *Self-esteem and self-modeling: The impact of (and upon) self-concept during structured video replay training.* Video presentation at the 15th annual Conference of European Association for Advancement of Behaviour Therapy, Munich.

Gibling, F., & Davies, G. (1988). Reinstatement of context following exposure to post-event information. *British Journal of Psychology, 79,* 129–141.

Gil, K. M., Collins, F. L., Jr., & Odom, J. V. (1986). The effects of behavioral vision training on multiple aspects of visual functioning in myopic adults. *Journal of Behavioral Medicine, 9,* 373–387.

Ginsburg, G. P. (Ed.). (1979). *Emerging strategies in social psychological research.* New York: Wiley.

Ginther, L. J., & Roberts, M. C. (1982). A test of mastery versus coping modeling in the reduction of children's dental fears. *Child and Family Behavior Therapy, 4,* 41–52.

Glasrud, P. H. (1984). Dentists' characteristics and child behavior management techniques. *Journal of Dentistry for Children, 51,* 337–343.

Golinkoff, R. M., Hirsh-Pasek, K., Cauley, K. M., & Gordon, L. (1987). The eyes have it: Lexical and syntactic comprehension in a new paradigm. *Journal of Child Language, 14,* 23–45.

Gonzales, F. P. (1982). *The mechanism of self-modeling: Skills acquisition versus raised self-efficacy.* Unpublished master's thesis, University of Alaska, Anchorage.

Gonzales, F. P. (1988). *The behavioral treatment of hospitalized conduct disorder children using video self-modeling.* Unpublished doctoral dissertation, Fuller Graduate School of Psychology, Pasadena, CA.

Gonzales, F. P., & Dowrick, P. W. (1982, November). *The mechanism of self-modeling: Skills acquisition versus raised self-efficacy.* Paper presented at 16th annual convention of the Association for Advancement of Behavior Therapy, Los Angeles.

Gonzales, F. P., & Pigott, H. E. (1986, February). *The efficacy of video self-modeling to treat a 2½-year-old preschool child with Down's syndrome.* Paper presented at the annual convention of the California State Psychological Association, San Francisco.

Gordon, R. A., Rozelle, R. M., & Baxter, J. C. (1988). The effect of applicant age, job level, and accountability on the evaluation of job applicants. *Organizational Behavior & Human Decision Processes, 41,* 20–33.

Gothard, S. (1987). The admissibility of evidence in child sexual abuse cases. *Child Welfare, 66,* 13–24.

Gould, D., & Roberts, G. (1982). Modeling and motor skill acquisition. *Quest, 33*, 214–230.

Gould, D., & Weiss, M. (1981). The effects of model similarity and model talk on self-efficacy and muscular endurance. *Journal of Sport Psychology, 3*, 17–29.

Gould, M. S., & Shaffer, D. (1986). The impact of suicide in television movies: Evidence of imitation. *The New England Journal of Medicine, 315*, 690–694.

Grabe, M., & Tabor, L. (1981). The use of videotaped material in the instruction and evaluation of developmental psychology students. *Teaching of Psychology, 8*, 115–117.

Graffi, S., & Minnes, P. M. (1988). Attitudes of primary school children toward the physical appearance and labels associated with Down syndrome. *American Journal on Mental Retardation, 93*, 28–35.

Greelis, M., & Kazaoka, K. (1979). The therapeutic use of edited videotapes with an exceptional child. *Academic Therapy, 15*, 37–44.

Greenbaum, P. E., & Melamed, B. G. (1988). Pretreatment modeling: A technique for reducing children's fear in the dental operatory. *Dental Clinics of North America, 32*, 693–704.

Griffiths, R. D. P. (1974). Videotape feedback as a therapeutic technique: Retrospect and prospect. *Behaviour Research and Therapy, 12*, 1–8.

Griggs, C. A., Jones, P. M., & Lee, R. E. (1989). Videofluoroscopic investigation of feeding disorders of children with multiple handicaps. *Developmental Medicine and Child Neurology, 31*, 303–308.

Gunderson, J. G., Autry, J. H., & Mosher, L. R. (1974). Special report: Schizophrenia 1973. *Schizophrenia Bulletin*, 15–54.

Gunter, B. (1987). Psychological influences of television. In H. Beloff & A. Colman (Eds.), *Psychology Survey Six* (pp. 276–305). Letchworth: British Psychological Society.

Gurtman, M. B. (1987). Depressive affect and disclosures as factors in interpersonal rejection. *Cognitive Therapy and Research, 11*, 87–100.

Hager, J. C., & Ekman, P. (1985). The asymmetry of facial actions is inconsistent with models of hemispheric specialization. *Psychophysiology, 22*, 307–318.

Hall, E. G., & Erffmeyer, E. S. (1983). The effect of visuomotor behavior rehearsal with videotaped modeling on free throw accuracy of intercollegiate female basketball players. *Journal of Sport Psychology, 5*, 343–346.

Hallett, R., & Sutton, S. R. (1988). Intervening against smoking in the workplace. *Psychology & Health, 2*, 13–29.

Hannah, G. T., Christian, W. P., & Clark, H. B. (1981). *Preservation of client rights*. New York: The Free Press.

Hannu, R. W. (1990). Interactive television networking. *Technological Horizons in Education Journal, 17*, 60–61.

Hargie, O. D. W. (1988). From teaching to counselling: An evaluation of the role of microcounselling in the training of school counsellors. *Counselling Psychology Quarterly, 1*, 75–83.

Haring, T. G., Kennedy, C. H., Adams, M. J., & Pitts-Conway, V. (1987). Teaching generalization of purchasing skills across community settings to autistic youth using videotape modeling. *Journal of Applied Behavior Analysis, 20*, 89–96.

Harless, W. G. (1986). An interactive videodisc drama: The case of Frank Hall. *Journal of Computer-Based Instruction, 13*, 113–116.

Harmon, R. J., Glicken, A. D., & Gaensbau, J. J. (1980). The relationship between infant play with inanimate objects and social interest in mother. *Journal of the American Academy of Child Psychiatry, 21,* 549–554.

Hatze, H. (1976). Biomechanical aspects of a successful motion optimization. In P. V. Koni (Ed.), *Biomechanics V-B.* Baltimore: University Park Press.

Hazel, J. S., Schumaker, J. B., Sherman, J. A., & Sheldon-Wildgen, J. (Producers). (1983). *ASSET: Adolescent social skills evaluation and training.* [Film or video and manual]. Champaign, IL: Research Press.

Heilveil, I. (1983). *Video in mental health practice: An activities handbook.* New York: Springer.

Heinich, R., Molenda, S., & Russell, R. (1982). *Instructional media and the new technologies of instruction.* New York: Wiley.

Helffenstein, D. A. (1981). *The effects of IPR (interpersonal process recall) on the interpersonal and communications skills of newly brain injured.* Unpublished doctoral dissertation, University of Virginia, Charlottesville.

"HELPIS" Database. (1988). British Universities Film and Video Council. 19.2.88.

Henderson, R. W., Landesman, E. M., & Kachuck, I. (1985). Computer-video instruction in mathematics: Field test of an interactive approach. *Journal for Research in Mathematics Education, 16,* 207–224.

Henny, L. (1983). Video and the community. In P. W. Dowrick & S. J. Biggs (Eds.), *Using video: Psychological and social applications* (pp. 167–177). Chichester, UK: Wiley.

Henny, L. (Ed.) (1987). *International Journal of Visual Sociology and Visual Anthropology, 1.*

Henry, G. K. (1987). Symbolic modeling and parent behavioral training: Effects on noncompliance of hyperactive children. *Journal of Behavior Therapy & Experimental Psychiatry, 18,* 105–113.

Herbert, D. L., Nelson, R. O., & Herbert, J. D. (1988). Effects of psychodiagnostic labels, depression severity, and instructions on assessment. *Professional Psychology: Research & Practice, 19,* 496–502.

Hersen, M., & Bellack, A. S. (1981). *Behavioral assessment: A practical handbook* (2nd ed.). New York: Pergamon Press.

Hill, S. D., & Tomlin, C. (1981). Self-recognition in retarded children. *Child Development, 52,* 145–150.

Hirschman, R., & Procter, R. (1985). *How to shoot better video.* Milwaukee, WI: Leonard Publishing.

Ho, C. P., Savenye, W., & Haas, N. (1986). The effects of orienting objectives and review on learning from interactive video. *Journal of Computer-Based Instruction, 13,* 126–129.

Hobson, R. P. (1987). The autistic child's recognition of age- and sex-related characteristics of people. *Journal of Autism & Developmental Disorders, 17,* 63–79.

Hoffman, S. (1987). The language of teaching: Responses to children's developing literacy. *Childhood Education, 63,* 356–361.

Holman, L. (1990). *Self-efficacy and video feedforward: A new technology in teaching beginning swimming.* Unpublished master's thesis, University of Alaska, Anchorage.

Holmes, G. L., McKeever, M., & Russman, B. S. (1983). Abnormal behavior or epilepsy? Use of long-term EEG and video monitoring with severely to profoundly mentally retarded patients with seizures. *American Journal of Mental Deficiency, 87,* 456–458.

Horney, K. (1945). *Our inner conflicts: A constructive theory of neurosis.* New York: Norton.

Hosford, R. E. (1980). Self-as-a-model: A cognitive social learning technique. *The Counseling Psychologist, 9,* 45–62.

Hosford, R. E., & Johnson, M. E. (1983). A comparison of self-observation, self-modeling, and practice without video feedback for improving counselor interviewing behaviors. *Counselor Education and Supervision, 23,* 62–70.

Hosford, R., & Krumboltz, J. (1969). Behavioral counseling: A contemporary overview. *The Counseling Psychologist, 1,* 1–33.

Hosford, R. E., & Mills, M. E. (1983). Video in social skills training. In P. W. Dowrick & S. J. Biggs (Eds.), *Using video: Psychological and social applications* (pp. 125–150). Chichester, UK: Wiley.

Hosford, R., Moss, C. S., & Morrell, G. (1976). The self-as-a-model technique: Helping prison inmates change. In J. D. Krumboltz & C. E. Thoresen (Eds.), *Counseling methods.* New York: Holt, Rinehart and Winston.

Hosford, R. E., & Polly, S. J. (1976). *The effect of vicarious self-observation on teaching skills.* (Tech. Rep. Contract No. 8-407674-07427). Santa Barbara: University of California Innovative Teaching Project.

Houts, A. C., Whelan, J. P., & Peterson, J. K. (1987). Filmed versus live delivery of full-spectrum home training for primary enuresis: Presenting the information is not enough. *Journal of Consulting and Clinical Psychology, 55,* 902–906.

Howe, G. W. (1987). Attributions of complex cause and the perception of marital conflict. *Journal of Personality and Social Psychology, 53,* 1119–1128.

Huczynski, A. (1982). Trigger films. *The Journal of Management Development, 1,* 10–21.

Hung, J. H. F., & Rosenthal, T. L. (1978). Therapeutic videotaped playback: A critical review. *Advances in Behaviour Research and Therapy, 1,* 103–135.

Huwiler, P. F. (1983). Teaching systematic video production. *Educational Technology, 23*(12), 39–42.

International Powerlifting Federation (1982). *1982 official handbook.* Hagersten, Sweden: Author.

Israel, A. C., & Brown, M. S. (1977). Correspondence training, prior verbal training, and control of nonverbal behavior via control of verbal behavior. *Journal of Applied Behavior Analysis, 10,* 333–338.

Ivey, A. E., & Authier, R. J. (1978). *Microcounselling: Innovations in interviewing, counselling, psychotherapy and psychoeducation.* Springfield, IL: Charles C. Thomas.

Izard, C. E. (1971). *The face of emotion.* New York: Appleton-Century-Crofts.

Izard, C. E. (1972). *Patterns of emotion: A new analysis of anxiety and depression.* New York: Academic Press.

Izard, C. E. (1977). *Human emotions.* New York: Plenum.

Izard, C. E. (1980). *The maximally discriminative facial movement coding system (MAX).* Newark: Instructional Resources Center, University of Delaware.

Izard, C. E., & Dougherty, L. M. (1980). *System for identifying affect expressions by holistic judgment (AFFEX).* Newark: Instructional Resources Center, University of Delaware.

Jackson, M. W. (1988). Lay and professional perceptions of dangerousness and other forensic issues. *Canadian Journal of Criminology, 30,* 215–229.

Jackson, R. L., & Beers, P. A. (1988). Focused videotape feedback psychotherapy: An integrated treatment for emotionally and behaviorally disturbed children. *Counselling Psychology Quarterly, 1,* 11–23.

Johnson, M. E. (in press). Effects of self-observation and self-as-a-model on counselor trainees' anxiety and self-evaluations. *The Clinical Supervisor.*

Johnston-O'Connor, E. J., & Kirschenbaum, D. S. (1986). Something succeeds like success: Positive self-monitoring for unskilled golfers. *Cognitive Therapy and Research, 10,* 123–136.

Jones, M. B. (1981). Convergence-divergence with extended practice: Three applications. *U.S. Naval Biodynamics Laboratory,* 6–9.

Jones, P. M. (1989). Feeding disorders in children with multiple handicaps. *Developmental Medicine and Child Neurology, 31,* 404–406.

Jordan, T., & Martin, C. (1987). The importance of visual angle in word recognition: A "shrinking screen" modification for visual displays. *Behavior Research Methods, Instruments, & Computers, 19,* 307–310.

Kagan, J. (1958). The concept of identification. *Psychological Review, 65,* 296–305.

Kagan, N. (1975). Influencing human interaction: Eleven years with IPR. *Canadian Counsellor, 9,* 75–97.

Kagan, N. (1978). Interpersonal process recall: Media in clinical and human interaction supervision. In M. M. Berger (Ed.), *Videotape techniques in psychiatric training and treatment* (2nd ed.) (pp. 70–84). New York: Brunner/Mazel.

Kagan, N. (1980). *Interpersonal process recall. A method of influencing human interaction: Instructor's manual.* Houston, TX: Mason Media.

Kagan, N. (1984). Interpersonal process recall: Basic methods and recent research. In D. Larsen (Ed.), *Teaching psychological skills.* Monterey, CA: Brooks Cole.

Kagan, N. (1988). Teaching counseling skills. In K. R. Cox & C. E. Ewan (Eds.), *The medical teacher.* Edinburgh: Churchill Livingston.

Kagan, N. & Krathwohl, D. R. (1967). *Studies in human interaction: Interpersonal process recall stimulated by videotape. (Research Report 20).* East Lansing, MI: Educational Publication Services.

Kagan, N., Krathwohl, D. R., & Miller, R. (1963). Stimulated recall in therapy using videotape—a case study. *Journal of Counseling Psychology, 10,* 237–243.

Kahn, G. S., Cohen, B., & Jason, H. (1979). The teaching of interpersonal skills in U.S. medical schools. *Journal of Medical Education, 54,* 29–35.

Kahn, J. S., Kehle, T. J., Jenson, W. R., & Clark, E. (1990). Comparison of cognitive-behavioral, relaxation, and self-modeling interventions for depression among middle-school students. *School Psychology Review, 19,* 196–211.

Kauffman, J. (1985). *Characteristics of children's behavior disorders* (3rd ed.). Columbus, OH: Charles Merrill.

Kazdin, A. E. (1974a). Covert modeling, model similarity, and reduction of avoidance behavior. *Behavior Therapy, 5,* 325–340.

Kazdin, A. E. (1974b). The effect of model identity and fear-relevant similarity on covert modeling. *Behavior Therapy, 5,* 624–635.

Kazdin, A. (1977). Assessing the clinical or applied importance of behavior change through social validation. *Behavior Modification, 1,* 427–452.

Kazdin, A. (1982). *Single-case research designs.* New York: Oxford University Press.

Kazdin, A. E., Esveldt-Dawson, K., Sherick, R. B., & Colbus, D. (1985). Assessment of overt behavior and childhood depression among psychiatrically hospitalized children. *Journal of Consulting and Clinical Psychology, 53,* 201–210.

Keane, S. P., Nelson, R. O., & Herbert, D. L. (1987). The role of contextual variables in maternal reactions to children's compliance and noncompliance. *Journal of Psychopathology and Behavioral Assessment, 9,* 49–65.

Kehle, T. J., Clark, E., Jenson, W. R., & Wampold, B. E. (1986). Effectiveness of self-observation with behavior disordered elementary school children. *School Psychology Review, 15,* 289–295.

Kehle, T. J., Owen, S. V., & Cressy, E. T. (1990). The use of self-modeling as an intervention in school psychology: A case study of an elective mute. *School Psychology Review, 19,* 115–121.

Kelley, H. H. (1973). The process of causal attribution. *American Psychologist, 28,* 107–128.

Kelley, M. A. (1986). *Three mediums of practice and the maintenance of pursuit rotor performance: Self-efficacy and imagery ability.* Unpublished master's thesis, University of Alaska, Anchorage.

Kelly, B. F. (1987). The relative effectiveness of instructional design features in two fractions curricula with mildly handicapped and remedial high school students. *Dissertation Abstracts International, 47,* 3394A–3395A.

Kendall, P. C., & Hollon, S. D. (1983). Calibrating the quality of therapy: Collaborative archiving of tape samples from therapy outcome trials. *Cognitive Therapy and Research, 7,* 199–204.

Kernan, W. J., Mullenix, P. J., & Hopper, D. L. (1987). Pattern recognition of rat behavior. *Pharmacology Biochemistry and Behavior, 27,* 559–564.

Kirschenbaum, D. S. (1984). Self-regulation and sport psychology: Nurturing and emerging symbiosis. *Journal of Sport Psychology, 6,* 159–183.

Kivlighan, D. M., Corazzini, J. G., & McGovern, T. V. (1985). Pregroup training. *Small Group Behavior, 16,* 500–514.

Kleck, R. E., Vaughan, R. C., Cartwright-Smith, J., Vaughan, K. B., Colby, C. Z., & Lanzetta, J. T. (1976). Effects of being observed on expressive, subjective, and physiological responses to painful stimuli. *Journal of Personality and Social Psychology, 34,* 1211–1218.

Kleinke, C. L., Wallis, R., & Stadler, K. (1990). *Evaluation of rapists as a function of expressed intent and remorse.* Manuscript submitted for publication.

Klingman, A., Melamed, B. G., Cuthbert, M. I., & Hermecz, D. A. (1984). Effects of participant modeling on information acquisition and skill utilization. *Journal of Consulting and Clinical Psychology, 52,* 414–422.

Kohut, H. (1978). Creativeness, charisma, group psychology. In P. Ornstein (Ed.), *The search for the self* (Vol. 2). New York: International Universities Press.

Kohr, M., Parrish, J., Neef, N., Driessen, J., & Hallanan, P. (1988). Communication skills training for parents: Experimental analysis and social validation. *Journal of Applied Behavior Analysis, 21,* 21–30.

Kolko, D. J. (1988). Educational programs to promote awareness and prevention of child sexual victimization: A review and methodological critique. *Clinical Psychology Review, 8,* 195–209.

Krajcik, J. S., Simmons, P. E., & Lunetta, V. N. (1988). A research strategy for the dynamic study of students' concepts and problem solving strategies using science software. *Journal of Research in Science Teaching, 25,* 147–155.

Krauss, R. M., Morrel-Samuels, P., & Hochberg, J. (1988). VIDEOLOGGER: A computerized multichannel event recorder for analyzing videotapes. *Behavior Research Methods, Instruments, and Computers, 20,* 37–40.

Kuczynski, L., Kochanska, G., Radke-Yarrow, M., & Girnius-Brown, O. (1987). A developmental interpretation of young children's noncompliance. *Developmental Psychology, 23,* 799–806.

Lambert, M. E. (1987). Mr. Howard: A behavior therapy simulation. *The Behavior Therapist, 10,* 139–140.

Landers, D. M. (1975). Observational learning of a motor skill: Temporal spacing of demonstrations and audience presence. *Journal of Motor Behavior, 7,* 281–287.

Landers, D. M., & Landers, D. M. (1973). Teacher versus peer models: Effects of model's presence- and performance level on motor behavior. *Journal of Motor Behavior, 5,* 129–139.

Latham, V. M. (1987). Interviewee training: A review of some empirical literature. *Journal of Career Development, 14,* 96-107.

Lawrence, P. (1979). *Exploring individual and organisational boundaries.* Chichester, UK: Wiley.

Leaky, R. E. (1979). *People of the lake.* New York: Avon.

Levy, M. R. (1987). Some problems of VCR research. *American Behavioral Scientist, 30,* 461–470.

Lewinsohn, P. M., & Clarke, G. N. (1984). *Coping with depression course: A psychoeducational intervention for unipolar depression.* Eugene, OR: Castalia Publishing.

Lewis, J. L., Stokes, D. R., Fischetti, L. R., & Rutledge, A. L. (1988). Using the patient as teacher: A training method for family practice residents in behavioral science. *Professional Psychology: Research and Practice, 19,* 349-352.

Lewis, R. (1987). *The home videomaker's handbook.* New York: Crown.

Liberman, R. P. (1987). *Rehabilitating the chronically mentally-ill patient.* [Videotape]. Los Angeles: UCLA Research Dissemination Center.

Lindholm, L., & Wilson, G. T. (1988). Body image assessment in patients with bulimia nervosa and normal controls. *International Journal of Eating Disorders, 7,* 527–539.

Liske, E., & Davis, W. J. (1987). Courtship and mating behaviour of the Chinese praying mantis, "Tenodera aridifolia sinensis." *Animal Behaviour, 35,* 1524–1537.

Littrell, J. M., Caffrey, P., & Hopper, G. C. (1987). Counselor's reputation: An important precounseling variable for adolescents. *Journal of Counseling Psychology, 34,* 228–231.

Logemann, J. A. (1986). *Manual for the videofluorographic study of swallowing.* London: Taylor and Francis.

Lovell, T. (1980). *Pictures of reality.* London: British Film Institute.

Ludwick-Rosenthal, R., & Neufeld, R. W. J. (1988). Stress management during noxious medical procedures: An evaluative review of outcome studies. *Psychological Bulletin, 104,* 326–342.

Machen, J., & Johnson, R. (1974). Desensitization, model learning and the dental behavior of children. *Journal of Dental Research, 53,* 83–87.

Magill, R. A. (1989). *Motor learning: Concepts and applications* (3rd ed.). Dubuque, IA: W. C. Brown.

Maile, L. J. (1985). *Self-modeling and powerlifting: A new look at peak performance.* Unpublished master's thesis, University of Alaska, Anchorage.

Malatesta, C. Z., Izard, C. E., Culver, C., & Nicolich, M. (1987). Emotion communication skills in young, middle-aged, and older women. *Psychology and Aging, 2,* 193–203.

Manning, B. H. (1988). Application of cognitive behavior modification: First and third graders' self-management of classroom behaviors. *American Educational Research Journal, 25,* 193–212.

Manthei, R. J. (1983). Client choice of therapist or therapy. *Personnel & Guidance Journal, 61,* 334–340.

Mao, C., Bullock, C. S., Harway, E. C., & Khalsa, S. K. (1988). A workshop on ethnic and cultural awareness for second-year students. *Journal of Medical Education, 63,* 624–628.

Marey, E. J. (1895). *Movement.* London: Ayer Co.

MARIS. (1988). On-line information database. London. 11.3.88.

Markus, H., & Wurf, E. (1987). The dynamic self-concept: A social psychological perspective. *Annual Review of Psychology, 38,* 299–337.

Marshall, W. R., Rothenberger, L. A., & Bunnell, S. L. (1984). The efficacy of personalized audiovisual patient-education materials. *The Journal of Family Practice, 19,* 659–663.

Martens, R. (1970). Social reinforcement effects on preschool children's motor performance. *Perceptual and Motor Skills, 31,* 787–792.

Martens, R., Burwitz, L., & Zuckerman, J. (1976). Modeling effects on motor performance. *Research Quarterly, 47,* 277–291.

Martin, B. L. (1986). Aesthetics and media: Implications for the design of instruction. *Educational Technology, 26,* 15–21.

Marzillier, J. S., & Winter, K. (1978). Success and failure in social skills training: Individual differences. *Behaviour Research and Therapy, 16,* 67–84.

Mascelli, J. V. (1965). *The five C's of cinematography.* Hollywood, CA: Cine/Graphic Publications.

Masters, J. C., Burish, T. G., Hollon, S. D., & Rimm, D. C. (1987). *Behavior therapy: Techniques and empirical findings* (3rd ed.). Orlando, FL: Harcourt Brace Jovanovich.

Mastria, E. O., Mastria, M. A., & Harkins, J. C. (1979). The treatment of child abuse by behavioral intervention: A case report. *Child Welfare, 58,* 253–261.

Matsumoto, D., Haan, N., Yabrove, G., Theodorou, P., & Cooke-Carney, C. C. (1986). Preschoolers' moral actions and emotions in Prisoner's Dilemma. *Developmental Psychology, 22,* 663–670.

Matthey, S. (1988). Cognitive-behavioural treatment of a thunder-phobic child. *Behaviour Change, 5,* 80–84.

Mauser, B. (1953). Studies in social interaction: III. Effect of variation in one partner's prestige on the interaction of observer pairs. *Journal of Applied Psychology, 37,* 391–393.

Maxwell, G., & Pringle, J. (1983). The analysis of video records. In P. Dowrick & S. Biggs (Eds.), *Using video: Psychological and social applications.* Chichester, UK: Wiley.

Mayadas, N. S., & Duehn, W. D. (1981). Stimulus/modeling (SM) videotape formats in clinical practice and research. In J. L. Fryrear & B. Fleshman (Eds.), *Videotherapy in mental health* (pp. 146–162). Springfield, IL: Charles C. Thomas.

Mayhew, G. L., & Anderson, J. (1980). Delayed and immediate reinforcement: Retarded adolescents in an educational setting. *Behavior Modification, 4,* 527–545.

McAuley, E. (1985). Modeling and self-efficacy: A test of Bandura's model. *Journal of Sport Psychology, 7,* 283–295.

McCallum, J. (1987, April). Videotape is on a roll. *Sports Illustrated,* pp. 136–144.

McCann, T. E., & Sheehan, P. W. (1987). The breaching of pseudomemory under hypnotic instruction: Implications for original memory retrieval. *British Journal of Experimental and Clinical Hypnosis, 4,* 101–108.

McComb, G. (1988). *Troubleshooting and repairing VCRs.* Blue Ridge Summit, PA: TAB Books.

McConkey, R., & Templer, S. (1987). Videocourses for training staff in developing countries: An example with severely retarded and multiply handicapped children. *International Journal of Rehabilitation Research, 10,* 206–210.

McCrea, C., & Summerfield, A. B. (1988). A pilot study of the therapeutic usefulness of videofeedback for weight loss and improvement of body image in the treatment of obesity. *Behavioural Psychotherapy, 16,* 269–284.

McCue, K. (1980). Preparing children for medical procedures. In J. Kellerman (Ed.), *Psychological aspects of childhood cancer* (pp. 238–260). Springfield, IL: Charles C. Thomas.

McCullagh, P. (1986). Model status as a determinant of observational learning and performance. *Journal of Sport Psychology, 8,* 319–331.

McCurdy, B. L., & Shapiro, E. S. (1988). Self-observation and the reduction of inappropriate classroom behavior. *Journal of School Psychology, 26,* 371–378.

McElroy, E. M. (1987). Sources of distress among families of the hospitalized mentally ill. *New Directions for Mental Health Services, 34,* 61–72.

McGuire, J., & Priestley, P. (1983). Life skills training in prisons and the community. In S. Spence & G. Shepherd (Eds.), *Developments in social skills training* (pp. 103–117). London: Academic Press.

McLeod, P. (1987). Visual reaction time and high-speed ball games. *Perception, 16,* 49–59.

McMahon, R. J., & Forehand, R. (1982). Suggestions for evaluating self-administered materials in parent training. *Child Behavior Therapy, 3,* 65–68.

McRea, C. (1983). Impact on body-image. In P. W. Dowrick & S. J. Biggs (Eds.), *Using video: Psychological and social applications* (pp. 95–103). Chichester, UK: Wiley.

Mead, G. H. (1934). *Mind, self, and society.* Chicago: University of Chicago Press.

Medoff, N. J., & Tanquary, T. (1986). *Portable video: ENG and EFP.* White Plains, NY: Knowledge Industry Publications.

Meichenbaum, D. H. (1971). Examination of model characteristics in reducing avoidance behavior. *Journal of Personality and Social Psychology, 17,* 298–307.

Meichenbaum, D. H. (1975). Self-instructional methods. In F. Kanfer & A. Goldstein (Eds.), *Helping people change.* New York: Pergamon.

Melamed, B. G. (1989, August). *Innovations in preparation media for patients undergoing surgery.* Workshop presented at 97th Annual Convention of the American Psychological Association, New Orleans.

Melamed, B. G., Dearborn, M., & Hermecz, D. A. (1983). Necessary considerations for surgery preparation: Age and previous experience. *Psychosomatic Medicine, 45,* 517–525.

Melamed, B. G., Hawes, R. R., Heiby, E., & Glick, J. (1975). Use of filmed modeling to reduce uncooperative behavior of children during dental treatment. *Journal of Dental Research, 54,* 797–801.

Melamed, B. G., Robbins, R. L., & Graves, S. (1982). Preparation for surgery and medical procedures. In D. Russo & J. Varni (Eds.), *Behavioral pediatrics: Research and practice,* (pp. 225–265). New York: Plenum.

Melamed, B., & Siegel, L. (1975). Reduction of anxiety in children facing hospitalization and surgery by use of filmed modeling. *Journal of Consulting and Clinical Psychology, 43,* 511–521.

Melamed, B. G., Yurcheson, R., Fleece, E. L., Hutcherson, S., & Hawes, R. (1978). Effects of film modeling on the reduction of anxiety-related behaviors in individuals varying in level of previous experience in the stress situation. *Journal of Consulting and Clinical Psychology, 46,* 1357–1367.

Melin, E. (1987). Neck-shoulder loading characteristics and work technique. *Ergonomics, 30,* 281–285.

Menzies, I. (1970). *The functioning of social systems as a defense against anxiety.* London: Tavistock.

Mercer, D., Correa, V. I., & Sowell, V. (1985). Teaching visually impaired students word processing competencies: The use of the Viewscan Textline. *Education of the Visually Handicapped, 17,* 17–29.

Metzner, R. J. (1978). Videotape self-confrontation after narcotherapy. In M. M. Berger (Ed.), *Videotape techniques in psychiatric training and treatment* (2nd ed.) (pp. 279–291). New York: Brunner/Mazel.

Meyer, M. (1988, June 30). Videos promoting child safety cover all bases. *Anchorage Daily News,* p. F20.

Michael, B. (1984). Using home video equipment for the handicapped child: Suggestion from the field. *Physical Therapy, 40,* 1691.

Microsoft Press. (1986). *CD-ROM: The new papyrus.* Redmond, WA: Author.

Microsoft Press. (1988). *Interactive multimedia.* Redmond, WA: Author.

Miklich, D., Chida, T., & Danker-Brown, P. (1977). Behavior modification by self-modeling without subject awareness. *Journal of Behavior Therapy and Experimental Psychiatry, 8,* 125–130.

Millar, S. (1988). Prose reading by touch: The role of stimulus quality, orthography and context. *British Journal of Psychology, 79,* 87–103.

Miller, C. R. (1987). *Essential guide to interactive videodisc hardware and applications.* Westport, CT: Meckler.

Miller, G., & Gwynne, G. (1982). *A life apart.* London: Tavistock.

Miller, S. B., & Ditto, B. (1988). Cardiovascular responses to an extended aversive video game task. *Psychophysiology, 25,* 200–208.

Minton, P. N. (1983). Video-tape instruction: An effective way to learn. *Rehabilitation Nursing,* 15–17.

Mirenda, P. L., Donnellan, A. M., & Yoder, D. E. (1983). Gaze behavior: A new look at an old problem. *Journal of Autism and Developmental Disorders, 13,* 397–409.

Mischel, W., & Grusec, J. (1966). Determinants of the rehearsal and transmission of neutral and aversive behaviors. *Journal of Personality and Social Psychology, 3,* 197–205.

Moldofsky, H., Broder, I., Davies, G., & Leznoff, A. (1979). Videotape educational program for people with asthma. *Canadian Medical Association Journal, 120,* 669–672.

Morokoff, P. J., Baum, A., McKinnon, W.R., & Gilliland, R. (1987). Effects of chronic unemployment and acute psychological stress on sexual arousal in men. *Health Psychology, 6,* 545–560.

Mulder, T., & Hulstijn, W. (1984). The effects of fatigue and task repetition on the surface electromyographic signal. *Psychophysiology, 21,* 528–534.

Mullen, P. D., Green, L. W., & Persinger, G. S. (1985). Clinical trials of patient education for chronic conditions: A comparative meta-analysis of intervention types. *Preventive Medicine, 14,* 753–781.

Mungny, G., & Perez, J. (1988). Minority influence and constructivism in social psychology [Henry Tajfel Memorial Lecture]. *British Psychological Society, Social Psychology Section Newsletter, 19,* 56–78.

Murphy, J. K., Alpert, B. S., Willey, E. S., & Somes, G. W. (1988). Cardiovascular reactivity to psychological stress in healthy children. *Psychophysiology, 25,* 144–152.

Murphy, K. R., & Constans, J. I. (1987). Behavioral anchors as a source of bias in rating. *Journal of Applied Psychology, 72,* 573–577.

Murray, A. (1982). *Impact of self-modeling or peer modeling on classroom behavior of inattentive elementary school boys.* Unpublished doctoral dissertation, Fordham University, New York.

National Association of Social Workers. (1980). *Code of ethics.* Washington, DC: Author.

National Commission for the Protection of Human Subjects of Biomedical and Behavioral Research (1978). Protection of human subjects: Research involving children. *Federal Register,* July 1978, 43 (No. 141).

Neumann, C. E. (1987, May). *The effect of videotape exemplars on the accuracy and reliability of observers coding childrens' free play behavior.* Paper presented at the annual meeting of the Association for Behavior Analysis. Nashville, TN.

Neef, N., Parrish, J., & Holbrook, C. (1988). *Respite care [Film].* Baltimore, MD: Johns Hopkins Medical Institutes.

Newell, K. M. (1981). Skill learning. In D. Holding (Ed.), *Human skills.* New York: Wiley.

Newell, W. J., Sims, D., & Myers, T. (1983). Principles and requisites of computer-assisted interactive video instruction: A sign language lesson. *American Annals of the Deaf, 128,* 662–672.

Nielsen, E., & Sheppard, M. A. (1988). Television as a patient education tool: A review of its effectiveness. *Patient Education and Counseling, 11,* 3–16.

Noble, G. (1975). *Children in front of the small screen.* London: Constable.

Noller, P., & Callan, V. J. (1988). Understanding parent adolescent interactions: Perceptions of family members and outsiders. *Developmental Psychology, 24,* 707–714.

O'Connor, R. D. (1969). Modification of social withdrawal through symbolic modeling. *Journal of Applied Behavior Analysis, 2,* 15–22.

O'Connor, T., & Smith, P. B. (1987). The labelling of schizophrenics by professionals and lay-persons. *British Journal of Clinical Psychology, 26,* 311–312.

O'Dell, S. L. (1984). Using videotape to train behavioral skills. *The Behavior Therapist, 7,* 149–150.

O'Dell, S. L., Blackwell, L. J., Larcen, S. W., & Hogan, J. L. (1977). Competency-based training for severely behaviorally handicapped children and their parents. *Journal of Autism and Childhood Schizophrenia, 7,* 231–242.

O'Dell, S. L., O'Quin, J. A., Alford, B. A., O'Briant, A. L., Bradlyn, A. S., & Giebenhain, J. E. (1982). Predicting the acquisition of parenting skills via four training methods. *Behavior Therapy, 13,* 194–208.

O'Leary, K. D., Romanczyk, R. G., Kass, R. E., Dietz, A., & Santogrossi, D. (1979). *Procedures for classroom observation of teachers and children.* Unpublished manuscript, SUNY at Stony Brook, Stony Brook, NY.

Olson, K. A., & Rardin, M. W. (1977, March). *Reducing hyperactive behavior in the classroom by photographic mediated self-modeling.* Paper presented at Banff 9th International Conference on Behavior Modification, Alberta, Canada.

Optical Recording Project/3M. (1981). *Premastering/postproduction procedures for Scotch videodiscs* (5/86 reprint). St. Paul, MN: Author.

Pace, P. W., Henske, J. C., Whitfill, B. J., Andrews, S. M., Russell, M. L., Probstfield, J. L., & Insull, W. Jr. (1981). Producing videocassette programs for diet instruction. *Journal of the American Dietetic Association, 79,* 689–692.

Pace, P. W., Henske, J. C., Whitfill, B. J., Andrews, S. M., Russell, M. L., Probstfield, J. L., & Insull, W., Jr. (1983). Videocassette use in diet instruction. *Journal of the American Dietetic Association, 83,* 166–169.

Padilla, G. V., Grant, M. M., Rains, B. L., Hansen, B. C., Bergstrom, N., Wong, H. L., Hanson, R., & Kubo, W. (1981). Distress reduction and the effects of preparatory teaching films and patient control. *Research in Nursing and Health, 4,* 375–387.

Palmer, P. B., Henry, J. N., & Rohe, D. A. (1985). Effect of videotape replay on the quality and accuracy of student self-evaluation. *Physical Therapy, 65,* 497–501.

Paniagua, F. A. (1987). Management of hyperactive children through correspondence training procedures: A preliminary study. *Behavioral Residential Treatment, 2,* 1–23.

Parrish, J., Egel, A., & Neef, N. (1986). Respite care provider training: A competency-based approach. In C. Salisbury (Ed.), *Respite care provider training: Current practices and directions for research* (pp. 117–142). New York: Paul Brookes.

Pauker, S. L. (1986). A new use for videotape in liaison psychiatry: A case from the burn unit. *General Hospital Psychiatry, 8*(1), 11–17.

Paulker, L. A., & Olgren, C. H. (1986). *Teleconferencing and electronic communications 5: Applications, technologies and human factors.* Madison, WI: Center for Interactive Programs.

Pear, J. J., & Legris, J. A. (1987). Shaping by automated tracking of an arbitrary operant response. *Journal of the Experimental Analysis of Behavior, 47,* 241–247.

Perry, M. A., & Furukawa, M. J. (1986). Modeling methods. In F. H. Kanfer & A. P. Goldstein (Eds.), *Helping people change: A textbook of methods* (pp. 66–110). New York: Pergamon.

Perry, S. (1989). *The development of self-modeling of social safety skills for the developmentally disabled.* Unpublished master's thesis, University of Alaska, Anchorage.

Perry, S., Dennis, A., Bolivar, C., & Dowrick, P. (1988, August). *Staying safe with strangers: An effective training package for DD young adults.* Paper presented at 3rd World Congress on Behaviour Therapy, Edinburgh.

Peterson, D. (1987). The effect of video-assisted instruction on student achievement and attitude in first grade math (Doctoral dissertation, Brigham Young University, 1986). *Dissertation Abstracts International, 47,* 4068A.

Peterson, L., Schultheis, K., Ridley-Johnson, R., Miller, D. J., & Tracy, K. (1984). Comparison of three modeling procedures on the presurgical and postsurgical reactions of children. *Behavior Therapy, 15,* 197–203.

Peterson, P. L., & Comeaux, M. A. (1987). Teachers' schemata for classroom events: The mental scaffolding of teachers' thinking during classroom instruction. *Teaching & Teacher Education, 3,* 319–331.

Petroski, R. A., Craighead, L. W., & Horan, J. J. (1983). Separate and combined effects of behavior rehearsal and self-other modeling variations on the grooming skill acquisition of mentally retarded women. *Journal of Counseling Psychology, 30,* 279-282.

Petty, L. C., & Rosen, E. F. (1987). Computer-based interactive video systems. *Behavior Research Methods, Instruments, & Computers, 19,* 160-166.

Pigott, H. E., & Gonzales, F. P. (1987). The efficacy of videotape self-modeling to treat an electively mute child. *Journal of Clinical Child Psychology, 16,* 106–110.

Pitcher, S. E., Rule, S., Cocklin, M., Stowitschek, J. J., & Swezey, K. (1987). Using telecommunications media to provide inservice training for special ed instructors in rural communities. *Technological Horizons in Education Journal, 14,* 72–76.

Plavin, M. H. (1988). Effects of presurgical preparation on anxiety of children and their mothers: Support versus information. *Dissertation Abstracts International, 49,* 223A–224A.

Powell, J. D. (1977). The use of trigger films in developing teaching skills. In L. Elton & K. Simmonds (Eds.), *Staff development in higher education.* Guildford: Society for Research in Higher Education.

Powell, L. A. (1988). The effects of learner control versus program control of corrective feedback on listening comprehension and vocabulary assimilation of low versus high performers in beginning college Spanish (Doctoral dissertation, Ohio State University, 1987). *Dissertation Abstracts International, 49,* 239A.

Powers, M. D., & Handleman, J. S. (1984). *Behavioral assessment of severe developmental disabilities.* Rockville, MD: Aspen Systems Corporation.

Prager, E., & Hantman, S. (1987). Adding an experimental dimension to undergraduate gerontological education: The "video thesis." *Educational Gerontology, 13,* 479–486.

Prince, D., & Dowrick, P. W. (1984, November). *Self-modeling in the treatment of depression: Implications for video in behavior therapy.* Paper presented at the 18th Annual Conference of the Association for the Advancement of Behavior Therapy, Philadelphia, PA.

Probst, M., Vandereycken, W., & Van Coppenolle, H. (1988). The body-image in anorexia nervosa: The use of videoconfrontation in the psychomotor therapy. *Acta Psychiatrika Belgique, 88,* 117-126.

Pyszczynski, T., & Greenberg, J. (1985). Depression and preference for self-focusing stimuli after success and failure. *Journal of Personality and Social Psychology, 49,* 1066–1075.

Quackenbush, R. L. (1987). Sex roles and social perception. *Human Relations, 40,* 659–669.

Quay, H. C., & Werry, J. S. (Eds.). (1986). *Psychopathological disorders of childhood* (3rd ed.). New York: Wiley.

Rand, R. (1987). Behavioral police assessment device: The development and validation of an interactive, preemployment, job-related, video psychological test. (Doctoral dissertation, University of San Francisco, 1987). *Dissertation Abstracts International, 48,* 610A–611A.

Rasnake, L. K. (1987). Anxiety reduction with children receiving medical care: Cognitive developmental considerations. (Doctoral dissertation, Ohio State University, 1987). *Dissertation Abstracts International, 48,* 286B–287B.

Raymond, D. D., Dowrick, P. W., & Kleinke, C. L. (1990). *Women's affective response to seeing themselves for the first time on unedited videotape.* Manuscript submitted for publication.

Reese, C. C. (1981). Use of video and super-8 film with drug dependent adolescents. In J. L. Fryrear & B. Fleshman (Eds.), *Videotherapy in mental health* (pp. 224–243). Springfield, IL: Charles C. Thomas.

Reith, S., Graham, J. L., McEwan, C., & Fraser, K. J. (1984). Video as a teaching aid. *British Medical Journal, 289,* 250.

Reivich, R. S., & Geertsma, R. H. (1968). Experiences with video-tape self-observation by psychiatric in-patients. *Journal of the Kansas Medical Society, 69,* 39–44.

Resch, R. C. (1981). Natural observation studies: Methodology and video recording in spontaneous behavior settings. *Infant Mental Health Journal, 2,* 176–187.

Rickert, V., Sottolano, D., Parrish, J., Riley, A., Hunt, F., & Pelco, L. (1988). Training parents to become better behavior managers: The need for a competency-based approach. *Behavior Modification, 12,* 475–496.

Riley, A. W., Parrish, J. M., & Cataldo, M. F. (1989). Training parents to meet the needs of children with medical or physical handicaps. In C. E. Schaefer, & J. M. Breismeister, (Eds.), *Handbook of parent training* (pp. 306–336). New York: Wiley.

Ripoll, H. (1988). Analysis of visual scanning patterns of volleyball players in a problem solving task. *International Journal of Sports Psychology, 19,* 9–25.

Risley, T. R., & Hart, B. (1968). Developing correspondence between the non-verbal and verbal behavior of preschool children. *Journal of Applied Behavior Analysis, 1,* 267–281.

Robbins, A. S., Fink, A., Kosecoff, J., Vivell, S., & Beck, J. C. (1982). Studies in geriatric education: II. Educational materials and programs. *Journal of the American Geriatrics Society, 30,* 340–347.

Robertson, M. C. (1988). Effectiveness of a videotaped behavioral intervention in reducing anxiety in emergency oral surgery patients. (Doctoral dissertation, University of Texas Health Science Center at Dallas, 1987). *Dissertation Abstracts International, 48,* 2107B.

Robinson, J. F. (1981). *Videotape recording: Theory and practice.* London: Focal Press.

Robinson, S. E., Kurpius, D. J., & Froehle, T. C. (1979). Self-generated performance feedback in interviewing training. *Counselor Education and Supervision, 29,* 91–100.

Rodolfa, E. R. (1987). Training university faculty to assist emotionally troubled students. *Journal of College Student Personnel, 28,* 183–184.

Rogers-Warren, A., & Baer, D. M. (1976). Correspondence between saying and doing: Teaching children to share and praise. *Journal of Applied Behavior Analysis, 9,* 335–354.

Rosenthal, T. L., & Bandura, A. (1978). Psychological modeling: Theory and practice. In S. Garfield & A. E. Bergin (Eds.), *Handbook of psychotherapy and behavior change* (pp. 621–658). New York: Wiley.

Rosenthal, T. L., Montgomery, L. M., Shadish, W. R., Edwards, N. B., Hutcherson, H. W., Follette, W. C., & Lichstein, K. L. (1989). Two new, brief, practical stressor tasks for research purposes. *Behavior Therapy, 20,* 545–562.

Ross, A. S., Anderson, R., & Gaulton, R. (1987). Methods of teaching introductory psychology: A Canadian survey. *Canadian Psychology, 28,* 266–273.

Ross, C. A., & Leichner, P. (1988). Residents performance on the mental status examination. *Canadian Journal of Psychiatry, 33,* 108–111.

Ross, D., Bird, A. M., Doody, S. G., & Zoeller, M. (1985). Effects of modeling and videotape feedback with knowledge results on motor performance. *Human Movement Science, 4,* 149–157.

Rothstein, A. L. (1981, August). Using feedback to enhance learning and performance with emphasis on videotape replay. *Science Periodical on Research and Technology in Sport, BU-1.*

Rothstein, A. L., & Arnold, R. K. (1976). Bridging the gap: Application of research on videotape feedback and bowling. *Motor Skills: Theory into Practice, 1,* 35–62.

Rowe, R. K. (1972). *A 50-hour intensified IPR training program for counselors.* Unpublished doctoral dissertation, Michigan State University.

Rubin, J. H., & Locascio, K. (1985). A model for communication skills group using structured exercises and audiovisual equipment. *International Journal of Group Psychotherapy, 35,* 569–584.

Rule, S., DeWulf, M. J., & Stowitschek, J. J. (1988). An economic analysis of inservice teacher training. *The American Journal of Distance Education, 2,* 12-22.

Runco, M. A., & Schreibman, L. (1988). Children's judgments of autism and social validation of behavior therapy efficacy. *Behavior Therapy, 19,* 565–576.

Rusalova, M. N., Izard, C. E., & Simonov, P. V. (1975). Comparative analysis of mimical and autonomic components of man's autonomic state. *Aviation, Space, and Environmental Medicine, 46,* 1132–1134.

Rynearson, R. R. (1982). Profile self-confrontation. *Psychiatric Annals, 12,* 1060–1064.

Safer, D. J. (1982). *Blaming the victim.* New York: Vintage Books.

Safran, J. S., & Safran, S. P. (1987). Teachers' judgments of problem behaviors. *Exceptional Children, 54,* 240–244.

Salmoni, A. W., Schmidt, R. A., & Walter, C. B. (1984). Knowledge of results and motor learning: A review and critical reappraisal. *Psychological Bulletin, 95,* 355–386.

Salvemini, N. J. (1988). The effects of rater rewards and prior ratee performance upon rating accuracy: An investigation of the motivational component in performance appraisal. *Dissertation Abstracts International, 48,* 1713A.

Saylor, K. E. (1988). Enhancing a videocassette weight loss program through self-directed adherence training. *Dissertation Abstracts International, 49,* 920B.

Schaefer, H. H., Sobell, M. B., & Mills, K. C. (1971). Some sobering data on the use of self-confrontation with alcoholics. *Behavior Therapy, 2,* 28–39.

Schaefer, J. H. (1975). Videotape: New techniques of observation and analysis in anthropology. In P. Hocking (Ed.), *Principles of visual anthropology* (pp. 253–282). The Hague: Mouton.

Scherer, K., & Ekman, P. (Eds.). (1982). *Handbook on methods of nonverbal behavior research.* New York: Cambridge University Press.

Schlosberg, H. (1941). A scale for the judgment of facial expression. *Journal of Experimental Psychology, 29,* 497–510.

Schlosberg, H. (1952). The description of facial expressions in terms of two dimensions. *Journal of Experimental Psychology, 44,* 229–237.

Schlosberg, H. (1954). Three dimensions of emotion. *Psychological Review, 61,* 81–88.

Schmidt, R. A. (1988). *Motor control and learning: A behavioral emphasis* (2nd ed.). Champaign, IL: Human Kinetics Publishers.

Schneider, B. H., Raycraft, S., Poirier, C. A., & Oliver, J. (1986). *Procedures manual: Individualized intervention for social competence program.* Unpublished manuscript, University of Ottawa, Child Study Center, Ottawa, Ontario.

Schoonover, S. C., Bassuk, E. L., Smith, R., & Gaskill, D. (1983). The use of videotape programs to teach interpersonal skills. *Journal of Medical Education, 58,* 804–810.

Schroeder, J. E., Dyer, F. N., Czerny, P., Youngling, E. W., & Gillott, D. P. (1986). Videodisc Interpersonal Skills Training and Assessment (VISTA): Overview and findings, Volume 1. *U.S. Army Research Institute for the Behavioral and Social Sciences Report* (Tech. Rep. 703 45 p). Ft. Benning Field Unit, GA: U.S. Army Research Institute for the Behavioral and Social Sciences.

Schunk, D. H., & Hanson, A. R. (1987, August). *Self-modeling and cognitive skill learning.* Paper presented at the annual meeting of the American Psychological Association, New York.

Schutz, A. (1967). *The phenomenology of the social world.* London: Heinemann.

Schwartz, G. E., Brown, S. L., & Ahern, G. L. (1980). Facial muscle patterning and subjective experience during affective imagery. *Psychophysiology, 17,* 75–82.

Schwarz, M. L., & Hawkins, R. P. (1970). Application of delayed reinforcement procedures to the behavior of an elementary school child, *Journal of Applied Behavior Analysis, 3,* 85–96.

Scraba, P. J. (1989). *Self-modeling for teaching swimming to children with physical disabilities.* Unpublished doctoral dissertation, University of Connecticut, Storrs.

Seal-Warner, C. (1988). Interactive video systems: Their promise and educational potential. *Teachers College Record, 89,* 373–383.

Shank, M. D., & Haywood, K. M. (1987). Eye movements while viewing a baseball pitch. *Perceptual & Motor Skills, 64,* 1191–1197.

Sharp, G. (1981). Acquisition of lecturing skills by university teaching assistants: Some effects of interest, topic relevance, and viewing a model videotape. *American Educational Research Journal, 18,* 491–502.

Sherwood, R. D., Kinzer, C. K., Bransford, J. D., & Franks, J. J. (1987). Some benefits of creating macro-contents for science instruction: Initial findings. *Journal of Research in Science Teaching, 24,* 417–435.

Shipley, R. H., Butt, J. H., & Horwitz, E. A. (1979). Preparation to reexperience a stressful medical examination: Effect of repetitious videotape exposure and coping style. *Journal of Consulting and Clinical Psychology, 47,* 485–492.

Shipley, R. H., Butt, J. H., Horwitz, B., & Farbry, J. E. (1978). Preparation for a stressful medical procedure: Effect of amount of stimulus preexposure and coping style. *Journal of Consulting and Clinical Psychology, 46,* 499–507.

Shotland, R. L., & Craig, J. M. (1988). Can men and women differentiate between friendly and sexually interested behavior? *Social Psychology Quarterly, 51,* 66–73.

Shotter, J. (1983). On viewing videotape records of oneself and others. In P. W. Dowrick & S. J. Biggs (Eds.), *Using video: Psychological and social applications* (pp. 199–210). Chichester, UK: Wiley.

Siegal, M. (1988). Children's knowledge of contagion and contamination as causes of illness. *Child Development, 59,* 1353–1359.

Siegal, M., Waters, L. J., & Dinwiddy, L. S. (1988). Misleading children: Causal attributions inconsistency under repeated questioning. *Journal of Experimental Child Psychology, 45,* 438–456.

Siegel, L. J. (1986). Measuring children's adjustment to hospitalization and to medical procedures. In P. Karoly (Ed.), *Handbook of child health assessment: Biosocial perspectives.* New York: Wiley.

Sigal, J., Hsu, L., Foodim, S., & Betman, J. (1988). Factors affecting perceptions of political candidates accused of sexual and financial misconduct. *Political Psychology, 9,* 273–280.

Sigurdson, E., Strang, M., & Doig, T. (1987). What do children know about preventing sexual assault? How can their awareness be increased? *Canadian Journal of Psychiatry, 32,* 551–557.

Silverstein, M. A. (1987). Social interaction analysis of elementary school students and a level one videodisc system in an educational environment (Doctoral dissertation, University of Wisconsin-Madison, 1987). *Dissertation Abstracts International, 49,* 35A.

Sims, H. P., & Manz, C. C. (1980). Categories of observed leader communication behaviors. *Proceedings: Southwest Academy of Management,* San Antonio, Texas.

Sipps, G. J., Sugden, G. J., & Faiver, C. M. (1988). Counselor training level and verbal response type: Their relationship to efficacy and outcome expectations. *Journal of Counseling Psychology, 35,* 397–401.

Skafte, D. (1987). Video in groups: Implications for a social theory of the self. *International Journal of Group Psychotherapy, 37,* 389–402.

Smith, V. L., & Ellsworth, P. C. (1987). The social psychology of eyewitness accuracy: Misleading questions and communicator expertise. *Journal of Applied Psychology, 72,* 294–300.

Snyder, C. R. (1985). The excuse: An amazing grace? In B. R. Schlenker (Ed.), *The self and social life* (pp. 235–260). New York: McGraw-Hill.

Solomon, M. Z., DeJong, W., & Jodrie, T. A. (1988). Improving drug regimen adherence among patients with sexually transmitted disease. *Journal of Compliance in Health Care, 3,* 41-56.

Speed, A. H. (1988). *Desktop video: A guide to personal and small business video production.* New York: Harcourt Brace Jovanovich.

Spence, S., & Shepherd, G. (1983). *Social skills training in practice.* London: Academic Press.

Spiegel, E. D. (1977). *The effects of self-observation on the social behavior of hyperactive children.* Unpublished doctoral dissertation, University of Southern California, Los Angeles.

Spindler, C. E. (1984). Audiovisual preoperative teaching for the total hip patient. *Orthopaedic Nursing, 3*(1), 30–40.

Sponder, B., & Schall, D. (1990, April). The Yugtarvik Museum project: Using interactive multimedia for cross-cultural distance education. *Academic Computing,* pp. 6–9, 42–44.

Srinivas, S., & Motowidlo, S. J. (1987). Effects of raters' stress on the dispersion and favorability of performance ratings. *Journal of Applied Psychology, 72,* 247–251.

St. Lawrence, J. (1986). DSM III: Diagnostic interview examples. *The Behavior Therapist, 6,* 39.

Stalonas, P. M., Keane, T. M., & Foy, D. W. (1979). Alcohol education for inpatient alcoholics: A comparison of live, videotape and written presentation modalities. *Addictive Behaviors, 4,* 223–229.

Stapleton, M. L. (1985). Computer-assisted video instruction at Moore-Norman Vocational Technical School. *American Annals of the Deaf, 130,* 371–373.

Stern, M., & Karraker, K. H. (1988). Prematurity stereotyping by mothers of premature infants. *Journal of Pediatric Psychology, 13,* 255–263.

Stokes, T. F., & Kennedy, S. H. (1980). Reducing child uncooperative behavior during dental treatment through modeling and reinforcement. *Journal of Applied Behavior Analysis, 13,* 41–49.

Stone, G. L., Wolraich, M. L., & Hillerbrand, E. (1988). Communicating distressful information: A video training program in a special education setting. *Journal of Counseling & Development, 66,* 438–441.

Stowitscheck, J. J., Mangus, B., & Rule, S. (1986). Inservice training via telecommunications: Out of the workshop and into the classroom. *Educational Technology, 26,* 28–33.

Strassberg, D. S., Kelly, M. P., Carroll, C., & Kircher, J. C. (1987). The psychophysiological nature of premature ejaculation. *Archives of Sexual Behavior, 16,* 327–336.

Stuart, C. K., & Stuart, V. W. (1981). Sexual assault: Disabled perspective. *Sexuality and Disability, 4,* 246–253.

Sulzer-Azaroff, B., & Mayer, G. R. (1977). *Applying behavior-analysis procedures with children and youth.* New York: Holt, Rinehart, & Winston.

Sumitsuji, N., Matsumoto, K., Tanaka, M., Kashiwagi, T., & Kaneko, Z. (1977). An attempt to systematize human emotion from EMG study of the facial expression. *Proceedings of the 4th Congress of the International College of Psychosomatic Medicine,* Kyoto, Japan.

Summerfield, A. (1983). Recording social interaction. In P. W. Dowrick & S. J. Biggs (Eds.), *Using video: Psychological and social applications* (pp. 3–11). Chichester, UK: Wiley.

Sutton, S., & Hallet, R. (1988). Understanding the effects of fear-arousing communications: The role of cognitive factors and amount of fear aroused. *Journal of Behavioral Medicine, 11,* 353–360.

Tanford, S., & Cox, M. (1987). Decision processes in civil cases: The impact of impeachment evidence on liability and credibility judgements. *Social Behaviour, 2,* 165–183.

Taylor, A. (1985). Technology and mediator training: Using videotaping for experiential learning. [Special issue: Divorce mediation]. *Journal of Divorce, 8,* 119–130.

Taylor, M. J., & Cooper, P. J. (1988, September). *Body size perception and depression: A mood induction study.* Paper presented at the 3rd World Congress on Behaviour Therapy, Edinburgh.

Teasdale, J. D., & Rezin, V. (1978). Effect of thought-stopping on thoughts, mood and corrugator EMG in depressed patients. *Behaviour Research and Therapy, 16,* 97–102.

Tedesco, J. F., & Schnell, S. V. (1987). Children's reactions to sex abuse investigation and litigation. *Child Abuse & Neglect, 11,* 267–272.

Tetreault, P. A., & Barnett, M. A. (1987). Reactions to stranger and acquaintance rape. *Psychology of Women Quarterly, 11,* 353–358.

Thelen, M., Fry, R., Fehrenbach, P., & Frautschi, N. (1979). Therapeutic videotape and film modeling: A review. *Psychological Bulletin, 86,* 701–720.

Thomas, S. (1989). *How to keep your VCR alive: VCR repair for the total klutz.* Tampa, FL: Worthington Publishing.

Tietge, N. S., Bender, S. J., & Scutchfield, D. (1987). Influence of teaching techniques on infant car seat use. *Patient Education and Counseling, 9,* 167–175.

Tinsley, H. E. A., Bowman, S. L., & Ray, S. B. (1988). Manipulation of expectancies about counseling and psychotherapy: Review and analysis of expectancy manipulation strategies and results. *Journal of Counseling Psychology, 35,* 99–108.

Traughber, B., & Cataldo, M. F. (1983). Biobehavioral effects of pediatric hospitalization. In P. Firestone & P. McGrath (Eds.), *Pediatric Behavioral Medicine,* (pp. 107–131). New York: Springer.

Trower, P., Bryant, B., & Argyle, M. (1978). *Social skills and mental health.* London: Methuen.

Trower, P., & Kiely, B. (1983). Video feedback: Help or hindrance? A review and analysis. In P. Dowrick & S. Biggs (Eds.), *Using video: Psychological and social applications* (pp. 181–197). Chichester, UK: Wiley.

Turner, J. R., Carroll, D., Dean, S., & Harris, M. G. (1987). Heart rate reactions to standard laboratory challenges and a naturalistic stressor. *International Journal of Psychophysiology, 5,* 151–152.

Twardosz, S., Weddle, K., Borden, L., & Stevens, E. (1986). A comparison of three methods of preparing children for surgery. *Behavior Therapy, 17,* 14–25.

Utz, P. (1982). *Video user's handbook* (2nd. ed.). Englewood Cliffs, NJ: Prentice-Hall.

Van Bourgondien, M. E. (1987). Children's responses to retarded peers as a function of social behaviors, labeling, and age. *Exceptional Children, 53,* 432–439.

Van der Meere, J., & Sergeant, J. (1988). Controlled processing and vigilance in hyperactivity: Time will tell. *Journal of Abnormal Child Psychology, 16,* 641–655.

Van Houten, R., & Rolider, A. (1988). Recreating the scene: An effective way to provide delayed punishment for inappropriate motor behavior. *Journal of Applied Behavior Analysis, 21,* 187–192.

Vaughan, K. B., & Lanzetta, J. T. (1980). Vicarious instigation and conditioning of facial expressive and autonomic responses to a model's expressive display of pain. *Journal of Personality and Social Psychology, 38,* 909–923.

Vernon, D. T. (1974). Modeling and birth order in response to painful stimuli. *Journal of Personality and Social Psychology, 29,* 794–799.

Vernon, D. T., & Bailey, W. C. (1974). The use of motion pictures in the psychological preparation of children for induction of anesthesia. *Anesthesiology, 40*(1), 68–72.

Vuchinich, S. (1984). Sequencing and social structure in family conflict. *Social Psychology Quarterly, 47,* 217–234.

Wachowiak, D., & Diaz, S. (1987). Influence of client characteristics on initial counselor perceptions. *Journal of Counseling Psychology, 34,* 90–92.

Walbott, H. G. (1982). Audiovisual recording: Procedures, equipment, and troubleshooting. In K. R. Scherer & P. Ekman (Eds.), *Handbook of methods in nonverbal behaviour research* (pp. 542–579). Cambridge: Cambridge University Press.

Walk, R. D., & Samuel, J. M. (1988). Sex differences in motion perception of Adler's six great ideas and their opposites. *Bulletin of the Psychonomic Society, 26,* 232–235.

Walker, H. M., McConnell, S., Holmes, D., Todis, B., Walker, J., & Golden, J. (1983). *The Walker social skills curriculum: The ACCEPTS program.* [Videotapes and manual]. Austin, TX: Pro-Ed.

Walker, H. M., Reavis, H. K., Rhode, G., & Jenson, W. R. (1985). A conceptual model for delivery of behavioral services to behavior disordered children in educational settings. In P. Bernstein & A. Kazdin (Eds.), *Handbook of clinical behavior therapy with children.* Homewood, IL: Irwin.

Walker, H. M., Severson, H., Stiller, B., Williams, G., Haring, N., Shinn, M., & Todis, B. (1987). *Systematic screening of pupils in the elementary age range at risk for behavior disorders: Development and trial testing of a multiple gating model.* Unpublished manuscript, University of Oregon.

Ward, J. D., Garlant, J. F., Paterson, G., Bone, V., & Hicks, B. H. (1984). Video cassette programmes in diabetes education. *The Diabetes Educator,* 48–50.

Watson, J. B., & Williams, S. E. (1987). Laryngectomees' and nonlaryngectomees' perceptions of three methods of alaryngeal voicing. *Journal of Communication Disorders, 20,* 295–304.

Weaver, J. B., Masland, J. L., Kharazmi, S., & Zillman, D. (1985). Effect of alcoholic intoxication on the appreciation of different types of humor. *Journal of Personality and Social Psychology, 49,* 781–787.

Webster-Stratton, C. (1984). Randomized trial of two parent-training programs for families with conduct disordered children. *Journal of Consulting and Clinical Psychology, 52,* 666–678.

Webster-Stratton, C. (1989). Systematic comparison of consumer satisfaction of three cost-effective parent training programs for conduct problem children. *Behavior Therapy, 20,* 103–115.

Webster-Stratton, C., Kolpacoff, M., & Hollinsworth, T. (1988). Self-administered videotape therapy for families with conduct-problem children: Comparison with two cost-effective treatments and a control group. *Journal of Consulting & Clinical Psychology, 56,* 558–566.

Weil, S., Charles, J., & King, R. (1985). *Through a hundred pairs of eyes.* London: Centre for Staff Development in Higher Education.

Weil, S., & Schofield, A. (1985). *The use of trigger video within professional education and training.* Unpublished manuscript, Center for Staff Development in Higher Education, London.

Weil, S., & Schofield, A. (1986). Integrating theory and practice: The use of trigger video. *Curricula and Teaching Methods,* 76–87.

Weinrach, S. G. (1986). Ellis and Gloria: Positive or negative model? *Psychotherapy: Theory, Research, Practice, Training, 23,* 642–647.

Weiser, J. (in press). *The secret lives of snapshots: A practical guide to phototherapy* (tentative title). New York: Brunner/Mazel.

Wessitsh, A. (1988). Effects of a heuristic and tutored video-instruction on problem solving in human rights. *Dissertation Abstracts International, 48,* 1716A.

White, M. J., & Lilly, D. L. (1989). Teaching attribution theory with a videotaped illustration. *Teaching of Psychology, 16,* 218–219.

Whiting, H. T., Bijlard, M. J., & den Brinker, B. P. (1987). The effect of the availability of a dynamic model on the acquisition of a complex cyclical action. *Quarterly Journal of Experimental Psychology, 39A,* 43–59.

Whitaker, C. (1978). The use of videotape in family therapy with special relation to the therapeutic impasse. In M. M. Berger (Ed.), *Videotape techniques in psychiatric training and treatment* (2nd ed.) (pp. 253–257). New York: Brunner/Mazel.

Wilkinson, G. (1988). A comparison of psychiatric decision-making by trainee psychiatrists using a simulated consultation model. *Psychological Medicine, 18,* 167–177.

Willener, A., Millard, G., & Ganty, R. (1976). *Videology and utopia.* London: Routledge.

Williams, C. L., & Kendall, P. C. (1985). Psychological aspects of patient education for stressful medical procedures. *Health Education Quarterly, 12,* 135–150.

Williams, S. L. (1987). The use of video games in studying nonhuman primate behavior (Doctoral dissertation, University of Montana, 1987). *Dissertation Abstracts International, 48,* 3139B.

Wolf, M. M. (1978). Social validity: The case for subjective measurement or how applied behavior analysis is finding its heart. *Journal of Applied Behavior Analysis, 11,* 203–214.

Woltersdorf, M. A. (1989). *Using videotape self-modeling in the treatment of attention deficit-hyperactivity disorder.* Unpublished doctoral dissertation, Fuller Graduate School of Psychology, Pasadena, CA.

Wood, F. H., & Larkin, K. C. (1979). *Disturbing, disordered, or disturbed?* Minneapolis: Special Education Programs, University of Minnesota.

Woodruff, J. C. (1988). Effects of an educational videotape presentation on the attitudes toward utilization of mental health professionals in a group of elderly persons. (Doctoral Dissertation, Auburn University, 1987). *Dissertation Abstracts International, 49,* 203A–204A.

Woolfolk, A. E., Woolfolk, R. L., & Wilson, G. T. (1977). A rose by any other name. . . : Labeling bias and attitudes toward behavior modification. *Journal of Consulting and Clinical Psychology, 45,* 184–191.

Worden, P. E., Kee, D. W., & Ingle, M. J. (1987). Parental teaching strategies with preschoolers: A comparison of mothers and fathers within different alphabet tasks. *Contemporary Educational Psychology, 12,* 95–109.

Yates, A. (1987). Should young children testify in cases of sexual abuse? *American Journal of Psychiatry, 144,* 476–480.

Young, S., & Getty, C. (1987). Visually guided feeding behaviour in the filter feeding cladoceran, "Daphnia magna." *Animal Behaviour, 35,* 541–548.

Ysseldyke, J. E., Algozzine, B., & Richey, L. (1982). Judgment under uncertainty: How many children are handicapped? *Exceptional Children, 48,* 531–534.

Zachary, R. A., Friedlander, S., Huang, L. N., Silverstein, S., & Leggott, P. (1985). Effects of stress-relevant and -irrelevant filmed modeling on children's responses to dental treatment. *Journal of Pediatric Psychology, 10,* 383–401.

Zettl, H. (1987). The anatomy of a television commercial: A media aesthetic analysis. *Semiotics of Advertisements, 1,* 99–115.

Ziarnik, J. P., & Bernstein, G. (1982). A critical examination of the effect of in-service training on staff performance. *Mental Retardation, 20,* 109–114.

Zygmont, J. (1988, February). Face to face. *Sky,* pp. 10–16.

Author Index

Subject Index

Action axis, 189
Adaptors, 269
Address code, 269
Advanced training, 55-56
Aesthetic presentation, 79-80
Affective disorders
  and facial behaviors, 162-65
Ambient, 269
Amplifier, 269
Analog, 269
Analysis applications, 31-41
  equipment considerations, 35
  medical diagnosis, 31-32
    example, 34
  motor activities, 31
    examples of movement analysis,
      32-33
  nonverbal expression and
    communication, 31
  example of facial expression analysis,
    33
  setting up the target events, 34-35
  social interaction, 31
    example of family interaction
      analysis, 33-34
  subsequent analysis (*See* Follow-up
    analysis)
  surveillance, 32, 40-41
Anxiety disorders, 83, 121
Aperture, 269
Aspect ratio, 269
Attention, 50
Audio level, 269
Audio mix, 269
Audio track, 270
Authoring, 270
Autism
  self-modeling for (*See* Developmentally
    disabled learner self-modeling, for
    children with autism)
Auto focus, 270
Automatic gain control, 270

Awareness, 115-16

Back lighting, 23, 270
Backtime, 270
Balanced line, 270
Band, 270
Behavior-disordered children, 248-49
Beta, 20
Bias, 43
Black body, 270
Black box, 270
Black level, 270
Blanking, 270
Bleed, 270
Blocking, 270
BNC (*See* Connectors)
Boom, 270
Bridge, 270
Broadcast quality, 270
Burn, 271
Bus, 271
Busy, 271

C-mount, 271
Cable compensation, 271
CAI, 271
Camcorder, 9
Cameo, 271
Camera transitions, 23
Capstan, 271
Capture, 271
Cassette, 271
Cathode ray tube (CRT), 271
CAV (*See* Disc)
CCD, 271
CCTV, 271
CD-ROM applications, 150-51
Chapter, 271
Character generator, 271
Child care, 60
Child self-management, 72-73